ANTONY
AND
CLEOPATRA

Edited by
JOHN WILDERS

LONDON AND NEW YORK

The general editors of the Arden Shakespeare have been
W. J. Craig and R. H. Case (first series 1899–1944)
Una Ellis-Fermor, Harold F. Brooks, Harold Jenkins
and Brian Morris (second series 1946–82)

Present general editors (third series)
Richard Proudfoot, Ann Thompson and
David Scott Kastan

This edition of *Antony and Cleopatra*, by John Wilders,
first published 1995 by Routledge
11 New Fetter Lane, London EC4P 4EE

Simultaneously published in the USA and Canada
by Routledge
29 West 35th Street, New York, NY 10001

Editorial material © 1995 John Wilders

Typeset in Ehrhardt by
Selwood Systems, Midsomer Norton, Avon
Printed in Great Britain by
Clays Ltd, St Ives plc

British Library Cataloguing in Publication Data
A catalogue record for this book is available from the British Library

Library of Congress Cataloging in Publication Data
A catalog record for this book has been requested

ISBN 0–415–01102–7 (hbk)
ISBN 0–415–01103–5 (pbk)

THIRD SERIES

General Editors: Richard Proudfoot, Ann Thompson
and David Scott Kastan

ANTONY
AND
CLEOPATRA

THE ARDEN SHAKESPEARE

*Third Series

To Benedikte

CONTENTS

LIST OF
ILLUSTRATIONS

List of illustrations

GENERAL EDITORS' PREFACE

The Arden Shakespeare is now nearly one hundred years old. The earliest volume in the first series, Edward Dowden's edition of *Hamlet*, was published in 1899. Since then, the Arden Shakespeare has become internationally recognized and respected. It is now widely acknowledged as the pre-eminent Shakespeare series, valued by scholars, students, actors, and 'the great variety of readers' alike for its readable and reliable texts, its full annotation and its richly informative introductions.

We have aimed in the third Arden series to maintain the quality and general character of its predecessors, preserving the commitment to presenting the play as it has been shaped in history. While each individual edition will necessarily have its own emphasis in the light of the unique possibilities and problems posed by the play, the series as a whole, like the earlier Ardens, insists upon the highest standards of scholarship and upon attractive and accessible presentation.

Newly edited from the original quarto and folio editions, the texts are presented in fully modernized form, with a textual apparatus that records all substantial divergences from those early printings. The notes and introductions focus on the conditions and possibilities of meaning that editors, critics and performers (on stage and screen) have discovered in the play. While building upon the rich history of scholarly and theatrical activity that has long shaped our understanding of the texts of Shakespeare's plays, the third series of the Arden Shakespeare is made necessary and possible by a new generation's encounter with Shakespeare, engaging with the plays and their complex relation to the culture in which they were – and continue to be – produced.

THE TEXT

On each page of the play itself, readers will find a passage of text followed by commentary and, finally, textual notes. Act and scene divisions (seldom present in the early editions and often the product of eighteenth-century or later scholarship) have been retained for ease of reference, but have been given less prominence than in the previous series. Chorus speeches are numbered as e.g. 2.0 when they precede the first scene of an act. Editorial indications of scene location have been removed to the textual notes or commentary.

In the text itself, unfamiliar typographic conventions have been avoided in order to minimize obstacles to the reader. Elided forms in the early texts are spelt out in full in verse lines wherever they indicate a usual late twentieth-century pronunciation that requires no special indication and wherever they occur in prose (except when they indicate non-standard pronunciation). In verse speeches, marks of elision are retained where they are necessary guides to the scansion and pro-nunciation of the line. Final -ed in past tense and participial forms of verbs is always printed as -ed, without accent, never as -'d, but wherever the required pronunciation diverges from modern usage a note in the commentary draws attention to the fact. Where the final -ed should be given syllabic value contrary to modern usage, e.g.

> Doth Silvia know that I am banished?
>
> (*TGV* 3.1.221)

the note will take the form

221 **banished** banishèd

Conventional lineation of divided verse lines shared by two or more speakers has been reconsidered and sometimes rearranged. Except for the familiar *Exit* and *Exeunt*, Latin forms in stage directions and speech prefixes have been translated into English, and the original Latin forms recorded in the textual notes.

COMMENTARY AND TEXTUAL NOTES

Notes in the commentary, for which a major source will be the *Oxford English Dictionary*, offer glossarial and other explication of verbal difficulties; they may also include discussion of points of theatrical interpretation and, in relevant cases, substantial extracts from Shakespeare's source material. Editors will not usually offer glossarial notes for words adequately defined in the *Concise Oxford Dictionary* or *Webster's Ninth New Collegiate Dictionary*, but in cases of doubt they will include notes. Attention, however, will be drawn to places where more than one likely interpretation can be proposed and to significant verbal and syntactic complexity. Notes preceded by an asterisk* involve readings altered from the early edition(s) on which the text is based.

Headnotes to acts or scenes discuss, where appropriate, questions of scene location, Shakespeare's handling of his source materials, and major difficulties of staging. The list of roles (so headed to emphasize the play's status as a text for performance) is also considered in commentary notes. These may include comment on plausible patterns of casting with the resources of an Elizabethan or Jacobean acting company and also on any variation in the description of roles in their speech prefixes in the early editions.

The textual notes are designed to let readers know when the edited text diverges from the early edition(s) on which it is based. Wherever this happens the note will record the rejected reading of the early edition(s), in original spelling, and the source of the reading adopted in this edition. Other forms from the early edition(s) recorded in these notes will include some spellings of particular interest or significance and original forms of translated stage directions. Where two early editions are involved, for instance with *Othello*, the notes will also record all important differences between them. The textual notes take a form that has been in use since the nineteenth century. This comprises, first: line reference, reading adopted in the text and closing square bracket; then: abbreviated reference, in italic, to the earliest edition to adopt the accepted reading, italic semi-colon and noteworthy alternative reading(s), each with abbreviated italic reference to its source.

Conventions used in these notes include the following. The solidus / is used, in notes quoting verse or discussing verse lining, to indicate line endings. Distinctive spellings of the basic text (Q or F) follow the square bracket without indication of source and are enclosed in italic brackets. An editor's name in brackets indicates the originator of a textual emendation. Stage directions (SDs) are referred to by the number of the line within or immediately after which they are placed. Line numbers with a decimal point relate to SDs more than one line long, with the number after the point indicating the line within the SD: e.g. 78.4 refers to the fourth line of the SD following line 78. Lines of SDs at the start of a scene are numbered 0.1, 0.2, etc. Where only a line number precedes the square bracket, e.g. 128], the note relates to the whole line; where SD is added to the number, it relates to the whole of a SD within or immediately following the line. Speech prefixes (SPs) follow similar conventions, 203 SP], referring to the speaker's name for line 203. Where a SP reference takes the form e.g. 38+ SP, it relates to all subsequent speeches assigned to that speaker in the scene in question.

Where, as with *King Henry V*, one of the early editions is a so-called 'bad quarto' (that is, a text either heavily adapted, or reconstructed from memory, or both), the divergences from the present edition are too great to be recorded in full in the notes. In these cases the editions will include a reduced photographic facsimile of the 'bad quarto' in an appendix.

PREFACE

This edition of *Antony and Cleopatra* is based on the only authoritative text we have, that of the First Folio (which I discuss in detail on pages 75–84). Like most modern editors I have retained the Folio readings where they make good sense, but in passages where the Folio seems faulty I have adopted the most plausible emendations made by previous editors or have introduced emendations of my own. The spelling has been modernized throughout in accordance with the principles set out by Stanley Wells in his *Modernizing Shakespeare's Spelling* (Oxford, 1979). The spelling of proper names has been regularized, a process which, although it has generally presented no problems, has in some cases been more difficult. (See commentary notes on Canidius, Dercetus and Thidias in the List of Roles.)

The Folio punctuation, which appears to have been largely the work of the compositors, is often faulty, misleading or ambiguous, as in

What sayes the married woman you may goe?
(TLN 325)

and

What was he sad, or merry?
(TLN 581)

In passages such as these the punctuation can be remedied in various ways. It is, of course, the editor's responsibility to emend the punctuation consistently with modern practice, but in many cases, such as the two quoted above, a decision about punctuation is essentially a decision about meaning. All editors can do is use their judgement, but when departures from the Folio punctuation affect the sense, I have recorded the punctuation of the Folio in the textual footnotes, and when previous editors have used a convincing punctuation which differs from my own I have recorded theirs as well as that of the Folio.

I have not attempted to record all the textual emendations made by previous editors but when I have adopted one I have noted its source in the textual footnotes, and when a previous scholar has introduced a reading which, though plausible, I have rejected, I have also recorded this.

In the commentary notes I have generally glossed obscure and obsolete words when they do not appear in the *Concise Oxford Dictionary*. Unless otherwise stated, definitions have been taken from the first edition of the *Oxford English Dictionary*, to which precise reference is given only if it records two or more distinct and different uses of the same word.

In the Introduction I have not attempted to provide anything like a complete survey either of the theatrical productions or of the criticism of the play. Readers who wish to know more about its history in the theatre should consult Margaret Lamb's excellent *Antony and Cleopatra on the English Stage* (London and Toronto, 1980), to which I am very much indebted. There is a survey of all the major criticism in Marvin Spevack's Variorum edition (1990), an analysis of the early criticism in Michael Steppat's *The Critical Reception of Shakespeare's 'Antony and Cleopatra' from 1607 to 1905*, *Bochum Studies in English*, vol. 9 (Amsterdam, 1980), and a guide to more recent studies in John W. Velz's *Shakespeare and the Classical Tradition 1660–1960* (Minneapolis, 1968). R. J. A. Weis gives a briefer account in his essay '*Julius Caesar* and *Antony and Cleopatra*', in *Shakespeare: A Bibliographical Guide*, ed. Stanley Wells (2nd edn, Oxford, 1990), pp. 275–94.

ACKNOWLEDGEMENTS

Like all Shakespearean editors I am indebted chiefly to my predecessors who have either solved the problems I should otherwise have had to deal with alone or have stimulated what I hope has been constructive disagreement. In particular I have learned a great deal from the two most recent editors of *Antony and Cleopatra*, Marvin Spevack, whose Variorum edition directed me towards a great deal of material of which I might otherwise have been ignorant, and David Bevington, whose New Cambridge edition is a model of thoroughness and good sense. I was unable to consult Michael Neill's Oxford edition which appeared when my own had been completed. The Provost and Fellows of Worcester College, Oxford, granted me a year's leave during which I began work on this edition and spent three months at the Huntington Library where the warm hospitality of the former Director, James Thorpe, helped to make my visit an enjoyable one. I am grateful to the staffs of the Huntington, Bodleian and Middlebury College libraries for their willing assistance, and I must thank John Pitcher for his permission to quote from his unpublished edition of the poems of Samuel Daniel. Passages from Janet Adelman's *The Common Liar* are quoted by permission of Yale University Press (© 1973), from Margaret Lamb's *Antony and Cleopatra on the English Stage* by permission of the Associated University Presses (© 1980), from Ernest Schanzer's *The Problem Plays of Shakespeare* by permission of Routledge, Chapman and Hall (© 1963) and from E. A. J. Honigmann's *Shakespeare: Seven Tragedies* by permission of the Macmillan Press (© 1976). Linden Stafford copy-edited this edition with exemplary thoroughness. My greatest debt, however, is to Richard Proudfoot and Ann Thompson, General Editors of the Arden Shakespeare, who read my edition in typescript with extraordinary and scrupulous care, pointed out many errors and made countless valuable suggestions.

John Wilders
Middlebury College, Vermont

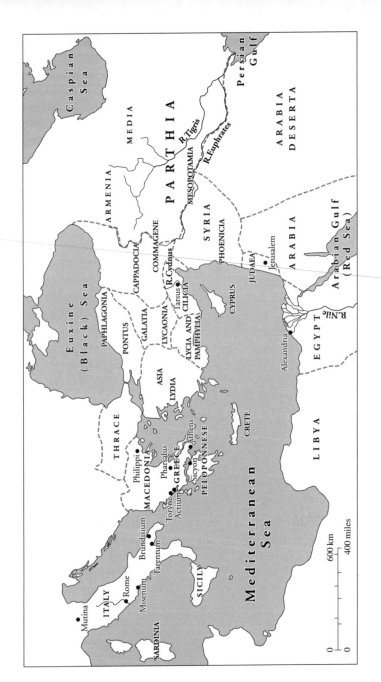

1 The Eastern Mediterranean, *c.* 31 BC

INTRODUCTION

Shakespeare probably completed *Antony and Cleopatra* towards the end of 1606 or early in 1607, after he had finished *Macbeth* and before he embarked on *Coriolanus* (see pages 69–75). He was then in his early forties and had been writing for the theatre for about seventeen years. The play is a dramatization of a tragic and celebrated love affair, the story of which had been well known to writers and readers for centuries before Shakespeare created his version of it. The story had been told in detail by the first-century biographer Plutarch and his account translated into both French and English. Virgil had referred to it in the eighth book of the *Aeneid*, Horace had written an ode on the courage and dignity of Cleopatra's suicide (*Odes* 1.37), and Chaucer had described her death in *The Legend of Good Women*. The story had been the subject of many paintings, and at least two dramatizations had been written in English before Shakespeare embarked on his. In attempting to write a play on such a celebrated subject, Shakespeare clearly set a challenge for himself. He rose to it so splendidly that in most of our minds Antony and Cleopatra actually were the people he created.

They impress us as exceptional people partly because we are conscious of their legendary status, a status which, in the play, they cultivate by the public extravagance of their lives. They are also extravagant in the range and intensity of their feelings. Both of them, but especially Cleopatra, shift rapidly from tenderness to fury and grief and the emotions of the one are largely determined by those of the other. What they seldom express, however, is love and when they do so it is a love which is seldom experienced in the present but remembered from the past:

> When you sued staying,
> Then was the time for words; no going then.
> Eternity was in our lips and eyes,
> Bliss in our brows' bent; none our parts so poor
> But was a race of heaven.
>
> (1.3.34–8)

We are willing to believe in their love, moreover, not simply because they recollect it so movingly but because the violence of their frequent quarrels testifies to their total absorption in each other. At a much lower emotional pitch, we sense Beatrice and Benedick's fascination with each other because of their repeated denials that they are fascinated.

Unlike Shakespeare's early romantic tragedy, *Romeo and Juliet*, *Antony and Cleopatra* is also a play about international politics, a public as well as a private drama in which Antony and Octavius compete for mastery over the Roman empire which, at the time, extended from Britain in the west to what is now Turkey in the east, and the battles in which this contest was fought out occupy much of the third and fourth acts. As in all his political plays, Shakespeare portrays this struggle in terms of the central personalities engaged in it. In other words, Caesar ultimately wins and Antony loses because of the kind of people they are and because of the irresistible power which Cleopatra exercises over Antony. This gives to the relationship between the lovers a sense of unusual weight and risk. Because Antony takes flight from the sea battle when Cleopatra has fled, we are readily convinced that a mere gesture from her would induce him to defy 'the bidding of the gods'. His dependency on her leads him to lose a battle the outcome of which affects the government of the Roman world. The political element in the drama is therefore not simply a background against which the love tragedy is played out but an inseparable part of it. Antony and Cleopatra seem to us larger than life because the future of the known world appears to depend on their relationship. They also see themselves as larger than life and it is typical of their self-dramatization that when Antony distributes the countries of the eastern empire to Cleopatra and her children he does so in a public ceremony at which the two of them sit in 'chairs of gold' on a silver platform and she is decked out in the habiliments of the goddess Isis (3.6.1–19). Her suicide, dressed in her royal vestments, is a last and entirely characteristic attempt to display herself as an extraordinary phenomenon, a 'wonderful piece of work'.

This last scene is unlike anything in Shakespeare's other tragedies and its uniqueness arises in part from the deliberately spectacular nature of Cleopatra's death. On the one hand it is a scene of absolute defeat in which the queen is shown as having lost everything apart from the two waiting women who have supported her throughout the play and when it concludes, all three of them are dead. In her last moments, however, she asserts that by her death she will be reunited with her lover in a world where they will be immune to time and change:

> Methinks I hear
> Antony call. I see him rouse himself
> To praise my noble act. I hear him mock
> The luck of Caesar, which the gods give men
> To excuse their after wrath. Husband, I come!
>   (5.2.282–6)

What Caesar, the Roman onlooker, regards as a tragedy is seen by Cleopatra as an apotheosis and we are left in doubt as to whether her death is a defeat or a kind of victory. The end of *Antony and Cleopatra* seems also like a beginning and it leaves us with simultaneous feelings of loss and exhilaration.

Shakespeare, then, created his two central characters as

people who are conscious of and seek to perpetuate their legendary status. At the same time they are intimately human. In the aftermath of their most violent row, Cleopatra remembers that it is her birthday (3.13.190). She is not only the more-than-Venus who contrives an astonishing entrance in her barge but the woman who hops forty paces in the public street and was carried to Julius Caesar in a mattress. Similarly Antony can join boisterously in the drinking bout on Pompey's galley and tease the drunken Lepidus. Left alone on his throne in the empty market place near Cydnus, we are told, he shows his embarrassment by whistling to the air (2.2.226).

Extraordinary though the tragedy is, it has seldom been performed satisfactorily on the stage. This is partly because few actresses have managed to encompass the full range of Cleopatra's personality, but much more damaging has been the ponderous, grandiose style in which, for over a century, it was produced. Such heavy-handedness tended to swamp the fineness of Shakespeare's dialogue which, for all the geographical scope of the play, is often private and intimate. It also stretched out the playing time to an intolerable length, as the reviewers complained, and broke up into disconnected episodes a work which was designed to be acted without interruption. The most successful productions have been on the uncluttered kind of stage for which Shakespeare designed it, and the likely features of a production in his own time are the subject of the next part of this introduction. Closely related to questions of staging are the objections made to the play by academic critics who thought it lacked unity and coherence and these criticisms are the subject of the section which follows. Criticism of the play's coherence is essentially criticism of its construction, the next general topic to be discussed, and the complexity of its structure gives rise to the complex, ambiguous impressions which it creates on an audience – our uncertainty as to how we should judge the major characters, the subject of another section. Such ambiguities, which are deeper and more sustained than those created by Shakespeare's other tragedies, preclude the possibility of any clear, simple response to the play, to the extent that some critics, notably A. C. Bradley, have doubted whether it is actually tragic, a subject considered in the next section. The introduction proceeds to a discussion of the play's distinctive language and style and an account of the sources from which Shakespeare took his material. It concludes with the more specialized topics of the probable date when the play was written and the state of the text as it was printed in the First Folio.

JACOBEAN PERFORMANCE

Continuity and speed

Jacobean public stages were very simple – not much more than an empty wooden platform about 43 feet wide and 27 feet deep thrust into the middle of the spectators with no scenery to raise or lower. There was a wall at the back with two doors through which the actors could make swift entrances and exits so that one group could walk on as another went off. The division of *Antony and Cleopatra* into five acts and forty-two scenes, begun by Nicholas Rowe in his edition of Shakespeare's works in 1709 and elaborated by subsequent editors, conveys an entirely false impression of the continuity and speed of performance which was possible in the theatre of Shakespeare's time. In the first printed text, the Folio of 1623, there are no act or scene divisions, and it is not difficult to imagine how in a Jacobean playhouse it could be performed as one single, uninterrupted action. Although in *Romeo and Juliet* (1. Prologue 12) the Chorus refers to 'the two hours' traffic of our stage', some of Shakespeare's contemporaries estimate three hours as the average playing time (Gurr, 33), and *Antony and Cleopatra* when performed on the Jacobean stage would have lasted no longer than that. A recent English production (by the Royal

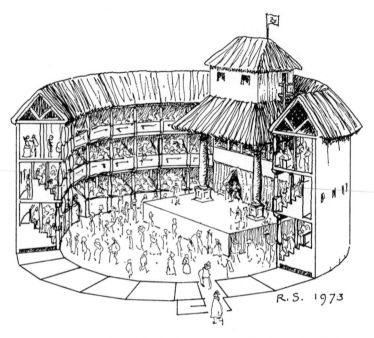

2 An artist's impression of the kind of playhouse (the Swan) for which
Antony and Cleopatra was written (see also p. 21 and p. 24, Fig. 5)

Shakespeare Company in 1992) in which the scene changes
were quick and simple lasted three and a quarter hours.

Visual language

The sheer emptiness of Shakespeare's stage and the absence
of scenery focused the audience's attention on the actors, who
were, presumably, dressed in a combination of contemporary
and 'classical' costumes of the kind depicted in the Longleat
manuscript (Fig. 3). This drawing, by Henry Peacham, the
only known portrayal of a performance in Shakespeare's own
time, shows an episode from *Titus Andronicus*, in which Queen
Tamora pleads with Titus for the lives of two of her sons. The
two pikemen on the left of the drawing wear the normal dress

3 Drawing of a scene from *Titus Andronicus* dated 1595

of soldiers of the time, including breeches and feathered helmets. Titus, Aaron and the two sons, however, wear stage versions of classical costume: buskins, cuirasses and, in the case of Titus and one of the sons, cloaks or skimpy togas. Titus wears a laurel wreath on his head, the Roman token of victory in battle. Tamora is dressed in a tall crown and an ample, full-length gown with embroidered sleeves, which, according to Muriel St Clare Byrne, 'characterise the stage heroine or tragedy queen until the end of the eighteenth century. There is nothing classical about her' (Byrne, 3.291). Although Cleopatra's command to Charmian, 'cut my lace', indicates that she wore the kind of tight bodice recently favoured by Queen Elizabeth and other fashionable ladies, there was probably some attempt to provide her and her entourage with 'Egyptian' clothes as well as the 'divers coloured fans' held by the eunuchs who attend her on her first entrance. Clothing is significant as an indication of nationality, rank and gender, as when an episode is devoted to the arming of Antony by Cleopatra before battle (4.4) and another to his disarming by Eros after his defeat (4.14). Antony and Cleopatra's exchange of clothing which she recalls with amusement during his absence in Rome (2.5.21–3) is, to Caesar, a sign of their degeneracy (1.4.5–7). Dress conveys information as well as creating spectacle and it is important that Philo and Demetrius, with whose conversation the tragedy begins, should be identifiably Roman soldiers commenting on their leader's enslavement by an Egyptian queen. Again, when, as the play moves towards its conclusion, Cleopatra ceremoniously puts on her queenly robes and crown, her dress helps to confirm her belief that she is not a defeated but a triumphant woman.

Though no visual impressions were created by scenery, the play is full of expressive groupings of characters on which the audience could concentrate without distraction, most notably when Cleopatra and her gentlewomen raise Antony aloft into the temporarily private haven of her monument. Shakespeare is, moreover, often quite specific in his stage directions, as when Pompey and Menas enter '*at one door with drum and trumpet*' and the triumvirs and their supporters come on '*at another ... with Soldiers marching*' (2.6). This first encounter between the opposing sides is thus accompanied by the sounds and sights of war. In their next (and last) meeting (2.7) the representatives of both sides, placed 'hand in hand', join in the singing of a drunken song before helping one another to stagger off Pompey's galley. Again, the entry direction to 2.3 specifically instructs Antony and Caesar to come on with Octavia '*between them*', a visible expression of the divided loyalties which are to trouble her more deeply as the action develops. The Longleat manuscript, which shows the two Roman soldiers to the left and the two captive sons to the right of the principal characters, suggests that 'the stage groupings were kept symmetrical as much as possible' (Lamb, 28). Such normally symmetrical arrangements would, of course, have highlighted occasional asymmetries, as at the end of Pompey's feast when a conference which has begun formally concludes in disorder.

Aural language

To be present at a performance of this tragedy is an aural as well as a visual experience created not simply by the counterpointing of the various voices but by the musical accompaniment which Shakespeare's stage directions require. The initial entrance of Antony and Cleopatra is heralded by a 'Flourish' which (ironically, in its context) 'proclaims the imperial theme' (Long, 202), as does the flourish which accompanies the exit of the triumvirs at the end of their conference (2.2.180). Drums and trumpets are brought playing on to the stage after the initial flourish which signals the arrival of Pompey, Menas and the triumvirs in 2.6. Music of a different kind – probably hautboys (ancestors of the modern oboe) – introduces the banquet on Pompey's galley, and the dance which concludes it was probably played by a 'loud consort' combining hautboys, fifes, drums and trumpets (Long, 212). '*Hautboys ... under the stage*' are specifically asked for in the eerie, mysterious episode (4.3) in which the 'god Hercules' is said to desert Antony on the night before battle. This may be compared to another supernatural moment when, in *Macbeth*, the witches' cauldron sinks beneath the stage and 'hautboys' are again required (Jones, 255). When, in the next scene (4.4.23) Antony, having been armed, greets his troops on the morning of battle, there is a flourish of trumpets, and each one of the battle scenes which follow is introduced by the sound either of drums and trumpets or of trumpets alone. The music not only creates a suitably martial impression but provides bridges which link these short, swiftly moving episodes together (Long, 217). Hence, although the resources of the Shakespearean playhouse were limited, Shakespeare used them with an expressive variety which nevertheless did not prevent the performance from moving quickly and without interruption.

Casting

Antony and Cleopatra is one of the longest of Shakespeare's plays (only *Richard III*, the Second Quarto of *Hamlet*, *Coriolanus* and *Cymbeline* are longer) and, in addition to an indeterminate number of extras (the sentries, soldiers and messengers who make brief, sometimes silent appearances), has an unusually large number of speaking parts. There is, however, ample evidence to show that in the Jacobean playhouse the doubling of roles was customary. Some of the characters, such as Philo, Demetrius, the Soothsayer, Menecrates and Menas, appear only in the early scenes, and the actors who played them could reappear as Taurus, Diomedes, Seleucus, the Ambassador or the Clown. In the most recent and detailed study of the casting of Shakespeare's plays, it is estimated that twelve men could play the nineteen principal male roles and four boys the four female roles (King, 91). This corresponds to what appears to have been the average number of principal actors in the company (ibid., 6). The minor roles would be played by hired men or playhouse attendants who probably joined the company late in the rehearsal period. In Adrian Noble's production for the Royal Shakespeare Company in 1982 in which there was some doubling, the company consisted of nineteen men and four women.

The role of Cleopatra was presumably designed for a boy. If it were not, her reference to some future 'squeaking Cleopatra' who would 'boy' her greatness 'i'th' posture of a whore' would lose most of its point. This extraordinarily daring image of an incompetent boy actor failing to do justice to the stature of the actual woman shows that the adolescent for whom Shakespeare created the role would be well able to fulfil the demands it made on him.[1] Our sense of Cleopatra's uniqueness, her power, is created as much by what the other characters –

1 Three of the most challenging women's roles that Shakespeare created – Lady Macbeth, Cleopatra and Volumnia – were in plays written within the same period. They may have been created for the same actor, a boy of exceptional talent.

especially Enobarbus – say about her as by what she herself says and does. Shakespeare would not have written such accounts of her effect on others, however, unless he had known that the boy could himself convey something of her magic to the audience, and in the prolonged final scene he had to display Cleopatra's greatness more or less on his own. If we are sceptical about an adolescent boy's ability to do justice to the role, it is probably because we underestimate the intelligence of children of that age. Moreover the boy actors were the products of a tradition which went back well beyond the playing of John Lyly's sophisticated court comedies to the performances put on by choristers during the course of the two previous centuries. With the introduction of women on to the stage this tradition was broken, but a comparable musical tradition still survives in the choir schools of British colleges and cathedrals. In the ease and professionalism with which these diminutive singers perform Renaissance polyphonic music we can still glimpse something of the skill of the original Cleopatra.

The foregoing attempt to reconstruct some of the features of the earliest performances must, of necessity, be hypothetical not simply because our knowledge of theatrical conditions in Shakespeare's time is very limited but because no record exists of any performance of the play before the middle of the eighteenth century. It is possible, but unlikely, that it was never put on at all during Shakespeare's lifetime. Two early seventeenth-century writers, however, seem to allude to performances of a play about Antony and Cleopatra. Robert Anton in *The Philosophers Satyrs* talks about immodest women who 'gad' to 'base *Playes*' where 'They shall see the *vices* of the *times*, / *Orestes* incest, *Cleopatres* crimes' (Anton, 46), and Richard Brathwait in *The English Gentlewoman* remarks that 'Loues enteruiew betwixt *Cleopatra* and *Marke Anthony*, promised to it selfe as much secure freedome as fading fancy could tender; yet the last Scene clozed all those Comicke passages with a Tragicke conclusion' (Brathwait, 196–7). The first of these comments was made before the publication of the First Folio, but the second (if it does refer to Shakespeare's play) could have been based on a reading rather than a performance.

With the closing of the theatres by Act of Parliament in 1642 the kinds of playhouse for which Shakespeare wrote were obliterated. The Globe was demolished in 1644 and the Blackfriars was pulled down eleven years later in order to make way for 'tenements'. When, after the restoration of Charles II, new theatres were built, they were of a different design and served audiences of different tastes.

THE QUESTION OF UNITY

Unities of place and time

After the Restoration, criticism of the drama, and especially of tragedy, was still dominated by a respect for the 'rules' or 'unities', often attributed to Aristotle but fully formulated in the late sixteenth century by the Italian scholar Castelvetro. The drama, he declared, 'cannot represent places very far apart, while the narrative method joins together places which are widely separated'. Similarly, whereas 'the narrative method joins together diverse times', this is something which the drama cannot do, since it 'cannot represent more things than those which come about in the space of time that the comedies and tragedies themselves require' (Castelvetro, 309). As Sir Philip Sidney put it, 'the stage should always represent but one place, and the uttermost time presupposed in it should be, both by Aristotle's precept and common reason, but one day' (Sidney, *Defence*, 113). With its constant shifting from one part of the Mediterranean to another and its time-span of ten years, *Antony and Cleopatra* clearly violated these principles and thereby offended contemporary educated tastes.

Before *Antony and Cleopatra* was written, several tragedies on the same subject had already been published both in England

and on the continent in which Castelvetro's principles had been faithfully observed. These included *Antonius* (1592) by Mary, Countess of Pembroke, Sidney's sister (an adaptation of Robert Garnier's *Marc Antoine*, 1578), and Samuel Daniel's *Tragedie of Cleopatra* (1594), with both of which Shakespeare was probably acquainted (see pages 61–3). If we consider how influential the rules were, it is clear, as Bevington points out (Cam[2] 46), that Shakespeare's was 'the truly innovative interpretation'.

John Dryden had the greatest admiration for Shakespeare but also realized, of course, that he was always breaking the rules, and especially in *Antony and Cleopatra*. As a kind of tribute, but also an implied criticism of Shakespeare, he wrote his own version of the tragedy, *All for Love*, a play based on Shakespeare's source, North's translation of Plutarch, and much influenced by Shakespeare but so radically rewritten as to constitute an original work and designed to suit contemporary taste. Dryden recast the action so as to keep it within the neoclassical unities and rewrote the dialogue in plainer, more lucid, decorous language. His tragedy occupies only the last day of the protagonists' lives and is confined throughout to Alexandria. Dryden also congratulated himself on maintaining the unity of action which is, as he himself wrote, 'so much one, that it is the only of the kind without Episode, or Underplot; every Scene in the Tragedy conducing to the main design, and every Act concluding with a turn of it' (Dryden, *Love*, 10). There is therefore no tragedy of Enobarbus, who is, indeed, absent from the play. Although *All for Love* cannot help but suffer by comparison with Shakespeare's play, it is an excellent tragedy of its kind and Dryden had good reason to be satisfied with it. It contains some of his most vigorous writing, as in Antony's expression of his deep affection for Dolabella:

> I was his Soul; he liv'd not but in me:
> We were so clos'd within each other's brests,

> The rivets were not found, that join'd us first.
> That does not reach us yet: we were so mixt,
> As meeting streams, both to ourselves were lost;
> We were one mass; we could not give or take,
> But from the same; for he was I, I he.
>
> (3.1.91–7; Dryden, *Love*, 58)

Although the language is plainer than Shakespeare's, it is seldom prosaic. It is more 'natural' but, as Dryden said in another context, it is 'exalted above the level of common converse, as high as the imagination can carry [it] with proportion to verisimility' (Dryden, *Essays*, 1.100–1). *All for Love* was first performed in 1677 and, though it was not successful initially, it grew in popularity and was played fairly regularly until the early nineteenth century. In 1977 the Prospect Theatre Company alternated performances of Dryden's tragedy with Shakespeare's and Barbara Jefford played Cleopatra in both plays.

The eighteenth century

The first critics of *Antony and Cleopatra* deplored Shakespeare's violation of the rules. 'Almost all his Historical Plays', Nicholas Rowe complained in 1709, 'comprehend a great length of Time, and very different and distinct Places: And in his *Antony* and *Cleopatra*, the Scene travels over the greatest Part of the *Roman* Empire' (Rowe, 1.xviii). 'If one undertook to examine the greatest part of these [tragedies] by those Rules which are establish'd by Aristotle ... it would be no very hard Task to find a great many Faults' (Rowe, 1.xxvi). Such 'faults' could be explained, though not justified, by Shakespeare's having lived in 'a state of almost universal licence and ignorance'. His was a time in which everyone 'took the liberty to write according to the dictates of his own fancy.' Under the circumstances it was surprising that he managed to write as well as he did.

It is significant that Rowe, the first critical biographer of Shakespeare, was also his first scholarly editor. It was he who first divided the text consistently into acts and scenes, thereby breaking up the continuity which it had displayed in the First Folio, and he who gave to each scene a geographical location (Charney, 94). Hence the first scene, according to Rowe, is set in 'Alexandria in Egypt', the fourth in 'Rome' and 4.15 in 'A magnificent Monument'. Subsequent editors became more specific. Theobald in 1733 notes at the beginning of 1.4 that '*the scene changes to* Caesar's *Palace in* Rome' and in 4.5 that it '*changes to a Camp*'. Clearly the editors were beginning to visualise the play in terms of performance on the eighteenth-century and not the Jacobean stage. In printed editions such irrelevant directions for staging became increasingly elaborate to the extent that by 1950 Dover Wilson located 4.15 in 'Cleopatra's monument; a square stone building with a flat roof and a heavily barred gateway in the centre of the outer wall'.

The increasing fragmentation of the play as it appeared in print happened simultaneously with the growing realism of theatrical scenery. By the time David Garrick mounted what was the first recorded production (at the Drury Lane Theatre in 1759), movable scenery had been introduced into the London theatres, consisting both of 'flats' which could be rolled on and off the stage in grooves, and 'drops' which were lowered from above (Southern, 32–4, 269, plates 39–41). Some adaptation of the text had therefore to be made in order to reduce the number of scenes and to avoid frequent scene changes, a process which went on up to the end of the nineteenth century. Hence some of the Roman scenes were omitted and the many short battle scenes conflated. Since the role of Cleopatra remained substantially intact, however (the last act was performed in its entirety), the emphasis of the play was significantly altered. It became essentially a tragedy of love played out within a sketchy political context. The failure of the production – which was given only six times – was attributed by one of the actors, Thomas Davies, to Garrick's inadequacy as Antony. Garrick, he recalled, 'from his passionate desire to give the public as much of their admired poet as possible, revived it ... with all the advantages of new scenes, habits, and other decorations proper to the play.' Nevertheless 'it did not answer his own and the public expectation' because Garrick 'wanted one necessary accomplishment: his person was not sufficiently important and commanding to represent the part' (T. Davies, 2.368). Garrick was a small man but his height was not, apparently, a handicap when he played Hamlet and Richard III, his most successful Shakespearean roles.

Of the style of Garrick's production we know practically nothing, but the only published notice suggests that it was visually striking: 'Upon the whole we think this play now better suited for the stage, than the closet, as scenery, dresses, and parade strike the eye, and divert one's attention from the poet.'[1] The prompter at Drury Lane, Richard Cross, noted in his record book that the play was 'all new dress'd and had fine Scenes' but 'did not seem to give the audience any great pleasure or draw any Applause' (Stone, 27). We have no pictures of the costumes but there are drawings of a Drury Lane *Julius Caesar* from that period which show that care was taken to reproduce Roman military dress (Merchant, 72–3), a first step towards the historical authenticity which much preoccupied nineteenth-century designers.

It may be that, when Samuel Johnson commented on *Antony and Cleopatra* in his edition of Shakespeare published six years later, he was influenced by the production put on by his close friend and former pupil David Garrick. Although he elsewhere dismissed the unities as irrelevant to the experience of a play in the theatre and used *Antony and Cleopatra* to illustrate his argument, he nevertheless protested that 'the events, of which the principal are described according to history, are produced

1   *A letter to the Hon. Author of the New Farce, Called the Rout ... Containing some remarks upon the New-revived Play of Antony and Cleopatra*, 1759 (Lamb, 45).

without any art of connection or care of disposition' (Johnson, 180).

The nineteenth century

During the course of the nineteenth century, productions became increasingly elaborate. John Philip Kemble's at Covent Garden in 1813, according to a correspondent in *Bell's Weekly Messenger* (19 December), was 'accompanied with a peculiar pomp and taste in the scenery and decorations' and he doubted whether 'Greece in all her elegance, and Rome, in all her luxury, possessed a stage which could rival Covent Garden, in pure refinement, and classical splendour'. There was an actual sea fight in which galleys were brought on to the stage and, at the conclusion of the performance, a funeral oration delivered by Dolabella ('His legs bestrid the ocean ...') was followed by a 'grand funeral procession' and an Epicedium sung by a choir of forty-five singers grouped round the sarcophagus (Davies; Lamb, 54–9). To accommodate this additional spectacle, Shakespeare's text had to be substantially cut, but further excisions were needed to make room for extracts from *All for Love*. Kemble no doubt hoped that his extravagant entertainment would fill the three thousand seats at the theatre (Odell, 2.13) but he was disappointed. The production, which was followed (as was the custom) by a comedy, *The Invisible Bridegroom*, was performed only nine times. Hazlitt, in the *Morning Chronicle* (16 November 1813), devoted most of his review to attacking the rearrangement and cutting of the text and the mixing of Shakespeare with Dryden.

Further extravaganzas followed. The most striking feature of the revival at Drury Lane in 1833, in which Macready appeared as Antony, was the designs of Charles Stanfield which, according to the playbill, included 'A Garden of Cleopatra's palace', 'a portico attached to the house of Octavius Caesar with the Capitol in the distance' and 'the promontory of Actium with views of the fleets of Caesar and Antony' (Odell, 2.176). Samuel Phelps at Sadler's Wells in 1849 created a vast procession (unsupported by the text, of course) out of Antony's victorious return to Alexandria (4.8). 'Phelps entered marching, followed by his lieutenants, many officers in ranks of four, trophies, then "*21 troops 3 abreast*". To greet him Miss Glyn [the Cleopatra] entered with "*12 Amazonian guards*" as well as her Egyptian guards, who ranged across the back of the stage' (Lamb, 67). To accommodate such lavish additions twelve of the forty-two scenes (mostly the political and military ones) were cut.

Opulent spectacle had, however, not yet reached its greatest extravagance and, as Lamb points out, with 'the increasing use of three-dimensional pieces for realistically detailed scenery, the sets could no longer be changed in view of the audience' (73). The number of scenes had, consequently, to be further reduced, the number of intervals increased and the continuity of playing further abandoned. The audiences were, in general, delighted. After the naval battle, again performed in full view, in Frederick Chatterton's 1873 production (Fig. 4), they reached a pitch of excitement 'which would not be calmed till Mr. Chatterton came before the curtain' (*The Times*, 22 September 1873). The critics, however, were not enthusiastic. The *Illustrated London News* protested 'we cannot but suffer with regret the mutilation of a classic and colossal work.... We venture to hope that in these days of spiritualism, the shade of the Bard of Avon was not present to witness these proceedings that pay so little respect to the gorgeous poetry which they interrupt and show a disposition to substitute' (27 September). Dutton Cook observed that, with so many stage effects, the actors 'occupy a rather subordinate position. Their services cannot be wholly dispensed with; still they are felt to be but the stopgaps of the representation, the aids and vehicles of the scene painter and the designer' (Cook, 208).

Such protests, unheeded by the theatre managers, grew

4 The death of Antony in Frederick Chatterton's production at Drury
  Lane, 1873, with James Anderson as Antony and Ellen Wallis as Cleopatra

stronger. Both critics and audiences agreed that in his production of 1890 Lewis Wingfield had gone too far. According
to *The Times* (19 November 1890) Shakespeare was 'merely
the pretext for a huge Oriental pantomime' and by the end of
the performance, which lasted for over four hours, 'the house
was indifferent to all but its own exhaustion'. The critic of the
Illustrated London News (22 November) agreed that, after 'an
intolerable deal of pomp, procession, ballet, chorus, tableau
and general glitter.... The mind slumbers and the eyes, weary
with watching, gradually close.'

The twentieth century

At the time when the reviewers were objecting to the wearisome
pomp of *Antony and Cleopatra* as it was presented in the
theatre, the critics continued to say that the play lacked unity.
A. C. Bradley singles out as the first of Shakespeare's 'real

defects' his tendency to 'string together a number of scenes in which the *dramatis personae* are frequently changed'. Like Castelvetro he finds such a method acceptable in a narrative but not in a play, and particularly 'where the historical material [is] undramatic, as in the middle part of *Antony and Cleopatra*'. He concedes that it 'was made possible by the absence of scenery' but insists that, 'considered abstractly, it is a defective method' (Bradley, 71). While admitting that the play might create a different effect on the Jacobean stage, he still seems to visualize it in terms of the realistic theatre of the late nineteenth century where *Antony and Cleopatra*, 'the most faultily constructed of all the tragedies', 'imposes the necessity of taking frequent and fatiguing journeys over thousands of miles' (ibid., 260).

It is astonishing to see that even E. K. Chambers, to whom, more than anyone, we owe our knowledge and understanding of the Elizabethan playhouse, should nevertheless continue to think of *Antony and Cleopatra* in terms of scenes and locations:

> Rome, Misenum, Athens, Actium, Syria, Egypt are the localities, with much further subdivision in the Egyptian scenes. The second act has four changes of locality, the third no less than eight, and it is noteworthy that these changes are often for quite short bits of dialogue, which no modern manager would regard as justifying a resetting of the stage. Shakespeare must surely have been in some danger, in this case, of outrunning the apprehension of his auditory.
>
> (Chambers, *Stage*, 3.124)

The discrepancy between Chambers's formidable knowledge of Elizabethan playhouses and his conception of a play in performance was thoroughly exposed in an article by Harley Granville-Barker:

> When [Chambers] speaks of 'the various types of scene which the sixteenth-century managers were called upon

to produce' [and] of 'the degree of use which they make of a structural background' ... well, I protest that the sixteenth-century manager, at any rate, would not have known what he meant by such talk. The play was acted on a stage. The actors came on the stage and went off it. That was the basis of the business.... Having made use of it, the dramatist would neglect and obliterate a locality without further consideration.

(Granville-Barker, 'Note', 63–4)

Paradoxically Granville-Barker owed his grasp of the Elizabethan stage largely to the researches of Chambers, though scholarly inquiry into the subject had begun in the eighteenth century with the work of Edmond Malone. It had taken a great leap forward in 1888 when the so-called De Witt drawing was discovered in the library of the University of Utrecht. This only surviving representation of the interior of an Elizabethan playhouse (the Swan) showed for the first time the thrust stage, the two entrance doors, the surrounding galleries and the auditorium open to the sky. The consequent impulse to mount the plays under conditions similar to those shown in the drawing came initially from William Poel, the founder of the Elizabethan Stage Society, who believed they should be acted with the same simplicity and pace as in Shakespeare's time. Poel himself never put on productions in a regular theatre. For lack of money, he had to be content with using mostly amateur actors and to construct temporary platform stages in halls designed for other purposes, but Granville-Barker, who had taken part in some of Poel's productions and was already distinguished for his performances in the plays of Shaw and Ibsen, took Poel's principles into the professional theatre with his simply staged, largely uncut versions of *The Winter's Tale* (1912), *Twelfth Night* (1912) and *A Midsummer Night's Dream* (1914) at the Savoy. Neither Poel nor Granville-Barker directed *Antony and Cleopatra*, but Barker wrote an extensive Preface to it (and to eight of Shakespeare's other plays) which had a profound effect on the style of all subsequent productions and is still felt today. When the cast of *Antony and Cleopatra* assembled for rehearsals at the National Theatre in 1987, the director, Sir Peter Hall, began by reading to them extracts from Granville-Barker's Preface, and its influence was everywhere evident in the production (Lowen, 1–2).

In his Preface Granville-Barker insisted that a director must free his mind from the act and scene divisions imposed by Rowe. 'There is no juncture', he says, 'where the play's acting will be made more effective by a pause' (Granville-Barker, *Prefaces*, 127). The division of the Folio texts into scenes, he explains, did not commit the editors to 'an imagined change of place, nor connote any check to the action':

> By Rowe's time ... painted scenery, of a more or less conventional sort, was in current use. This defined locality; and a change of scene meant a change of place, was a diversion and a check to the action in every sense. The old fluidity of the Elizabethan stage, which really could 'call the mind forward without inter-mission', was gone.

The Elizabethan stage, he continues, gave to its dramatists a freedom 'which the promise of the scenic stage gradually sapped; but Shakespeare, at least, never surrendered to it.' In *Antony and Cleopatra* 'we find him in the maturity of his craftsmanship, enjoying and exploiting it to the full' (135).

The first production of the tragedy to be done according to the principles of Poel and Granville-Barker was directed by Robert Atkins at the Old Vic in 1922. The scenery was very simple and consisted chiefly of wooden cut-outs and movable steps set against a cyclorama (Lamb, 106–7). The text was only slightly cut and the performance ran rapidly. It received few notices, however (presumably because the Waterloo Road was thought less worthy of attention than the West End), and those who did review it seemed unaware that anything unusual had happened. The full effect of Granville-Barker's ideas was not evident until after the Second World War, in, for example, Glen Byam Shaw's production at the Shakespeare Memorial Theatre in 1953. Working with the designers Motley, Shaw constructed a set of stairs close to the front of the stage and spanning its entire width, which brought the actors closer to the audience and created an impression of spaciousness appropriate for the 'ranged empire' which the action encompasses. This sense of space was further accentuated by limiting the furniture to a minimum and was most apparent when the entire depth of the stage was revealed to the cyclorama at the back. The emptiness of the stage also allowed the performance to be taken at speed. As the *New Statesman* reported (9 May 1953),

> The scenes shuttle in unbroken succession, the luxurious glow of the East giving instant place to the cold white of Rome, and it is only a second and closer look that assures one that this is pure illusion created by light alone on the cyclorama. Never again does one want to see the cluttered stage which most productions need to employ to suggest the necessary pomp.

Simplicity of setting and rapidity of performance also characterized the production at Stratford in 1972 when, under the direction of Trevor Nunn, *Antony and Cleopatra* was presented as part of a season which included all four of Shakespeare's Roman tragedies. The productions acquired a certain unity by being played within the same set, an austere white box. Locations were suggested by stage furniture (large, luxurious cushions in Egypt; a massive table for the political negotiations in Rome) and by the contrast between the military dress and white togas of the Romans and the pink, mauve and orange robes of the Egyptians (Fig. 6). This simplicity of style allowed it to be transferred very successfully to television, where, on

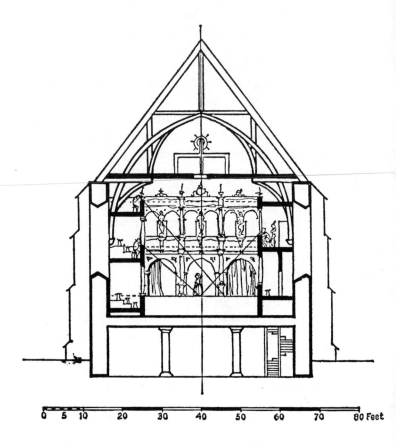

5 An artist's impression of a Jacobean indoor theatre, the Blackfriars

the small screen, it became a much more domestic drama. This may, in fact, have been closer to the style in which Shakespeare conceived it. Emrys Jones suggests that the play could have been designed originally for the Blackfriars theatre, a relatively small, indoor auditorium:

> [It] certainly should never be thought of in terms of cinematic or operatic spectacle. Although it abounds

24

6 Royal Shakespeare Company production by Trevor Nunn, 1972, with Janet Suzman as Cleopatra

in imagery of cosmic vastness, it works through short scenes and small groups of characters and through effects of often minute delicacy. Unlike Shakespeare's other Roman plays, it has no crowd scenes: it is in many ways a quiet play, conversational rather than declamatory.

(Jones, 7–8)

These were certainly the effects created by Nunn's television version and by Jonathan Miller's for the BBC in 1980. Both directors were compelled by the nature of the medium to reveal elements in the play which the Victorian actor managers had obscured.

Once a style of production approximating to that of Shakespeare's own time had been thoroughly established, the question of unity was not again raised by the critics, who now began to consider the construction of *Antony and Cleopatra* on its own terms. The extravagant nineteenth-century way of staging it did not die out entirely, however, but reappeared, complete with sea fight, in Charlton Heston's film (1972).

THE QUESTION OF STRUCTURE

Shifts of location

The dramatic construction of *Antony and Cleopatra*, with its constant shifts of location, is one which Shakespeare had already used in the two parts of *Henry IV* with their oscillations between the court, the tavern and the battlefield and their excursions into Wales and Gloucestershire. This in turn grew out of the mode he had used in the comedies, where one location is set off against another: the house of Baptista against that of Petruchio in *The Taming of the Shrew*, the city and the wood in *A Midsummer Night's Dream*, Venice and Belmont in *The Merchant of Venice*. It had, in fact, been Shakespeare's way of working from the very beginning. As Emrys Jones points out,

A striking feature of a play like *1 Henry VI* is the constant comparativeness of its method: we are never allowed to become identified with the point of view of any one of its characters. Although Talbot is a famous soldier-hero, he is only one of several main figures. The play's vision of reality is never less than complex:

26

all viewpoints are partial. Hence the endless oscillation
from one group, one individual, to another.

(Jones, *Origins*, 13–14)

By the time he wrote the two *Henry IV* plays, this kind of
construction was a means whereby he presented the audience
with a number of different assumptions, attitudes and ways of
life. The civil war, for example, which to King Henry is a
source of continual anxiety, to Falstaff is an opportunity to line
his own pockets, and the interview between the King and the
Prince, which in the court takes place in earnest, is the subject
of a charade in the tavern. The audience is offered several
different and conflicting attitudes to the same experience, and
is invited to weigh the public responsibilities of war and politics
against the personal desire for pleasure, comradeship and self-
satisfaction. During the greater part of the two plays the
conflicting attitudes are kept equally in view, chiefly in the
figure of the Prince, who manages to encompass both, but
towards the end of each play he is compelled to make a choice,
first when he pledges himself to defeat Hotspur in Part 1, and
again when he casts off Falstaff in Part 2. On the second
occasion, however, the impression is created that in dismissing
Falstaff he repudiates a part of himself. There is no wholly
'correct' choice. England's gain is Falstaff's loss and, though
we do not feel that his decision is wholly laudable, the
alternative – to embrace Falstaff – would have been far worse.

In *Antony and Cleopatra* Shakespeare created a similar kind
of structure but used it with greater complexity and carried its
implications further. Throughout the play, Roman attitudes
and principles, expressed mainly by Octavius Caesar, are placed
in opposition to the Egyptian, represented chiefly by Cleopatra.
Antony is in a similar position to Prince Hal, equally at home
in either world but compelled eventually to choose between
them, and the critics, as we shall see, have continued to argue
whether or not he chose correctly. As Maurice Charney says,

27

Rome and Egypt 'represent crucial moral choices and they function as symbolic locales in a manner not unlike Henry James's Europe and America' (Charney, 93).

Egypt and Rome

Rome is represented by a predominantly male society in which the only woman, Octavia, is regarded as a ' "cement" to promote and consolidate male relations' (Erickson, 128). For the Romans the ideal is measured in masculine, political, pragmatic, military terms, the subservience of the individual to the common good of the state, of personal pleasure to public duty, of private, domestic loyalties to the demands of empire. Alexandria, on the other hand, is a predominantly female society for which the ideal is measured in terms of the intensity of emotion, of physical sensation, the subservience of social responsibility to the demands of feeling. Hence Cleopatra must send to Antony every day a several greeting or she'll unpeople Egypt, and, at Actium, Antony deserts his own men and takes flight with Cleopatra because his heart is tied to her rudder. Adelman points out the extreme contrast between the two eulogies of Antony, the first delivered by Caesar in praise of the hardened soldier he once was (1.4.56–72), the second by Cleopatra in celebration of the Antony who has died (5.2.78–91). Since both are retrospective and neither corresponds with the man we are actually shown, both are idealizations, but, in describing the ideal, both speakers reveal the values they espouse. Whereas Caesar, says Adelman, 'locates Antony in the Timonesque landscape of absolute deprivation', a winter landscape in which he survives by exercising the manly virtues of fortitude and endurance, Cleopatra places him in a setting of 'immense abundance' with 'no winter in it': 'The contest between Caesar and Cleopatra, Rome and Egypt, is in part a contest between male scarcity and female bounty as the defining site of Antony's heroic masculinity' (Adelman, *Mothers*, 176–

7). For Caesar, as for Coriolanus, manliness entails the repression of all that is female, but for Cleopatra Antony is visualized as like herself, 'feeding and renewing the appetite in an endless cycle of gratification and desire, making hungry where most she satisfies' (ibid., 190). Caesar regards his 'great competitor' as a man who has betrayed his own ideals (as, indeed, does Antony from time to time) but Cleopatra sees him as a man who has become at one with herself. As Erickson puts it, 'Octavius finds in Antony a heightened image of his own abstemiousness, Cleopatra's celebration of the bountiful Antony projects a model in which she discovers her own bounty' (Erickson, 142). As so often in Shakespeare, every gain is a different kind of loss and every asset a different kind of liability. 'We are left at the end with a painfully divided response, for which there is no resolution' (ibid., 145).

Shifts within scenes

These contrasts and contradictions form the basis on which the play is constructed and also determine the shape of individual scenes. In the opening scene the 'flourish' or fanfare of trumpets leads us to expect the formal entry of some distinguished leader but it is followed by the arrival of Antony and Cleopatra with her maids, 'with eunuchs fanning her'. The 'triple pillar of the world' is exhibited to us as what the Roman Philo calls 'a strumpet's fool'. Again, the formal reconciliation between Antony and Caesar (2.2.18–180) is immediately followed by a private conversation between Maecenas and Enobarbus about the excesses of Alexandrian social life (2.2.185–99), and the former's belief that Antony must now leave Cleopatra is followed by the latter's assurance that he will not. The official feast which is held to celebrate the success of the peace conference (2.7) is preceded by the chatter among the servants about the drunkenness of the guests. The poignancy of Caesar's farewell to his sister (3.2) is undermined by the cynical observations of Agrippa and Enobarbus which introduce it, and their sarcastic asides during the course of the scene prevent us from taking it wholly seriously. This counterpointing of the poignant, the solemn and the tragic against the ironical, the sceptical and the absurd is most apparent in Shakespeare's treatment of Antony's suicide. Believing that he has suffered his ultimate defeat and that Cleopatra has killed herself, he realizes that the two ideals to which he has devoted his life have been destroyed and he therefore resolves to die in the Roman, stoical manner by falling on his sword. His ineffectual attempt to do so, however, is both painful and ridiculous: his servant Eros, instead of assisting his master, falls on his own sword; when Antony tries to kill himself he fails; the guards, refusing to complete the job, walk away, and it is now when he is at his most abject that he learns that Cleopatra is still alive. Nevertheless he insists on giving her the heroic version of the story:

> [I] do now not basely die,
> Not cowardly put off my helmet to
> My countryman; a Roman by a Roman
> Valiantly vanquished.
>
> (4.15.57–60)

This is – and is not – a faithful account of the scene we have witnessed. Even the most transcendentally moving moment in the play, the suicide of Cleopatra towards which the whole of the final scene has been moving, is interrupted by the entry of the Clown with his basket of figs. His garrulous chatter and his reluctance to leave (perhaps, as Bowers suggests, he's hoping for a tip) delay Cleopatra's death and thereby create suspense but they also modify our impression of her final speeches during which, as Mack remarks, 'we also hear echoing between the lines the gritty accents of the opposing voice' (Mack, 23).

Instability of characters

Such radically differing attitudes are expressed not only by different individuals but by the same person, depending on the mood and circumstances in which characters find themselves. To Antony, Cleopatra is at one moment 'this enchanting queen' and at another a 'triple-turned whore', and to Cleopatra the messenger from Rome is at first a 'horrible villain' and later 'a fellow of good judgement', 'a proper man'. These conflicting ways of interpreting experience had long preoccupied Shakespeare but in this play they are also a preoccupation of the characters. On hearing of Fulvia's death, Antony reflects, as though it were axiomatic.

> The present pleasure,
> By revolution lowering, does become
> The opposite of itself
>
> (1.2.131–3)

and Caesar, contemplating the growing support for Pompey, states it as a law of nature that

> he which is was wished until he were,
> And the ebbed man, ne'er loved till ne'er worth love,
> Comes deared by being lacked.
>
> (1.4.42–4)

It is when he himself hears of Antony's death that his contempt for the 'old ruffian' turns into grief and he weeps for the loss of his 'brother', his 'mate in empire' and the heart which kindled his own thoughts (5.1.40–8). Nowhere else in Shakespeare do we meet

> characters given to such persistent oscillation of feel-
> ings, such violent veering between emotional extremes.
> In the case of Cleopatra it is at times deliberately

31

practised, part of her technique of exhibiting her infinite variety in order to keep monotony at bay, her method of tantalising Antony by providing moods that are emotional foils to his own.

(Schanzer, *Problem Plays*, 143)

The actress who by all accounts conveyed this quality most faithfully was Dorothy Green, who played the role in three major productions between 1912 and 1930. Of the second of these, the *Times* critic wrote (25 April 1921):

She realises, as few players of the part in recent years have done, the 'infinite variety' of the Queen's moods. Stately, sinuous, arrogant, seductive, pleading, passionate – Miss Green is everything in turn, but she rises to her greatest height in the scene of sheer fury when she learns from the Messenger of Antony's marriage to Octavia, and all but strangles him in her madness.

Judging from the photographs, she was also sinister, a *femme fatale* like Swinburne's Dolores or Wilde's Salomé (Fig. 7), and the reviewers sensed this: 'What evil there is in the woman, gathered scene by scene as one might gather flowers, and what superb and dreadful tenderness when the asp is at her breast' (*The Times*, 25 November 1930). She was very much the actress, fascinating, temperamental, and dangerous, as was also the great nineteenth-century Cleopatra, Isabella Glyn, though she was a good deal more majestic:

Gorgeous in person, in costume, and in her style of action, she moved, the Egyptian Venus, Minerva, Juno – now pleased, now angry, now eloquent, now silent – capricious and resolved, according to the situation and sentiment to be rendered. Withal she was

7 Dorothy Green as Cleopatra at the Shakespeare Memorial Theatre, 1912

classical, and her *poses* severely statuesque. Her death was sublime.... Altogether Miss Glyn's performance of *Cleopatra* is the most superb thing ever witnessed on the modern stage.

(*Illustrated London News*, 27 October 1849)

A contemporary illustration shows her in one of her poses offering her hand to Thidias (Fig. 8).

Images of instability

The sense of the inconstant, shifting nature of our impressions that is expressed by the structure of the play and the pre-occupations of the characters extends also to its distinctive images, which, as Charney points out, are of 'melting, fading, dissolving, discandying, disponging and losing of form': 'Shakespeare seems to be creating his own vocabulary to establish the feeling of disintegration in the Roman world' (Charney, 140). Indeed the whole play portrays the gradual process of Antony's disintegration to the point when 'The crown o'th' earth doth melt' (4.15.65). Shakespeare's playhouse was probably better able than ours to convey this impression to an audience. What was in front of them was, of course, an empty platform with the tiring-house wall at the back, but Shakespeare could transform it into wherever he chose, as when in *A Midsummer Night's Dream* (another play much preoccupied with the fluid nature of reality) Theseus' court melts into a forest. Similarly in *Antony and Cleopatra* Alexandria melts into Rome and the battlefield becomes Cleopatra's monument. This effect is well described by Granville-Barker, who says that the Elizabethan dramatist, having made use of a location, 'would neglect and obliterate it without further consideration. The consciousness of it in the audience's imagination might be compared to a mirage, suddenly appearing, imperceptibly fading' (Granville-

8 Isabella Glyn as Cleopatra with, in the background, Samuel Phelps as Antony at Sadler's Wells, 1849

Barker, 'Note', 64). On a realistic, nineteenth-century stage with its solid sets and frequent scene changes this was no longer possible. The actor in Chatterton's production, James Anderson, describes the effect of such scene changes on an actor:

> I must ... acknowledge my own inability to make a serious impression on the audience; I could do nothing, being stunned and cowed by the furious noise of preparation for 'heavy sets' behind the scenes that destroyed all power of acting in front.
>
> (J. Anderson, 316–17)

The fullest expression of the melting, dissolving nature of

perception is given by Antony in one of those insights which Shakespeare's tragic heroes experience shortly before their deaths. As a great soldier who knows he has undergone his final defeat, he contemplates the shifting patterns of the clouds and feels that he, too, is no longer 'himself':

> That which is now a horse, even with a thought
> The rack dislimns and makes it indistinct
> As water is in water.
>
> My good knave Eros, now thy captain is
> Even such a body. Here I am Antony,
> Yet cannot hold this visible shape, my knave.
>
> (4.14.9–11, 12–14)

The philosophy of instability

This idea was not unique to Shakespeare but also preoccupied some of his contemporaries. Bacon was certainly aware of each individual's tendency to interpret the world subjectively, 'owing either to his own proper and peculiar nature' or 'to the differences of impression, accordingly as they take place in a mind preoccupied and predisposed or in a mind indifferent and settled'. 'The spirit of man', he concludes, 'is in fact a thing variable and full of perturbation' (Bacon, 54). The writer who most immediately comes to mind is, however, Montaigne, with whose *Essayes* Shakespeare was certainly acquainted by the time he came to write *The Tempest* and who contemplated with a melancholy curiosity the transience both of the world and of mankind:

> There is no constant existence, neither of our being, nor of the objects. And we and our judgement, and all mortall things else do uncessantly rowle, turne and passe away. Thus can be nothing certainely established, nor of the one, nor of the other; both the judgeing

and the judged being in continuall alteration and motion.... Thus, seeing all things are subject to passe from one change to another; reason, which therein seeketh a reall subsistence, findes her selfe deceived as unable to apprehend any thing subsistent and permanent; forsomuch as each thing either commeth to a being, and is not yet altogether: or beginneth to dy before it be borne.

(Montaigne, 323)

Both Bacon and Montaigne express the renewed influence of philosophical scepticism which appeared in Europe towards the end of the seventeenth century, but transformation is also the central theme of Ovid's *Metamorphoses*, perhaps the most lasting influence on all Shakespeare's work and which he must have read as a schoolboy. The Roman poet's prolonged meditation in the last book of the *Metamorphoses* on the ceaseless flux of creation probably lies behind this distinctive element of the play.

The desire for stability

Against such an irresistible force, Shakespeare's characters attempt to create some sort of defence which will keep them stable and upon which they can rely. Caesar, foreseeing that his own and Antony's temperaments are so incompatible that their friendship is unlikely to last, longs for a 'hoop' which will hold them 'staunch' or watertight (2.2.121–3); Antony, ashamed of his lost reputation and his pitifully botched suicide, hopes that his fame as 'the greatest prince o'th' world' will remain intact (4.15.53–7), and Enobarbus recognizes that a servant willing to remain loyal to a 'fallen lord' will '[earn] a place i'th' story' (3.13.44–7) as, by his death, he does. Similarly the poet of the *Sonnets* hopes that the beauty of the fair youth will be eternalized in his verse when all other things have changed or been forgotten. Finally, Cleopatra becomes 'marble-constant' in her resolve to leave 'the varying shore o'th' world' and find eternal stability with Antony in an existence beyond change. Whether or not she does so we have no means of knowing. We know only that she is convinced that she will, and that by her suicide she has earned a place in the story which Plutarch and Shakespeare and others have repeatedly told.

THE QUESTION OF MORAL JUDGEMENT

In the principal source of *Antony and Cleopatra*, the 'Life of Antony', Plutarch displays a disinterested attitude towards the two major figures (see page 60). He acknowledges their strengths and virtues – Antony's courage and magnanimity, Cleopatra's vitality, her magnetism – yet this responsive sympathy does not prevent him from judging them. Even in his youth, says Plutarch, Antony was lured into 'great follies and vain expences upon women, in rioting and banketing' (North, 255) and he lays the blame for Antony's decline squarely on Cleopatra (North, 273).

Shakespeare's judgement of his characters is less easy to discern. This is partly because, whereas Plutarch tells his story as a narrative on which he comments from time to time in his own person, Shakespeare transformed it into a play in which each character expresses him or her self and no character speaks with the voice of the dramatist. There are characters such as Philo, Pompey, Enobarbus and especially Caesar who unhesitatingly criticize Antony:

>   If he filled
> His vacancy with his voluptuousness,
> Full surfeits and the dryness of his bones
> Call on him for't. But to confound such time
> That drums him from his sport, and speaks as loud

As his own state and ours, 'tis to be chid
As we rate boys who, being mature in knowledge,
Pawn their experience to their present pleasure
And so rebel to judgement.

(1.4.25–33)

Against such passages, however, Shakespeare places Cleopatra's adoration of 'my man of men':

Nature wants stuff
To vie strange forms with fancy; yet t'imagine
An Antony were nature's piece 'gainst fancy,
Condemning shadows quite.

(5.2.96–9)

To complicate matters, these same characters change their opinions of one another. Although Enobarbus acts as a commentator on the characters and action of the play, his opinions are complex and he, too, changes his mind.

Clearly with a play as paradoxical and self-contradictory as this, any attempt to determine the opinion of the author is necessarily difficult if not impossible. The only account which does justice to its complexity is the play itself and, though criticism may (and often does) illuminate, in the face of this particular work it is almost bound to simplify. Nevertheless some critics, while admitting the play's intricacy, have attempted to locate and define Shakespeare's attitude towards his material. None has been more simple and reductive than Dryden, who approved 'the excellency of the moral' which he believed the story illustrated, 'for the chief persons represented were famous patterns of unlawful love; and their end accordingly was unfortunate' (Dryden, *Love*, 10). Dowden acknowledges that 'the passion and the pleasure of the Egyptian queen, and of her paramour, toil after the infinite', but concludes that, finally, what Shakespeare 'would seem to say to us ... is that this sensuous infinite is but a dream, a deceit, a snare.... The severity of Shakespeare, in his own dramatic fashion, is as absolute as that of Milton' (Dowden, 311–13).

More recent critics have, after considerable hesitation, come to a similar conclusion. Franklin M. Dickey attempts to reach towards Shakespeare's judgement by examining *Antony and Cleopatra* in the context of earlier treatments of the same subject from Virgil's and Chaucer's onwards. He decides that, although, unlike his predecessors, the dramatist has little to say about the power of Fortune and the insecurity of princes, nevertheless, like them, he says a great deal about 'the dire consequences of indecorum on the part of princes and the terrible end of excessive passion' (Dickey, 76). For him, Antony and Cleopatra are examples of rulers who threw away a kingdom for lust, 'and this is how, despite the pity and terror that Shakespeare makes us feel, they appear in the play' (ibid., 179).

Such an interpretation was in part a protest against the opposite, romantic view, 'the elevation claimed by those critics who insist[ed] on seeing Cleopatra as a seventeenth-century precursor of Wagner's Isolde' (Riemer, 101). After all, Swinburne had called Cleopatra 'the perfect and everlasting woman' (Swinburne, *Shakespeare*, 76) and *Antony and Cleopatra* 'the greatest love-poem of all time' (Swinburne, *Study*, 191). Wilson Knight sometimes repeats what Swinburne has said, though at more length and with considerably more evidence. For him, Cleopatra is 'love absolute and incarnate' (Knight, 318), at once 'Rosalind, Beatrice, Ophelia, Gertrude, Cressida, Desdemona, Cordelia and Lady Macbeth' (ibid., 290). He arrives at his transcendental view of the tragedy by consciously discarding any attention to character and action, preferring to invoke 'certain symbolic images' which, for him, are 'the only elements in Shakespeare which will lead us from multiplicity and chaos towards unity, simplicity and coherence' (ibid., 19). He by no means overlooks the images of sensuality, eroticism and the physical but, largely by emphasizing Enobarbus' eulogy of

Cleopatra on the Cydnus and Cleopatra's idealizing vision of Antony after his death, comes to the conclusion that, in Shakespeare's treatment of them, the lovers are finally transfigured and thereby vindicated:

> We see the protagonists, in love and war and sport, in death or life or that mystery containing both, transfigured in a transfigured universe, themselves that universe and more, outpacing the wheeling orbs of earth and heaven.... So Cleopatra and Antony find not death but life.
>
> (Knight, 262)

Knight was certainly justified in calling our attention to the language and images of the play which the moralizing critics had tended generally to overlook, but in so doing he took little or no account of the characters who express themselves in these images and the context in which they occur. Enobarbus' 'barge' speech is placed immediately after Antony's agreement to marry Octavia, and the effect of this placing is to make us realize that Antony will ultimately desert her for Cleopatra and thereby give Caesar a pretext to turn against him. The magnetism of Cleopatra is shown to be disastrous politically. Again, Cleopatra's final vision of Antony, magnificent in itself, is also subjective (as is everyone's opinion in this play). As Janet Adelman pertinently asks, 'Is this the vision of the play or her own peculiar brand of delusion?' (Adelman, *Essay*, 7). The Antony she celebrates does not correspond with the one we have seen, nor is her view of him shared by any other character. Her final insight may be her ultimate delusion. Shakespeare's critics, like his characters, tend to interpret this play in accordance with the predispositions they bring to it. They can find ample support for their arguments in whatever evidence they care to select from the text.

Are all attempts to reach some final understanding simply otiose, an inevitable simplification of a challengingly complex work? This may be so, but the desire to respond to the challenge is nevertheless irresistible. 'The whole play', as Adelman says, 'can be seen as a series of attempts on the part of the characters to understand and judge each other and themselves' (Adelman, *Essay*, 20). It is scarcely surprising, then, that we should be compelled to judge them ourselves – or, at any rate, to discover how Shakespeare judged them.

Ultimately the difficulty arises out of Shakespeare's uniquely copious powers of empathy, his capacity not simply to understand people unlike himself but in his imagination to become them, as Hazlitt observed:

> He was the least of an egotist that it was possible to be. He was nothing in himself; but he was all that others were, or that they could become. He not only had in himself the germs of every faculty and feeling, but he could follow them by anticipation, intuitively, into all their conceivable ramifications, through every change of fortune or conflict of passion, or turn of thought.... He had only to think of any thing in order to become that thing, with all the circumstances belonging to it.
>
> (Hazlitt, 47–8)

Shakespeare could also identify himself with every kind of ideal, especially the Roman, with which he must have become familiar from his schooldays onwards. The two principles on which the play is built are irreconcilable, and to ask which of them Shakespeare favoured (which is what, essentially, some of the critics are doing) is not a question that should be asked.

A few critics, however, have done justice to the irreconcilable nature of the opposites with which Shakespeare presents us. Schanzer, for example, recognizes that, as a consequence of the structure of the play, 'we are confronted with these opposed evaluations, and in such a way as to exclude ... a simple or consistent response' (Schanzer, *Problem Plays*, 146), and

Bullough agrees that 'the breadth and intensity of Shakespeare's vision are such as to make us accept both moral judgements against and passionate approval of Antony and Cleopatra' (Bullough, 252). Adelman, who has explored the play more fully and subtly than anyone, concludes that 'this is the final contrariety that the play demands of us: that the extreme of skepticism must be balanced by an extreme of assent' (Adelman, *Essay*, 110).

THE QUESTION OF THE TRAGIC

In certain obvious and general ways *Antony and Cleopatra* resembles Shakespeare's other tragedies. Like *Richard II, Julius Caesar* and *Coriolanus* it is both a tragedy and a history play, a work of the imagination based largely on historical accounts and portraying people who once lived in situations in which they actually found themselves. Together with *Romeo and Juliet* it is a double tragedy, but, whereas in the earlier work the two principal characters die swiftly one after the other and for much the same reasons (a combination of self-sacrificial love and bad luck), in the later tragedy each of them undergoes a prolonged final suffering on which Shakespeare lingers. Each of their suicides constitutes a separate episode; their motives for suicide differ and produce different effects on an audience.

In some ways Antony resembles Shakespeare's other tragic heroes, exceptional men in that their fate, as Bradley says, 'affects the welfare of a whole nation or empire' (Bradley, *Tragedy*, 10). Both he and Cleopatra are exceptional too in their capacity for extreme and spontaneous feeling which manifests itself most powerfully when they are responding, whether in fury or delight, to each other. For this reason Octavius, though he becomes the supreme ruler of the Roman empire, seems a lesser person. Antony, like Brutus, Macbeth and Coriolanus, finds himself in a position in which he must make a choice which has far-reaching consequences both for himself and his country. His choice occurs fairly early in the play at the point when (2.3.37) he resolves to return from Rome to Egypt. Although his decision seems sudden, it is not, to the audience, unexpected in view of the hold which we know Cleopatra has over him, and especially because it occurs less than a hundred lines after Enobarbus' testimony to her magnetism (2.2.201–28). Unlike the other tragic heroes, however, he undergoes no apparent struggle, never defines or articulates the nature of his choice (which is, again, perfectly clear to the audience) or seems to foresee its consequences. Like Coriolanus, Shakespeare's other great Roman soldier, he never intellectualizes, has practically no soliloquies and acts always upon impulse. His decline is prolonged but follows no steady, descending line – his catastrophic flight at Actium is followed by a spectacular victory – and his insights into his predicament come to him spasmodically, in flashes:

> O, whither hast thou led me, Egypt? See
> How I convey my shame out of thine eyes
> By looking back what I have left behind
> 'Stroyed in dishonour.
>
> (3.11.51–4)

Within moments he casts such painful thoughts out of his mind. He buries them and prefers to think of what he has gained:

> Fall not a tear, I say; one of them rates
> All that is won and lost. Give me a kiss.
> (3.11.69–70)

It is only after his final defeat and what he believes to be Cleopatra's betrayal that he is forced to confront the truth of his situation and then he acts on it by committing suicide.

In his inability (or refusal) to recognize the momentous nature of his choice or to face up to and learn from its consequences, Antony is unlike Shakespeare's other tragic heroes. Macbeth, by contrast, is entirely aware of the significance of Duncan's murder even before he commits it. Antony is shown to be limited intellectually and even imaginatively, and for this reason it was not difficult for the moralizing critics to see him as a great warrior who was blinded by the charms of a woman. These are, moreover, by no means his only limitations. He is often shown in situations in which he is overshadowed or worsted by sharper intellects such as Caesar's and especially by Cleopatra's. Whereas Plutarch depicted him as a sociable entertaining man, Shakespeare's Antony, as Honigmann points out, is in the early scenes not so self-assured:

It is Cleopatra who rails and mocks, and Antony is always at the receiving end, and not amused. She laughs, he glooms. . . . Long before Actium . . . Antony impresses us in scene after scene as a loser; Herculean, but still a loser; and his defeats in conversation, added by Shakespeare, distinguish him equally from Plutarch's Antonius and from the other tragic heroes.

(Honigmann, 150, 153)

He is most miserably degraded, of course, in his failure to perform the decorous suicide which he attempts and which, in retrospect, he likes to think he has accomplished. One has only to recall the death of Brutus to see the difference.

Superficially Cleopatra appears to be possessed of that 'fatal tendency to identify the whole being with one interest, object, passion or habit of mind' which for Bradley distinguished Shakespeare's tragic figures (Bradley, *Tragedy*, 20–1). Certainly her attention in the first three scenes is fixed on Antony and on the means – any means – to discourage him from leaving her, and during his absence in Rome he is her exclusive preoccupation. His presence is necessary, however, in order to satisfy her political as well as her emotional needs. He is both her lover and the commander of her military forces, and when his fortunes decline she at least toys with the idea of settling on favourable terms with Caesar. Her possible shift of allegiance appears first in the interview with Thidias (3.13) and, although her subsequent protestations of loyalty to Antony seem to satisfy him (3.13.163–72), the audience may not be so easily assured. As Adelman says, 'Is Cleopatra merely exercising her powers over Thidias for the sake of the game, or does she really hope to woo Octavius through him?' (Adelman, *Essay*, 15). Her uppermost thought may well be of self-preservation. This is undoubtedly her impulse when, terrified of Antony's rage against her, she flees to the monument and sends him the false news of her suicide (4.13), but whether or not it is self-preservation she has in mind after Antony's death is more difficult to determine. Certainly she begins to contemplate suicide immediately after he is gone:

> Then is it sin
> To rush into the secret house of death
> Ere death dare come to us?
>
> (4.15.84–6)

and at the beginning of the final scene she appears positively resolved to take this course (5.2.4–8). In the interview with Seleucus, however, her intentions are not so clear and Shakespeare here clouds the motives which in Plutarch's account were explicit. According to Plutarch, Cleopatra deliberately allowed Caesar to discover that she had kept half her treasure in order to create the false impression that she planned to survive. In Shakespeare's version, however, it is uncertain whether she wishes to give this impression or genuinely hopes to come to terms with Caesar. In other words, her intention may be to kill herself out of devotion to Antony or to 'pack cards with Caesar' and enjoy a comfortable life in retirement. It is only when she discovers from Dolabella that the latter option is not open that she resolves finally on suicide. Honigmann sums up the situation admirably:

> Though Cleopatra's choice of death seems unconditional when Antony dies, she has time to think again, and her final decision affects us differently. She learns that Octavius will lead her in triumph, and that he can resist her charms, and again her vanity comes into play. Her actions, not necessarily all of a piece, suggest that she *may* still wish to live.
>
> (Honigmann, 166)

A similar inconsistency surrounds the suicide itself. Both she and Antony like to imagine themselves dying 'after the high Roman fashion'. Neither of them achieves this ideal and, moreover, the two suicides are utterly unlike, 'his – unplanned, messy, a man alone; hers – a basket of figs prepared with an asp, supported by her women – thrillingly beautiful. The difference is brought home to us by Antony's unbearable physical pain, succeeded by her death "As sweet as balm, as soft as air, as gentle"' (Honigmann, 166–7). She had, we learn later, 'pursued conclusions infinite / Of *easy* ways to die' (5.2.354–5; my italics). Her final act may be seen, as she wants us to see it, as a supreme and glorious sacrifice or as an extreme self-indulgence. As in his portrayal of Antony, Shakespeare does not allow us to respond in any simple way. We are at the same time drawn to and distanced from them both. Such uncertainties have been perceived only in the twentieth century, when criticism has concentrated on tensions, ambiguities, counter-cultures and self-contradiction. It was these uncertainties, however, which made the play unsatisfactory to the great interpreter of tragedy of an earlier generation, A. C. Bradley.

Bradley excluded *Antony and Cleopatra* from his study of Shakespearean tragedy, and in his *Oxford Lectures on Poetry* he stated categorically that 'to regard this tragedy as a rival of the famous four, is surely an error' (Bradley, *Lectures*, 282). He accounts for this conviction by saying that it is 'not painful', 'not as exciting dramatically' as the other four tragedies and has 'no scenes of action or passion which agitate the audience with alarm, horror, painful expectation, or absorbing sympathies and antipathies'. Eventually he identifies the quality in the play which causes his unease and, in so doing, glimpses the complex, paradoxical nature of its fabric:

> The first half of the play, though it forebodes tragedy, is not decisively tragic in tone. Certainly the Cleopatra scenes are not so. We read them, and we should witness them, in delighted wonder and even with amusement. The only scene that can vie with them, that of the revel on Pompey's ship, though full of menace, is in great part humorous. Enobarbus, in this part of the play, is always humorous. Even later, when the tragic tone is deepening, the whipping of Thyreus, in spite of Antony's rage, moves mirth.
>
> (Bradley, *Lectures*, 284–5)

He concedes that such a play may well be as 'masterly' as the four great tragedies and 'more delightful', but 'it cannot possibly excite the same emotions'. There is, he says 'something half-hearted in Shakespeare's appeal here, something even ironical in his presentation of this conflict' (ibid., 290).

That Bradley identified the distinguishing element in *Antony and Cleopatra* there can be little doubt. He senses the lack of that consistently tragic high seriousness to which he responded in *Lear* and *Macbeth*, but accepts the fact that in this play Shakespeare attempted 'something different'. One cannot help feeling, however, that by 'something different' Bradley really meant 'something inferior'. As G. K. Hunter points out in an illuminating essay on Bradley (Hunter, 270–85), he thought of himself as a philosopher-critic. As the son of an evangelical clergyman, he reacted violently against the kind of faith in which he had been brought up and found that literature, and especially Shakespearean tragedy, could fill the void once occupied in his mind by religion. In so doing he fulfilled the prediction made almost thirty years earlier by Matthew Arnold that more and more 'mankind will discover that we have to turn to poetry to interpret life for us, to console us, to sustain us' (Arnold, 2). Bradley valued Shakespeare's tragedies for their capacity to interpret the world and man's place in it without recourse to Christian theology. 'We remain confronted', as he says at the end of his lecture on 'The Substance of Tragedy',

> with the inexplicable fact, or the no less inexplicable appearance, of a world travailing for perfection, but bringing to birth, together with glorious good, an evil which it is able to overcome only by self-torture and self-waste. And this fact or appearance is tragedy.
>
> (Bradley, Tragedy, 39)

Such a description may well apply to *Othello* and *Macbeth*, where good and evil are precisely located, but to *Antony and Cleopatra*, where the perfection for which the two principal characters strive is also shown to be a waste and a delusion, it seems irrelevant. Nothing purely good or evil can be found in the play and what seems admirable in one context is shown as ridiculous in another – or, rather, appears as both admirable and ridiculous at one and the same time. A tragedy founded on such assumptions could not satisfy Victorian readers who looked to it to console and sustain them. In the sceptical twentieth century it has been better appreciated.

LANGUAGE AND STYLE

The 'Asiatic' style

The distinctive language and style in which Antony and

Cleopatra express themselves may have been created by Shakespeare in response to a remark made by Plutarch in his 'Life of Marcus Antonius'. As a young man, says Plutarch, Antony left Italy and went to Greece where he spent much of his time in 'the studie of eloquence'. As a result of this early training he 'used a manner of phrase in his speeche, called Asiatik, which caried the best grace and estimation of that time, and was much like to his manners and life: for it was full of ostentation, foolish braverie, and vaine ambition' (North, 225). Plutarch, although a Greek, here speaks in the austerely disapproving tone of the Romans (whom he much admired) and, consistently with the rhetorical principles established by Aristotle, regards Antony's eloquence not simply as a verbal style but as a moral quality, an expression of his personality and way of life. Perhaps picking up this hint from Plutarch, Shakespeare fashioned for Antony and Cleopatra a way of speaking which he used in no other play and which contributes more than anything to the extreme contrast between Egypt and Rome discussed earlier (p. 28). As Rosalie Colie explains,

> The Greeks had, naturally enough, characterized Persians and others to the East of Athens as 'Asiatic', meaning sensuous, sybaritic, self-indulgent, rich, materialist, decorated, soft. According to the paradigm, Asiatics lived a life of ease, delicacy, even of sloth, surrounded by ornate works of art and elaborate amusements for body and spirit. Gradually the moral disapproval leveled at their eastern neighbors came to be applied to a style of oratory conceived as 'like' Persian life, a style formally complex, ornate, decorated and elaborate.
>
> (Colie, 171)

In *Antony and Cleopatra* Shakespeare reversed the process and created an 'Asiatic' style to reflect the Alexandrian way of life.

Hyperbole

The most distinctive feature of this style is its hyperbole, its
exaggeration. Cleopatra expresses every possible emotion from
rapturous joy and uncontrollable rage to suicidal despair, but
seems incapable of moderation, the Roman 'measure' or golden
mean, and she expresses this intensity of feeling, which she
cultivates and pursues as though it were a moral absolute, in a
correspondingly heightened language. Looking back on the
love she has shared with Antony, she conceives of it in terms
which are nothing less than transcendental:

> Eternity was in our lips and eyes,
> Bliss in our brows' bent; none our parts so poor
> But was a race of heaven.
>
> (1.3.36–8)

On hearing of Antony's marriage, she calls for the collapse of
her empire into chaos:

> Melt Egypt into Nile, and kindly creatures
> Turn all to serpents!
>
> (2.5.78–9)

After Antony's death, she does not say, simply, that she has
lost all sense of purpose, but that creation itself has ceased to
exist:

> All's but naught;
> Patience is sottish, and impatience does
> Become a dog that's mad.
>
> (4.15.82–4)

It is, of course, her nature to change rapidly from one extreme
of feeling to another but even when, in the final scene, she
settles herself in her determination to die, she speaks of this
newly-found stability in typically absolute terms:

> My resolution's placed, and I have nothing
> Of woman in me. Now from head to foot
> I am marble-constant.
>
> (5.2.237–9)

This heightened form of speech appears at its most extreme and prolonged in her eulogy of the dead Antony with its series of hyperbolic metaphors: Antony's legs 'bestrid the ocean; his reared arm / Crested the world' and his voice was 'as rattling thunder' (5.2.81–5).

World imagery

This passage is also notable for what Charney calls its 'words of cosmic reference' (80), the 'world imagery' which 'represents the most general pattern of imagery in the play' (93). This occurs so frequently that it is impossible to illustrate it fully here (but see Charney, 80–93). In the opening speech of the play Antony is described as 'The triple pillar of the world'; during the feast on Pompey's galley, Menas calls the triumvirs 'these three world-sharers' (2.7.71), and before his final victory, Caesar prophesies that a 'time of universal peace' is coming in which 'the three nooked world / Shall bear the olive freely' (4.6.5–7). In the mouths of the Romans such references are not simply metaphorical, for in their eyes the Roman empire, which the triumvirs governed, extended throughout the known world. For Antony and Cleopatra, on the other hand, their relationship itself constitutes the world, an all-encompassing universe of feeling which they see as an alternative to the lesser Roman world of conquest and empire. Hence, for Antony, Cleopatra is the 'day o'th' world' (4.8.13) and, for Cleopatra, Antony is 'the crown o'th' earth' without which it is 'no better than a sty' (4.15.64–5). The impression that the play encompasses vast expanses of territory and that the conflict is one in which the politics of the world are at stake was one which the nineteenth-century actor–managers hoped to create by dramatic spectacle, but in fact such extravagant and cumbersome means were unnecessary. The impression is created more than sufficiently by Shakespeare's language.

Antony's kind of rhetoric, his 'Asiatic' style, is often as heightened as Cleopatra's to the extent that Shakespeare seems to imply that he has acquired it from her as a mode of expressing feelings which she, and only she, has awakened in him. His way of speaking to Octavia is a great deal more sober and factual. His grandiose dismissal of Rome and its messengers (an example of what Plutarch calls his 'foolish bravery') prefigures Cleopatra's injunction that Egypt should melt into the Nile:

> Let Rome in Tiber melt, and the wide arch
> Of the ranged empire fall! Here is my space!
>
> (1.1.34–5)

The oneness which they occasionally achieve is suggested by their tendency to use similar words and figures of speech. Like her he expresses himself in extreme and heightened language ('Kingdoms are clay') and the fury with which he attacks Thidias, the messenger from Caesar, is as violent as hers towards the messenger from Rome (3.13.100–9; 2.5.62–72). Such extremes of emotion, diction and behaviour unite them to each other and distinguish them from the Romans. They are a quality which Cleopatra recognizes in Antony and admires in him:

> Be'st thou sad or merry,
> The violence of either thee becomes,
> So does it no man else.
>
> (1.5.62–4)

Egyptian and Roman imagery

The language of Cleopatra and her court is distinguished by a series of recurring images which make us constantly aware of the way they live. Egypt is associated with the Nile as Rome is with the Tiber, and the Nile is visualized as the source both of fruitfulness and of carrion-eating insects, harvest and deadly serpents. Cleopatra is herself the 'serpent of old Nile' (1.5.26) and the river reflects something of her paradoxical nature, both life-enhancing and fatally poisonous. Egypt is also a place of feeding and drinking to excess, where eight wild boars are roasted for a breakfast for twelve people (2.2.189–90) and Antony calls for wine both in defiance of his defeat (3.13.189–90) and in celebration of his victory (4.8.32–5). When Pompey thinks of Antony in Egypt, he imagines him sitting at a dinner prepared by 'Epicurean cooks' who sharpen his appetite with 'cloyless sauce' (2.1.24–5). Cleopatra is also repeatedly described in terms of food which, according to Enobarbus, is always enticing and never satisfying:

> Other people cloy
> The appetites they feed, but she makes hungry
> Where most she satisfies.
>
> (2.2.246–8)

That there are relatively few distinctive images associated with Rome is itself significant, for the Romans are characterized by their moderation, their temperance and ability to control their feelings. Temperance is a virtue which Caesar admired in Antony before he encountered Cleopatra. In his campaigns in northern Italy the young Antony was able to endure famine 'with patience more / Than savages could suffer' and could survive on wild berries and 'the barks of trees' (1.4.59–69). Caesar's own intemperance at the feast on Pompey's galley disgusts him and he confesses that rather than drink so much in a day he would prefer to fast for four (2.7.102–3). Whereas Egypt is associated with feeling and sensuality, as in the playful chatter among Cleopatra's servants (1.2.1–80) which is openly sexual, Rome is associated with action, especially military and political action. It is, says Charney, 'a place of conference tables, armor, political decisions and hard material objects' (102), and Caesar's speeches are much concerned with conveying information, devising strategy and issuing commands. The only woman to appear in the Roman scenes is Octavia who is of 'a holy, cold and still conversation' (2.6.124–5) whereas Cleopatra sees herself as black from the 'amorous pinches' of the sun god (1.5.29).

Although the two worlds of the play are thus differentiated by the kind of style and diction associated with them, the characters who inhabit them are at the same time individuals with their own distinctive forms of speech. Whereas Charmian, always loyal to her mistress, is frankly outspoken, Mardian is hesitant and deferential. Lepidus, the dupe among the triumvirs, scarcely says anything in the company of the other two and when he does it is in those balanced, antithetical clauses favoured by Brutus in *Julius Caesar*, which express thoughtfulness, rationality and moderation:

> That which combined us was most great, and let not
> A leaner action rend us. What's amiss,
> May it be gently heard. When we debate
> Our trivial difference loud, we do commit
> Murder in healing wounds. Then, noble partners,
> The rather for I earnestly beseech,
> Touch you the sourest points with sweetest terms,
> Nor curstness grow to th' matter.

> (2.2.19–26)

The two men whose lives and loyalties are initially divided between Egypt and Rome, Antony and Enobarbus, instinctively shift from one mode to another depending on their circumstances and situation. Once Antony has heard the news from Rome, he reprimands Enobarbus for his sexual 'Egyptian' banter ('No more light answers') and embarks on a speech as factual and politically observant as any of Caesar's (1.2.183–203). Enobarbus, at any rate in the early scenes, tends to speak prose and as his first extensive interview with Antony begins, the dialogue changes abruptly from verse to prose, an appropriate medium for the knowing, pragmatic, experienced soldier (the kind of man which Iago, another tried campaigner, pretends to be), but once he recalls Cleopatra's spectacular arrival in her barge (2.2.201–28) he modulates into the heightened, figurative speech associated with Egypt. The divided personalities of the two men are reflected in the two distinct modes in which they speak. Shakespeare, like Aristotle and Plutarch, believed that style was an expression of character, conduct and morality. As Ben Jonson declared, 'Language most shows a man: speak that I may see thee.'

THE SOURCES

Plutarch

The main source from which Shakespeare took the material for *Antony and Cleopatra* was the *Parallel Lives of the Greeks and Romans* by the first-century biographer and moralist Plutarch. He did not read the *Lives* in the original Greek but used an English translation by Sir Thomas North (1579), itself taken from a French version by Jacques Amyot (1559). He had already used North's Plutarch for some of the details in *A Midsummer Night's Dream*, and as a major source for *Julius Caesar* and *Timon of Athens*; after completing *Antony and Cleopatra*, he drew on it again for *Coriolanus*.

The two writers, though separated by a space of more than fifteen centuries, formed one of the most fruitful of all literary collaborations, and it is not difficult to see why Shakespeare found Plutarch's biographies congenial. They supplied him not only with narratives of some of the most critical periods in Roman history, but with detailed, intimate accounts of the protagonists. Hence we learn that Julius Caesar was 'leane, white, and soft skinned, and often subject to headache, and otherwhile to the falling sicknes' (North, 66), that Cleopatra was carried to Julius Caesar wrapped in a mattress (North, 74), and that Antony resembled Hercules not only 'in the likenes of his bodye ... but also in the wearing of his garments' (North, 257). Such details were invaluable to the dramatist and he seized on them and incorporated them into his plays. Moreover, both men wrote on the assumption that the course of history was shaped by the actions of men in power and, for that reason, both were curious to penetrate into the subtleties of human character and to trace the alliances and rivalries between powerful people.

Shakespeare's reshaping of Plutarch

Plutarch's biography of Antony is the longest of the *Lives*. It begins with a description of his ancestry and education and ends with an account of his children. Although his relationship with Cleopatra is by far the most important element, Plutarch also describes Antony's alliance with Julius Caesar against Pompey, his campaign against Cassius following the murder of Caesar and his protracted and disastrous incursions into Parthia. Some of the looseness of Plutarch's narrative remains in the play with its ten-year time-span and its constant shifts between continents, but Shakespeare gives to his play a much tighter dramatic structure by concentrating his attention largely on the relationship between the two major characters. Hence it opens with Antony already captivated by Cleopatra and all previous events are either omitted or, as in the case of the murder of Julius Caesar, mentioned briefly in retrospect (2.6.10–19; 3.2.53–6). Apart from the victory of Ventidius over Pacorus (3.1), the Parthian campaigns, which occupy about a fifth of the 'Life', are omitted entirely, and other events which in Plutarch occupy several years are tightly compressed, particularly in 1.2, where the wars of Lucius and Fulvia against Octavius, the conquests of Labienus, and Fulvia's death are dealt with in about forty lines (1.2.93–128). On the other hand the episodes in the 'Life' which lead up to Cleopatra's suicide are dramatized in full and unfolded gradually to extend almost over a complete act. With his emphasis on the two major characters, Shakespeare reduced the role of Octavia and moved her into the background. In Plutarch's version she is a much stronger, more independent figure. She has a daughter by Antony before leaving with him for Athens and is pregnant with a second when she goes to mediate between him and Octavius. It is she, moreover, who after Antony's death takes care of his children, including those he has had by Cleopatra. In the play it is implied that she is childless (3.13.111–14). Both writers create an implicit contrast between Octavia and Cleopatra, but, whereas Plutarch admires the former's matronly, domestic virtues, she is sometimes, in Shakespeare's play, the object of ridicule especially by Cleopatra (3.3). This shift of emphasis makes Antony's attraction to Cleopatra more understandable.

Shakespeare's task, however, was not simply to shorten and give shape to Plutarch's biography but to transpose a narrative into a play and that, of course, entailed the removal of the narrator. Plutarch frequently comments on and judges the major characters, as when he describes the 'wonderfull love' which Antony inspired among his soldiers or condemns his 'naughty life', and his 'extreme wasteful expences upon vaine light huswives' (North, 261). Such comments are, in the drama, either exemplified in action, as when Antony's servants weep when he dismisses them (4.2.34–5), or placed in the mouths of the Roman characters, Philo, Demetrius, Pompey and especially Octavius. As a result of this transposition the unfavourable comments on Antony become distinctively Roman and lose something of the authoritative force and objectivity they had when delivered by Plutarch himself. They become only one of several ways in which he may be assessed.

It was presumably the need to incorporate into the play someone who would take on the role of Plutarch that led Shakespeare to create Enobarbus (Pelling, 41). In the 'Life' 'Domitius', as he is called, is a very minor figure who is 'sicke of an agewe' when he deserts to Caesar and is subsequently sent 'all his caryage, trayne, and men' by Antony, and 'though he gave [Antony] to understand that he repented his open treason, he died immediatly after' (North, 298). Out of this incident Shakespeare created Enobarbus, who has much of Plutarch's open-mindedness and detachment. It is he who, in what are almost entirely Plutarch's words, testifies in the 'barge' speech to Cleopatra's extravagance and magnetism (2.2.201–28), who, like Plutarch, foresees the folly of Antony's decision to fight by sea (3.7.34–48) and perceives his increasing foolhardiness (3.13.29–37) as Plutarch does throughout the latter part of the 'Life'. As an ironic and detached commentator he opens and closes many scenes, but he is, of course, far more than a choric figure who fulfils a dramatic function. He is a fully realized character, loyal, sociable, sceptical, pragmatic, popular and ultimately tragic. He dies not of an ague but of remorse at his own disloyalty.

Plutarch saw himself as a moralist. In his introduction to the 'Parallel Lives of Demetrius and Antony' he observes that

the great Ladies of all [the] arts, Temperaunce, justice and wisdom, doe not only consider honestie, upright-

> nes, and profit: but examine withall, the nature and
> effects of lewdnes, corruption and damage.... So
> thinke I, we shall be the forwarder in reading and
> following the good, if we know the lives, and see the
> deformity of the wicked.
>
>   (*Lives*, 5.372–3)

In other words he saw his function as an instructive one in
which he exhibited to his readers examples of virtue or vice
for them to follow or avoid. Hence he condemns Antony's
degeneracy without hesitation and is in no doubt that Cleopatra's influence on him was disastrous: 'if any sparke of
goodnesse or hope of rising were left in him, Cleopatra
quenched it straight, and made it worse then before' (North,
273). Yet he is by no means a simple moralist. He is aware of
and fascinated by the complex, paradoxical nature of his
characters, the coexistence within the same person of strengths
and weaknesses. Though certainly aware of Antony's flaws, he
does full justice to his courage and stamina, his magnanimity
towards his troops and the affection which he inspires in
them. He shows a similar open-mindedness towards Cleopatra.
Although he disapproves of the artfulness with which she gains
control over her lover, he also shows how her early flirtation
deepens into love and conveys very movingly her sense of
desolation after Antony's death. Both of them illustrate 'the
saying of Plato: That from great minds, both great vertues
and great vices do procede' (*Lives*, 5.373). Something of the
ambiguous, self-contradictory quality of *Antony and Cleopatra*
was already present in Plutarch's narrative waiting to be
developed.

    Since the two writers were so similar in temperament and
outlook – even in their sense of the theatrical – it is not
surprising that at times Shakespeare incorporated quite long
passages from the 'Life' into the dialogue with little alteration

(e.g. 2.2.201–28; 5.1.35–48). Nevertheless, as MacCallum points out, there is one major element in *Antony and Cleopatra* which Shakespeare did not find in Plutarch and that is the sense of transcendence which both lovers experience as their lives draw to a close. MacCallum pertinently reminds us that the title of Dryden's tragedy on the same subject is *All for Love, or the World Well Lost*. 'We have', he says, 'something of the same feeling in reading Shakespeare and we do not have it in reading Plutarch' (MacCallum, 340).

Octavius in the 'Life' is scarcely described at all but is revealed more by what he does than by what is said of him. In the glimpses we see of him he appears as a brilliantly efficient soldier and a careful politician who deliberately discredits Antony in order to win support for himself and tries to deceive Cleopatra, after her defeat, in order to dissuade her from committing suicide. Nevertheless he is unequivocally portrayed as the instrument of Fate, into whose hands 'the government of all the world' was predestined to fall (North, 292) at what Shakespeare's Octavius calls the 'time of universal peace' (4.6.5). It may be that Shakespeare formed an impression of his aloofness and restraint from Simon Goulart's *Life of Augustus*, translated by North for the 1603 edition of Plutarch's *Lives* (North, 247). Shakespeare has also been shown to have consulted the 1578 translation of Appian's *Civil Wars* for details of Pompey's rebellion and death and the uprisings of Lucius and Fulvia (MacCallum, 648–52; Appian, xxiii–xxviii).

Dramatic sources

It is clear, then, that in preparation for the writing of *Antony and Cleopatra*, as for his other historical plays, Shakespeare did a certain amount of research. He also appears to have read the Countess of Pembroke's tragedy *Antonius* (1592), an adaptation of Robert Garnier's *Marc Antoine* (1578), itself based on Plutarch. There are enough verbal similarities to show that the countess's tragedy lingered in Shakespeare's mind (Wilson, x; Schanzer, 'Pembroke', 154–7; Schanzer, *Problem Plays*, 150–2; Bullough, 228–31), but more significant is her portrayal of Cleopatra which, unlike Plutarch's, is consistently sympathetic. Antony alone is said to have been responsible for his downfall and the only condemnation of Cleopatra comes from herself. Moreover her suicide is motivated not, as in Plutarch and Shakespeare, by a desire to avoid public humiliation but by a simple, passionate wish to be reunited in death with her lover,

> To be in one selfe tombe, and one selfe chest,
> And wrapt with thee in one selfe sheete to rest.
> (Bullough, 405)

Although, as Schanzer remarks (*Problem Plays*, 151), Shakespeare could find nothing in *Antonius* of the calculating, self-indulgent woman he depicts in the first four acts, nevertheless he may have been influenced by it when he created the resolute, idealizing Cleopatra of the final scene.

It is more certain that he read and remembered Samuel Daniel's tragedy *Cleopatra* (1594), which was designed as a companion piece to *Antonius* and dedicated to the Countess of Pembroke. Once again, the influence is confined almost entirely to the final scene of Shakespeare's play, for *Cleopatra* opens after Antony's death and is devoted chiefly to the heroine's expression of her feelings as she contemplates suicide. There are quite a lot of phrases and expressions which bring *Antony and Cleopatra* to mind (Farnham, 157–71; Dickey, 169–71; Schanzer, *Problem Plays*, 152–4; Bullough, 231–6; Brower, 346–8). For example, Cleopatra describes Antony as 'My *Atlas*, and supporter of my pride' (compare 'demi-Atlas', 1.5.24) and declares: 'I have both hands, and will, and I can die' (Bullough, 408–9; compare 4.15.51). Like Shakespeare's heroine (5.2.69) she tells Proculeius that she wants 'leave to die' (ibid., 415), and when she prepares for death she dresses herself in her richest clothes,

> Even as she was when on thy crystall streames,
> Cleere *Cydnos* she did shew what earth could shew.
> (Bullough, 443; compare 5.2.227–8)

Daniel's Cleopatra is, moreover, driven to suicide for a variety of reasons: a desire to redeem her past infamy by choosing an honourable death, a longing to be with Antony, and, above all, a wish to avoid the shame of appearing in Caesar's triumph, an idea not much developed by Plutarch but repeated several times by Shakespeare (5.2.51–6; 5.2.206–20). She is therefore not a simple character, and her complexity is deepened by the fact that her emotional tensions are expressed both by herself and by the Chorus. The latter delivers a moralizing commentary at the end of each act, condemning her 'luxurie', remarking on the vanity of human wishes and observing the tendency of pride to destroy itself. Hence our impression of Cleopatra is created both subjectively by the heroine and objectively by the Chorus. It has to be said, however, that *Cleopatra* is an entirely different kind of play from *Antony and Cleopatra*. It is, like *Antonius*, a strictly classical Senecan tragedy which consists mostly of extended speeches like operatic arias. All action, including Cleopatra's death, takes place off the stage and the language is consistently decorous. Daniel's Cleopatra, as Reimer says (15), has none of the vulgarity of Shakespeare's heroine. Had Shakespeare not read Daniel or the Countess of Pembroke, *Antony and Cleopatra* would probably have been much as it is; without Plutarch it could not have existed.

Introduction

Mythological sources

As well as drawing on these literary and dramatic sources, Shakespeare also associates his hero and heroine with several mythological archetypes, sometimes explicitly, sometimes by implication.[1] Several times in the play Antony is compared to Mars (1.1.4; 2.2.6; 2.5.117) and Cleopatra to Venus (2.2.210), and Mardian the eunuch confesses that he thinks 'What Venus did with Mars' (1.5.19). There are two myths, both very well known in the Renaissance, about the relationship between these deities. In one of them, told by Homer (*Odyssey*, 8.266–328), Venus and Mars, lying in bed together, are trapped in a net made by Vulcan, the husband of Venus, and are exposed to the laughter of the gods. Shakespeare is more probably thinking, however, of the story told by Lucretius (*De Rerum Natura*, 1.29–40) where Mars, vanquished by love, lies unarmed in Venus' lap and is wooed to peace (Adelman, *Essay*, 91; Bono, 176; Waddington). Shakespeare had told this story at some length in *Venus and Adonis* (ll.97–114) and it was a popular subject of Renaissance iconography, where it shows the power of love to overcome strife (Wind, 89–90). On the other hand, the myth can also be interpreted in a contrary manner as an example of how valour can be enslaved by lust. In other words, it is capable of both an 'Egyptian' and a 'Roman' reading.

The story closely resembles another classical myth, the account given by Ovid (*Heroides*, 9.55–118; *Fasti*, 2.305–58) of Hercules' subjugation by Omphale, the Amazonian Queen of Lydia. Antony, according to Plutarch, claimed to be descended from 'one Anton, the sonne of Hercules', and he resembled his heroic ancestor both in 'the likenes of his bodye' and 'the wearing of his garments' (North, 257). Moreover in Shakespeare's play it is Hercules who leaves him on the night

1 R. K. Root points out that 'in the series of great tragedies, classical mythology plays quite an insignificant part; but in *Antony and Cleopatra* and *Coriolanus* it suddenly reasserts itself with surprising vigour. ... A chief characteristic is the frequent allusion to the greater divinities' (Root, 130).

64

before battle (4.3.21–2) and not Bacchus as in Plutarch. While infatuated by Omphale, according to Ovid, Hercules allowed her to dress him in her clothes and was compelled to spin among her women while she wore his lion's skin and armed herself with his club (Adelman, *Essay*, 81–3; Bevington, 9–10). The similarity between Antony's and Hercules' predicaments had been pointed out by Plutarch in his 'Comparison of Demetrius with Antonius': 'We see in painted tables, where Omphale secretlie stealeth away Hercules clubbe, and tooke his Lyons skinne from him. Even so Cleopatra oftentimes unarmed Antonius, and intised him to her, making him lose matters of great importaunce' (North, 319). Hercules and Antony were also paired together as types of the lust–enslaved hero by Tasso (*Gerusalemme Liberata*, 16.3–7) and in Spenser's *Faerie Queene* (5.8.2; Waddington, 225). The comparison appears to have been in Shakespeare's mind when Cleopatra recalls how she put her tires and mantles on Antony while she wore his sword Philippan (2.5.22–3).

   Another episode in the legend of Hercules is implicit in *Antony and Cleopatra*. This is the story of *Hercules in Bivio* or 'Hercules at the Crossroads', originally told by Xenophon (Schanzer, *Problem Plays*, 155–8; Coates, 45–52; Bevington, 9). Hercules, says Xenophon, went out to a quiet place and 'sat pondering which road to take'. He was approached by two women, one modest, sober and dressed in white, the other plump, soft and dressed 'so as to disclose all her charms'. Whereas the latter, Vice, invites him to follow her, offering a life free from hardship, effortlessly devoted to the pleasures of food, drink and love, Virtue offers only the toil and hardship which lead to glory (*Memorabilia*, 2.1.21–34). The legend was the subject of countless pictorial and literary representations (Panofsky, *passim*) including Ben Jonson's masque *Pleasure Reconciled to Virtue* (performed 1618), where, as in some other versions, the two opposites are united. The situation is clearly analogous to Antony's in the first two acts of the play, particularly when he has to choose between Cleopatra and Octavia, and the implied allusion reflects both favourably on him in that he is associated with a demi-god, and at the same time unfavourably, since, unlike his supposed ancestor, he ultimately chooses the path of 'Vice'. His predicament is such that he is unable to reconcile the two.

The most celebrated of such choices in classical literature, however, was that of Aeneas in the fourth book of Virgil's *Aeneid* (Schanzer, *Problem Plays*, 158–9; Brower, 350–2; Adelman, 68–74), where, struggling between his love for Dido and his divinely appointed mission to found a new Troy, he follows his sacred destiny and forsakes Dido, who, in grief, destroys herself. Virgil himself had already made connections between the two pairs of lovers, for, as Pelling (17) points out, his Dido was in part modelled on the historical Cleopatra, and on the shield which is given to Aeneas by Venus is embossed a representation of Antony's defeat at Actium (*Aeneid*, 8.675–713). The similarities between Virgil's narrative and Shakespeare's play are quite close.[1] Not only is Antony, like Aeneas, lured from his duty to Rome by his love of a woman, but Cleopatra, like Dido (whom in her grief she much resembles), is a queen of a North African people and stages her own suicide after her lover has gone. Indeed, as Antony prepares for his own death, he imagines himself reunited with Cleopatra in the Elysian Fields in the presence of Dido and Aeneas:

> Where souls do couch on flowers we'll hand in hand
> And with our sprightly port make the ghosts gaze.
> Dido and her Aeneas shall want troops,
> And all the haunt be ours.
>
> (4.14.52–5)

1   There are enough detailed similarities between *Antony and Cleopatra* and Marlowe's treatment of the story of Dido and Aeneas, *Dido, Queen of Carthage*, to indicate that Marlowe's tragedy as well as Virgil's epic poem were in Shakespeare's mind as he wrote the play (Spevack, 603–4; Adelman, *Essay*, 177–83).

Antony's recollection of Virgil, however, is highly selective – indeed distorted. In the *Aeneid*, as Adelman points out (*Essay*, 68–9), Dido and Aeneas do meet in the other world but he finds her wandering with other disconsolate lovers in the plains of mourning and, when she sees Aeneas, she turns away from him. He grieves for her only briefly before going on to the Elysian Fields where he is shown the spirits of the future heroes of Rome. 'The Aeneas whom [Antony] recalls is the lover, not the hero, Dido's Aeneas, not Rome's' (ibid., 68).

The association of Antony and Cleopatra with these classical archetypes creates a number of contradictory effects. The idea that Antony is another Hercules, another Aeneas, and that Cleopatra is a greater Venus, a second Dido, clearly adds to that sense of their own magnitude which they themselves deliberately create, both in Shakespeare's account of them and in Plutarch's, and it cannot help but make its impression on an audience. At the same time, if we reflect on these allusions, we realize that, by Roman standards, they discredit the protagonists, particularly Antony, who, like Mars with Venus and Hercules with Omphale, abandons heroic virtue for the blandishments of a woman but, unlike Hercules at the crossroads, turns away from the path of Roman virtue and, unlike Aeneas, gives up his obligations to his country for the sake of his love for a foreign queen. The paradoxical, ambivalent nature of the lovers which is central to Shakespeare's play is deepened by their association with their mythological archetypes.

There is another parallel which, according to Plutarch, Cleopatra created in her own lifetime, her identification with the Egyptian goddess Isis (Lloyd; Fisch; Bono, 199–219; Adelman, *Mothers*, 183–4). At the ceremony where Antony divides the Asian kingdoms between Cleopatra and her children, says Plutarch, she 'did not onely weare at that time (but at all other times els when she came abroad) the apparell of the goddesse Isis, and so gave audience unto all her subjects, as a new Isis' (North, 290–1). Whereas Plutarch's disapproval of this ceremony is merely implicit, Shakespeare, by giving this passage almost verbatim to Caesar (3.6.1–19), turns it into an expression of outrage and contempt.[1] Both writers report the episode from a Roman standpoint but it may be that Shakespeare realized there was a significance to it of which Caesar was unaware but which Plutarch, as the author of the long essay *Concerning Isis and Osiris*, must have known. One of the characteristics which distinguishes the Egyptians in Shakespeare's play is their oaths by and prayers to Isis (1.2.66, 69, 75; 1.5.73; 3.3.15) and Cleopatra in certain ways resembles the Egyptian goddess. Plutarch, whose essay was available to Shakespeare in the English translation by Philemon Holland (1603), visited Alexandria himself and writes at length about the significance which she had for the Egyptians. They believe that the earth is 'the body of Isis' which is annually flooded and made fertile by the Nile which is her brother Osiris (Holland, 1300). Isis is a deity who presides over love affairs, and is the female principle of nature (ibid., 1309). The 'different tinctures and colours' of her robes perhaps suggested to Shakespeare the ever-changing moods of Cleopatra, 'for her whole power consisteth and is emploied in matter which receiveth all formes, and becommeth all maner of things, to wit, light, darkness, day, night, fire, water, life, death, beginning and end' (ibid., 1318). In her multi-faceted personality, Isis

1 In Beerbohm Tree's production at Her Majesty's theatre in 1906 this ceremony was actually shown on the stage. It was, recalled the Cleopatra, Constance Collier, 'the most spectacular scene in the play'.

> Cleopatra, robed in silver, crowned in silver, carrying a golden sceptre and a symbol of the sacred golden calf in her hand, went in procession through the streets of Alexandria, the ragged, screaming populace acclaiming the Queen, half in hate, half in superstitious fear and joy, as she made her sacrilegious ascent to her high throne in the market place.
>
> (Collier, 186)

By transforming Caesar's contemptuous account of the episode into a spectacular show, Tree totally changed its effect. In John Caird's 1992 production for the Royal Shakespeare Company the ceremony was again mounted on the stage but in the background and as an accompaniment to Caesar's words.

resembles Shakespeare's 'wrangling queen'.

Shakespeare was familiar with the *Golden Ass* of Apuleius which had been translated into English by William Adlington (1566) and was a source for *A Midsummer Night's Dream*. Towards the end (Book 11) Apuleius describes a vision of Isis in which she appears to him wearing a crown woven of flowers and surrounded with coiled serpents and holds in her hand a golden cup 'out of the mouth wherof the serpent Aspis lifted up its head, with a swelling throat' (Apuleius, 192). The asp, it appears, was associated specifically with Isis, and Cleopatra may in fact have chosen to die from its sting partly for this reason. Shakespeare may not have known this but he could have read in *De Iside et Osiride* about the appearance and habits of the crocodile or 'serpent' which is discussed at the feast on Pompey's galley (2.7.24–8).

The central myth of Isis concerns her devotion to her husband and brother Osiris. Osiris was killed by their brother Typhon, who cut up his body into pieces and scattered them over the land. Isis searched for and found them, all except the genitals, of which she made a replica to take their place and thereby enabled him to gain immortality. It may be that Shakespeare had this legend in his mind in the final scene of the play where Cleopatra 'reconstructs' the dead Antony and, like Isis, looks forward to joining her lover in the afterlife (Bono, 199–219; Bevington, 11; Adelman, *Mothers*, 184). It would be highly appropriate if, in donning her robes and crown in preparation for suicide, Cleopatra once more appeared as 'the goddess Isis' about to be reunited with Osiris: 'Husband, I come.'

THE DATE OF COMPOSITION

When, having become king, Macbeth reveals a sense of inferiority towards Banquo, he recalls Mark Antony's similar uneasiness towards Octavius Caesar:

> under him
> My Genius is rebuk'd, as it is said
> Mark Antony's was by Caesar.
> (3.1.54–6)

As Shakespeare wrote these words, Plutarch's 'Life of Marcus Antonius' clearly came into his mind and he might already have been considering a play in which Antony and Octavius were brought into opposition. Indeed he probably wrote *Antony and Cleopatra* immediately after *Macbeth*, but precisely when he composed it is a matter for conjecture.

The only certain fact is that on 20 May 1608 the publisher Edward Blount acquired the rights to two works, one of which was called *Antony and Cleopatra*:

> **Edw. Blount.** Entred for his copie vnder thand*es* of Sr Geo. Buck knight & m^r warden Seton a booke called. The booke of Pericles Prynce of Tyre $\quad$ vj^d

> **Edw. Blunt** Entred also for his copie by the lyke Aucthoritie. A booke Called. Anthony. & Cleopatra
> $$vj^d$$
> (Greg, *Bibliography*, 24)

Neither work is described as a play, nor are they attributed to Shakespeare, and it is possible that either or both of them were written by someone else. Nevertheless they are almost certainly his, if only because Blount was unlikely to have acquired the rights to two non-Shakespearean works with titles identical to those of plays by Shakespeare (Spevack, 380). If they were, then the entry establishes that *Antony and Cleopatra* had been completed before 20 May 1608.

Having acquired the right to publish the play, however, Blount did not, apparently, do so, unless, of course, no copy of his edition has survived. A more likely explanation is that

Blount had no intention of publishing it and that the entry was a 'blocking' entry, 'an attempt on the part of Shakespeare's company to protect themselves against an anticipated piracy by employing a friendly publisher ... to register his copyright in the plays named' (Cam[1], 1). It is also possible that, for some reason, Blount's entry was cancelled (Greg, *Pericles*, 1). If, incidentally, Blount did hope to forestall unauthorized publication, his attempt failed in the case of *Pericles* which was published twice in the following year without authorization.

Several scholars believe, however, that the play was written earlier. This theory was first put forward by R. H. Case, the editor of the first Arden edition (1906), who saw signs of the influence of *Antony and Cleopatra* on the revised version of Samuel Daniel's *Cleopatra*. Daniel's Senecan tragedy, which had first appeared in 1594, was reissued three times with minor alterations and then published with extensive revisions in his *Certaine Small Workes* some time (exactly when is not known) in 1607. Shakespeare's influence on the last of these versions could be seen, according to Case, in the more dramatic nature of Daniel's revised text, 'the replacing of relation and soliloquy by dialogue', the greater part played by 'characters familiar to us in *Antony and Cleopatra*' such as Charmian and Iras, the introduction of two new characters, 'Dircetus' and Diomedes, and the addition of an episode in which 'Dircetus' brings to Ceasar the sword of Mark Antony as he does in Shakespeare's play (Ard[1], x–xi). If *Antony and Cleopatra* does lie behind these revisions but was not yet in print, then, Case concludes, Daniel must have seen a performance of Shakespeare's tragedy in 1606 or early 1607.

It would be misleading, however, to imagine that Daniel, suddenly inspired by a performance of *Antony and Cleopatra*, radically transformed his tragedy into a more 'Shakespearean' drama. *Cleopatra* is only one of many works which he revised at this period, and even in its new form it is still a strictly formal, neoclassical tragedy. As his biographer Joan Rees remarks, it 'hardly ranks as theatrical drama either in point of action presented or speed or liveliness of dialogue' (Rees, 107–8). Moreover it has been argued by Schanzer that the revisions could all have been derived not from Shakespeare but from Plutarch and another Senecan tragedy, *Antonius* (1592), by Daniel's patron, Mary, Countess of Pembroke, to whom *Cleopatra* was dedicated (Schanzer, 'Daniel's revision', 379).

A more plausible connection between Daniel's and Shakespeare's tragedy has been revealed by Barroll, and this consists not of any major revisions to *Cleopatra* of the kind adduced by Case, but of one small detail. In the revised version, as Barroll points out, Eros, the servant whom Antony asks to kill him, is described as Antony's 'late enfranchis'd servant', a detail supplied not by Plutarch, who calls him simply 'a man of his ... whom he loved and trusted' (North, 309), but by Shakespeare, whose Antony says to Eros:

> When I did make thee free, swor'st thou not then
> To do this when I bade thee?
>
> (4.14.82–3)

Small though the connection is, it does indicate that Daniel had become acquainted with *Antony and Cleopatra* at some time before the publication of his revised *Cleopatra* in 1607 (Barroll, *Politics*, 161–4). The influence of Shakespeare is, incidentally, apparent in some of Daniel's other works. In his *Funeral Poem upon the Death of the late noble Earl of Devonshire* there are recognizable echoes of *Henry V*, and Daniel's editor, John Pitcher, remarks that 'many of the revised poems and plays in Daniel's 1607 collected edition (in which the *Funeral Poem* appeared) show signs of Shakespeare's influence' (Pitcher 1978).

There remains the question of how he could have become

familiar with Shakespeare's tragedy. Most scholars have assumed that he must have seen a performance of it at the Globe, but, as Barroll points out, there were few performances in 1607 at the public theatres, which were closed for long periods on account of the plague. He concludes that it was probably shown at court during the Christmas season of 1606–7. No one, however, seems to have considered the possibility that Daniel saw the play in manuscript. For just over a year (4 February 1604 to 28 April 1605) he held an appointment as the licenser of plays submitted for performance at court by the Children of the Queen's Revels (Rees, 96–7), and, as such, would regularly see the manuscripts of new plays. It may be that one of them was *Antony and Cleopatra*.[1] If this was so, then Shakespeare's tragedy must have been completed, though not necessarily performed, three or four years earlier than has hitherto been supposed.

Other evidence in favour of an earlier date – possible allusions to *Antony and Cleopatra* in the writings of other authors – is far from strong. The most striking is a passage in Barnabe Barnes's tragedy *The Devil's Charter* which was performed at court by Shakespeare's company on 2 February 1607 and printed later in the same year (Ard[1], xii–xiii). In one episode, Alexander Borgia murders two princes as they lie asleep by applying 'aspiks' to their breasts:

> *He draweth out of his boxes aspiks.*
> Come out here now you *Cleopatraes* birds.
> Fed fat and plump with proud *Egiptian* slime,
> Of seauen mouth'd *Nylus* but now turn'd leane:
> *He putteth to either of their brests an* Aspike.
> Take your repast vpon these Princely paps.
> Now *Ptolamies* wife is highly magnified,
> Ensigning these faire princely twins their death,

1 This idea was suggested to me privately by Dr John Pitcher.

> And you my louely boys competitors,
> With *Cleopatra* share in death and fate.
>
> (Barnes, 71)

The passage is significant in that, whereas Plutarch says specifically that Cleopatra applied the asps to her arm (North, 316), Barnes seems to assume that she put them on her breasts. He need not necessarily have taken this detail from Shakespeare, however, for the notion had been widespread at least since the middle of the sixteenth century and was common in pictorial representations of Cleopatra's suicide (Hughes-Hallett, 193), as the physician James Primrose pointed out: '*Petrus Victorius* blames the Painters, that paint *Cleopatra* applying the Aspe to her paps, seeing it is manifest out of *Plutarch* in the life of *Antonius*, and out of *Plinie* likewise, that she applied it to her arme' (Primrose, 29).[1] Barnes's assumption could have been derived not from *Antony and Cleopatra* but simply from popular belief.

To summarize, the entry in the Stationers' Register, assuming that it refers to Shakespeare's play, shows that *Antony and Cleopatra* had been completed by 20 May 1608, and the revision made by Daniel to his *Cleopatra* strongly suggests that it was finished by the Christmas of 1606–7. If Daniel read the play in manuscript, however, it could have been completed between 4 February 1604 and 28 April 1605, the period during which he was the licenser of plays for the court, but this hypothesis is not strong enough to place the date of composition so early.

On 8 November 1623 *Antony and Cleopatra* reappeared in the Stationers' Register when, together with fifteen other plays by Shakespeare, it was again assigned to Blount and to the printer Isaac Jaggard. This entry was of Shakespeare's comedies, histories and tragedies, 'soe many of the said Copies as

1 Primrose's *Popular Errours, or the Errours of the People in Physick* was first published in Latin (Amsterdam, 1639) and then in an English translation (London, 1651).

are not formerly entred to other men' (Arber, 4.69). It was, in other words, part of the process whereby Blount and Jaggard prepared the way for the publication of the First Folio. Why *Antony and Cleopatra* was included in the list when Blount already held the right to it is a mystery. It may be, as Greg believed, that the original entry had been cancelled or, during the course of fifteen years, simply forgotten (Chambers, *Study*, 1.477). Be that as it may, the play first appeared in print in the First Folio and it is on this text that all subsequent editions must of necessity be based.

A copy of the First Folio has survived in which one page (352) has been proof-corrected in manuscript, and there are other copies in which the page appears in its corrected state. This and other pages which exist both in uncorrected and corrected states were once taken as evidence that considerable trouble had been taken to ensure that the text was as accurate as possible. Closer examination by Hinman, however, has revealed that few pages were actually corrected and that reference to the manuscript copy was seldom made. The errors corrected on page 352 were all obvious typographical ones and one error ('weepe' instead of 'wept' in TLN 1607) was left uncorrected. As Hinman concludes, 'textual accuracy was not the goal aimed at and ... the proof-correction to which the Folio was now and again subject did little to achieve it.' Nevertheless the Folio 'presents not only the only authoritative text of this great play but a reasonably satisfactory one as well' (Facsimile xxvii).

THE TEXT

Many features of the Folio text indicate that the copy used in Jaggard's printing house was not Shakespeare's 'foul papers' but a transcript of them, and not one prepared by the prompter for use in the theatre. The most obvious of these is the presence of the 'ghost' characters Lamprius, Rannius and Lucillius, who, having been brought on to the stage at the opening of the second scene, are given nothing to say and make no further appearance in the play. It seems that the dramatist, having introduced them, found he had no use for them but omitted to remove their names from the entry direction. This oversight would have been remedied by the prompter when he prepared the script for performance. The prompter could also have sorted out the confusion, which has given much trouble to editors, later in the same scene (1.2.118–28) when the First Messenger is required to speak after he has left the stage and the Second Messenger is ordered by Antony to fetch the messenger from Sicyon who then appears without having been summoned (see Fig. 9). Shakespeare clearly wanted to create the bustle of messengers entering and leaving but failed to work out precisely when or how they should do it.

There are passages in which characters who have not entered are required to speak (as in the case of Iras at 3.11.26, Thidias at 3.12.33 and Proculeius at 5.1.68), and others where characters must obviously leave but are not provided with an exit (as with Alexas at 1.3.6, Gallus towards the end of 5.1 and Scarus at 4.12.17). Other oversights include the general *Exeunt* directions at 3.13.199 and 4.6.11 after which Enobarbus must remain to deliver his soliloquies. Such minor omissions could also be put right by the prompter and have caused no problems for the editors, but the absence of any instructions as to how Cleopatra should be captured in her monument (5.2.34) has compelled editors to devise a stage direction from the details supplied by Plutarch. This particular omission, however, was probably the responsibility not of the author but of the compositor, who, as a result of misjudgement in casting off his copy, found himself with too much material to fit on to the page and cut the stage direction as being more dispensable than the dialogue.[1]

---

1   Hinman points out that this is a very 'tight' page on which the entry directions have far fewer white lines above and below them than those on the page opposite. It is also (zzl recto) the last page to be composed in the first half of the quire (Hinman, 508–9).

Enter Anthony, with a Messenger.

  Cleo. We will not looke vpon him:
Go with vs.   *Exeunt.*
  Messen. Fuluia thy Wife,
First came into the Field.
  Ant. Against my Brother *Lucius?*
  Messen. I : but soone that Warre had end,
And the times state
Made friends of them, ioynting their force 'gainst *Cæsar,*
Whose better issue in the warre from Italy,
Vpon the first encounter draue them.
  Ant. Well, what worst.
  Mess. The Nature of bad newes infects the Teller.
  Ant. When it concernes the Foole or Coward: On.
Things that are past, are done with me. 'Tis thus,
Who tels me true, though in his Tale lye death,
I heare him as he flatter'd.
  Mes. Labienus (this is stiffe-newes)
Hath with his Parthian Force
Extended Asia : from Euphrates his conquering
Banner shooke, from Syria to Lydia,
And to Ionia, whil'st——
  Ant. Anthony thou would'st say.
  Mes. Oh my Lord.
  Ant. Speake to me home,
Mince not the generall tongue, name
Cleopatra as she is call'd in Rome :
Raile thou in *Fuluia's* phrase, and taunt my faults
With such full License, as both Truth and Malice
Haue power to vtter. Oh then we bring forth weeds,
When our quicke windes lye still, and our illes told vs
Is as our earing : fare thee well awhlle.
  Mes. At your Noble pleasure.   *Exit Messenger.*
        Enter another Messenger.
  Ant. From *Scicion* how the newes? Speake there.
  1. *Mes.* The man from *Scicion,*
Is there such an one?
  2. *Mes.* He stayes vpon your will.
  Ant. Let him appeare :
These strong Egyptian Fetters I must breake,
Or loose my selfe in dotage.

    Enter another Messenger with a Letter.

What are you?
  3. *Mes. Fuluia* thy wife is dead.
  Ant. Where dyed she.
  Mes. In *Scicion,* her length of sicknesse,
With what else more serious,
Importeth thee to know, this beares.
  Antho. Forbeare me
There's a great Spirit gone, thus did I desire it :
What our contempts doth of ten hurle from vs,
                 x

9 *Antony and Cleopatra* 1.2.92–130 (TLN 170–220),
First Folio

Elsewhere there are what Greg calls 'indefinite and permissive stage directions' characteristic of foul papers (Greg, *First Folio*, 142), such as the entry of '*two or three Servants*' at the opening of 2.7 and of the '*Company of Soldiours*' and the '*Centerie, and his Company*' at the beginning of 4.3 and 4.9. In entries of this kind, Shakespeare supplied the general idea and left it to the players to decide how many people were available.

These features point strongly to the author's manuscript as the copy used for setting the Folio text, as do certain distinctively Shakespearean spellings, especially the predominant use of 'oh' instead of the shorter 'o' noted by the Oxford editors (Wells, *Companion*, 142). Since there are relatively few misreadings, however, the manuscript was not, by the standards of the day, difficult to decipher. 'It might', concludes Spevack, 'be the kind of transcript intermediate between foul papers and the promptbook' (Spevack, 379). The play is one of six in the Folio which are not divided into acts or scenes (the others are *Troilus and Cressida*, *2* and *3 Henry VI*, *Romeo and Juliet* and *Timon of Athens*).

Antony and Cleopatra was printed in twenty-nine double-column pages: signatures vv6 verso (page 340), quire xx, mistakenly signed x (pages 341–52), quire yy (yy2 and yy3, mistakenly signed y2 and y3) (pages 353–64) and signatures zz1–zz2 verso (pages 365–8). Hinman has shown that, like the rest of the Folio, it was not set page by page in sequence, but by formes, and that the formes were composed and printed 'from the inside outward', starting with the two immediately contiguous pages, 4 recto and 3 verso, and finishing with 1 recto and 6 verso of each quire. Developing a method which had been applied by previous scholars, Hinman was also able to discriminate, largely by their distinctive spelling habits, between the work of the various compositors and, on this evidence, deduced that *Antony and Cleopatra* was composed entirely by compositor B, the man who set the greater part of the volume. More recently, however, Howard-Hill has shown that part of the text was set by compositor E, whom Hinman had identified as a novice, competent to set from printed copy but not from manuscript. Howard-Hill's deduction was reached partly from the evidence of additional spelling habits and also from the use of spaces after commas. 'Whereas compositor B preferred to insert a space after a comma in a short line, compositor E even more consistently omitted spaces' (Howard-Hill, 7). His argument is particularly strong because it relies not simply on spelling, which could be influenced by the manuscript copy, but on habits which are distinctively personal. His conclusion is that compositor E was responsible for signatures xx3 verso to xx5 recto, xx6 recto and verso and yy1 recto (pages 346–9 and 351–3; TLN 744–1266 and 1395–1785; 2.2.59–2.6.72 and 2.7.57–3.6.33). Compositor B set the remainder – and by far the greater portion – of the text, as befitted the more experienced, faster workman.

It is difficult to compare their skills because some passages offer more possibilities for error than others. A large number of misreadings appear, for example, in 3.6.70–6, the work of compositor B, but these lines include the names and kingdoms of Antony's Near Eastern allies, words less familiar than those in the rest of the play. If, however, the first seven pages set by B are compared with the seven set by E, it becomes clear that E's punctuation is less accurate than B's. 'Errors in punctuation are common,' notes Bevington, 'suggesting that the compositors not only did what they could with Shakespeare's sparsely-pointed manuscript but regarded punctuation as their responsibility' (Cam², 266). The editor may therefore more confidently emend the punctuation of pages set by E. On the other hand, B was more inclined to make 'graphic errors' (simple misreadings of the manuscript), perhaps because, working faster, he read less accurately than E.

The text does contain a few notorious cruces, such as the problem of the 'Arm-gaunt Steede' in 1.5.50, the 'ribaudred Nagge of Egypt' in 3.10.10 and the question whether Antony's bounty was, as the Folio says, 'An *Antony*' or, as Theobald proposed, 'an autumn' (5.2.86), but many of the other textual problems can be solved with some degree of certainty and, indeed, had been solved by the end of the eighteenth century.

These do not include problems of lineation. The text of *Antony and Cleopatra* contains an exceptionally large number of passages in which the lineation seems either odd or obviously wrong. As is usual in his later plays, Shakespeare does not write consistently in pentameters but often in short and, less frequently, hypermetric lines for expressive, dramatic effect. Moreover, in addition to episodes which are written entirely in prose, such as the dialogue between Enobarbus and Menas (2.6.82–138) and the conversation between the servants before the banquet on Pompey's galley (2.7.1–16), there are short prose interjections in scenes which are otherwise written in verse, of which those by Enobarbus at 2.2.109–12 and 114–15 are examples. In these passages, prose is appropriate for the plain-speaking soldier and gives substance to Caesar's complaint that he does not 'dislike the matter but the manner of his speech'. These alone should make the editor cautious of trying to arrange as verse any passage printed as prose. Yet, as McKerrow observed, 'modern editors have, as a general rule, tended to treat all lines which *could* be metrical, or could be *made* metrical by a slight alteration, as verse and to print them as such' (McKerrow, 45). This tendency is apparent in the editorial treatment of the following passage in the Folio (2.2.29–33; TLN 713–17):

Caes.	Welcome to Rome.
Ant.	Thanke you.
Caes.	Sit.
Ant.	Sit sir.
Caes.	Nay then.

Most editors have presented this as a single verse line (into which it easily falls) but it is doubtful that the listener is conscious of the iambics and it could as well be printed, as in this edition, as a series of prose interjections.

On the other hand, at 2.6.62–5 (TLN 1254–6), the dialogue, which has hitherto been in verse, suddenly shifts into prose for no obvious dramatic reason:

> No *Anthony* take the lot: but first or last, your fine Egyptian cookerie shall haue the fame, I haue heard that *Iulius Caesar*, grew fat with feasting there.

Another feature of the text is the running on of what appear to be one line and one half-line to form a single hypermetric line, as in 2.2.35–6 (TLN 720):

> I must be laught at, if or for nothing, or a little, I

and 5.2.305–6 (TLN 3559):

> That I might heare thee call great *Caesar* Asse, vnpolicied.

Conversely, there are more frequent examples of what are presumably single lines of verse which are printed as two short lines, as in 2.7.119 (TLN 1472–3):

> What would you more?
> *Pompey* goodnight. Good Brother

and, a few lines later (2.7.130; TLN 1484–5),

> But what, we are Friends?
> Come downe into the Boate.

Again, the Folio sometimes presents the reader with a succession of short lines which may be regarded as split full lines of verse or brief exchanges of prose, such as the following (3.3.7–8; TLN 1630–4):

Mes.	Most gratious Maiestie.
Cleo.	Didst thou behold *Octauia*?
Mes.	I dread Queene.
Cleo.	Where?
Mes.	Madam in Rome

This problem is compounded by the compositor's practice, normal in this period, of starting every new speech without indenting it, even if it begins in the middle of a verse line. In other words, half-lines which we are accustomed to seeing in modern editions at the right of the page are placed at the left, so that, for example, the following (presumably) divided line (1.3.25)

ANTONY   The gods best know –
CLEOPATRA   O, never was there queen

appears in the Folio (TLN 329–30) as

Ant.	The Gods best know.
Cleo.	Oh neuer was there Queene

It is not immediately clear whether these two short lines should be considered parts of a single line or simply short interjections which should stand on their own. Once the reader becomes accustomed to the compositors' practice of not indenting, this particular problem can be solved (it is a single, divided line), but it is harder to reach a decision when three short lines appear in succession, as in the following from the opening scene of the play (1.1.18–20; TLN 27–9; see Cam[2], 266):

Mes.	Newes (my good Lord) from Rome.
Ant.	Grates me, the summe.
Cleo.	Nay heare them *Anthony*.

> *Cæfar.* What would you more?
> *Pompey* goodnight. Good Brother
> Let me requeſt you of our grauer buſineſſe
> Frownes at this leuitie. Gentle Lords let's part,
> You ſee we haue burnt our cheekes. Strong *Enobarbe*
> Is weaker then the Wine, and mine owne tongue
> Spleet's what it ſpeakeſt: he wilde diſguiſe hath almoſt
> Antickt vs all. What needs more words? goodnight.
> Good *Anthony* your hand,
>   *Pom.* Ile try you on the ſhore.
>   *Anth.* And ſhall Sir, giues your hand.
>   *Pom.* Oh *Anthony*, you haue my Father houſe.
> But what, we are Friends?
> Come downe into the Boate.

>   *Mef.* Moſt gratious Maieſtie.
>   *Cleo.* Did'ſt thou behold *Octauia* ?
>   *Mef.* I dread Queene.
>   *Cleo.* Where?
>   *Mef.* Madam in Rome, I lookt her in the face: and
> ſaw her led betweene her Brother, and *Marke Anthony.*

10 *Antony and Cleopatra* 2.7.119–30 (TLN 1472–85)
    and 3.3.7–10 (TLN 1630–5), First Folio

This particular problem is described by McKerrow:

> There are a number of passages consisting of an uneven
> number of part-lines in which little difference is made
> metrically if we begin with a part-line or if we rearrange
> the passage throughout so as to end with one.
>
>   (McKerrow, 44)

Some of these problems have been clarified, though not
necessarily solved, by the knowledge we have recently acquired
about the working practices of the compositors. If we can
understand why a compositor chose to depart from what we
suppose to have been the lineation of the manuscript copy, we
may be in a better position to emend it with some confidence.
It was once thought that mislining was derived from the
manuscript (Greg, *Editorial Problem*, 147), but, thanks to the
work of Hinman, we now realise that it was often created by
the need for the compositor to accommodate the text within
the limits of the page. Mislining of this kind was brought

about for two reasons. The first was the necessity to fit long verse lines into the narrow double columns which were used throughout the Folio. Hence the two short lines quoted earlier were a way of dealing with one long line –

What would you more? Pompey, goodnight. Good brother

– which was too long to fit into the Folio column. A similar solution was found by the compositor in dealing with the other long line:

But what? We are friends! Come down into the boat.

The second reason was the need to fit the text not into the column but the page. Having divided up the manuscript copy into sections, each of which he thought could be accommodated on a page ('casting-off copy'), the compositor discovered when he came to set the pages that he had miscalculated and had to set more verse lines than the pages could accommodate. The solution was to set verse as prose, which occupies less space. This is almost certainly what happened when, in the passage quoted above, the dialogue suddenly changes from verse to prose. The manuscript was presumably lined as follows:

No *Anthony* take the lot:
But first or last, your fine Egyptian cookerie
Shall haue the fame, I haue heard that *Iulius Caesar*
Grew fat with feasting there.

Not all problems of lineation can be solved by this means, however, and in all cases where two or more equally acceptable solutions are possible (as in 1.1.18–20 quoted above) the editor must either choose between them, knowing that his choice may or may not reflect the manuscript copy, or, like Bevington and the Oxford editors, retain the lineation of the Folio.

THE TRAGEDY OF

ANTONY
AND
CLEOPATRA

LIST OF ROLES

MARK ANTONY
OCTAVIUS CAESAR   } *triumvirs*
LEPIDUS

CLEOPATRA   *Queen of Egypt*

SEXTUS POMPEIUS *or* POMPEY   *rebel against the triumvirs*   5

DEMETRIUS
PHILO
DOMITIUS ENOBARBUS
VENTIDIUS
SILIUS
EROS   *followers of Antony*   10
CANIDIUS
SCARUS
DERCETUS
A *Schoolmaster, Antony's* AMBASSADOR   15

OCTAVIA   *sister of Octavius Caesar*

MAECENAS
AGRIPPA
TAURUS
DOLABELLA   *followers of Caesar*   20
THIDIAS
GALLUS
PROCULEIUS

CHARMIAN
IRAS   25
ALEXAS
MARDIAN, *a eunuch*   *attendants on Cleopatra*
DIOMEDES
SELEUCUS

MENAS   30
MENECRATES   *followers of Pompey*
VARRIUS

MESSENGERS
A SOOTHSAYER
SERVANTS *of Pompey*   35
A BOY SINGER
A CAPTAIN *in Antony's army*
SENTRIES *and* GUARDS
A CLOWN

Eunuchs, attendants, captains, soldiers, servants

1 MARK ANTONY In 40 BC, the year in which the play starts, he was forty-two. He died ten years later. Following the defeat of Brutus and Cassius, with which *Julius Caesar* concludes, Antony, Octavius and Lepidus became triumvirs and Antony proceeded with an army into Greece and Asia Minor where, in Cilicia, he summoned Cleopatra to appear before him to answer the accusation that she had assisted Brutus and Cassius in their war against him. She 'disdained to set forward otherwise, but to take her barge on the river of Cydnus' (North, 274; 2.2.196–7; *OCD*).

2 OCTAVIUS CAESAR At the time when the play opens he was twenty-three; hence Cleopatra's reference to 'the scarce-bearded Caesar' (1.1.22) and Antony's to 'the boy Caesar' (3.13.17). His mother was the niece of Julius Caesar, who, in his will, declared Octavius his adopted heir. In 43 BC he became a triumvir with Lepidus and Antony, but, with the enforced retirement of Lepidus and the defeat and death of Antony, he effectively became master of the Roman empire. He died at the age of fifty-one (*OCD*).

3 LEPIDUS The son of a celebrated father, he sided with Antony after the murder of Julius Caesar and was made a triumvir with Antony and Octavius. In the year when the play opens he was about fifty. He played an independent part in the campaign against Sextus Pompeius and laid claim to Sicily but was relieved of his responsibilities by Octavius, who forced him to retire into private life (3.5.6–11). He died aged about seventy-eight.

4 CLEOPATRA Born in 69 BC; at the time of the opening of the play she was twenty-nine. Shakespeare seems to imagine her as older than this (1.5.28–30). Before meeting Antony she had been the mistress of Julius Caesar, who, following his defeat of her brother Ptolemy XIII (who, in

accordance with Egyptian custom, was also her husband), returned her to the throne from which Ptolemy had expelled her. She followed Julius Caesar (by whom she had had a son) on his return to Rome, but came back to Alexandria after his assassination and met Antony three years later (*OCD*). According to Plutarch, she had 'accesse and credit with Cneus Pompey (the sonne of Pompey the great)' (1.5.32–5; 3.13.121–3; North, 273).

5 SEXTUS POMPEIUS The younger son of Pompey the Great, and aged about twenty-seven at the time the play opens. Following the defeat and murder of his father by Julius Caesar, he was outlawed but occupied Sicily, from where he used his ships to rescue his father's former supporters and, with their help, raided and blockaded the Italian coast (1.2.190–2; 1.3.46–55). By the treaty of Misenum he was made governor of Sicily, Sardinia and Achaea (2.6.34–9; North, 279) but was later defeated by Octavius at the battle of Naulochus. He escaped to Asia Minor, where, at the age of forty, he was captured and executed on Antony's orders (3.5.16–19) (*OCD*; Appian, 76–7, 95).

8 DOMITIUS ENOBARBUS Plutarch mentions two men named Domitius: Domitius Aenobarbus, who accompanied Antony on his Parthian campaigns and later married one of his daughters; and Domitius, a soldier who deserted Antony (but was not called Aenobarbus) (North, 298, 317; Norman, 59–61). Dawson suggests that Shakespeare transferred to the deserter the name *Aenobarbus* because its meaning, 'red-bearded', associates him with the traditionally red-haired Judas Iscariot, the most celebrated traitor and suicide.

9 VENTIDIUS Publius Ventidius (born *c*.98 BC), one of Antony's leading officers, 'a meane man borne, and of no noble house nor family: who only

came to that he attained unto, through Antonius frendshippe, the which delivered him happie occasion to achieve great matters' (North, 281). In 39 BC he was sent by Antony to drive the Parthians out of Syria (2.3.39–40) where he won a series of brilliant victories and was rewarded with an official triumph (3.1.1–11; North, 279, 281). He died shortly afterwards (*OCD*).

11 EROS Described by Plutarch as a man of Antony's 'whom he loved and trusted much, and whom he had long before caused to sweare unto him, that he should kill him when he did commaunde him' (North, 309). Barroll (*Politics*) points out that Shakespeare conflates Eros with 'one Rhamnus, one of his slaves enfranchised that was of his guard, and made him give him his faith that he would thrust his sword through him when he [Antony] would bid him' (Barroll, *Politics*, 161–3; *Lives*, 6.51).

12 CANIDIUS Canidius Crassus, 'a man of great estimacion about Antonius' (North, 286), and one of Antony's most trusted officers. He served with him in the Parthian campaigns and was commander of Antony's army at Actium but escaped before it surrendered. Contrary to Shakespeare's account (3.10.33–5; 4.6.16–18) he did not desert to Caesar, but rejoined Antony in Egypt, where he was later put to death by Octavius (*OCD*). Of the various spellings of his name in F (see textual notes) 'Camidius' appears most frequently but there is no apparent reason why Shakespeare should have changed the spelling *Canidius* which he found in North's Plutarch. It was easy enough for Compositor B to misread manuscript 'ni' as 'mi'.

13 SCARUS Not mentioned by Plutarch but identified by some editors as Marcus Aemilius Scaurus who accompanied Sextus Pompeius into Asia after the latter's defeat but betrayed him into the hands of Antony's generals. After the battle of Actium he was condemned to death by Octavius but was later pardoned (Furness; *OCD*). Barroll ('Scarrus': 31–9) argues that Scarus is the same character as the 'scarred soldier' of 3.7.60–81 and 4.5.

14 DERCETUS North, who spells his name 'Dercetaeus' (310), describes him as one of Antony's guard. The Folio offers the editor a choice between *Dercetus* and *Decretas*. The latter spelling occurs more frequently but the former is closer to North. Bevington points out (225) that Compositor B, who set this page, had difficulty in spelling unfamiliar names.

16 OCTAVIA Sister to Octavius and, at the time of the opening of the play, aged about thirty. She married Antony after the death of her first husband Caius Marcellus (2.6.112; North, 278). Although in the play it is implied that she was childless (3.13.111–13), she actually had two daughters by Antony as well as a son and two daughters by her first husband (North, 280, 282; *OCD*).

17 MAECENAS Caius Maecenas (died 8 BC), one of the 'chiefe frendes' of Octavius (North, 282) and a celebrated patron of literature. He was the friend and benefactor of Horace and Virgil and took part in the negotiations between Antony and Octavius which led to Antony's marriage to Octavia (2.2; *OCD*).

18 AGRIPPA Marcus Vipsanius Agrippa (*c.*64–12 BC), a strong supporter of Octavius and a distinguished naval commander. He was admiral of the Roman fleet at Actium (Furness; *OCD*).

19 TAURUS Titus Statilius Taurus, 'the greatest Roman marshal after Agrippa' (*OCD: Statilius*) and commander of the land army at Actium (3.7.77–8; North, 299). The F spelling, *Towrus*, indicates how his name should be pronounced.

20 DOLABELLA Cornelius Dolabella, probably the son of Publius Cor-

nelius Dolabella, a consul with Antony in 44 BC (*OCD*). Plutarch calls him 'one of Caesars very great familiars, and besides did beare no evil will unto Cleopatra' (North, 314). Little is known of him other than what is recorded by Plutarch.

21 THIDIAS Spelled *Thyreus* by North but *Thidias* or *Thidius* in F. Described by Plutarch as one of Caesar's men, 'a verie wise and discreete man, who bringing letters of credit from a young Lorde unto a noble Ladie, and that besides greatly liked her beawtie, might easely by his eloquence have perswaded her' (North, 306; 3.13).

22 GALLUS Caius Cornelius Gallus (*c*.69–26 BC), poet, politician and friend of Octavius. Virgil dedicated his tenth Eclogue to him. As a consequence of his support for Octavius in the war against Antony and Cleopatra he was made first Governor of Egypt (*OCD*).

23 PROCULEIUS Little is known of him beyond what is given by Plutarch. He is said to have been, with Maecenas, the principal friend of Octavius (Furness).

24–5 CHARMIAN, IRAS According to Plutarch, Caesar declared that 'Iras, a woman of Cleopatraes bedchamber, that friseled her heare, and dressed her head, and Charmion ... were those that ruled all the affaires of Antonius Empire' (North, 295).

26 ALEXAS 'Alexas Laodician', says Plutarch, 'was in greater credit with [Antony] then any other Grecian. ... He had alway bene one of Cleopatraes ministers to win Antonius, and to overthrow all his good deter-

minations to use his wife Octavia well' (North, 306). As a man of higher status than a servant he is addressed by Charmian as 'Lord' (1.2.1).

27 MARDIAN described by Plutarch as Cleopatra's eunuch (North, 295).

28 DIOMEDES identified by Plutarch as 'a secretarie' who was commanded by Cleopatra to bring Antony 'into the tombe or monument' where she had taken refuge (North, 309; 4.14.115–32).

29 SELEUCUS 'one of [Cleopatra's] Treasorers' (North, 314).

30–1 MENAS, MENECRATES According to Plutarch, 'two notable pirats' and supporters of Sextus Pompeius who 'scoored all the sea thereabouts, that none durst peepe out with a sayle' (1.4.49–56; North, 279). Menas was a freedman of Pompey the Great and captured Sardinia for Sextus in 40 BC but surrendered it to Octavius and was rewarded with equestrian rank. He was killed while campaigning in Illyria (*OCD: Menodorus*). Menecrates was a freedman and naval commander of Sextus Pompeius who was sent against Octavius' fleet. He also fought against Menas after the latter had deserted to Octavius but, seeing that the enemy was about to capture his vessel, he threw himself overboard and was drowned (Furness; Spevack).

32 VARRIUS Possibly so named after (or confused with) Varius Cotyla, an officer and companion of Antony's 'that would drinke lustely with him' (Spevack; North, 268). In the play he is a supporter of Pompey.

LIST OF ROLES] *first given, imperfectly, by Rowe* 1 ANTONY] F (*Anthony*) *passim, except Anthonio 2.2.7; Anthonyo 2.5.26* 9 VENTIDIUS] *F 3.1, F2, North; Ventigius F 2.3.30, 39 SD, 39* 12 CANIDIUS] *North, Rowe; Camidias F 3.7.19 SD; Camidius F 3.7.20; Camindius F 4.6.16* 14 DERCETUS] *F 4.14.112 SP; Decretas F 5.1.3 SD, 5.1.5; Decre. F 4.14.116 SP; Dec. F 5.1.5 SP; Dercetaeus North* 19 TAURUS] *North, Theobald; Towrus F* 21 THIDIAS] *F 3.12.31; Thidius F 3.13.109 SD;* Thyreus *North, Theobald*

ANTONY AND
CLEOPATRA

　　　　　Enter DEMETRIUS *and* PHILO.

PHILO

　　Nay, but this dotage of our general's
　　O'erflows the measure. Those his goodly eyes,
　　That o'er the files and musters of the war
　　Have glowed like plated Mars, now bend, now turn
　　The office and devotion of their view　　　　　　5

1.1 Location: Alexandria. The play begins in the middle of a crisis with Antony already captivated by Cleopatra and messengers summoning him back to Rome. In this short opening scene much of the play is contained: Antony's romantic adoration of Cleopatra and his neglect of his political duties, her power to control him by provoking him, the disapproval of the Roman characters and their regret for his decline from his former greatness (repeated more fully by Octavius in 1.4) and the tensions between Egypt and Rome which grow into open war in Act 3.

1 **dotage** infatuation. The word has connotations of folly but not necessarily of old age.

2 **O'erflows the measure** 'exceeds the limit. But the expression suggests abundance as well as prodigality' (Jones). 'Implicit in the word "measure" are two related concepts: *moderation* and *measurement* ... Octavius is the exemplar of measure' (Adelman, *Essay*, 122–3).

2–10 **Those ... lust** 'Antony has been Mars in battle; now he, like Mars, has turned from his proper business and become captive to love.... The bellows and fan suggest a humbler, more domestic fire than the glow of war' (Adelman, *Essay*, 83). On allusions to Venus and Mars in the play generally, see p. 64.

3 **files and musters** assembled ranks

4 **plated** clad in armour. Shakespeare may have been acquainted with Cartari's *Imagines Deorum*, Lyon, 1581 (see note to 5.2.78–91), in which the brightness of Mars's armour is emphasized: 'He wore ... on his head a helmet most bright and shining, and of so fierie a hue and glister, as it seemed there issued out of it great flashes of lightning, his breastplate was of solid gold, reflecting with a most glorious and eye-delighting lustre' (trans. Richard Linche as *The Fountaine of Ancient Fiction*, 1599, p. viii).

5 **office** service, duty

1.1] *F (Actus Primus. Scoena Prima.)*

90

Upon a tawny front. His captain's heart,
Which in the scuffles of great fights hath burst
The buckles on his breast, reneges all temper
And is become the bellows and the fan
To cool a gipsy's lust.

Flourish. Enter ANTONY, CLEOPATRA, *her Ladies*
[CHARMIAN *and* IRAS], *the train, with Eunuchs fanning her.*

                    Look where they come!   10
Take but good note, and you shall see in him
The triple pillar of the world transformed
Into a strumpet's fool. Behold and see.

CLEOPATRA
If it be love indeed, tell me how much.

ANTONY
There's beggary in the love that can be reckoned.   15

CLEOPATRA
I'll set a bourn how far to be beloved.

---

6 **front** forehead, and hence face, with a pun on 'battle-front'. 'Shakespeare equates "a brow of Egypt" with a dark complexion in *MND* 5.1.11. Cleopatra calls herself "black" at 1.5.29' (Bevington).

8 **reneges all temper** abandons all restraint. *Temper* could also mean 'the particular degree of hardness and elasticity or resiliency imparted to steel by tempering' (*OED* Temper *sb.* 5).

9 **bellows ... fan** Antony simultaneously both arouses and satisfies her. Cf. 2.2.213–15.

10 **gipsy's lust** Gipsies began to appear in England in the early sixteenth century and were thought to have come from Egypt. 'Gipsy' was also a contemptuous term for a promiscuous woman. Hence Cleopatra is here described as a gipsy, an Egyptian and a whore. 'In the next scene her maids are given another gipsy-like trait – an

interest in fortune-telling' (Jones).

10.2 SD *Eunuchs* The presence of the eunuchs not only provides local oriental colour but also suggests the sexual ambiguities of Cleopatra's court, an idea developed by Caesar in 1.4.5–7 where he describes Cleopatra as *manlike* and Antony as *womanly*.

12 **triple** one of three. As a triumvir, Antony is one of the three rulers of the Roman empire.

13 **fool** 'one who is made to appear a fool ... a dupe' (*OED sb.* 3)

14 **tell** Cleopatra uses the word in the sense of 'inform', but Antony interprets it in the sense of 'count'.

15 **There's ... reckoned** 'Love which can be computed (i.e. is less than infinite) is contemptibly poor.' Cf. *RJ* 2.6.32, 'They are but beggars that can count their worth.'

16 **bourn ... beloved** 'limit on how much you may love me'

10 SD CHARMIAN *and* IRAS] *Jones*   12 The ... world] *F2;* (The ... world) *F*

ANTONY

Then must thou needs find out new heaven, new earth.

Enter a Messenger.

MESSENGER

News, my good lord, from Rome.

ANTONY

Grates me! The sum.

CLEOPATRA

Nay, hear them, Antony.   20

Fulvia perchance is angry, or who knows
If the scarce-bearded Caesar have not sent
His powerful mandate to you: 'Do this, or this;
Take in that kingdom and enfranchise that.
Perform't, or else we damn thee.'

ANTONY   How, my love?   25

CLEOPATRA

Perchance? Nay, and most like.
You must not stay here longer; your dismission
Is come from Caesar; therefore hear it, Antony.
Where's Fulvia's process? – Caesar's, I would say.
    Both?

---

17 **new ... earth** Cf. Revelation 21:1, 'I
sawe a new heaven, and a new earth';
2 Peter 3:13, 'We, according to his
promise, look for a newe heaven, and
a newe earth.'

19 **Grates ... sum** 'It irritates me but
tell me briefly.'

21 **Fulvia** Antony's wife who, according
to Plutarch, was 'somewhat sower,
and crooked of condition' and was
'not contented to master her husband
at home, but would also rule him in
his office abroad, and commaund him,
that commaunded legions and great
armies' (North, 262).

22 **scarce-bearded** At the time the play
opens, Octavius was twenty-three and
Antony forty-two. Later (4.12.48)

Antony calls him 'the young Roman
boy'.

24 **Take in** take possession of
enfranchise liberate

25 **we** 'The "royal we" implies royal
authority in addressing one who owes
duty' (Bevington).
How 'What did you say?'

27 **dismission** dismissal; order to leave

29 **process** a summons to appear in a
court of law (*OED sb.* 7)
Both 'Cleopatra makes, or pretends
to make, a slip of the tongue – she
meant *Caesar*, but says *Fulvia* by
mistake, and then adds that *Both*
might have their reasons for wanting
Antony in Rome' (Jones).

19 Grates me!] *Johnson subst.;* Grates me, *F;* Rate me, *F2*

Call in the messengers! As I am Egypt's Queen,   30
Thou blushest, Antony, and that blood of thine
Is Caesar's homager; else so thy cheek pays shame
When shrill-tongued Fulvia scolds. The messengers!

ANTONY

Let Rome in Tiber melt, and the wide arch
Of the ranged empire fall! Here is my space!   35
Kingdoms are clay! Our dungy earth alike
Feeds beast as man. The nobleness of life
Is to do thus, when such a mutual pair
And such a twain can do't, in which I bind,
On pain of punishment, the world to weet   40
We stand up peerless.

CLEOPATRA   Excellent falsehood!
Why did he marry Fulvia and not love her?
I'll seem the fool I am not. Antony
Will be himself.

32 **homager** vassal; 'one who owes
homage or fealty' (*OED*)
else so or else
33 **scolds** 'quarrels noisily, brawls' (*OED*
Scold *v.* 1)
34 **arch** Shakespeare here develops the
idea of the 'triple pillar[s] of the
world' in 1.12. 'Antony seems to
imagine that when he takes his
support from the world, a significant
portion of it will collapse' (Adelman,
Essay, 117).
35 **ranged** ordered, with connotations of
an army arranged in ranks. Compare
ranges 3.13.5.
37–41 **The nobleness ... peerless**
'They made an order betwene them,
which they called Amimetobion (as
much [as] to say, no life comparable
and matcheable with it) one feasting
ech other by turnes, and in cost,
exceeding all measure and reason'
(North, 275).
38 * **thus** The SD *Embracing* which Pope
introduced here, though perfectly

acceptable, limits the significance of
Antony's statement, which refers not
simply to a physical embrace but to
their whole way of life.
mutual well-matched
39–41 **I bind ... peerless** 'I command
the world to recognise (*weet*), on pain
of punishment if they do not, that
we stand unequalled.' 'On pain of
punishment' was a formula used in
official statutes, and, as Jones comments, Antony uses the style of a
public proclamation.
41–3 * **Excellent ... not** The *aside* with
which Johnson marked these lines is
unnecessary. Spoken directly to
Antony, they are consistent with the
taunting attitude Cleopatra adopts
towards him throughout the scene.
42 **Why ... her** She implies that Antony,
having married Fulvia, loves his wife
and not herself.
44 **be himself** 'be the fool, or deceiver,
he is'

38 thus] *F;* thus (*Embracing*) *Pope*   40 On] *F2;* One *F*

ANTONY   But stirred by Cleopatra.
    Now, for the love of Love and her soft hours,   45
    Let's not confound the time with conference harsh.
    There's not a minute of our lives should stretch
    Without some pleasure now. What sport tonight?
CLEOPATRA
    Hear the ambassadors.
ANTONY   Fie, wrangling queen,
    Whom everything becomes – to chide, to laugh,   50
    To weep; whose every passion fully strives
    To make itself, in thee, fair and admired!
    No messenger but thine, and all alone
    Tonight we'll wander through the streets and note
    The qualities of people. Come, my queen!   55
    Last night you did desire it. [*to the Messenger*] Speak
        not to us.
                    Exeunt [*Antony and Cleopatra*] *with the train.*
DEMETRIUS
    Is Caesar with Antonius prized so slight?
PHILO
    Sir, sometimes, when he is not Antony,
    He comes too short of that great property
    Which still should go with Antony.
DEMETRIUS   I am full sorry   60

44 **But stirred** 'only if inspired'.
   Antony's reply means 'I'll be a fool
   only if I am captivated by Cleopatra'
   or, more probably, 'I shall be fully
   myself only if inspired by Cleopatra.'
   Throughout this dialogue Cleopatra
   provokes Antony and he turns her
   taunts in such a way as to flatter her.
46 **confound** waste. Compare 1.4.28.
   conference conversation
48 **pleasure now** immediate pleasure
   sport pastime, recreation
49 **wrangling** contentious
50–2 **Whom** ... **admired** Compare

2.2.248–50.
53–5 **all alone ... people** 'He would
   goe up and downe the citie disguised
   like a slave in the night, and would
   peere into poore mens windowes and
   their shops, and scold and brawle with
   them within the house: Cleopatra
   would be also in a chamber maides
   array, and amble up and downe the
   streets with him' (North, 276).
56 SD *train* retinue
57 **prized** estimated, judged
59 **property** distinctive quality
60 **still** always

48 now] *F*; new *Warburton*   51 whose] *F2*; who *F*; how *Ard²*   56 SD *to the Messenger*] *Cam¹*
subst.   Antony and Cleopatra] *Capell*

94

That he approves the common liar who
Thus speaks of him at Rome, but I will hope
Of better deeds tomorrow. Rest you happy!   *Exeunt.*

[1.2]   *Enter* ENOBARBUS *[and other Roman Officers], a*
Soothsayer, CHARMIAN, IRAS, MARDIAN *the Eunuch, and*
ALEXAS.

CHARMIAN   Lord Alexas, sweet Alexas, most anything
Alexas, almost most absolute Alexas, where's the
soothsayer that you praised so to th' Queen? O, that
I knew this husband which you say must charge his
horns with garlands!   5
ALEXAS   Soothsayer!
SOOTHSAYER   Your will?

61 **approves ... liar** 'confirms that
common gossip is actually true'
63 **happy** fortunate (*OED a.* 2)

1.2 Location: Alexandria. The tension
between Antony's political obligations
and his love for Cleopatra, already
present in 1.1, now increases as more
messengers arrive from Rome, compelling him to confront his dilemma
and making his departure from Egypt
inescapable. The scene is divided into
an 'Egyptian' and a 'Roman' section
(1–80 and 93–204), with Cleopatra's
brief appearance acting as a bridge
between them. Later (138–82) Enobarbus jokes lightheartedly (as
Antony has done in 1.1) about issues
which his master is now forced to
take seriously.
0.1 * Three of the named characters in
the F entry, Lamprius, Rannius and
Lucillius, say nothing throughout the
scene and never reappear. Shakespeare presumably intended to make
use of them later but found he had
no need for them. Nevertheless he
apparently intended Enobarbus to be
accompanied by other Roman officers

to match the Egyptians and in order
to create a contrast between the fairly
full stage with which the scene opens
and the more private, serious
exchanges between Antony and the
messengers after the stage has been
cleared at line 92. 'The two groups',
suggests Ridley, 'come in simultaneously but by different doors.'
Plutarch refers to his 'grandfather
Lampryas' as the authority for one of
his stories but does not mention the
other two characters.
4–5 * **charge ... garlands** It appears
that the Soothsayer has been characteristically enigmatic in predicting a
husband for Charmian, and the
editors too have been baffled by him.
If we retain F's 'change' and interpret
with as 'for', the reference is to a
cuckold who will exchange his horns
for the garlands of a bridegroom (cf.
Cym 1.5.55, 'to exchange one misery
with another'). If we accept Theobald's emendation it is to a cuckold
whose horns are laden (*charged*) with
the wreath of victory as 'the champion
cuckold of all Egypt' (Wilson).

1.2] Pope   0.1 and ... Officers] this edn; Lamprius, a Southsayer, Rannius, Lucillius F
1 Lord] Johnson; L. F   4 charge] Theobald (Warburton); change F

CHARMIAN   Is this the man? Is't you, sir, that know
    things?
SOOTHSAYER
    In nature's infinite book of secrecy   10
    A little I can read.
ALEXAS   Show him your hand.
ENOBARBUS
    Bring in the banquet quickly; wine enough
    Cleopatra's health to drink.

[Enter Servants with wine and other refreshments and exeunt.]

CHARMIAN   *[Gives her hand to the Soothsayer.]* Good
    sir, give me good fortune.   15
SOOTHSAYER   I make not, but foresee.
CHARMIAN   Pray then, foresee me one.
SOOTHSAYER   You shall be yet far fairer than you are.
CHARMIAN   He means in flesh.
IRAS   No, you shall paint when you are old.   20
CHARMIAN   Wrinkles forbid!
ALEXAS   Vex not his prescience. Be attentive.
CHARMIAN   Hush!
SOOTHSAYER   You shall be more beloving than beloved.
CHARMIAN   I had rather heat my liver with drinking.   25
ALEXAS   Nay, hear him.
CHARMIAN   Good now, some excellent fortune! Let me

12–13 **Bring ... drink** F gives no SD
    following this order, but, to judge
    from Enobarbus' next remark (47–8),
    he, and possibly the others, have been
    helping themselves liberally to the
    wine during the dialogue with the
    Soothsayer.
12 **banquet** 'a course of sweetmeats, fruit
    and wine ... a dessert' (*OED sb.*[1] 3)
18 **fairer** 'The present prediction is
    perhaps fulfilled in Charmian's
    character, by the fairer, nobler qual-
    ities displayed in Act 5 ... Charmian
    takes *fair* in the sense "plump, in
    good condition". Cf *AYL* 1.1.11–12,
    "His horses ... are fair with their
    feeding" ' (Case).
22 **prescience** foreknowledge
25 **I ... drinking** 'I had rather my liver
    was warmed with drink than with
    love.' Love, like drink, was thought
    to inflame the liver. Compare *MWW*
    2.1.116–17, 'Love my wife? With liver
    burning hot.'

13 SD] *Cam*[1] *subst.*   14 SD] *Cam*[2] *subst.*

be married to three kings in a forenoon and widow
them all. Let me have a child at fifty to whom Herod
of Jewry may do homage. Find me to marry me with   30
Octavius Caesar and companion me with my mistress.

SOOTHSAYER

You shall outlive the lady whom you serve.

CHARMIAN   O, excellent! I love long life better than
figs.

SOOTHSAYER

You have seen and proved a fairer former fortune   35
Than that which is to approach.

CHARMIAN   Then belike my children shall have no
names. Prithee, how many boys and wenches must I
have?

SOOTHSAYER

If every of your wishes had a womb,   40
And fertile every wish, a million.

CHARMIAN   Out, fool! I forgive thee for a witch.

ALEXAS   You think none but your sheets are privy to
your wishes.

CHARMIAN   Nay, come, tell Iras hers.   45

ALEXAS   We'll know all our fortunes.

28–30 **three kings ... Herod of Jewry**
This reference to the birth of Christ,
the three kings and King Herod of
Judaea 'accentuates the ironic contrast
between Charmian's vivacious hedon-
ism and the sacred story to which she
unconsciously alludes' (Bevington).
Herod was regarded as a type of brutal
tyrant and was so portrayed in the
miracle plays. He was 'the last person
in the world to do homage to an
infant' (Wilson).

32 **You ... serve** Charmian does outlive
Cleopatra but only by a few moments.
She understandably takes this state-
ment as a prophecy of long life.

33–4 **I ... figs** This may be no more
than a statement of preference and a

foreshadowing of the figs which
conceal the asps in 5.2, but, in view
of the cheerfully erotic tone of this
conversation, the meaning is more
probably sexual, since figs resemble
the male genitals. Compare the 'sexually allusive imprecation "fig me" '
(Partridge) and *2H4* 5.3.118–19, 'fig
me like / The bragging Spaniard.'

35 **proved** experienced

37–8 **have no names** be bastards.
Compare *TGV* 3.1.317–18.

42 **I ... witch** 'I absolve thee from the
sin of witchcraft (i.e. You are no
prophet!)' (Wilson)

43–4 **You ... wishes** a variation of the
proverbial expression 'Take counsel
of your pillow' (Tilley, C696)

41 fertile] *Warburton (Theobald);* fore-tell *F*

97

ENOBARBUS   Mine, and most of our fortunes tonight,
      shall be drunk to bed.

IRAS [*Holds out her hand.*] There's a palm presages
      chastity, if nothing else.   50

CHARMIAN   E'en as the o'erflowing Nilus presageth
      famine.

IRAS   Go, you wild bedfellow, you cannot soothsay!

CHARMIAN   Nay, if an oily palm be not a fruitful
      prognostication, I cannot scratch mine ear. Prithee,   55
      tell her but a workaday fortune.

SOOTHSAYER   Your fortunes are alike.

IRAS   But how? But how? Give me particulars!

SOOTHSAYER   I have said.

IRAS   Am I not an inch of fortune better than she?   60

CHARMIAN   Well, if you were but an inch of fortune
      better than I, where would you choose it?

IRAS   Not in my husband's nose.

CHARMIAN   Our worser thoughts heavens mend!
      Alexas – come, his fortune, his fortune! O, let him   65
      marry a woman that cannot go, sweet Isis I beseech

---

48 **drunk to bed** to go to bed drunk

51 **E'en ... famine** ironical. The over-
flowing of the Nile irrigated the soil
and made it fertile. See 2.7.20–3.

54 **oily palm** Compare Tilley, H86, 'A
moist hand argues an amorous
nature.' Of Desdemona's moist hand
Othello observes, 'This argues fruitfulness and liberal heart' (*Oth* 3.4.38).

55 **I cannot ... ear** 'I'm no true woman.'
'To have itching ears is to enjoy the
traditional female relish for hearing
novelties (See *OED* Ear *sb.*[1] 3d)'
(Bevington).

63 **Not ... nose** Charmian implies that
she would prefer the inch to be in
her husband's penis. Cf. Tilley, 155:
'An inch in a man's nose is much.'

65–71 *** Alexas ... thee** Since in F (and,
presumably, in F's copy text) proper
names and speech prefixes are both

italicised, the compositor mistook the
name 'Alexas' for a speech prefix and
assigned the rest of the speech to
him. Theobald's emendation has been
generally accepted.

66 **go** meaning uncertain. Possible
interpretations are (1) 'cannot die'
(*OED* Go *v.* 28, 'To "depart this
life"'); Charmian prays that Alexas
will have a wife he can't get rid of,
and then, as an afterthought, thinks
of a worse fate and says 'and let her
die too'; (2) cannot become pregnant
(*OED* 7); (3) 'cannot "go all the way"
with her sexual partner' (Partridge,
121–2).

Isis originally the Egyptian goddess
of the earth and of fertility. For
allusions to Isis in the play generally,
see pp. 67–9.

49 SD] *Cam*[1]   56 workaday] *F (worky day)*   65–71 Alexas – come ... thee] *Theobald; Alexas.*
Come ... thee *F (assigning the speech to Alexas)*

thee, and let her die too, and give him a worse, and
let worse follow worse, till the worst of all follow him
laughing to his grave, fiftyfold a cuckold! Good Isis,
hear me this prayer, though thou deny me a matter   70
of more weight; good Isis, I beseech thee!

IRAS Amen. Dear goddess, hear that prayer of the
people! For as it is a heartbreaking to see a handsome
man loose-wived, so it is a deadly sorrow to behold
a foul knave uncuckolded. Therefore, dear Isis, keep   75
decorum and fortune him accordingly!

CHARMIAN Amen.

ALEXAS Lo now, if it lay in their hands to make me a
cuckold, they would make themselves whores, but
they'd do't.   80

Enter CLEOPATRA.

ENOBARBUS Hush, here comes Antony.
CHARMIAN Not he, the Queen.
CLEOPATRA Saw you my lord?
ENOBARBUS No, lady.
CLEOPATRA Was he not here?   85
CHARMIAN No, madam.

72–3 **prayer of the people** probably an
allusion to one of the Collects in the
Elizabethan Book of Common Prayer
(1594). The Collect for the First
Sunday after Epiphany, for example,
includes the words 'Lorde, we
beseche thee, mercyfully to receyve
the prayers of the people' (Folio xx),
and the Collect for Septuagesima
Sunday begins 'O Lorde we beseche
thee favourably to heare the prayers
of thy people' (Folio xxiiii verso).
75–6 **keep decorum** act appropriately.
Compare 5.2.17.
76 **accordingly** correspondingly
81 **here comes Antony** It is highly

unlikely that Enobarbus mistakes the
arriving Cleopatra for Antony, as
some commentators have supposed.
More probably he describes Cleopatra
as 'Antony' because he sees the latter
as totally under her control. Some
editors, overlooking this implication,
delay her entrance until after l. 82.
83 * **Saw** 'The F reading "Saue" is an
easy error for "Saw". Compositor B
mistakenly read the conventional
greeting, "Saue you, my lord",
though it is plainly inappropriate here
since it provides no question for
Enobarbus to answer' (Bevington).

80 SD *Enter* CLEOPATRA] *F; opp.* Queen *l.82 / Capell*   83 Saw you my lord?] *F2; Saue you,
my Lord. F*

99

CLEOPATRA
   He was disposed to mirth, but on the sudden
   A Roman thought hath struck him. Enobarbus!
ENOBARBUS   Madam?
CLEOPATRA
   Seek him and bring him hither.   [*Exit Enobarbus.*]
                                  Where's Alexas?   90
ALEXAS   Here, at your service. My lord approaches.

                 Enter ANTONY *with a* Messenger.

CLEOPATRA
   We will not look upon him. Go with us.
                    Exeunt [all but Antony and Messenger].

MESSENGER
   Fulvia thy wife first came into the field.
ANTONY
   Against my brother Lucius?
MESSENGER
   Ay,   95
   But soon that war had end, and the time's state
   Made friends of them, jointing their force 'gainst
      Caesar,
   Whose better issue in the war from Italy
   Upon the first encounter drave them.
ANTONY
   Well, what worst?   100
MESSENGER
   The nature of bad news infects the teller.
ANTONY
   When it concerns the fool or coward. On!

93–9 **Fulvia ... them** 'His brother
Lucius, and Fulvia his wife, fell out
first betwene them selves, and afterwards fell to open warre with Caesar,
and had brought all to nought, that
they were both driven to flie out of

Italie' (North, 277).
96 **time's state** situation at the time
97 **jointing** uniting
98 **better issue** greater success
100 **what worst?** 'what's the worst
   news?'

90 SD *Cam¹ subst.*   91 SD Messenger] *F; Messenger and Attendants / Rowe*   92 SD *all ...
Messenger*] *Capell subst.*   100 worst?] *Rowe;* worst. *F;* worse? *Hanmer*

Things that are past are done with me. 'Tis thus:
Who tells me true, though in his tale lie death,
I hear him as he flattered.

MESSENGER   Labienus –   105
This is stiff news – hath with his Parthian force
Extended Asia. From Euphrates
His conquering banner shook, from Syria
To Lydia, and to Ionia,
Whilst –

ANTONY   'Antony', thou wouldst say –

MESSENGER   O, my lord!   110

ANTONY

Speak to me home; mince not the general tongue;
Name Cleopatra as she is called in Rome;
Rail thou in Fulvia's phrase, and taunt my faults
With such full licence as both truth and malice
Have power to utter. Oh, then we bring forth weeds   115
When our quick minds lie still, and our ills told us
Is as our earing. Fare thee well awhile.

105–9 **Labienus ... Ionia** 'The seconde
newes, [was] as bad as the first: that
Labienus conquered all Asia with the
armie of the Parthians, from the river
of Euphrates, and from Syria, unto
the contries of Lydia and Ionia. Then
began Antonius with much a doe, a
litle to rouse him selfe as if he had
bene wakened out of a deepe sleepe,
and as a man may say, comming out
of a great dronkennes' (North, 277).
Quintus Labienus was sent to Parthia
by Cassius in order to raise troops to
fight against Antony and Octavius,
but with Cassius' defeat and suicide
he was stranded there. In 41–40 BC
(just before the opening of the play)
he invaded Syria with Parthian help
and defeated Antony's governor. He
then proceeded to invade Asia Minor,
as the Messenger reports (*OCD*).

107 **Extended** seized upon; a legal term
signifying 'to take possession of by a

writ of extent; to seize upon (land
etc.) in satisfaction for a debt' (*OED*
Extend *v.* 11)
Euphrates accented on the first syllable

111 **home** directly, frankly. Compare
Cor 3.3.1–2, 'In this point charge him
home, that he affects / Tyrannical
power.'

115–17 * **Oh ... earing** 'When the soil
of our minds lies fallow, it produces
weeds, but when we are told our
faults it is as though the soil were
ploughed.' *Earing* = ploughing (*OED*
Ear *v.*¹). Compare the proverb 'Weeds
come forth on the fattest soil if it is
untilled' (Dent, W241). 'The proverb
tends to support Warburton's emendation of F's *windes* to *minds*, cor-
recting an easy minim error'
(Bevington).

116 **quick** lively

---

103 done ... 'Tis] *F*; done. With me 'tis *Cam¹*   116 minds] *Hanmer (Warburton)*; windes *F*

MESSENGER

    At your noble pleasure.

                            Exit Messenger.

                Enter another Messenger.

ANTONY

    From Sicyon how the news? Speak there!

2 MESSENGER

    The man from Sicyon –

ANTONY   Is there such a one?   120

2 MESSENGER

    He stays upon your will.

ANTONY   Let him appear.

                [Exit Second Messenger.]

    These strong Egyptian fetters I must break,

    Or lose myself in dotage.

          Enter another Messenger *with a letter.*

                    What are you?

3 MESSENGER   Fulvia thy wife is dead.

ANTONY   Where died she?   125

3 MESSENGER   In Sicyon.

    Her length of sickness, with what else more serious

    Importeth thee to know, this bears. *[Gives him the letter.]*

ANTONY   Forbear me.

                 [Exit Third Messenger.]

118–21 * **At ... appear** See LN,
p. 303.
119 **Sicyon** a Greek city in northern
Peloponnesus, north-west of Corinth
121 **stays ... will** awaits your orders
124–8 **Fulvia ... bears** 'By good

fortune, his wife Fulvia going to
meete with Antonius, sickened by the
way, and dyed in the citie of Sicyone'
(North, 278).

128 **Forbear me** leave me

118 SD *Exit Messenger*] F; *Rowe omits Enter another* Messenger] F; *Rowe, Capell omit; Enter ...
a third attends at the door Cam²* 119 Sicyon] *Pope; Scicion* F (*passim*) how the] F; ho, the
Dyce 120 SP 2 MESSENGER] *Oxf, Cam²; 1. Mes.* F; *Mes. / Rowe; 1.A / Capell* ANTONY Is
... one?] *Oxf;* F *assigns the whole line to the Messenger* a one] *Capell;* an one F 121 SP 2
MESSENGER] F (*2. Mes.*); *Attend. / Rowe; 2.A / Capell; Sec. Att. Ard¹*; 3 MESSENGER *Cam²* SD
Exit Second Messenger] *Oxf; Exeunt Second and Third Messengers Cam²* 123 SD *another*] F; *a fourth
Cam²* 124 SP 3 MESSENGER] F (*3. Mes.*); *2. Mes. / Rowe; 4* MESSENGER *Cam²* 127 SD *Gives
... letter*] *Johnson* 128 SD *Exit Third Messenger*] *Oxf; Exit Messenger / Theobald subst.*

There's a great spirit gone! Thus did I desire it.
What our contempts doth often hurl from us   130
We wish it ours again. The present pleasure,
By revolution lowering, does become
The opposite of itself. She's good, being gone.
The hand could pluck her back that shoved her on.
I must from this enchanting queen break off.   135
Ten thousand harms, more than the ills I know,
My idleness doth hatch. How now, Enobarbus!

Enter ENOBARBUS.

ENOBARBUS What's your pleasure, sir?
ANTONY I must with haste from hence.
ENOBARBUS Why then we kill all our women. We see   140
how mortal an unkindness is to them. If they suffer
our departure, death's the word.
ANTONY I must be gone.
ENOBARBUS Under a compelling occasion let women
die. It were pity to cast them away for nothing,   145
though between them and a great cause they should
be esteemed nothing. Cleopatra, catching but the

130–1 **What ... again** 'We wish we
had kept those things which we have
thrown away in contempt.' Compare
1.4.41–4 and the proverbs 'The worth
of a thing is best known by the want'
(Dent, W924) and 'The good is not
known until lost' (Dent, G298.1).
Doth is an example of the old third
person plural of the verb ending in
'th' (Abbott, 334).
132 **By revolution** 'in due course of
time' (*OED* Revolution *sb.* 2).
Compare *2H4* 3.1.45–7, 'O God, that
one might read the book of fate, /
And see the revolution of the times /
Make mountains level.' The image
also suggests the turning of the wheel
of Fortune whereby pleasure becomes

pain. Bevington compares the
expression to Daniel, *Cleopatra*
3.1.549–50, 'Thus doth the ever-
changing course of things / Runne a
perpetuall circle, ever turning'
(Bullough, 421).
134 **could** would like to. Antony, having
neglected his wife, feels guilty and
responsible for her death.
137 **idleness** folly (*OED* 2) and also
inactivity, indolence (*OED* 4)
145 **die** As well as using the word in
the literal sense, Enobarbus plays on
it in the sense of 'experience sexual
climax' ('to be consumed with longing
desire' *OED v.* 7). His dialogue
during the rest of this scene is full of
sexual innuendoes.

130 contempts doth] *F*; contempts doe *F2*   137 SD *Enter* ENOBARBUS] *as Dyce; after* hatch
F   144 a compelling occasion] *Rowe*; a compelling an occasion *F*

103

least noise of this, dies instantly. I have seen her die
twenty times upon far poorer moment. I do think
there is mettle in death which commits some loving   150
act upon her, she hath such a celerity in dying.

ANTONY   She is cunning past man's thought.

ENOBARBUS   Alack, sir, no; her passions are made of
nothing but the finest part of pure love. We cannot
call her winds and waters sighs and tears; they are   155
greater storms and tempests than almanacs can report.
This cannot be cunning in her. If it be, she makes a
shower of rain as well as Jove.

ANTONY   Would I had never seen her!

ENOBARBUS   O, sir, you had then left unseen a won-   160
derful piece of work, which not to have been blest
withal would have discredited your travel.

ANTONY   Fulvia is dead.

ENOBARBUS   Sir?

ANTONY   Fulvia is dead.   165

ENOBARBUS   Fulvia?

ANTONY   Dead.

ENOBARBUS   Why, sir, give the gods a thankful sacrifice.
When it pleaseth their deities to take the wife of a
man from him, it shows to man the tailors of the   170
earth; comforting therein, that when old robes are
worn out, there are members to make new. If there
were no more women but Fulvia, then had you indeed

---

150 **mettle** spirit, vitality, as in *1H4*
2.4.12, 'a Corinthian, a lad of mettle'

156 **almanacs** sold by pedlars and containing calendars, astrological fore-
casts and predictions about the
weather. In *MND* (3.1.53–4) Bottom
consults an almanac to discover when
the moon will shine.

158 **Jove** believed to be responsible for
the weather and was worshipped as
a rain god. Shakespeare must have
known Ovid's account (*Metamorphoses*, 1.262–73) of the flood cast
upon the earth by Jove.

161 **piece** **of** **work** masterpiece.

Compare *Ham* 2.2.303–4, 'What a
piece of work is a man.'

162 **discredited your travel** 'lowered
your reputation as a traveller'

170–1 **shows … earth** 'shows men that
the gods are the world's tailors'.
Enobarbus argues that a dead wife,
like a worn-out suit, can be replaced.
There are further sexual innuendoes
in this speech, as in *members* and *case*
(the male and female organs). For *case*
used in this bawdy sense, see *AW*
1.3.21.

171 **therein** to this extent

a cut, and the case to be lamented. This grief is
crowned with consolation: your old smock brings   175
forth a new petticoat, and indeed the tears live in an
onion that should water this sorrow.

ANTONY

The business she hath broached in the state
Cannot endure my absence.

ENOBARBUS   And the business you have broached here   180
cannot be without you, especially that of Cleopatra's,
which wholly depends on your abode.

ANTONY

No more light answers. Let our officers
Have notice what we purpose. I shall break
The cause of our expedience to the Queen   185
And get her leave to part. For not alone
The death of Fulvia, with more urgent touches,
Do strongly speak to us, but the letters too
Of many our contriving friends in Rome
Petition us at home. Sextus Pompeius   190
Hath given the dare to Caesar and commands
The empire of the sea. Our slippery people,

---

174 **cut** 'severe disaster or misfortune; a blow, shock' (*OED sb.* 4)

175 **smock** a woman's petticoat; here the woman herself. Compare the proverb 'His old coat will buy you a new kirtle' (Tilley, B607).

176–7 **tears ... onion** proverbial: 'To weep with an onion' (Dent, O67)

178 **broached** broachèd; another bawdy pun. Antony uses the word to mean 'set on foot, started', but Enobarbus in the sense of 'pierced, stabbed, thrust through' (*OED* Broach *v.*[1] 1; Broached 2).

182 **abode** staying. Compare *Oth* 4.2.226.

183 **light** indecent. Antony is aware that both 'business' and 'broached' have sexual implications.
   officers subordinates

184 **break** disclose, as in 'break the news' (*OED v.* 22)

185 **expedience** 'that which requires speed; an enterprise, expedition' (*OED sb.* 1a)

186 * **leave** 'Several editors retain "love", understanding with Steevens: "And prevail on her love to consent to our separation"; but strong probability favours *leave*, and Malone remarked a similar misprint ("loves" for "leaves") in *Tit* 3.1.291' (Case).
   part depart

187 **more ... touches** 'things that touch us more sensibly, more pressing motives' (Johnson)

189 **contriving** 'skilfully or artfully devising; scheming' (*OED ppl. a*)

190 **at home** 'to come home'

192 **slippery** unstable, fickle (*OED* 3, 4)

186 leave] *Pope;* loue *F*   191 Hath] *F2;* Haue *F*

Whose love is never linked to the deserver
Till his deserts are past, begin to throw
Pompey the Great and all his dignities   195
Upon his son, who, high in name and power,
Higher than both in blood and life, stands up
For the main soldier; whose quality going on,
The sides o'th' world may danger. Much is breeding
Which, like the courser's hair, hath yet but life   200
And not a serpent's poison. Say our pleasure,
To such whose place is under us, requires
Our quick remove from hence.
ENOBARBUS   I shall do't.   [*Exeunt.*]

[1.3]   *Enter* CLEOPATRA, CHARMIAN, ALEXAS *and* IRAS.

CLEOPATRA   Where is he?
CHARMIAN   I did not see him since.

194–5 **throw ... Great** 'give the title "Pompey the Great"'. Sextus Pompeius was the younger son of Pompey the Great. See note on Sextus Pompeius, p. 87.
197 **blood and life** spirit and energy
197–8 **stands ... soldier** 'shows himself to be the greatest soldier'. Compare 1.1.41.
198 **quality** party, supporters (*OED sb.* 5c). Cf. *1H4* 4.3.36–7, 'You are not of our quality, / But stand against us like an enemy.'
199 **sides** bounds; limits
danger endanger
200–1 **like ... poison** Theobald explains this allusion by referring to a popular belief, recorded by Holinshed, that a horse hair put into a bucket of river water 'will in short time stirre and become a living creature' (*Chronicles*, 1587, 3.2.224). Coleridge remarks that this was 'a common experiment with schoolboys in Cumberland and

Westmorland' (Coleridge, 1.87).
201–2 * **Say ... requires** The F2 emendation of this passage is the simplest and most plausible that has been offered. Manuscript *place is* could easily have been misread as *places* (F).

1.3 Location: Alexandria. The necessity for Antony to leave Cleopatra, which has become increasingly urgent in the two previous scenes, now reaches a crisis as he announces his decision to her. Her opening conversation with Charmian (1–13) reveals the strategy – deliberately not to give way to his moods – she will adopt later in the scene (as she already has in 1.1). It is only at l. 100 that she accepts his departure as inevitable.
2 **did not see** have not seen. Abbott (62) points out that we still say 'I never saw him *after* that' and that *since* has the meaning of *after*.

200 hair] *Rowe;* heire *F;* hare *F3*   202 place is ... requires] *F2;* places ... require *F*   204 SD] *F2*

1.3] *Capell*

CLEOPATRA [*to Alexas*]

See where he is, who's with him, what he does.
I did not send you. If you find him sad,
Say I am dancing; if in mirth, report   5
That I am sudden sick. Quick, and return. [*Exit Alexas.*]

CHARMIAN

Madam, methinks if you did love him dearly,
You do not hold the method to enforce
The like from him.

CLEOPATRA   What should I do I do not?

CHARMIAN

In each thing give him way; cross him in nothing.   10

CLEOPATRA

Thou teachest like a fool: the way to lose him.

CHARMIAN

Tempt him not so too far; I wish, forbear.
In time we hate that which we often fear.

Enter ANTONY.

But here comes Antony.

CLEOPATRA   I am sick and sullen.

ANTONY

I am sorry to give breathing to my purpose –   15

CLEOPATRA

Help me away, dear Charmian! I shall fall!
It cannot be thus long; the sides of nature

---

4 **I ... you** 'Don't tell him I sent you.'

6 SD * *Exit Alexas* F does not indicate to whom Cleopatra's speech is addressed or who obeys her order. Capell's SD has been generally accepted. Alexas does not speak during this scene.

8 **hold** 'follow, pursue ... practice' (Schmidt)

12 **Tempt** provoke

13 **In ... fear** Bevington compares this with the proverb 'He cannot love me

that is afraid of me' (Dent, L556).

14 **sick and sullen** To be 'sick of the sullens' was a proverbial expression (Dent, S964). *Sullen* means 'solemn, serious' (*OED a., adv.* 2).

15 **breathing** utterance, voice, as in the 1611 translation of Lamentations 3:56, 'Hide not thine ear at my breathing, at my cry.'

17–18 **sides ... it** The implicit idea is that the body is able to contain only a certain degree of emotion beyond

---

3 SD] *Jones*   6 SD] *Capell*   12 I wish] *F;* iwis *Cam¹*

Will not sustain it.

ANTONY   Now, my dearest queen –

CLEOPATRA

Pray you, stand farther from me!

ANTONY   What's the matter?

CLEOPATRA

I know by that same eye there's some good news.   20
What, says the married woman you may go?
Would she had never given you leave to come!
Let her not say 'tis I that keep you here.
I have no power upon you; hers you are.

ANTONY

The gods best know –

CLEOPATRA   Oh, never was there queen   25
So mightily betrayed! Yet at the first
I saw the treasons planted.

ANTONY   Cleopatra –

CLEOPATRA

Why should I think you can be mine and true –
Though you in swearing shake the throned gods –
Who have been false to Fulvia? Riotous madness,   30

which it must give way. Compare
4.14.40–2 where a similar idea is
present and *TN* 2.4.93–4, 'There is
no woman's sides / Can bide the
beating of so strong a passion.'

21 * **What ... go** Apart from the question mark at the end, F gives no
punctuation to this line, which can
be punctuated in various ways (see
collation), each producing a slightly
different meaning. F4's solution is the
most plausible.

21–2 **What ... come** These lines may
be derived from the 'Epistle of Dido
to Aeneas' in Ovid, *Heroides*, Epistle
7.139: 'sed iubet ire deus. vellem,
vetuisset adire' ('"But your god
orders you to go." I wish he had

forbidden you to come'). Antony's
situation here, torn between his political obligations and his love for Cleopatra, has much in common with
that of Aeneas in relation to Dido in
Virgil's *Aeneid* 4. For comparisons
between Antony and Cleopatra and
Dido and Aeneas generally, see pp.
66–7. The 'married woman' is Fulvia.

27 **planted** 'either in the gardener's
sense ... or = placed (like mines
etc.)' (Case)

29 **Though ... gods** an allusion to the
belief that when Jupiter swore an oath
'the whole of Olympus shuddered to
its foundations' (Jones)
throned thronèd

30 **Riotous madness** i.e. 'on my part'

21 What, says ... go?] *F4 subst.;* What sayes ... goe? *F;* What says the marry'd Woman? you may
go; *Rowe*

To be entangled with those mouth-made vows
Which break themselves in swearing!
ANTONY   Most sweet queen –
CLEOPATRA

Nay, pray you seek no colour for your going,
But bid farewell and go. When you sued staying,
Then was the time for words; no going then.   35
Eternity was in our lips and eyes,
Bliss in our brows' bent; none our parts so poor
But was a race of heaven. They are so still,
Or thou, the greatest soldier of the world,
Art turned the greatest liar.

ANTONY   How now, lady?   40
CLEOPATRA

I would I had thy inches! Thou shouldst know
There were a heart in Egypt!
ANTONY   Hear me, queen.

The strong necessity of time commands
Our services awhile, but my full heart
Remains in use with you. Our Italy   45
Shines o'er with civil swords; Sextus Pompeius

31 **mouth-made** 'coming from the lips and not the heart'. Shakespeare often makes the distinction between words and thoughts (or deeds) as in *TC* 5.3.108, 'Words, words, mere words, no matter from the heart.'

33 **colour** pretext. Compare *TGV* 4.2.3, 'under the colour of commending him'.

34 **sued staying** begged to stay

36–8 **Eternity ... heaven** It is clear from Cleopatra's statement in 39–40 that she is here quoting Antony's former protestations of love; *our* may be the royal plural but could also refer to the 'mutual pair'.

37 **our brows' bent** the arch of my eyebrows

38 **a race of heaven** 'of heavenly origin' (Malone). Warburton, however, paraphrases it as 'had a smack or flavour of heaven.'

42 **a heart** courage. *Egypt* may refer to the country or its queen.

45 **in use** 'in your keeping'; a legal term meaning 'in trust'. *OED* (Use *sb.* 4c) quotes from a statute of Henry VIII, 'in use, confidence or trust'.

46 **civil swords** swords of civil war
Sextus Pompeius 'Out of Italy all things were not quiet, for *Pompey*, by resorte of condemned Citizens, and auntient possessioners, was greatly increased, both in might and estimation: for they that feared their life, or were spoyled of their goodes, or lyked not the present state, fledde all to hym.... Beside a repayre of yong men, desirous of gayne and service, not caring under whom they went, because they were all Romanes, sought unto him' (Appian, 76–7).

37 brows'] *Johnson;* browes *F*   44 services] *F2;* Seruicles *F*

Makes his approaches to the port of Rome;
Equality of two domestic powers
Breed scrupulous faction; the hated, grown to
    strength,
Are newly grown to love; the condemned Pompey,   50
Rich in his father's honour, creeps apace
Into the hearts of such as have not thrived
Upon the present state, whose numbers threaten;
And quietness, grown sick of rest, would purge
By any desperate change. My more particular,   55
And that which most with you should safe my going,
Is Fulvia's death.

CLEOPATRA
Though age from folly could not give me freedom,
It does from childishness. Can Fulvia die?

ANTONY
She's dead, my queen.   [*Gives her the letters.*]
Look here, and at thy sovereign leisure read   61
The garboils she awaked. At the last, best,
See when and where she died.

48–9 **Equality ... faction** 'The equal balance between two powers within the same country (*domestic*) creates factions which disagree over small details.'

49 * **Breed** Some editors, following Pope, read *breeds*, but the plural verb is used because of its proximity to the plural *powers* (Abbott, 412).

49–50 **the hated ... love** 'Now they have become powerful, those who were formerly hated are now loved.' Compare 1.2.193–5; 1.4.41–4.

53 **Upon ... state** 'under the present government'

54–5 **quietness ... change** Peace (*quietness*) is here visualized as a disease which must be purged by any means. A similar idea is expressed in *2H4* 4.1.63–6. *Purge* means 'cure by means of a laxative'.

55 **desperate** 'characterised by the recklessness or resolution of despair; applied *esp.* to actions done or means resorted to in the last extremity, when all else fails' (*OED* 5)
particular personal motive

56 **with ... going** 'make my departure unsuspected by you of dangerous consequences' (Abbott, 290). For *safe* used as a verb, see 4.6.27.

62 **garboils** commotions, disturbances. Shakespeare uses the word only in this play (here and in 2.2.72), but it is not uncommon among other writers of his time. See *OED* Garboil *sb.*
best This may refer to the news in the letter ('the last item is the best') or is a term of endearment addressed to Cleopatra. Compare *WT* 4.2.54, 'My best Camillo'.

49 Breed] *F;* Breeds *Pope*   60 SD] *Jones subst.*

CLEOPATRA   O most false love!
Where be the sacred vials thou shouldst fill
With sorrowful water? Now I see, I see,   65
In Fulvia's death how mine received shall be.

ANTONY

Quarrel no more, but be prepared to know
The purposes I bear; which are, or cease,
As you shall give th'advice. By the fire
That quickens Nilus' slime, I go from hence   70
Thy soldier, servant, making peace or war
As thou affects.

CLEOPATRA   Cut my lace, Charmian, come!
But let it be; I am quickly ill and well –
So Antony loves.

ANTONY   My precious queen, forbear,
And give true evidence to his love, which stands   75
An honourable trial.

CLEOPATRA   So Fulvia told me.
I prithee, turn aside and weep for her,
Then bid adieu to me, and say the tears
Belong to Egypt. Good now, play one scene

---

64 **sacred vials** tear bottles or lachry-
matories. These small vessels, found
in ancient Roman tombs and probably
designed to contain perfumes, were
thought to have been used by mourn-
ers to collect their tears in order to
deposit them as tributes to the dead.
Compare Donne, 'Twicknam Garden':
'Hither with crystal vials, lovers
come, / And take my tears, which are
love's wine.'
68 **bear** intend
69–70 **the fire ... slime** the sun which
fertilises the Nile valley. Shakespeare
was closely acquainted with Ovid's
Metamorphoses and must have read
there (1.495–522) about the growth
of vegetation by the action of the sun

on the soil which had been watered
by the Nile. For the myth of Isis as
the soil and her brother Osiris as the
Nile, see pp. 67–9.
72 **affects** art inclined
Cut my lace i.e. of her tightly laced
bodice as she pants for breath
74 **So Antony loves** 'Antony's love is as
changeable as my health' or 'depending on whether Antony loves me or
not'
75 **stands** 'will sustain' with a pun on
'stand trial'. The legal metaphor is
developed from *true evidence*.
76 **So Fulvia told me** 'So I've learned
from your behaviour toward Fulvia'
(Bevington)
79 **Egypt** i.e. the Queen of Egypt

72 affects] *F;* affectst *F2*   73 well –] *Theobald subst.;* well, *F*

111

Of excellent dissembling, and let it look   80
Like perfect honour.

ANTONY   You'll heat my blood. No more.

CLEOPATRA
You can do better yet, but this is meetly.

ANTONY
Now by my sword –

CLEOPATRA   And target. Still he mends,
But this is not the best. Look, prithee, Charmian,
How this Herculean Roman does become   85
The carriage of his chafe.

ANTONY
I'll leave you, lady.

CLEOPATRA
Courteous lord, one word:
Sir, you and I must part, but that's not it;
Sir, you and I have loved, but there's not it;   90
That you know well. Something it is I would –
Oh, my oblivion is a very Antony,
And I am all forgotten!

ANTONY   But that your royalty
Holds idleness your subject, I should take you
For idleness itself.

---

82 **meetly** 'fair, moderately good' (*OED adv.* 1)

83 **And target** Cleopatra's completion of Antony's phrase 'makes it a swashbuckler's oath' (Wilson). A target is a small shield.

85 **Herculean** Plutarch says there was a tradition that Antony's family was descended from Hercules and that Antony attempted to perpetuate it by the clothing he wore and the 'likenes of his bodye' (North, 257). For comparisons between Antony and Hercules in the play generally, see pp. 64–6.

85–6 **does ... chafe** 'with what grace he performs the role of the angry man'. *Carriage* conveys the sense of 'deportment' (*OED* 13).

93 **I ... forgotten** ambiguous, perhaps deliberately. It may mean (1) 'I am entirely forgotten by Antony' or (2) 'I have entirely forgotten (what I was going to say).' 'My oblivion' is also ambiguous and may mean either 'my forgetfulness' or 'my being forgotten'.

93–4 **But ... subject** 'If it were not that your highness were in control of these frivolities'. For *idleness*, see note to 1.2.137.

81 blood. No more.] *Rowe subst.;* blood no more? *F*   83 my sword] *F2;* Sword *F*

CLEOPATRA   'Tis sweating labour   95
To bear such idleness so near the heart
As Cleopatra this. But, sir, forgive me,
Since my becomings kill me when they do not
Eye well to you. Your honour calls you hence;
Therefore be deaf to my unpitied folly,   100
And all the gods go with you! Upon your sword
Sit laurel victory, and smooth success
Be strewed before your feet!

ANTONY   Let us go. Come.
Our separation so abides and flies
That thou, residing here, goes yet with me,   105
And I, hence fleeting, here remain with thee.
Away!   *Exeunt.*

[1.4]   *Enter* OCTAVIUS [CAESAR] *reading a letter,* LEPIDUS,
and their train.

CAESAR
You may see, Lepidus, and henceforth know,

95–6 **labour ... bear** She compares her feelings to those of a woman in childbirth. The so-called *idleness* is extremely painful to her.

98 **becomings** graces. Compare *Son* 150, 'Whence hast thou this becoming of things ill?'

99 **Eye well** look good in your eyes

102 **laurel victory** The image is of a victorious general who wears a crown of laurels in his triumphal procession, an idea developed in the next line with the reference to the rushes or flowers strewn in the victor's path.

104–6 **Our ... thee** The idea that the lovers, separated physically, remain united spiritually also occurs in Donne, 'Valediction Forbidding Mourning', 21–4.

1.4 Location: Rome. The disapproval of

Antony's conduct which Shakespeare found in Plutarch and is briefly expressed by Philo and Demetrius in 1.1 is now given full expression by Octavius, who, like them, laments Antony's decline from his former exemplary stature (57–72). The incompatibility between the two men is fully apparent and prepares us for the total split which occurs in Act 3. Caesar's puritanical view of Antony's indulgences contrasts with the playfully bawdy talk of the Egyptians at the opening of 1.2. Lepidus, in his more lenient attitude towards Antony, reveals himself as less decisive than Caesar, by whom he is dominated throughout the scene, and Caesar's dominance prepares us for his dismissal of Lepidus from the triumvirate (3.5.6–11).

105 goes] *F;* goest *F2*

1.4] *Capell*

It is not Caesar's natural vice to hate
Our great competitor. From Alexandria
This is the news: he fishes, drinks, and wastes
The lamps of night in revel; is not more manlike   5
Than Cleopatra, nor the Queen of Ptolemy
More womanly than he; hardly gave audience, or
Vouchsafed to think he had partners. You shall find
    there
A man who is the abstract of all faults
That all men follow.

LEPIDUS   I must not think there are   10
Evils enough to darken all his goodness.
His faults, in him, seem as the spots of heaven,
More fiery by night's blackness; hereditary
Rather than purchased; what he cannot change
Than what he chooses.   15

CAESAR
You are too indulgent. Let's grant it is not
Amiss to tumble on the bed of Ptolemy,
To give a kingdom for a mirth, to sit
And keep the turn of tippling with a slave,

---

3 **competitor** associate, as in 2.7.71
5 **lamps of night** This could be a
  metaphor for the stars, but *wastes*
  implies that Caesar is thinking literally of oil lamps.
6 **Ptolemy** Ptolemy XIV (*c*.59–44 BC),
  younger brother of Cleopatra, to
  whom, following Egyptian custom,
  he was married. His older brother,
  Ptolemy XIII, had also been married
  to her. Julius Caesar made him joint
  ruler of Egypt with Cleopatra in 47 BC.
  By the time the play opens (40 BC)
  he was already dead, murdered on her
  orders; hence the reference to 'Egypt's
  widow' at 2.1.38 (*OCD*).
7 **gave audience** i.e. received my messengers
8 * **Vouchsafed** Bevington compares

F's 'vouchsafe' with 'dumbe' in 1.5.52
as 'a similar mistaking of *d* for *e* by
Compositor B'.
there i.e. in the letter
9 **abstract** 'epitome, summary' (Schmidt)
12 **spots of heaven** i.e. the stars
14 **purchased** acquired. The distinction
  made here is a legal one between
  property acquired by inheritance
  (*hereditary*) and by other means.
  Compare *2H4* 4.5.199–200, 'what in
  me was purchas'd, / Falls upon thee
  in a more fairer sort.'
18 **mirth** joke (*OED sb.* 3)
19 **keep ... tippling** 'take turns in
  drinking toasts' (Wilson), but *tippling*
  also has connotations of 'habitual
  indulgence in liquor' (*OED sb.*[1] 2).
  Plutarch often describes Antony's

---

3 Our] *Johnson (Heath)*; One *F*   8 Vouchsafed] *Johnson;* vouchsafe *F*   9 abstract] *F2*; abstracts
F

To reel the streets at noon, and stand the buffet   20
With knaves that smells of sweat. Say this becomes
    him –
As his composure must be rare indeed
Whom these things cannot blemish – yet must
    Antony
No way excuse his foils, when we do bear
So great weight in his lightness. If he filled   25
His vacancy with his voluptuousness,
Full surfeits and the dryness of his bones
Call on him for't. But to confound such time
That drums him from his sport, and speaks as loud
As his own state and ours, 'tis to be chid   30
As we rate boys who, being mature in knowledge,
Pawn their experience to their present pleasure
And so rebel to judgement.

riotous behaviour, his tendency, for example, to 'drinke like a good fellow with every body, to sit with the souldiers when they dine, and to eate and drinke with them souldierlike' (North, 257), but Shakespeare is not here following any specific passage.

20 **reel** stagger, as though intoxicated, as in *Cym* 5.4.161, 'reeling with too much drink'
  stand the buffet 'endure the punches'

21 **smells** one of a great many instances in Shakespeare of 'the northern early English third person plural in -*s*' (Abbott, 333)

22 **As** though (*OED adv.* B.3b)
  composure character; literally the composition of the elements out of which a character is made. Compare *TC* 2.3.240, 'Thank the heavens, lord, thou art of sweet composure.' The more modern sense of 'poise, dignity' is also present.

24 **foils** blemishes; 'disgrace, stigma' (*OED* Foil *sb.*² 2b)

24–5 **we ... lightness** 'his trifling levity throws such a heavy burden on us'

26 **vacancy** leisure; spare time

27–8 **Full ... for't** 'let stomach disorders and syphilis call him to account' (Jones). A surfeit is 'a derangement of the system arising from intemperance' (*OED sb.* 5). One of the effects of syphilis was thought to be the drying up of the bones. Thomas Middleton, *Black Book* (1604), refers to 'monsieur Drybone, the Frenchman' (Middleton, 23).

28 **confound** waste. Compare 1.1.46.

29 **drums** 'summons as by a drum' (*OED* Drum *v.* 6)

30 **his ... ours** i.e. his and our positions as triumvirs
  'tis to be chid 'it deserves scolding'

31 **rate** 'chide, scold, reprove vehemently' (*OED v.*² 1)

32 **Pawn ... pleasure** 'abandon their judgement for the sake of immediate pleasure'

33 **to** against

21 smells] *F;* smell *F2*   30 chid] *Capell;* chid: *F*

Enter a Messenger.

LEPIDUS   Here's more news.

MESSENGER
Thy biddings have been done, and every hour,
Most noble Caesar, shalt thou have report   35
How 'tis abroad. Pompey is strong at sea,
And it appears he is beloved of those
That only have feared Caesar. To the ports
The discontents repair, and men's reports
Give him much wronged.

CAESAR   I should have known no less.   40
It hath been taught us from the primal state
That he which is was wished until he were,
And the ebbed man, ne'er loved till ne'er worth love,
Comes deared by being lacked. This common body,
Like to a vagabond flag upon the stream,   45
Goes to and back, lackeying the varying tide,
To rot itself with motion.

---

40 **Give him** say he [Pompey] is (*OED* Give *v.* 25)

41 **from ... state** 'since government began' (Wilson)

42 **That ... were** 'the man now in power had supporters until he gained power'. For a similar idea, see 1.2.130–1 and note.

43 **ebbed** 'on the way out'. This allusion to the movements of the tide develops into the *stream* and *varying tide* of 45–6.

44 * **Comes deared** 'becomes loved'. Theobald defends his emendation of F's *fear'd* by comparing the passage with *Cor* 4.1.15, 'I shall be lov'd when I am lack'd', and the idea is also consistent with the distinction between *beloved* and *feared* in 37–8.
common body commoners. In *Julius Caesar* and *Coriolanus* the notorious fickleness of the Roman mob is actu-

ally shown. In this play it is merely described.

45 **vagabond flag** 'drifting reed'. A *vagabond* is, literally, a wanderer. Some editors gloss *flag* as the iris but it could refer to any reed or rush (*OED sb.*[1] 1).

46 * **lackeying** Theobald glosses his emendation of F's 'lacking' as 'floating backwards and forward with the variation of the tide, like a page or lacquey, at his master's heels'.

47 SD * **Enter ... Messenger** There is no stage direction in F but the arrival of a second messenger is consistent with the previous messenger's assurance (34–6) that Caesar will receive reports 'every hour'. Caesar's prompt and efficient treatment of his messengers contrasts strongly with Antony's dismissal of those from Rome in 1.1.

44 deared] *Theobald (Warburton);* fear'd *F*   46 lackeying] *Theobald (Warburton);* lacking *F;* lashing *Pope*

[*Enter another* Messenger.]

2 MESSENGER
Caesar, I bring thee word
Menecrates and Menas, famous pirates,
Makes the sea serve them, which they ear and
    wound   50
With keels of every kind. Many hot inroads
They make in Italy – the borders maritime
Lack blood to think on't – and flush youth revolt.
No vessel can peep forth but 'tis as soon
Taken as seen; for Pompey's name strikes more   55
Than could his war resisted.

CAESAR   Antony,
Leave thy lascivious wassails! When thou once

49–55 **Menecrates ... seen** 'Sextus
Pompeius at that time kept in Sicilia,
and so made many an inrode into
Italie with a great number of pynn-
asies and other pirates shippes, of
the which were Captaines two notable
pirats, Menas and Menecrates, who
so scoored all the sea thereabouts, that
none durst peepe out with a sayle'
(North, 278–9).
49 **famous** 'notorious' (*OED a.* 3a).
Compare *TS* 1.2.252, 'famous for a
scolding tongue'.
50 **Makes** make. See 21 and note.
ear plough. Compare 1.2.117.
51 **hot inroads** violent incursions or
raids
52–3 **the ... on't** 'the coastal regions
turn pale at the thought of it'
53 **flush** 'full of life or spirit, lively, lusty,
vigorous. Hence self-confident, self-
conceited' (*OED a.*[1] 2). Appian (77)
records that Pompey's power and
reputation were increased by 'a
repayre of yong men, desirous of
gayne and service, not caring under

whom they went, because they were
all Romanes'.
55–6 **strikes ... resisted** 'creates more
trouble than if he attacked us and we
had to resist him'
57 * **wassails** Though F's reading
('Vassailes') has been defended as signifying 'slaves, commoners', most
editors have adopted Pope's emendation *wassails* ('riotous festivity',
OED Wassail *sb.* 4), which is supported by the contrast Caesar goes
on to make with Antony's former
abstemiousness.
57–72 **When ... not** 'Hircius and Pansa,
then Consuls ... together with
Caesar, who also had an armye, went
against Antonius that beseeged the
citie of Modena, and there overthrew
him in battell: but both the Consuls
were slaine there.... It was a wonderfull example to the souldiers, to
see Antonius that was brought up in
all finenes and superfluitie, so easily
to drinke puddle water, and to eate
wild frutes and rootes: and moreover

---

47 SD] *Capell*   49 Menecrates] *North, F4; Menacrates F*   50 Makes] *F; Make F4*   57 wassails]
Pope; Vassailes F

117

Was beaten from Modena, where thou slew'st
Hirtius and Pansa, consuls, at thy heel
Did famine follow, whom thou fought'st against,   60
Though daintily brought up, with patience more
Than savages could suffer. Thou didst drink
The stale of horses and the gilded puddle
Which beasts would cough at. Thy palate then did
    deign
The roughest berry on the rudest hedge.   65
Yea, like the stag when snow the pasture sheets,
The barks of trees thou browsed. On the Alps,
It is reported, thou didst eat strange flesh
Which some did die to look on. And all this –
It wounds thine honour that I speak it now –   70
Was borne so like a soldier that thy cheek
So much as lanked not.

LEPIDUS
    'Tis pity of him.

CAESAR   Let his shames quickly
Drive him to Rome. 'Tis time we twain
Did show ourselves i'th' field, and to that end   75
Assemble we immediate council. Pompey
Thrives in our idleness.

LEPIDUS   Tomorrow, Caesar,
I shall be furnished to inform you rightly
Both what by sea and land I can be able
To front this present time.

CAESAR   Till which encounter,   80

it is reported, that even as they passed
the Alpes, they did eate the barcks of
trees, and such beasts, as never man
tasted of their flesh before' (North,
267–8).

63 **stale** urine (*OED sb.* 5)
   gilded 'tinged with a golden colour'
   (*OED ppl. a.* 2)
64 **deign** 'condescend to take' (Schmidt);

the opposite of 'disdain'. Compare
TGV 1.1.152, 'Julia would not deign
my lines.'
65 **rudest** wildest, least cultivated
67 **browsed** browsèd
72 **So ... not** 'did not even become thin'
79 **can be able** 'am able to muster'
80 **front** 'face, confront; *esp.* to face in

58 Was] *F;* Wert *F2;* Wast *Steevens*   Modena] *North, Johnson; Medena F*   59 Hirtius] *F4; Hirsius*
F; Hircius / North   Pansa] *North, F2; Pausa F*   67 browsed] *F (*brows'd*);* browsedst *F2*   76
we] *F2;* me *F*

It is my business too. Farewell.

LEPIDUS

Farewell, my lord. What you shall know meantime
Of stirs abroad, I shall beseech you, sir,
To let me be partaker.

CAESAR   Doubt not, sir.

I knew it for my bond.   85

Exeunt [by different doors].

[1.5]   *Enter* CLEOPATRA, CHARMIAN, IRAS *and* MARDIAN.

CLEOPATRA   Charmian!

CHARMIAN   Madam?

CLEOPATRA   [*yawns*] Ha, ha.
Give me to drink mandragora.

CHARMIAN   Why, madam?

CLEOPATRA

That I might sleep out this great gap of time   5
My Antony is away.

defiance or hostility, present a bold
front to' (*OED v.*[1] 3)
83 **stirs** stirrings; events
85 * **knew** Dyce's emendation 'know',
followed by several editors, is unnecessary and removes the brusqueness
from Caesar's remark, the modern
equivalent of which would be 'Don't
tell me my duty, I knew it already.'
bond obligation; duty

1.5 Location: Alexandria. Whereas in
Rome messengers arrive thick and
fast, here Cleopatra, deprived of
Antony, is idle and bored. Her
longing for news of him (19–27) is
fulfilled by, and gives dramatic force
to, the arrival of Alexas. Her need of
him for personal reasons is contrasted
with Caesar's need for him for military reasons (1.4.56–7). Since Cleo-

patra does not reappear until 2.5,
Shakespeare may have created this
scene in order to keep her in our
minds during the Roman scenes that
follow it.

3 SD * *yawns* Wilson added this stage
direction and it is difficult to imagine,
in view of the context, that Cleopatra
expresses anything other than
boredom.

4 **mandragora** Shakespeare may have
learned of the narcotic power of this
plant (also called 'mandrake') from
Apuleius: 'I gave him no poison, but
a doling drinke of Mandragora, which
is of such force, that it will cause any
man to sleepe as though he were dead'
(*Golden Ass*, 10.44). For the possible
influence of Apuleius on the play, see
p. 69.

85 knew] *F;* know *Dyce*[2] SD *by … doors*] *this edn; separately Cam*[2]

1.5] *Capell* 3 SD] *Cam*[1] 5 time] *Rowe subst.;* time: *F*

CHARMIAN
  You think of him too much.
CLEOPATRA
  Oh, 'tis treason!
CHARMIAN   Madam, I trust not so.
CLEOPATRA
  Thou, eunuch Mardian!
MARDIAN   What's your highness' pleasure?
CLEOPATRA
  Not now to hear thee sing. I take no pleasure   10
  In aught an eunuch has. 'Tis well for thee
  That, being unseminared, thy freer thoughts
  May not fly forth of Egypt. Hast thou affections?
MARDIAN
  Yes, gracious madam.
CLEOPATRA
  Indeed?   15
MARDIAN
  Not in deed, madam, for I can do nothing
  But what indeed is honest to be done.
  Yet have I fierce affections, and think
  What Venus did with Mars.
CLEOPATRA   O, Charmian,
  Where think'st thou he is now? Stands he, or sits he?   20
  Or does he walk? Or is he on his horse?
  O happy horse, to bear the weight of Antony!

10 **sing** 'Mardian is the official singer; cf. 2.5.2 SD' (Ridley). 'In *TN* 1.2.55–9, Viola resolves to take on the disguise of a eunuch and singer to Duke Orsino' (Bevington).
12 **unseminared** emasculated; 'deprived of virility' (*OED*, which cites no other example). This is Shakespeare's only use of the word.
  freer less restrained, 'looser'
13 **affections** passions; 'feeling as opposed to reason; lust' (*OED* Affec-

tion *sb*. 3)
17 **honest** chaste. Compare *AYL* 3.3.28.
19 **What ... Mars** Mars and Venus had an irresistible passion for each other. Venus' husband, Vulcan, placed a net round the bed where the lovers lay and, having caught them in it, exposed them to the ridicule of the gods (Homer, *Odyssey*, 266–328; Ovid, *Metamorphoses*, 4.173–89; *Ars Amatoria*, 2.561–85). See also p. 64.

9 Thou, eunuch] *F;* Thou eunuch, *Pope*

Do bravely, horse, for wot'st thou whom thou mov'st?
The demi-Atlas of this earth, the arm
And burgonet of men! He's speaking now,   25
Or murmuring 'Where's my serpent of old Nile?'
For so he calls me. Now I feed myself
With most delicious poison. Think on me
That am with Phoebus' amorous pinches black
And wrinkled deep in time? Broad-fronted Caesar,   30
When thou wast here above the ground, I was
A morsel for a monarch; and great Pompey
Would stand and make his eyes grow in my brow;
There would he anchor his aspect, and die
With looking on his life.   35

23 **bravely** a difficult word to define in its seventeenth-century sense. It does not primarily mean 'with courage' but 'splendidly', as in *Cym* 2.2.15, 'How bravely thou becom'st thy bed.'
wot'st thou do you know

24 **demi-Atlas** In classical myth Atlas was said to support the world (sometimes the heavens) on his shoulders. Cleopatra so describes Antony because he shares the responsibility for the world with Octavius. 'The Queen, unlike Philo, 1.1.12, ignores Lepidus' (Case). Atlas was for a time relieved of his load by Hercules and it is generally thought that 'Hercules carrying the Globe' was depicted on the sign of the Globe theatre (*Hamlet*, ed. Harold Jenkins (1982), p. 473).

24–5 **arm / And burgonet** 'i.e. the complete soldier, "arm" standing for the offensive and "burgonet" for the defensive' (Wilson). A *burgonet* is 'a helmet with a visor, so fitted to the gorget or neck-piece, that the head could be turned without exposing the neck' (*OED*). It originally came from Burgundy.

28 * **Think on me** 'i.e. why should I suppose he thinks of me?' (Bevington). If the F reading is

retained (i.e. without the question mark) the sentence is an injunction to the absent Antony.

29 **Phoebus** the sun god (whose rays have tanned her skin)
amorous pinches Cleopatra clearly had experience of these; cf. 5.2.294–5.

30–5 **Broad-fronted … life** For Cleopatra's relationships with Julius Caesar and Gnaeus Pompey, see notes to List of Roles, p. 87.

30 **Broad-fronted** In his 'Life of Julius Caesar' (*De Vita Caesarum*, 1.xlv) Suetonius says he had a broad face and he is so depicted in Roman busts and coins. The *front* is the forehead.

32 **great Pompey** ambiguous because it is unclear whether *great* is a descriptive adjective or a title. Cleopatra's supposed affair was not with Pompey the Great but with Gnaeus Pompey, his younger son and brother to Sextus (who appears in the next scene) (North, 273). See also 3.13.121–3.

34 **aspect** gaze (*OED sb.* 1); accented on the second syllable
die 'to languish, pine away with passion; to be consumed with longing desire' (*OED v.*[1] 7)

30 time?] *Rowe;* time. F

Enter ALEXAS *from Antony.*

ALEXAS

Sovereign of Egypt, hail!

CLEOPATRA

How much unlike art thou Mark Antony!
Yet, coming from him, that great medicine hath
With his tinct gilded thee.
How goes it with my brave Mark Antony?   40

ALEXAS

Last thing he did, dear queen,
He kissed – the last of many doubled kisses –
This orient pearl. His speech sticks in my heart.

CLEOPATRA

Mine ear must pluck it thence.

ALEXAS   'Good friend,' quoth he,
'Say the firm Roman to great Egypt sends   45
This treasure of an oyster, at whose foot,
To mend this petty present, I will piece
Her opulent throne with kingdoms. All the East,
Say thou, shall call her mistress.' So he nodded
And soberly did mount an arm-gaunt steed   50

---

38 **great medicine** a technical term from alchemy for the elixir which, it was thought, could turn base metals into gold. Compare Jonson, *Alchemist* 2.1.27, 'When you see the effects of the great medicine', and *Tem* 5.1.280, 'This grand liquor that hath gilded 'em'. *Tinct*, which means 'colouring, dyeing', was also another term for the elixir (*OED* Tinct *sb.* 2).

40 **brave** See note to 23.

43 **orient** lustrous; originally applied to precious stones from the East, which were more brilliant than those found in the West (*OED sb.* and *a.* B.2)

45 **firm** 'constant, steadfast' (*OED a.* A.6)

47 **piece** 'mend, repair ... or complete by adding a piece or pieces; to patch' (*OED v.* 1b)

50 * **arm-gaunt** lean from service in battle (or 'arms'). The commentators have devoted much time to this expression (see textual notes), partly because it occurs nowhere else and may therefore be a misreading, partly because *gaunt* seems inappropriate for a horse which must bear a 'demi-Atlas' (Wilson). A *gaunt* steed, however, need not necessarily be a feeble one. See *OED* Gaunt *adj.* 1, 'In favourable or neutral sense: Slim, slender, not fat.' Hulme (297) persuasively interprets *gaunt* as 'fit, ready

---

35 SD *Antony*] *Collier MS, Ard¹; Caesar F*   42 kissed – the ... kisses –] *Theobald subst.;* kist the ... kisses *F*   50 arm-gaunt] *F;* arm-girt *Hanmer;* war-gaunt *Jackson;* ardent *Kinnear;* armigerent *John Samson,* TLS, *30 April 1920;* arrogant *Singer;* arm-jaunced *Oxf*

Who neighed so high that what I would have spoke
Was beastly dumbed by him.

CLEOPATRA

What, was he sad or merry?

ALEXAS

Like to the time o'th' year between the extremes
Of hot and cold, he was nor sad nor merry.   55

CLEOPATRA

O well-divided disposition! Note him,
Note him, good Charmian, 'tis the man; but note
    him!
He was not sad, for he would shine on those
That make their looks by his; he was not merry,
Which seemed to tell them his remembrance lay   60
In Egypt with his joy; but between both.
O heavenly mingle! Be'st thou sad or merry,
The violence of either thee becomes,
So does it no man else. Met'st thou my posts?

ALEXAS

Ay, madam, twenty several messengers.   65
Why do you send so thick?

CLEOPATRA   Who's born that day
When I forget to send to Antony
Shall die a beggar. Ink and paper, Charmian!
Welcome, my good Alexas! Did I, Charmian,
Ever love Caesar so?

for', and 'arm-gaunt' as 'ready for
armed conflict'. For full discussions
of the various emendations, see Ard²,
235–6; Spevack, 64–8.

52 **beastly dumbed** either 'rendered
inaudible by the beast's neigh' or
'reduced to silence like a dumb beast'
(*OED* Dumb *v.* 2). Compare *Per* 5
Chorus 5: 'Deep clerks she dumbs.'
* **dumbed** F's 'dumbe' is 'an *e:d*
misprint' (Wilson).

53 * **What ... merry** F's punctuation –
or, rather, lack of it – leaves this line

open to one of two interpretations, of
which Rowe adopts one and Wilson
the other (see collation). Either one is
acceptable.

57 **'tis the man** 'that's just like him'

63 **thee becomes** 'is becoming to you'.
Jones points out that this tribute to
Antony is similar to Antony's account
of Cleopatra in 1.1.49–52 and Enobarbus' description of her in 2.2.248–
50.

66 **thick** 'in crowds or throngs; numer-
ously' (*OED adv.* 2)

52 dumbed] *Theobald;* dumbe *F*   53 What, was he sad] *Rowe subst.;* What was he sad, *F;* What
was he, sad *Cam¹*   64 man] *F2;* mans *F*

123

CHARMIAN   O that brave Caesar!   70

CLEOPATRA

Be choked with such another emphasis!
Say, 'the brave Antony'.

CHARMIAN   The valiant Caesar!

CLEOPATRA

By Isis, I will give thee bloody teeth
If thou with Caesar paragon again
My man of men!

CHARMIAN   By your most gracious pardon,   75

I sing but after you.

CLEOPATRA   My salad days,

When I was green in judgement, cold in blood,
To say as I said then. But come, away,
Get me ink and paper!
He shall have every day a several greeting   80
Or I'll unpeople Egypt!   *Exeunt.*

[**2.1**]   *Enter* POMPEY, MENECRATES *and* MENAS *in warlike manner.*

POMPEY

If the great gods be just, they shall assist

---

70 **brave** splendid. Compare 23 and note.

74 **paragon** 'place side by side; parallel, compare' (*OED v.* 1)

76–7 **salad ... judgement** 'Caesar and Pompey knew her when she was but a young thing, and knew not then what the world ment: but nowe she went to Antonius at the age when a womans beawtie is at the prime, and she also of best judgement' (North, 273). Wilson suggests that 'salad days' means 'before I took to strong meat', but the image then leads to *green* and *cold*, which are characteristic of both salads and the young Cleopatra. *Green*, then as now, was used figuratively to mean 'immature'.

80–1 **He ... Egypt** Her extravagant impulses match those of Antony as reported in 44–9. *Several* means 'separate, different'.

2.1 Location: Sicily. Having aroused our curiosity about Pompey and his associates in 1.3 and 1.4, Shakespeare now satisfies it by introducing them. He creates dramatic tension by making them, unlike ourselves, initially unaware that Antony is on his way to Rome and then bringing on the Messenger to announce that he is expected there imminently. The scene prepares us well in advance for the conference between Pompey, Menas and the triumvirs in 2.6.

2.1] *Rowe*

The deeds of justest men.

MENECRATES   Know, worthy Pompey,
That what they do delay they not deny.

POMPEY
Whiles we are suitors to their throne, decays
The thing we sue for.

MENECRATES   We, ignorant of ourselves,   5
Beg often our own harms, which the wise powers
Deny us for our good; so find we profit
By losing of our prayers.

POMPEY   I shall do well.
The people love me, and the sea is mine;
My powers are crescent, and my auguring hope   10
Says it will come to th' full. Mark Antony
In Egypt sits at dinner, and will make
No wars without doors; Caesar gets money where
He loses hearts; Lepidus flatters both,
Of both is flattered; but he neither loves,   15
Nor either cares for him.

MENAS   Caesar and Lepidus
Are in the field. A mighty strength they carry.

POMPEY
Where have you this? 'Tis false.

MENAS   From Silvius, sir.

POMPEY
He dreams. I know they are in Rome together,
Looking for Antony. But all the charms of love,   20

3 **what ... deny** proverbial: 'Delays are not denials' (Dent, D198.1)
4–5 **Whiles ... for** 'While we pray to the gods, the thing we pray for wastes away.'
5–8 **We ... prayers** Compare Romans 8:26, 'Likewise the spirit also helpeth our infirmities. For we knowe not what to desyre as we ought.'
10 **crescent** growing (Latin *crescere*). Compare *Ham* 1.3.11–12, 'For nature crescent does not grow alone / In thews and bulk.' The metaphor of the

crescent or waxing moon is developed in the next line.
auguring 'divining, presaging, prophetic' (*OED*)
13 **without doors** 'out of doors (the only wars Antony will make are the wars of love)' (Jones)
15 **neither loves** loves neither
16, 18, 39 SP *MENAS See LN, pp. 303–4.
17 **in the field** 'engaged in military operations' (*OED* Field *sb*. 7)
20 **Looking for** hoping, on the lookout, for (*OED* Look *v*. 15)

16, 18, 39 SPs MENAS] *Malone (Capell); Mene. F*

125

Salt Cleopatra, soften thy waned lip!
Let witchcraft join with beauty, lust with both;
Tie up the libertine in a field of feasts;
Keep his brain fuming. Epicurean cooks
Sharpen with cloyless sauce his appetite   25
That sleep and feeding may prorogue his honour
Even till a Lethe'd dullness –

Enter VARRIUS.

How now, Varrius?

VARRIUS

This is most certain that I shall deliver:
Mark Antony is every hour in Rome
Expected. Since he went from Egypt 'tis   30
A space for farther travel.

POMPEY

I could have given less matter
A better ear. Menas, I did not think
This amorous surfeiter would have donned his helm
For such a petty war. His soldiership   35

---

21 **Salt** lecherous ('of bitches: in heat'
*OED a.*²). Compare *Tim* 4.3.86–8,
'Make use of thy salt hours, season
the slaves / For tubs and baths.'
* **waned** 'faded, declined, like the
waning moon'. Steevens, emending
F's 'wand' to 'wan'd', comments that
'wand' could either be 'a contraction
of *wanned* or "made wan" or of *waned*,
i.e. *decreased*, like the moon, in its
beauty'. Wilson conjectures that
Shakespeare wrote 'wane', an alternative spelling of 'wan' which, by
a minim error, became F's 'wand'.
'Wanned', 'wan' and 'waned' are all
possible but Cleopatra is elsewhere
described as dark rather than wan
and, since there are references to her
ageing (1.5.30; 2.2.245), *waned* seems
the most likely, especially in view of

the references to the crescent moon
in 10–11. While Pompey's powers are
waxing, hers are waning.
24 **fuming** 'clouded with the fumes of
alcohol'
Epicurean 'able to make refined and
delicious food'
25 **cloyless** 'that never cloys (or satiates)'
26 **prorogue his honour** 'postpone the
time when he will act on his sense of
honour'. *Prorogue* means 'put off for
a time, defer' (*OED v.* 2).
27 **Lethe'd** utterly forgetful. Those who
drank of the river Lethe in Hades
totally forgot their past. The word
('Lethied' in F) is pronounced with
two syllables.
30–1 **'tis ... for** 'he has had time for'
(*OED* Space *sb.*¹ 1)

21 waned] *Steevens³*; wand *F*; wan *Pope*   22 join] *F* (ioyne); joined *Cam²* (*Ard²*)

Is twice the other twain. But let us rear
The higher our opinion, that our stirring
Can from the lap of Egypt's widow pluck
The ne'er-lust-wearied Antony.

MENAS　　　　　　　　　　　　　I cannot hope
Caesar and Antony shall well greet together.　　　　40
His wife that's dead did trespasses to Caesar;
His brother warred upon him, although I think
Not moved by Antony.

POMPEY　　　　　　　　　　I know not, Menas,
How lesser enmities may give way to greater.
Were't not that we stand up against them all,　　　　45
'Twere pregnant they should square between
　themselves,
For they have entertained cause enough
To draw their swords. But how the fear of us
May cement their divisions, and bind up
The petty difference, we yet not know.　　　　　　50
Be't as our gods will have't! It only stands
Our lives upon to use our strongest hands.
Come, Menas.　　　　　　　　　　　　　　*Exeunt.*

36–7 **rear ... opinion** 'raise our opinion
　of ourselves'
38 **Egypt's widow** See note to 1.4.6.
39 * **ne'er-lust-wearied** Theobald's em-
　endation, generally accepted, makes
　Antony appear sexually insatiable. F's
　'neere', however, implies that he is
　'nearly' exhausted by lust. In its
　context the emendation seems right.
　hope 'suppose, think, suspect' (*OED
　v.* 4)
40 * **greet** No emendation is necessary
　but Furness's proposal of 'gree' (=
　agree) is an attractive one. The
　doubling of letters ('greet together'
　for 'gree together') is not uncommon.
　Compare F's 'should'st stowe' for
　'should'st tow' in 3.11.58.
41 **wife** i.e. Fulvia. See 1.2.93–9 and
　notes.

trespasses offences, wrongs (*OED
Trespass sb.* 1)
42 **brother** i.e. Lucius. See 1.2.93–9;
　2.2.47–56.
　* **warred** F's 'wan'd' is an easy mis-
　reading of manuscript 'war'd'.
44 **lesser ... greater** proverbial: 'The
　greater (one) grief (sorrow) drives out
　the less (another)' (Dent, G446)
46 **pregnant** 'clear, obvious' (*OED a.*[1])
　square 'fall out, disagree or quarrel'
　(*OED v.* 8). Cf. *MND* 2.1.28–30,
　'They never meet ... But they do
　square.'
47 **entertained** 'entertainèd'
49 **cement** accented on the first syllable
51–2 **It only ... upon** 'Only it is a
　question of life and death' (*OED
　Stand v.* 78p, 'It is a question of')

39 ne'er-] *Theobald;* neere *F;* ne're *Pope*[2]　40 greet] *F;* gree *Ard*[2] *(Furness)*　42 warred] *F2;* wan'd
F　44 greater.] *Rowe;* greater, *F*　45 all,] *Rowe;* all: *F*

[2.2]   *Enter* ENOBARBUS *and* LEPIDUS.

LEPIDUS

Good Enobarbus, 'tis a worthy deed,
And shall become you well, to entreat your captain
To soft and gentle speech.

ENOBARBUS   I shall entreat him
To answer like himself. If Caesar move him,
Let Antony look over Caesar's head   5
And speak as loud as Mars. By Jupiter,
Were I the wearer of Antonio's beard,
I would not shave't today!

LEPIDUS   'Tis not a time
For private stomaching.

2.2 Location: Rome. The play moves
from crisis to crisis. Having made the
difficult break with Cleopatra, Antony
now has to face Caesar's accusations
and, having patched up their differences, the triumvirs immediately
prepare to deal with Pompey. Antony
appears favourably in this scene,
frankly admitting his faults (97–100)
but also defending himself against
unfounded criticism (50–76). Caesar
is uncompromisingly in control. He
accepts no apologies and, having
raised one complaint (46–61), moves
immediately to others (76–9, 86–95).
Lepidus, in his few brief interjections
(104, 161) tries to look on the bright
side. The marriage proposal is made
not by Octavius but by his 'chiefe
frende' Agrippa and appears to have
been set up in advance. The warmth
of the greetings between Maecenas,
Agrippa and Enobarbus (181–4) contrasts strongly with the coldness of
the encounter between Caesar and
Antony, and Enobarbus' tribute to the
wonder of Cleopatra (201–28) significantly follows the arrangement of
Antony's marriage. The short final

section (243–53) prepares us for
Antony's desertion of Octavia.

4 **like himself** 'as beseems his greatness' (Wilson)
   move him stir him to anger

6 **as loud as Mars** Mars was celebrated
for the power of his voice: when
wounded, 'brazen Ares bellowed loud
as nine thousand warriors or ten thousand cry in battle, when they join in
the strife of the war god' (Homer,
Iliad, 5.859–61).

7 **Antonio's** This version of Antony's
name is also used by Cleopatra
(2.5.26) and is presumably a familiar
form.

7–8 **Were ... today** either 'I would meet
him undressed, without show of
respect' (Johnson) or 'I would dare
him to pluck it' (Wilson). To pluck
or shake an enemy's beard was a
gesture of defiance and contempt. Cf.
KL 3.7.76–7, 'If you did wear a beard
upon your chin, / I'd shake it on this
quarrel.'

9 **stomaching** resentment; 'Feeling or
cherishing indignation or bitterness'
(*OED*)

2.2] *Rowe*   7 Antonio's] F *(Anthonio's)*; Antonius' *Steevens*

ENOBARBUS   Every time
Serves for the matter that is then born in't.   10
LEPIDUS
But small to greater matters must give way.
ENOBARBUS
Not if the small come first.
LEPIDUS   Your speech is passion;
But pray you stir no embers up. Here comes
The noble Antony.

Enter ANTONY *and* VENTIDIUS.

ENOBARBUS   And yonder Caesar.

Enter CAESAR, MAECENAS *and* AGRIPPA.

ANTONY
If we compose well here, to Parthia.   15
Hark, Ventidius.
CAESAR
I do not know, Maecenas. Ask Agrippa.
LEPIDUS
Noble friends,
That which combined us was most great, and let not
A leaner action rend us. What's amiss,   20
May it be gently heard. When we debate
Our trivial difference loud, we do commit
Murder in healing wounds. Then, noble partners,
The rather for I earnestly beseech,
Touch you the sourest points with sweetest terms,   25
Nor curstness grow to th' matter.
ANTONY   'Tis spoken well.
Were we before our armies, and to fight,

9–10 **Every ... in't** a version of the
proverb 'There is a time for all things'
(Dent, T314), ultimately derived
from Ecclesiastes 3:1
15 **compose** 'come to a settlement'
20 **leaner** slighter

23 **healing** trying to heal
26 **Nor ... matter** 'Nor let ill temper
be added to our real problems.' See
OED Grow *v.* 11, 'to come or pass by
degrees into some state or condition'.

I should do thus.   *Flourish.*

CAESAR   Welcome to Rome.

ANTONY   Thank you.   30

CAESAR   Sit.

ANTONY   Sit, sir.

CAESAR   Nay then.   [*Caesar sits, then Antony.*]

ANTONY

I learn you take things ill which are not so,

Or being, concern you not.

CAESAR   I must be laughed at   35

If, or for nothing or a little, I

Should say myself offended, and with you

Chiefly i'th' world; more laughed at that I should

Once name you derogately when to sound your name

It not concerned me.

ANTONY   My being in Egypt, Caesar,   40

What was't to you?

CAESAR

No more than my residing here at Rome

Might be to you in Egypt. Yet if you there

Did practise on my state, your being in Egypt

Might be my question.

ANTONY   How intend you, 'practised'?   45

CAESAR

You may be pleased to catch at mine intent

---

28 **thus** It may be that Antony should here embrace Lepidus, but, more probably, he simply assures Lepidus that his words would be temperate anyway. Bevington suggests that Caesar signals for the flourish, 'thereby giving himself the edge in the politics of the situation'.

29–33 **Welcome ... then** a simple but subtle piece of dialogue. Caesar, as the host, invites Antony to sit, but Antony, refusing to accept a subordinate position, compels Caesar to accept *his* invitation. The conference opens with a tiff over the pecking order.

37 **say myself** say I was

39 **derogately** disparagingly; 'derogatorily' (*OED*, which supplies no other instance of this word)

44 **practise on my state** 'plot against my authority'

45 **my question** 'a matter of concern to me'

    intend mean, imply

46 **catch at** 'gather, infer' (Jones); 'to apprehend by the senses or intellect' (*OED* Catch v. 35). Compare 1.2.147.

33 SD] *this edn; They sit / Jones*

By what did here befall me. Your wife and brother
Made wars upon me, and their contestation
Was theme for you; you were the word of war.
ANTONY
You do mistake your business. My brother never   50
Did urge me in his act. I did enquire it,
And have my learning from some true reports
That drew their swords with you. Did he not rather
Discredit my authority with yours,
And make the wars alike against my stomach,   55
Having alike your cause? Of this my letters
Before did satisfy you. If you'll patch a quarrel,
As matter whole you have to make it with,
It must not be with this.
CAESAR   You praise yourself
By laying defects of judgement to me, but   60
You patched up your excuses.
ANTONY   Not so, not so!
I know you could not lack – I am certain on't –
Very necessity of this thought, that I,

47–9 **Your ... war** 'He was informed [by his friends], that his wife Fulvia was the only cause of this warre: who being of a peevish, crooked, and troublesome nature, had purposely raised this uprore in Italie, in hope thereby to withdraw him from Cleopatra' (North, 277).

48–9 * **their ... you** The various emendations proposed for this passage (see textual notes) all create a more or less similar meaning, namely that Antony's wife and brother started an uprising against Caesar for Antony's sake. This interpretation is confirmed by what follows ('you were the word of war'). See also the quotation from North's Plutarch in the previous note. The F text can, however, be interpreted in this way without emendation if 'for you' is taken in the sense

of 'on your behalf' and 'theme' has the sense given in *OED* Theme 1b, 'that which is the cause *of* or *for* specified action'. A paraphrase of the passage would be 'their uprising was an affair undertaken on your behalf'.

51 **urge me** 'use me as a pretext' (*OED* Urge *v.* 1)

52 **reports** reporters, sources

53 **with** against. Plutarch says that Antony heard the news from 'his frends ... that fled out of Italie' (North, 277).

55 **stomach** wishes, inclination

56 **Having ... cause** 'having the same cause as you have against me'

57 **patch** 'make up, put together or frame hastily' (*OED v.* 3)

58 **As ... with** 'though you have ample cause with which to create one'. For *as* meaning 'though', see 1.4.22.

49 Was theme for] *F (*Theame*);* Was theam'd for *Theobald;* Had theme from *Johnson*   58 you ... make] *F;* you ... take *F2;* you've not to make *Rowe*

131

Your partner in the cause 'gainst which he fought,
Could not with graceful eyes attend those wars   65
Which fronted mine own peace. As for my wife,
I would you had her spirit in such another.
The third o'th' world is yours, which with a snaffle
You may pace easy, but not such a wife.
ENOBARBUS   Would we had all such wives, that the men   70
might go to wars with the women!
ANTONY
So much uncurbable, her garboils, Caesar,
Made out of her impatience – which not wanted
Shrewdness of policy too – I grieving grant
Did you too much disquiet. For that, you must   75
But say I could not help it.
CAESAR   I wrote to you
When rioting in Alexandria. You
Did pocket up my letters, and with taunts
Did gibe my missive out of audience.
ANTONY   Sir,
He fell upon me ere admitted, then.   80
Three kings I had newly feasted, and did want
Of what I was i'th' morning. But next day
I told him of myself, which was as much
As to have asked him pardon. Let this fellow

---

65 **graceful** 'favourable, friendly' (*OED a.* 3)
   attend observe, take note of. Compare *TN* 1.4.27–8, 'She will attend it better in thy youth / Than in a nuntio's of more grave aspect.'
66 **fronted** opposed, challenged. Compare 1.4.80.
68 **snaffle** 'a simple form of bridle-bit, having less restraining power than one provided with a curb' (*OED sb.*[1] 1). 'To ride with a snaffle' is 'to rule

easily, to guide with a light hand' (*OED* 1c). To *pace* a horse is to train and hence control it.
72 **garboils** See note to 1.3.62.
79 **missive** messenger. Compare *Mac* 1.5.6–7, 'came missives from the King'.
80 **admitted** formally received
   then as opposed to 'next day' (82)
81–2 **want … morning** 'was not myself as I had been in the morning'
83 **of myself** 'how I had been'

65 graceful] *F;* grateful *Pope*   75 disquiet. For … must] *Theobald subst.;* disquiet, for … must, *F*   76–7 you / When … Alexandria. You] *Steevens*[2] *subst.;* you, when … Alexandria you *F;* you. / When … you *Cam*[1]*;* you / When, … Alexandria, you *Oxf*   80 admitted, then.] *F subst. (*then:*);* admitted: then *Rowe*

132

Be nothing of our strife; if we contend,   85
Out of our question wipe him.

CAESAR   You have broken
The article of your oath, which you shall never
Have tongue to charge me with.

LEPIDUS
Soft, Caesar!

ANTONY
No, Lepidus, let him speak.   90
The honour is sacred which he talks on now,
Supposing that I lacked it. But on, Caesar:
'The article of my oath –'

CAESAR
To lend me arms and aid when I required them,
The which you both denied.

ANTONY   Neglected, rather;   95
And then when poisoned hours had bound me up
From mine own knowledge. As nearly as I may
I'll play the penitent to you, but mine honesty
Shall not make poor my greatness, nor my power
Work without it. Truth is that Fulvia,   100
To have me out of Egypt, made wars here,
For which myself, the ignorant motive, do
So far ask pardon as befits mine honour
To stoop in such a case.

LEPIDUS   'Tis noble spoken.

MAECENAS
If it might please you to enforce no further   105
The griefs between ye; to forget them quite

---

85 **Be nothing of** 'have nothing to do
   with' (Jones)
89 **Soft** 'Go carefully'
94 **required** requested
96–7 **bound ... knowledge** 'so para-
   lysed my senses that I lost all knowledge of myself' (Wilson)

98–100 **mine honesty ... it** 'my honesty
   (in admitting this) shall not detract
   from my authority, nor will that authority be dishonestly or dishonourably
   used' (Bevington)
106 **griefs** grievances (*OED* Grief *sb*. 2b)

93 oath –] *Theobald;* oath. *F;* oath? *(Furness)*

Were to remember that the present need
Speaks to atone you.

LEPIDUS   Worthily spoken, Maecenas.

ENOBARBUS   Or, if you borrow one another's love for
the instant, you may, when you hear no more words   110
of Pompey, return it again. You shall have time to
wrangle in when you have nothing else to do.

ANTONY
Thou art a soldier only. Speak no more.

ENOBARBUS   That truth should be silent, I had almost
forgot.   115

ANTONY
You wrong this presence; therefore speak no more.

ENOBARBUS   Go to, then! Your considerate stone.

CAESAR
I do not much dislike the matter but
The manner of his speech; for't cannot be
We shall remain in friendship, our conditions   120
So differing in their acts. Yet, if I knew
What hoop should hold us staunch, from edge to
    edge
O'th' world I would pursue it.

AGRIPPA   Give me leave, Caesar.

CAESAR
Speak, Agrippa.

107–8 **the … you** 'the present emerg-
    ency requires you to be united'. *Atone*
    means 'be at one with'.
114 **That … silent** proverbial: 'All
    truths must not be told at all times'
    (Dent, T594)
116 **presence** 'noble company'
117 **considerate** not 'showing con-
    sideration' (*OED a.* 4) but 'thought-
    ful' (*OED* 2). Enobarbus means that
    though he will be silent he won't
    stop thinking. Compare the proverbial

expression 'as still as a stone' (Dent,
    S879).
120 **conditions** dispositions, characters.
    Compare *MV* 1.2.129–30, 'the con-
    dition of a saint, and complexion of a
    devil.'
122 **hoop … staunch** The image is of
    a hoop which holds together a barrel
    to prevent it from leaking. A similar
    metaphor occurs in *2H4* 4.4.41–8.
    staunch watertight

---

107 remember that] *Capell;* remember: that *F*   113 soldier only. Speak] *Theobald subst.;* Souldier,
onely speake *F*   122–3 staunch, from … world I] *Rowe subst.;* staunch from … world: I *F*

AGRIPPA
> Thou hast a sister by the mother's side, 125
> Admired Octavia. Great Mark Antony
> Is now a widower.

CAESAR   Say not so, Agrippa.
> If Cleopatra heard you, your reproof
> Were well deserved of rashness.

ANTONY
> I am not married, Caesar. Let me hear 130
> Agrippa further speak.

AGRIPPA
> To hold you in perpetual amity,
> To make you brothers, and to knit your hearts
> With an unslipping knot, take Antony
> Octavia to his wife; whose beauty claims 135
> No worse a husband than the best of men;
> Whose virtue and whose general graces speak
> That which none else can utter. By this marriage
> All little jealousies which now seem great,
> And all great fears which now import their dangers 140
> Would then be nothing. Truths would be tales,
> Where now half-tales be truths. Her love to both
> Would each to other, and all loves to both
> Draw after her. Pardon what I have spoke,
> For 'tis a studied, not a present thought, 145

---

125 **by ... side** i.e. a half-sister. Plutarch calls her 'the eldest sister of Caesar, not by one mother' (North, 278). Historically she was a younger sister and the child of both of Caesar's parents.
127 * **Say not so** F's 'Say not, say' presumably arose from simple repetition of the same word by either the dramatist or the compositor.
128–9 **your ... rashness** 'the reproof of your rashness would be well deserved'
130–1 **I ... speak** '[Antony] denied not that he kept Cleopatra, but so did he not confess that he had her as his wife' (North, 278).
137–8 **speak ... utter** 'show forth qualities which no other woman can express'
139 **jealousies** suspicions (*OED* Jealousy *sb.* 5)
140 **import** 'carry with them, involve' (Case)
141–2 **Truths ... truths** 'Unpleasant truths would be considered mere gossip whereas now rumours are taken for the truth.'
142 **both** i.e. Caesar and Antony
145 **present** sudden, spontaneous

By duty ruminated.

ANTONY   Will Caesar speak?

CAESAR

Not till he hears how Antony is touched
With what is spoke already.

ANTONY

What power is in Agrippa,
If I would say, 'Agrippa, be it so',   150
To make this good?

CAESAR   The power of Caesar, and
His power unto Octavia.

ANTONY   May I never,
To this good purpose that so fairly shows,
Dream of impediment! Let me have thy hand.
Further this act of grace, and from this hour   155
The heart of brothers govern in our loves
And sway our great designs!

CAESAR   There's my hand.

                              [*They clasp hands.*]

A sister I bequeath you, whom no brother
Did ever love so dearly. Let her live
To join our kingdoms and our hearts; and never   160
Fly off our loves again!

LEPIDUS   Happily, amen!

ANTONY

I did not think to draw my sword 'gainst Pompey,

154 **impediment** an echo of the words
spoken by the priest in the preamble
to the Solemnisation of Matrimony
in the *Book of Common Prayer*: 'I
require and charge you ... that if
eyther of you do know any impediment, why you may not be lawfully
ioyned together in Matrimonie, that
ye confesse it' (1578, sig. Rv recto)
154–5 * **Let ... grace** F has no punctuation mark after *hand* and, as it
stands, the statement means 'May our
handshake ratify this act of grace.'
Theobald's semicolon (here a full

stop) makes *Further* an imperative
('help forward; pursue') which Caesar
in fact does when he presents Octavia
to Antony.
154 **thy** 'Note the instant change to the
familiar "thy". Caesar is not so warm-
hearted; he retains the distant "you"
to the end' (Furness).
160–1 **never ... again** 'may our affection for each other never again desert
us'. For *fly off* meaning 'desert', see
KL 2.4.90, 'images of revolt and flying
off'.

154–5 hand. / Further] *Theobald subst.;* hand / Further F   157 SD] *Collier²subst.*

For he hath laid strange courtesies and great
Of late upon me. I must thank him, only
Lest my remembrance suffer ill report;   165
At heel of that, defy him.

LEPIDUS   Time calls upon's.
Of us must Pompey presently be sought
Or else he seeks out us.

ANTONY   Where lies he?

CAESAR   About the Mount Misena.   170

ANTONY   What is his strength by land?

CAESAR

Great and increasing, but by sea
He is an absolute master.

ANTONY   So is the fame.
Would we had spoke together! Haste we for it.
Yet, ere we put ourselves in arms, dispatch we   175
The business we have talked of.

CAESAR   With most gladness,
And do invite you to my sister's view,

---

163 **strange** unusual, extraordinary.
Compare *LLL* 4.3.374, 'We will with
some strange pastime solace them.'
One 'strange courtesy' is presumably
Pompey's reception in Sicily of
Antony's mother. 'Sextus Pompeius
had delt verie frendly with Antonius,
for he had curteously received his
mother, when she fled out of Italie
with Fulvia' (North, 279).

165 **remembrance** (bad) memory; forgetfulness

167 **presently** immediately

170 **Misena** a promontory, town and
harbour in the Bay of Naples, now
known as Punta di Miseno

171–3 * **What … master** Hanmer gave
'What is his strength?' to Antony
and 'By … master' to Caesar. Ridley
adopted the emendation on the
grounds that Antony 'was not likely

to narrow the scope of his questions to
the enemy's land forces', but Antony
already knows (1.2.190–2) about
Pompey's sea-power and there is no
reason to depart from F when it makes
good sense, as it does here.

173 **fame** report (Latin *fama*)

174 **spoke** Shakespeare sometimes uses
'speak' to mean 'join battle', as in
2.6.25, but it is unlikely that at this
point Antony would wish he had
already fought against Pompey. *Spoke*
is more probably used in the sense of
'had a conference', as in *R2* 2.3.29.
Wilson paraphrases this passage as 'If
only *you and I* had taken counsel
together (instead of quarrelling) this
disaster (Pomp.'s mastery of the sea)
would never have happened.'

177 **my sister's view** 'to see my sister'

---

164 him, only] *Collier²;* him only, *F*   170 Misena] *North, Ard¹;* Mesena *F*   171–2 strength by
land? / CAESAR Great] *F;* strength? / *Caes.* By land great *Hanmer*

Whither straight I'll lead you.

ANTONY

Let us, Lepidus, not lack your company.

LEPIDUS

Noble Antony, not sickness should detain me.   180

Flourish. Exeunt all except Enobarbus, Agrippa, Maecenas.

MAECENAS Welcome from Egypt, sir.

ENOBARBUS Half the heart of Caesar, worthy Maecenas! My honourable friend, Agrippa!

AGRIPPA Good Enobarbus!

MAECENAS We have cause to be glad that matters are   185
so well digested. You stayed well by't in Egypt.

ENOBARBUS Ay, sir, we did sleep day out of countenance
and made the night light with drinking.

MAECENAS Eight wild boars roasted whole at a breakfast, and but twelve persons there. Is this true?   190

ENOBARBUS This was but as a fly by an eagle. We had
much more monstrous matter of feast, which worthily
deserved noting.

MAECENAS She's a most triumphant lady, if report be
square to her.   195

182–3 **Half ... Agrippa** Plutarch calls
Maecenas and Agrippa Caesar's 'two
chiefe frendes' (North, 282).

186 **stayed well by't** 'stood up well to
things'. Apparently a military
expression: 'stood your ground'
(Schmidt).

187 **sleep ... countenance** To put
someone out of countenance was to
disconcert him. They 'put the day
out of countenance by sleeping
throughout it (so turning it into
night)' (Jones).

188 **light** 'light in a twofold sense, i.e.
bright and either of light behaviour
or light headed' (Case)

189–90 **Eight ... there** Plutarch says
that his grandfather was acquainted

with a physician who knew one of
Antony's cooks. 'When he was in the
kitchin, and saw a world of diversities
of meates, and amongst others, eight
wilde boares rosted whole: he began
to wonder at it, and sayd, Sure you
have a great number of ghests to
supper. The cooke fell a laughing,
and answered him, No (quoth he) not
many ghestes, nor above twelve in all'
(North, 276). By the time the gossip
had reached Rome, the 'supper' had
become a 'breakfast'.

191 **fly ... eagle** Compare the proverb
'The eagle does not catch flies' (Dent,
E1).

195 **square** fair, honest (*OED a.* 8)

186 digested] *F2;* disgested *F*

ENOBARBUS   When she first met Mark Antony, she
   pursed up his heart upon the river of Cydnus.
AGRIPPA   There she appeared indeed! Or my reporter
   devised well for her.
ENOBARBUS   I will tell you.   200
   The barge she sat in, like a burnished throne,
   Burned on the water; the poop was beaten gold;
   Purple the sails, and so perfumed that
   The winds were love-sick with them; the oars were
      silver,
   Which to the tune of flutes kept stroke, and made   205
   The water which they beat to follow faster,
   As amorous of their strokes. For her own person,

---

197 **Cydnus** not in Alexandria as is sometimes supposed, but in Cilicia in the south-east of what is now Turkey
199 **devised** invented (*OED* Devise *v.* 7b)
201–28 **The ... nature** In this passage Shakespeare follows Plutarch in closer detail than anywhere else in the play. 'When she was sent unto by divers letters, both from Antonius him selfe, and also from his frendes, she made so light of it, and mocked Antonius so much, that she disdained to set forward otherwise, but to take her barge in the river of Cydnus, the poope whereof was of gold, the sailes of purple, and the owers of silver, which kept stroke in rowing after the sounde of the musicke of flutes, howboyes, citherns, violls, and such other instruments as they played upon in the barge. And now for the person of her selfe: she was layed under a pavillion of cloth of gold of tissue, apparelled and attired like the goddesse Venus, commonly drawen in picture: and hard by her, on either hand of her, pretie faire boyes apparelled as painters doe set forth god

Cupide, with litle fannes in their handes, with the which they fanned wind upon her. Her Ladies and gentlewomen also, the fairest of them were apparelled like the nymphes Nereides (which are the mermaides of the waters) and like the Graces, some stearing the helme, others tending the tackle and ropes of the barge, out of which there came a wonderfull passing sweete savor of perfumes, that perfumed the wharfes side, pestered with innumerable multitudes of people.... So that in thend, there ranne such multitudes of people one after an other to see her, that Antonius was left post alone in the market place, in his Imperiall seate to geve audience' (North, 274). Closely though he follows this passage, Shakespeare also modifies and develops it. By comparing the two extracts we have an opportunity to observe his imagination working on his material.
203 **perfumèd** perfumèd. The accent is on the second syllable.
207 **strokes** both 'the beat of the oars' and 'caresses'

---

197 Cydnus] *North, F2;* Sidnis *F*   202 Burned] *Malone;* Burnt *F*   204 love-sick ... them; the] *Capell subst.;* Loue-sicke. / With them the *F*

139

It beggared all description: she did lie
In her pavilion, cloth-of-gold of tissue,
O'erpicturing that Venus where we see   210
The fancy outwork nature. On each side her
Stood pretty dimpled boys, like smiling cupids,
With divers-coloured fans, whose wind did seem
To glow the delicate cheeks which they did cool,
And what they undid did.

AGRIPPA   O, rare for Antony!   215

ENOBARBUS

Her gentlewomen, like the Nereides,
So many mermaids, tended her i'th' eyes,
And made their bends adornings. At the helm
A seeming mermaid steers. The silken tackle
Swell with the touches of those flower-soft hands   220
That yarely frame the office. From the barge
A strange invisible perfume hits the sense

---

209 **cloth-of-gold ... tissue** *Cloth-of-gold* and *tissue* are more or less the same thing, 'a rich kind of cloth often interwoven with gold or silver' (*OED* Tissue *sb*. 1a).

210–11 **O'erpicturing ... nature** 'more beautiful than a picture of Venus in which the artist's imagination surpasses the goddess herself'. Plutarch says, simply, that Cleopatra was 'apparelled and attired like the goddesse Venus, commonly drawen in picture'. There is no reason to suppose, as did Theobald, that Shakespeare had any specific painting in mind.

214 * **glow** make glow. Compare 'bellows and the fan' (1.1.9) and note. F's 'gloue' is a simple misreading of 'glow' or 'glowe'.

216 **Nereides** sea-nymphs; daughters of the sea-god Nereus. They were imagined as young girls who inhabited the water and were well disposed to mankind. The word is pronounced with four syllables with the emphasis

on the first one.

217 **i'th' eyes** in her sight or presence. Compare *Ham* 4.4.6, 'We shall express our duty in his eye.'

218 **made ... adornings** *Bends* has been variously interpreted as 'gestures of obeisance', 'Cleopatra's eyebrows', 'the several companies (bands) of Nereids', 'the thickest and strongest planks on the outward part of the ship's side', etc. The most likely meaning is 'obeisances': 'their bending postures were themselves decorative.' Another possibility is that, in view of the nautical terminology of the rest of the speech, *bends* may be 'knots used to unite one rope to another' (*OED* Bend *sb*.[1] 3).

219 **tackle** rigging and sails

221 **yarely** nimbly, briskly (a nautical expression). Compare 3.7.38.
    frame the office 'carry out their tasks'

222 **invisible perfume** Perfumes are, of course, invisible, but the adjective adds to the impression of the magical.

---

214 glow] *Rowe;* gloue *F*   216 gentlewomen] *F2;* Gentlewoman *F*

Of the adjacent wharfs. The city cast
Her people out upon her, and Antony,
Enthroned i'th' market-place, did sit alone,   225
Whistling to th'air, which, but for vacancy,
Had gone to gaze on Cleopatra, too,
And made a gap in nature.
AGRIPPA   Rare Egyptian!
ENOBARBUS
Upon her landing, Antony sent to her;
Invited her to supper. She replied   230
It should be better he became her guest,
Which she entreated. Our courteous Antony,
Whom ne'er the word of 'No' woman heard speak,
Being barbered ten times o'er, goes to the feast,
And, for his ordinary, pays his heart   235
For what his eyes eat only.
AGRIPPA   Royal wench!
She made great Caesar lay his sword to bed.
He ploughed her, and she cropped.
ENOBARBUS   I saw her once
Hop forty paces through the public street
And, having lost her breath, she spoke and panted,   240
That she did make defect perfection,
And, breathless, pour breath forth.

---

223 **wharfs** banks of the river (*OED* Wharf *sb.*¹ 2c)
226 **but for vacancy** 'except that it would have created a vacuum'. Nature proverbially 'abhors a vacuum' (Dent, N42).
227 **Had** would have
235 **ordinary** supper; a meal regularly provided in taverns for a fixed price (*OED sb.* 14)
238 **cropped** bore fruit. 'Caesar made Cleopatra ... Queene of Aegypt, who being great with childe by him, was shortly brought to bedde of a sonne, whom the Alexandrians named Cae-

sarion' (Plutarch, 'Life of Julius Caesar', North, 75).
242 * **breathless ... forth** The spelling and punctuation in F ('breathlesse powre breath forth') admits of two interpretations: (1) 'though breathless was yet able to pour forth breath', the version favoured by Staunton, and (2) 'though breathless, yet emanated power', the version adopted by Capell and others. The former, consistent as it is with Cleopatra's other paradoxical qualities, is the more likely (and more Shakespearean).

236 eat] F (eate); ate *Cam*² 242 breathless, pour breath] F (breathlesse powre); breathlesse power breath *F2;* breathless, power breathe *Hanmer*

MAECENAS

  Now Antony must leave her utterly.

ENOBARBUS

  Never! He will not.

  Age cannot wither her, nor custom stale   245

  Her infinite variety. Other women cloy

  The appetites they feed, but she makes hungry

  Where most she satisfies; for vilest things

  Become themselves in her, that the holy priests

  Bless her when she is riggish.   250

MAECENAS

  If beauty, wisdom, modesty can settle

  The heart of Antony, Octavia is

  A blessed lottery to him.

AGRIPPA   Let us go.

  Good Enobarbus, make yourself my guest

  Whilst you abide here.

ENOBARBUS   Humbly, sir, I thank you.   255

                                   Exeunt.

[2.3] *Enter* ANTONY, CAESAR; OCTAVIA *between them.*

ANTONY

  The world and my great office will sometimes

---

245 **custom stale** Compare with the proverbial expression 'as stale as custom' (Dent, C930).

246 **infinite variety** There is an echo here of the proverb 'Variety takes away satiety' (Dent, V18).

249 **Become themselves** are becoming

250 **riggish** 'wanton, licentious' (*OED*)

251 **beauty, wisdom, modesty** According to Plutarch, Octavia had 'an excellent grace, wisedom, and honestie, joined unto so rare a beawtie, that when she were with Antonius ... she should be a good meane to keepe good love and amitie

betwext her brother and him' (North, 278).

253 **blessed** blessèd

  lottery prize; 'portion fallen to his share' (Schmidt)

2.3 In all the editions before Capell's (1768) this is a continuation of the previous scene. Location: Rome. Antony's opening line, the first we hear after his marriage, is ominous and the Soothsayer's admonitions (14, 17) increase the likelihood of his returning to Cleopatra. By the end of the scene he has made his decision

244 Never! He] *this edn;* Neuer he *F*

2.3] *Capell*

Divide me from your bosom.
OCTAVIA   All which time
Before the gods my knee shall bow my prayers
To them for you.
ANTONY   Good night, sir. My Octavia,
Read not my blemishes in the world's report.   5
I have not kept my square, but that to come
Shall all be done by th' rule. Good night, dear lady.
OCTAVIA
Good night, sir.
CAESAR
Good night.   *Exeunt [Caesar and Octavia].*

                    Enter Soothsayer.

ANTONY
Now, sirrah! You do wish yourself in Egypt?   10
SOOTHSAYER
Would I had never come from thence, nor you thither!
ANTONY
If you can, your reason?

and thereby created another, and ultimately fatal, crisis. His decline originates from this moment (37–9). The entry of Ventidius (39), a man, unlike Antony, totally committed to his public duty, prepares us for 3.1, where Shakespeare deals summarily with the Parthian campaign.

5 **Read ... report** 'Don't believe popular accounts of my faults.'

6 **kept my square** Like a *rule* (or ruler), a *square* (or set-square) is a tool used in carpentry and the terms are here used metaphorically. *OED* defines 'Square' (*sb.* 2a) as 'a rule or guiding principle' and cites Thomas Wright, *Passions of the Minde*, 1601 (1621), 1.3.13: 'To governe the body ... by the square of prudence, and rule of reason'.

8 * **Good night, sir** F assigns this line

to Antony as the conclusion of his speech. F2, however, is almost certainly correct to give it to Octavia, since Antony has already said good night to Caesar at line 4.

10–22 **Now ... between you** 'With Antonius there was a soothsayer or astronomer of Aegypt .... He, either to please Cleopatra, or else for that he founde it so by his art, told Antonius plainly, that his fortune (which of it selfe was excellent good, and very great) was altogether bleamished, and obscured by Caesars fortune: and therefore he counselled him utterly to leave his company, and to get him as farre from him as he could' (North, 280).

10 **sirrah** a form of address used to inferiors

8 SP OCTAVIA] *F2; not in F* 9 SD *Exeunt ... Octavia] Rowe; Exit F* 11 thither] *F;* Gone thither *Oxf*

143

SOOTHSAYER

I see it in my motion; have it not in my tongue.
But yet hie you to Egypt again.

ANTONY   Say to me,

Whose fortunes shall rise higher, Caesar's or mine?   15

SOOTHSAYER

Caesar's.
Therefore, O Antony, stay not by his side.
Thy daemon – that thy spirit which keeps thee – is
Noble, courageous, high unmatchable,
Where Caesar's is not. But near him, thy angel   20
Becomes afeard, as being o'erpowered; therefore
Make space enough between you.

ANTONY   Speak this no more.

SOOTHSAYER

To none but thee; no more but when to thee.
If thou dost play with him at any game,
Thou art sure to lose; and of that natural luck   25
He beats thee 'gainst the odds. Thy lustre thickens
When he shines by. I say again, thy spirit
Is all afraid to govern thee near him;
But, he away, 'tis noble.

ANTONY   Get thee gone.

---

13 **in my motion** intuitively. See *OED* Motion, *sb.* 9, 'inward prompting'.
14 **hie you** hasten
18 **daemon ... thee** According to Plutarch, the soothsayer told Antony 'Thy Demon ... (that is to say, the good angell and spirit that kepeth thee) is affraied' of Caesar's (North, 280).
19 **unmatchable** 'incapable of being matched or equalled' (*OED* 1)
20 **Where** wherever, in whatever place
21 * **afeard** This emendation of F's 'a feare' is supported by North's 'Thy Demon ... is affraied of his', and by

the later (27–8) 'thy spirit / Is all afraid.' The mistaking of manuscript *d* for *e* is very common.
23 **no ... when** only when
26 **lustre** splendour, glory (*OED sb.*[1] 3, 4b)
   thickens 'grows dim', as in *Mac* 3.2.50, 'light thickens'
27 **by** near you
28 **govern** 'guide, direct, lead' (*OED* 2c)
29 * **away** F's 'alway' is a simple error and Pope's emendation, generally accepted, clearly fits the sense of the passage.

---

18 daemon – that ... thee –] *Jones;* Daemon that ... thee, *F;* Daemon (that's ... thee) *F2*   19 high unmatchable] *F;* high, unmatchable *F3*   21 afeard] *Collier²;* a feare *F*   23 thee; no ... but when] *Theobald subst.;* thee no ... but: when *F*   29 away, 'tis] *Pope;* alway 'tis *F*

144

Say to Ventidius I would speak with him.   30

Exit [Soothsayer].

He shall to Parthia. Be it art or hap,
He hath spoken true. The very dice obey him,
And in our sports my better cunning faints
Under his chance. If we draw lots, he speeds;
His cocks do win the battle still of mine   35
When it is all to naught, and his quails ever
Beat mine, inhooped, at odds. I will to Egypt;
And though I make this marriage for my peace,
I'th' East my pleasure lies.

Enter VENTIDIUS.

                    O come, Ventidius.
You must to Parthia. Your commission's ready.   40
Follow me and receive't.   *Exeunt.*

[2.4]   *Enter* LEPIDUS, MAECENAS *and* AGRIPPA.

LEPIDUS

Trouble yourselves no further. Pray you hasten
Your generals after.

31 **art or hap** skill or chance. *Art* was frequently used at this time to mean specifically magical art. Compare *Tem* 1.2.1.

33–4 **my ... chance** 'my superior skill is overcome by his luck'

34–7 **If we ... odds** 'It is said that as often as they two drew cuts for pastime, who should have any thing, or whether they plaied at dice, Antonius alway lost. Oftentimes when they were disposed to see cockefight, or quailes that were taught to fight one with an other: Caesars cockes or quailes did ever overcome' (North, 280).

34 **speeds** wins, prospers

35 **still** always

36 **When ... naught** 'even when the odds are all to nothing in my favour'

37 **inhooped** In cock fights the birds were enclosed in a circle or hoop to prevent them from escaping.

40 **commission** official appointment (as commander in Parthia)

2.4 Location: Rome. This scene, often omitted in performance, prepares us for the meeting with Pompey in 2.6 and creates the sense of impending battle, leaving the actual outcome uncertain as we return to Cleopatra.

30, 39 SD, 39 Ventidius] *F2; Ventigius F* 30 SD *Soothsayer] Rowe* 39 SD] *as Dyce; after Ventigius 1. 39 F*

2.4] *Capell*

AGRIPPA   Sir, Mark Antony
    Will e'en but kiss Octavia, and we'll follow.

LEPIDUS
    Till I shall see you in your soldiers' dress,
    Which will become you both, farewell.

MAECENAS   We shall,   5
    As I conceive the journey, be at the Mount
    Before you, Lepidus.

LEPIDUS   Your way is shorter;
    My purposes do draw me much about.
    You'll win two days upon me.

MAECENAS *and* AGRIPPA
    Sir, good success!   10

LEPIDUS
    Farewell.   *Exeunt.*

[2.5]   *Enter* CLEOPATRA, CHARMIAN, IRAS *and* ALEXAS.

CLEOPATRA
    Give me some music – music, moody food
    Of us that trade in love.

ALL   The music, ho!

Enter MARDIAN *the Eunuch.*

6 **the Mount** Mount Misena, where
Pompey's ships are riding at anchor
(North, 279) and the conference in
2.6 takes place. It is mentioned at
2.2.170.

8 **My .. about** 'My plans compel me
to go a long way round.'

10 **success** 'fortune, luck' (*OED sb.* 2)

2.5 Location: Alexandria. Unlike the triumvirs, Cleopatra, as in 1.5, has
nothing to do in Antony's absence.
Having followed Plutarch very closely
in 2.2 and 2.3, Shakespeare invented
this episode, taking a hint from Plu-

tarch's account of Cleopatra's anger
at her treasurer Seleucus (which he
dramatised in 5.2) with whom she
'was in such a rage ... that she flew
upon him, and tooke him by the
heare of the head, and boxed him
wellfavoredly' (North, 314). Her fury
at the messenger closely resembles
Antony's at the unfortunate Thidias
in 3.13. The episode is presented
ironically, since, unlike Cleopatra, we
know that Antony has already
resolved to return to Egypt (2.3.37).

1 **moody** melancholy

6 at the] *F2;* at *F*

2.5] *Pope*

CLEOPATRA

Let it alone. Let's to billiards. Come, Charmian.

CHARMIAN

My arm is sore. Best play with Mardian.

CLEOPATRA

As well a woman with an eunuch played   5
As with a woman. Come, you'll play with me, sir?

MARDIAN

As well as I can, madam.

CLEOPATRA

And when good will is showed, though't come
      too short,
The actor may plead pardon. I'll none now.
Give me mine angle; we'll to th' river. There,   10
My music playing far off, I will betray
Tawny-finned fishes. My bended hook shall pierce
Their slimy jaws, and, as I draw them up,
I'll think them every one an Antony,
And say 'Ah, ha! You're caught!'

CHARMIAN   'Twas merry when   15
You wagered on your angling; when your diver

---

3 **Let's to billiards** Objections have
been made that this reference is an
anachronism. Furness thinks that
Shakespeare may have known Chapman's *Blind Beggar of Alexandria*
(1598), a play in which ladies are
summoned to billiards, and have con-
cluded that the game was played by
Alexandrian women.

5–6 **As well ... with a woman**
Compare *PP* 18.47–8, 'Were kisses all
the joys in bed, / One woman would
another wed.'

7 **As ... madam** Mardian picks up
the sexual connotation of *play* in the
previous line and develops it as a joke
at his own expense.

8–9 **when ... pardon** Two proverbial
expressions are here conflated: 'The

good will is all' (Dent, G339) and 'To
take the will for the deed' (Dent,
W393). With *too short* Cleopatra may
be continuing the sexual innuendoes,
and alluding to the eunuch's physical
deficiency.

10 **angle** fishing rod (from the bent hook
with which the fish are caught)

11 **betray** 'entrap'. Compare *JC* 2.1.204:
'unicorns may be betray'd with trees.'

12 * **Tawny-finned** F's 'Tawny fine' is
another misreading of *d* for *e* as at
1.4.8 and 2.3.21.

15–18 **'Twas ... up** 'A number of people
came to the haven, and got into the
fisher boates to see this fishing.
Antonius then threw in his line and
Cleopatra straight commaunded one
of her men to dive under water ...

10–11 river. There, / My ... off,] *F4 subst.;* Riuer there / My ... off. *F*   12 Tawny-finned]
Theobald; Tawny fine *F*

Did hang a salt fish on his hook, which he
With fervency drew up.
CLEOPATRA   That time? O times!
I laughed him out of patience, and that night
I laughed him into patience, and next morn,   20
Ere the ninth hour, I drunk him to his bed,
Then put my tires and mantles on him, whilst
I wore his sword Philippan.

Enter a Messenger.

             Oh, from Italy!
Ram thou thy fruitful tidings in mine ears,
That long time have been barren!
MESSENGER   Madam, madam –   25
CLEOPATRA
Antonio's dead! If thou say so, villain,
Thou kill'st thy mistress; but well and free,
If thou so yield him, there is gold, and here
My bluest veins to kiss, a hand that kings
Have lipped, and trembled, kissing.   30
MESSENGER
First, madam, he is well.
CLEOPATRA   Why, there's more gold.
But sirrah, mark, we use
To say the dead are well. Bring it to that,

and to put some old salte fish upon
his baite .... Antonius thinking he
had taken a fishe in deede, snatched
up his line presently. Then they all
fell a laughing' (North, 277).

17 **salt fish** a fish which has been dried
and pickled in salt
22 **tires** head-dresses (*OED* Tire *sb.*[1] 3)
23 **sword Philippan** the sword used by
Antony at the Battle of Philippi in
which he and Octavius defeated
Brutus and Cassius. There is no evidence that 'Philippan' was the actual

name given to Antony's sword. The
exchange of clothing suggests Hercules' enslavement by Omphale. See
pp. 64–5.
26 **Antonio** Compare 2.2.7 and note.
27 **free** i.e. 'not captive' (44) to Caesar
28 **yield** report (*OED* v. 12b)
32–3 **we ... well** proverbial: 'He is well
since he is in heaven' (Dent, H347).
Shakespeare alludes to this idea quite
often, e.g. in *RJ* 4.5.76; *Mac* 4.3.176–
9. *Use* means 'are accustomed'.
33 **Bring ... that** 'If it comes to that'

23 SD] *as Collier; after* Italie *F*   26 Antonio's] *F (Anthonyo's); Anthony's F2*   28 him, there]
Pope²; him. / There *F*

The gold I give thee will I melt and pour
Down thy ill-uttering throat.

MESSENGER   Good madam, hear me.   35

CLEOPATRA

Well, go to, I will.
But there's no goodness in thy face if Antony
Be free and healthful. So tart a favour
To trumpet such good tidings! If not well,
Thou shouldst come like a Fury crowned with
        snakes,   40
Not like a formal man.

MESSENGER   Will't please you hear me?

CLEOPATRA

I have a mind to strike thee ere thou speak'st.
Yet if thou say Antony lives, is well,
Or friends with Caesar, or not captive to him,
I'll set thee in a shower of gold and hail   45
Rich pearls upon thee.

MESSENGER   Madam, he's well.

CLEOPATRA   Well said!

MESSENGER

And friends with Caesar.

CLEOPATRA   Thou'rt an honest man!

MESSENGER

Caesar and he are greater friends than ever.

---

35 **uttering** used not only in the sense
of 'speaking' but also 'announcing for
sale' (*OED* Utter *v.*[1] 1b). Cleopatra
visualizes the Messenger as a pedlar
offering his wares, as in 'pack of
matter' (54).

38 **So ... favour** 'so sour a look' (*OED*
Favour *sb.* 9). Cf. *MM* 4.2.33–4, 'A
good favour you have, but that you
have a hanging look.'

40 **Fury ... snakes** In Greek mythology
the Furies were spirits of vengeance
whose function was to avenge wrongs

done to kindred. They were represented with serpents springing from
their heads.

41 **formal** normal, sane (*OED a.* and *sb.*
4b, 4c)

45–6 **I'll ... upon thee** Bevington points
out that this is an allusion to the myth
of Danae. She was visited by Zeus in
the form of a shower of gold and
made pregnant by him (Ovid, *Metamorphoses*, 4.611).

47 **honest** worthy, as in *MND* 3.1.184,
'Your name, honest gentleman?'

43 is] *Capell;* 'tis *F*

149

CLEOPATRA
Make thee a fortune from me!

MESSENGER   But yet, madam —

CLEOPATRA
I do not like 'But yet'. It does allay   50
The good precedence. Fie upon 'But yet'!
'But yet' is as a gaoler to bring forth
Some monstrous malefactor. Prithee, friend,
Pour out the pack of matter to mine ear,
The good and bad together. He's friends with
     Caesar,   55
In state of health, thou say'st, and, thou sayst, free.

MESSENGER
Free, madam? No. I made no such report.
He's bound unto Octavia.

CLEOPATRA   For what good turn?

MESSENGER
For the best turn i'th' bed.

CLEOPATRA   I am pale, Charmian.

MESSENGER Madam, he's married to Octavia.   60

CLEOPATRA
The most infectious pestilence upon thee!

Strikes him down.

MESSENGER
Good madam, patience!

CLEOPATRA   What say you?

Strikes him.

                                   Hence,

Horrible villain, or I'll spurn thine eyes

50–1 **allay ... precedence** 'detract from the good news that preceded it' (*OED* Allay *v.*² 2). 'Precedence' is spoken with a long 'e' (as in 'precede') and the emphasis on the second syllable.

54 **Pour ... ear** 'Cleopatra thinks of the messenger with his news as like a pedlar with his pack, and elaborates the image later, in lines 104–6' (Ridley).

58 **He's ... turn** Cleopatra interprets the Messenger's *bound* as meaning 'indebted' (as a consequence of some 'good turn' Octavia has done for Antony) and not as 'united', the sense intended by the Messenger. The latter then twists Cleopatra's *turn* so that it has a sexual meaning, probably *OED* Turn *sb.* 24, ' stroke or spell of work; ... a task, job'.

63 **spurn** kick. Compare *CE* 2.1.83, 'like a football you do spurn me thus.'

Like balls before me! I'll unhair thy head!
                              She hales him up and down.
Thou shalt be whipped with wire and stewed in brine,   65
Smarting in lingering pickle!
MESSENGER   Gracious madam,
I that do bring the news made not the match.
CLEOPATRA
Say 'tis not so, a province I will give thee,
And make thy fortunes proud. The blow thou hadst
Shall make thy peace for moving me to rage,   70
And I will boot thee with what gift beside
Thy modesty can beg.
MESSENGER   He's married, madam.
CLEOPATRA
Rogue, thou hast lived too long!   *Draw a knife.*
MESSENGER   Nay then, I'll run.
What mean you, madam? I have made no fault.   *Exit.*
CHARMIAN
Good madam, keep yourself within yourself.   75
The man is innocent.
CLEOPATRA
Some innocents 'scape not the thunderbolt.
Melt Egypt into Nile, and kindly creatures
Turn all to serpents! Call the slave again!
Though I am mad, I will not bite him. Call!   80
CHARMIAN
He is afeard to come.
CLEOPATRA   I will not hurt him.
                              [*Exit Charmian.*]
These hands do lack nobility that they strike

---

64 SD *hales* drags (*OED* Hale *v.*[1] 1b); a
    variant form of 'haul', 'to draw or
    pull along with force or violence'
    (*OED* Haul *v.* 1)
66 **pickle** 'salt or acid liquor ... in which
    flesh, vegetables, etc. are prepared'
    (*OED sb.*[1] 1)

71 **boot** enrich (*OED v.*[1] 4)
78 **Melt ... Nile** Earlier (1.1.34) Antony
    has said 'Let Rome in Tiber melt.'
    kindly not 'benevolent' but 'natural'
    (*OED a.* 1). Cleopatra wants such
    creatures to turn into serpents and
    thereby become unnatural.

81 SD] *Dyce*

A meaner than myself, since I myself
Have given myself the cause.

Enter the Messenger *again* [*with* CHARMIAN].

                  Come hither, sir.
Though it be honest, it is never good   85
To bring bad news. Give to a gracious message
An host of tongues, but let ill tidings tell
Themselves when they be felt.

MESSENGER   I have done my duty.

CLEOPATRA

Is he married?
I cannot hate thee worser than I do   90
If thou again say 'Yes'.

MESSENGER   He's married, madam.

CLEOPATRA

The gods confound thee! Dost thou hold there still?

MESSENGER

Should I lie, madam?

CLEOPATRA   Oh, I would thou didst,
So half my Egypt were submerged and made
A cistern for scaled snakes! Go, get thee hence!   95
Hadst thou Narcissus in thy face, to me
Thou wouldst appear most ugly. He is married?

MESSENGER

I crave your highness' pardon.

CLEOPATRA   He is married?

MESSENGER

Take no offence that I would not offend you.

---

83 **A ... myself** 'someone socially my inferior'
92 **hold there** 'stick to that'
94 **So** even if
95 **cistern** pond or lake, as in *Oth* 4.2.61–2, 'a cistern for foul toads / To knot and gender in'.
96 **Narcissus** the ideal of male beauty.

In classical mythology he was a young man who fell in love with his own reflection in a fountain (Ovid, *Metamorphoses*, 3.346 ff.).
99 **Take ... you** 'Don't be offended that I am hesitant to offend you (by repeating the bad news)' (Bevington).

84 SD *Enter ... again*] *Cam²; after* Sir *l. 84* F   *with* CHARMIAN] *Dyce subst.*   96 face, to me] *F2;* face to me, *F*

To punish me for what you make me do   100
Seems much unequal. He's married to Octavia.
CLEOPATRA
Oh, that his fault should make a knave of thee
That act not what thou'rt sure of! Get thee hence!
The merchandise which thou hast brought from Rome
Are all too dear for me. Lie they upon thy hand   105
And be undone by 'em.   [*Exit Messenger.*]
CHARMIAN   Good your highness, patience.
CLEOPATRA
In praising Antony, I have dispraised Caesar.
CHARMIAN
Many times, madam.
CLEOPATRA   I am paid for't now.
Lead me from hence;
I faint! O Iras, Charmian! 'Tis no matter.   110
Go to the fellow, good Alexas, bid him
Report the feature of Octavia, her years,
Her inclination; let him not leave out
The colour of her hair. Bring me word quickly.
                                    [*Exit Alexas.*]
Let him for ever go! Let him not, Charmian.   115
Though he be painted one way like a Gorgon,

101 **much unequal** very unfair
103 * **That ... of** a passage subject
to many emendations, none of them
wholly satisfactory. I have adopted
the Oxford emendation of F's 'art',
originally suggested by Case, because
it makes somewhat better sense and,
as the Oxford editors point out, the
misreading of *act* as 'art' was easily
done and occurs in Q1 of *Oth* 3.3.328.
They comment that the Messenger
'does not *act*, or commit, the offence
that he knows of'. For a full discussion of this problem see Wells, *Re-
editing*, 38–9.
105–6 **Lie ... 'em** 'May you be unable

to sell them and may you be ruined
by them' (Jones)
112 **feature** physical characteristics.
Compare *AYL* 3.3.3, 'Doth my simple
feature content you?'
113 **inclination** temperament, personality
116–17 **Though ... Mars** The allusion
is to a 'perspective' picture of a kind
which was popular in Shakespeare's
time. They were painted on a fur-
rowed surface in such a way that if
looked at from the left they showed
one portrait and from the right they
showed another. Viewed straight from
the front they appeared confused.

103 act not] *Oxf (Ard¹); art not F* 106 SD] *Rowe* 114 SD] *Capell* 115 go! Let] *Cam¹;* go,
let *F*

The other way's a Mars. [*to Iras*] Bid you Alexas
Bring me word how tall she is. Pity me, Charmian,
But do not speak to me. Lead me to my chamber.

Exeunt.

[**2.6**] *Flourish. Enter* POMPEY *and* MENAS *at one door with
drum and trumpet; at another* CAESAR, LEPIDUS, ANTONY,
ENOBARBUS, MAECENAS, AGRIPPA, *with Soldiers marching.*

POMPEY
Your hostages I have, so have you mine,
And we shall talk before we fight.

CAESAR   Most meet
That first we come to words, and therefore have we
Our written purposes before us sent,

Robert Plot describes them in his
History of Staffordshire, 1686, p. 391.
There are references to them in *H5*
5.2.320–1 and *R2* 2.2.18–20, 'Like
perspectives, which rightly gazed
upon / Show nothing but confusion;
ey'd awry, / Distinguish form'. Cleopatra says that, seen from one point of
view, Antony appears like the Gorgon
Medusa (whose head was crowned
with snakes and whose gaze turned
men to stone), but seen from the other
he looks like the god of war. In a
sense the entire play is a perspective
in which characters and situations are
seen from different points of view.

2.6 Location: 'By the mount of Misena,
upon a hill that runneth farre into
the sea: Pompey having his shippes
ryding hard by at ancker, and Antonius and Caesar their armies upon the
shoare side, directly over against him'
(North, 279). The crisis created by
Pompey, one of the major reasons for
Antony's decision to return to Rome
(1.3.46–55), now comes to a head as
he and the triumvirs meet in conference, but with Pompey's unex-

pected agreement to the terms offered
him (57–9) the crisis evaporates and
turns into a celebration. Shakespeare
reproduces the unpredictable nature
of history, as when the defeat of
Antony which we have been expecting
in 4.7 turns out to be a victory. Having
disposed of Pompey, however, the
triumvirs are no longer united by a
common cause and the scene concludes with Enobarbus' prediction
(122–4) of the split between Antony
and Octavius which will turn out to
be the real crisis of the play.

0.1 * *and* MENAS In F Pompey enters
alone at one door and Menas comes
in with Caesar's party at the other.
Clearly Menas belongs not with
Caesar but with Pompey, and Rowe
rightly moved him there (see textual
notes). Wilson suggests that Shakespeare added Menas' name after he
had written the dialogue at the end
of the scene (82–136) in which Menas
takes part. Until then he does not
speak.

4 **purposes** proposals, 'propositions'
(*OED* Purpose *sb.* 4)

117 SD *to Iras*] *this edn; to Mardian / Capell*

2.6] *Pope*   0.1 POMPEY *and* MENAS ... AGRIPPA] *Rowe; Pompey ... Agrippa, Menas* F

Which if thou hast considered, let us know   5
If 'twill tie up thy discontented sword
And carry back to Sicily much tall youth
That else must perish here.
POMPEY   To you all three,
The senators alone of this great world,
Chief factors for the gods: I do not know   10
Wherefore my father should revengers want,
Having a son and friends, since Julius Caesar,
Who at Philippi the good Brutus ghosted,
There saw you labouring for him. What was't
That moved pale Cassius to conspire? And what   15
Made the all-honoured, honest Roman, Brutus,
With the armed rest, courtiers of beauteous freedom,
To drench the Capitol, but that they would
Have one man but a man? And that is it

7 **tall** 'brave, bold, valiant' (*OED a.* 3)
9 **senators alone** sole senators. As becomes clear in 15–19, the motive for Pompey's rebellion is that the three triumvirs have taken over the power which should belong to the Senate and have achieved the kind of political dominance for which Julius Caesar was assassinated.
10 **factors** agents, representatives (*OED* Factor *sb.* 3)
10–14 **I … him** Pompey attempts to justify his rebellion by drawing a parallel between Octavius and Antony on the one hand and himself on the other. As the former had avenged the death of Julius Caesar by overcoming his assassins Brutus and Cassius at Philippi, so Pompey now wishes to avenge the death of his father who had been overcome by Julius Caesar at Pharsalus.
11 **want** be in need of, lack
13 **Who … ghosted** Before his defeat at the Battle of Philippi, Brutus was

visited by the ghost of Julius Caesar (*JC* 4.3.275–86).
14 **labouring for him** striving on his behalf
15 **pale Cassius** Julius Caesar, according to Plutarch, did not like Cassius' 'pale lookes' ('Life of Julius Caesar', North, 82).
16 **honest** 'having honourable motives or principles; marked by uprightness or probity' (*OED a.* 3). Brutus prided himself on his sense of honour, as does Antony (2.2.91; 3.4.22–3, etc.). It was a distinctively Roman virtue.
17 **armed** (probably) armèd
   courtiers wooers
18 **drench** i.e. with Julius Caesar's blood
19 **but a man** 'only a man' (not a king or a dictator). It was because they believed that Julius Caesar was ambitious for supreme power that Brutus and Cassius formed the conspiracy against him (*JC* 1.2.152–61, 2.1.12–17).

7 Sicily] *North, F2;* Cicelie *F*   16 the] *F2; not in F*   honest Roman] *F2;* honest, Romaine *F*   19 is] *F2;* his *F*

Hath made me rig my navy, at whose burden   20
The angered ocean foams, with which I meant
To scourge th'ingratitude that despiteful Rome
Cast on my noble father.
CAESAR   Take your time.
ANTONY
Thou canst not fear us, Pompey, with thy sails.
We'll speak with thee at sea. At land thou know'st   25
How much we do o'ercount thee.
POMPEY   At land indeed
Thou dost o'ercount me of my father's house;
But since the cuckoo builds not for himself,
Remain in't as thou mayst.
LEPIDUS   Be pleased to tell us –
For this is from the present – how you take   30
The offers we have sent you.
CAESAR   There's the point.
ANTONY
Which do not be entreated to, but weigh
What it is worth embraced.
CAESAR   And what may follow

20 **burden** 'a "load" ... considered as a measure of quantity; ... the carrying capacity of a ship' (*OED sb.* 3). Compare *AWW* 2.3.205, 'a vessel of too great a burden'.

23 **Take your time** 'Don't hurry.' Caesar is telling Pompey to calm down.

24 **fear** frighten. Compare *MM* 2.1.1–2, 'We must not make a scarecrow of the law, / Setting it up to fear the birds of prey.'

25 **speak with** encounter. Compare 2.2.174 and *Cor* 1.4.4, 'They lie in view, but have not spoke as yet.'

27 **Thou ... house** The significance of Pompey's pun (on *o'ercount*) becomes clear if we consult North's Plutarch: 'When Pompeys house was put to

open sale, Antonius bought it: but when they asked him money for it, he made it very straung, and was offended with them' (North, 262).

29 **as thou mayst** 'while you can' (*OED* May *v.*[1] 2). Pompey not only compares Antony to a cuckoo (which lays its eggs in the nests of other birds) but hints, perhaps, that he may not be allowed to live there much longer.

30 **from the present** 'beside the point' **how you take** 'your reaction to'

32 **Which ... to** 'Don't be persuaded to accept them'

32–3 **weigh ... embraced** 'consider what it is worth to you if you accept them'

33–4 **what ... fortune** 'what the consequences may be if you attempt some-

29–30 us – / For ... present – how you take] *Theobald subst.*; vs, / (For ... present how you take) *F*

To try a larger fortune.

POMPEY   You have made me offer
Of Sicily, Sardinia; and I must   35
Rid all the sea of pirates; then to send
Measures of wheat to Rome. This 'greed upon,
To part with unhacked edges, and bear back
Our targes undinted.

CAESAR, ANTONY, LEPIDUS
                    That's our offer.

POMPEY   Know, then,
I came before you here a man prepared   40
To take this offer, but Mark Antony
Put me to some impatience. Though I lose
The praise of it by telling, you must know
When Caesar and your brother were at blows,
Your mother came to Sicily and did find   45
Her welcome friendly.

ANTONY   I have heard it, Pompey,
And am well studied for a liberal thanks
Which I do owe you.

POMPEY   Let me have your hand.

                    [*They shake hands.*]
I did not think, sir, to have met you here.

ANTONY
The beds i'th' East are soft; and thanks to you   50

thing more ambitious'. Caesar is
warning Pompey not to resort to war.
34–9 **You ... undinted** 'After they had
agreed that Sextus Pompeius should
have Sicile and Sardinia, with this
condicion, that he should ridde the
sea of all theeves and pirats, and make
it safe for passengers, and withall that
he should send a certaine [quantity]
of wheate to Rome: one of them did
feast an other, and drew cuts who
should beginne' (North, 279).
38 **part** depart

edges the cutting edges of their
swords and, hence, the swords themselves. Compare *Cor* 5.6.111–12: 'Cut
me in pieces, Volsces, men and lads,
/ Stain all your edges on me.'
39 **targes** shields. Both here and in *Cym*
5.5.5 the word is pronounced as a
monosyllable and with a hard 'g'.
44 **When ... blows** See 1.2.93–9 and
note.
your i.e. Antony's
47 **studied for** prepared to give (*OED*
Studied *ppl. a.* 2b)

39 SP CAESAR ... LEPIDUS] *Capell; Omnes. F*   43 telling, you] *Theobald; telling. You F*   48
SD] *Collier² subst.*

That called me timelier than my purpose hither,
For I have gained by't.

CAESAR   Since I saw you last,
There is a change upon you.

POMPEY   Well, I know not
What counts harsh Fortune casts upon my face,
But in my bosom shall she never come   55
To make my heart her vassal.

LEPIDUS   Well met here!

POMPEY

I hope so, Lepidus. Thus we are agreed.
I crave our composition may be written
And sealed between us.

CAESAR   That's the next to do.

POMPEY

We'll feast each other ere we part, and let's   60
Draw lots who shall begin.

ANTONY   That will I, Pompey.

POMPEY

No, Antony, take the lot.
But, first or last, your fine Egyptian cookery
Shall have the fame. I have heard that Julius Caesar
Grew fat with feasting there.

ANTONY   You have heard much.   65

---

51 **timelier ... purpose** 'sooner than I had intended'

54 **counts** sums, reckonings
casts 'to sum up or reckon accounts' (*OED* Cast *v.* 37c). Pompey compares his face to a board of the kind used in taverns on which Fortune has marked the price (in lines or scars) which he has had to pay for his experience.

55–6 **But ... vassal** 'I shall never allow bad luck to discourage (gain mastery over) me'

58 **composition** agreement; i.e. the peace treaty

62 **take the lot** 'accept the result of the lottery'

64–5 **I ... there** In his 'Life of Julius Caesar' Plutarch says that when Julius Caesar was in Alexandria he spent 'all the night long in feasting and bancketing' (North, 73). Now that they have reached an agreement, Pompey introduces a lighter topic, but, in view of the fact that Antony too has been feasting in Egypt, it is a delicate one and Antony (65) protests. Nevertheless Pompey continues to be tactless (68) and Enobarbus tries firmly to stop him (69).

53 There is] *Rowe;* ther's *F*   58 composition] *F2;* composion *F*

POMPEY

I have fair meanings, sir.

ANTONY   And fair words to them.

POMPEY

Then so much have I heard.

And I have heard Apollodorus carried –

ENOBARBUS

No more of that! He did so.

POMPEY   What, I pray you?

ENOBARBUS

A certain queen to Caesar in a mattress.   70

POMPEY

I know thee now. How far'st thou, soldier?

ENOBARBUS   Well;

And well am like to do, for I perceive

Four feasts are toward.

POMPEY   Let me shake thy hand.

                              [*They shake hands.*]

I never hated thee. I have seen thee fight

When I have envied thy behaviour.

ENOBARBUS   Sir,   75

I never loved you much, but I have praised ye

When you have well deserved ten times as much

As I have said you did.

POMPEY   Enjoy thy plainness;

It nothing ill becomes thee.

66 * **meanings** F's 'meaning' seems
acceptable out of its context but the
plural pronoun *them* in the next line
justifies the emendation to the plural
noun here.

68–70 **Apollodorus ... mattress** 'Caesar
... secretly sent for Cleopatra which
was in the contry to come to him.
She onely taking Apollodorus Sicilian
of all her friendes, took a litle bote
... and came and landed hard by the
foote of the castell. Then having no
other meane to come in to the court,

without being knowen, she laid her
selfe downe upon a mattresse ...
which Apollodorus her frend tied and
bound together like a bundel with a
great leather thong ... and brought
her thus hamperd in this fardell unto
Caesar' (Plutarch, 'Life of Julius
Caesar', North, 74).

73 **toward** (emphasized on the first
syllable) imminent, impending

78 **Enjoy** 'continue to indulge' (*OED*
v. 4)

66 meanings] *Malone (Heath);* meaning *F*   69 of that] *F3;* that *F*   73 SD] *Oxf subst.*

Aboard my galley I invite you all.   80
Will you lead, lords?

CAESAR, ANTONY, LEPIDUS
                                    Show's the way, sir.

POMPEY   Come.
                    Exeunt all but Enobarbus and Menas.

MENAS   [*aside*] Thy father, Pompey, would ne'er have
    made this treaty. [*to Enobarbus*] You and I have known,
    sir.

ENOBARBUS   At sea, I think.   85

MENAS   We have, sir.

ENOBARBUS   You have done well by water.

MENAS   And you by land.

ENOBARBUS   I will praise any man that will praise me,
    though it cannot be denied what I have done by land.   90

MENAS   Nor what I have done by water.

ENOBARBUS   Yes, something you can deny for your
    own safety: you have been a great thief by sea.

MENAS   And you by land.

ENOBARBUS   There I deny my land service. But give   95
    me your hand, Menas! [*They shake hands.*] If our eyes
    had authority, here they might take two thieves
    kissing.

MENAS   All men's faces are true, whatsome'er their
    hands are.   100

ENOBARBUS   But there is never a fair woman has a true
    face.

MENAS   No slander. They steal hearts.

ENOBARBUS   We came hither to fight with you.

---

83 **known** been acquainted; met.
Compare *Cym* 1.4.35, 'We have
known together in Orleans.'

95 **land service** a pun. It could mean
'military as opposed to naval service'
(*OED*).

97 **take** catch, arrest

two thieves i.e. their hands

99–101 **true … true** Menas uses the
word in the sense of 'honest' and
Enobarbus in the sense of 'not altered
by cosmetics'.

102 **No slander** 'You're absolutely
right.'

---

81 SP CAESAR … LEPIDUS] *Capell; All. F*   SD *all but*] *Ard¹; Manent F*   82 SD] *Johnson*
83 SD] *Hanmer*   96 SD] *Oxf*

MENAS   For my part, I am sorry it has turned to a   105
  drinking. Pompey doth this day laugh away his
  fortune.
ENOBARBUS   If he do, sure he cannot weep't back again.
MENAS   You've said, sir. We looked not for Mark Antony
  here. Pray you, is he married to Cleopatra?   110
ENOBARBUS   Caesar's sister is called Octavia.
MENAS   True, sir. She was the wife of Caius Marcellus.
ENOBARBUS   But she is now the wife of Marcus
  Antonius.
MENAS   Pray ye, sir?   115
ENOBARBUS   'Tis true.
MENAS   Then is Caesar and he for ever knit together.
ENOBARBUS   If I were bound to divine of this unity, I
  would not prophesy so.
MENAS   I think the policy of that purpose made more   120
  in the marriage than the love of the parties.
ENOBARBUS   I think so too. But you shall find the band
  that seems to tie their friendship together will be the
  very strangler of their amity. Octavia is of a holy,
  cold and still conversation.   125
MENAS   Who would not have his wife so?
ENOBARBUS   Not he that himself is not so; which is
  Mark Antony. He will to his Egyptian dish again.
  Then shall the sighs of Octavia blow the fire up in
  Caesar, and, as I said before, that which is the strength   130
  of their amity shall prove the immediate author of
  their variance. Antony will use his affection where it

---

109 **You've said** 'Quite right', as in *TN*
  3.1.11, *Oth* 4.2.201
112 **She ... Marcellus** According to
  Plutarch, Octavia was 'a noble Ladie,
  and left the widow of her first
  husband Caius Marcellus' (North,
  278).
115 **Pray ye, sir?** 'I beg your pardon?'
118 **bound to divine** 'forced to predict
  the outcome'
120 **policy ... purpose** 'political
  motives for that proposal'

made mattered
123–4 **be the very** 'actually be the'
125 **still** 'quiet, gentle in disposition;
  meek' (*OED a.* and *sb.*[2] A.4c)
  conversation behaviour. Compare
  Psalms 50:23: 'To him that ordereth
  his conversation ryght wyl I shewe
  the salvation of God.'
132 **affection** used in the sense of 'sexual
  appetite' (*OED sb.* 3). Hence 'use his
  affection' means 'satisfy his appetite'.

is. He married but his occasion here.

MENAS   And thus it may be. Come, sir, will you aboard?
     I have a health for you.   135

ENOBARBUS   I shall take it, sir. We have used our
     throats in Egypt.

MENAS   Come, let's away.

                                                              Exeunt.

[2.7]   *Music plays. Enter two or three* Servants *with a banquet.*

1 SERVANT   Here they'll be man. Some o' their plants
     are ill-rooted already; the least wind i'th' world will
     blow them down.

2 SERVANT   Lepidus is high-coloured.

1 SERVANT   They have made him drink alms-drink.   5

---

133 **occasion**   political   opportunity;
'necessity or need arising from circumstances' (*OED sb.*[1] 5)
136 **used** trained, practised

2.7 Location: on board Pompey's galley.
'[Pompey] cast ankers enowe into the
sea, to make his galley fast, and then
built a bridge of wodde to convey
them to his galley, from the heade of
mount Misena: and there he wel-
comed them, and made them great
cheere' (North, 279). Shakespeare
visualizes the guests leaving the
banquet by boat (130). The knowing
comments of the servants (1–16)
prepare us for the entry of the distinguished guests and provide a
different view of them from the one
we have seen in 2.6. Antony's light-
hearted talk about the Nile and the
crocodile (17–50), apparently a continuation of what he has been saying
off stage, keeps Egypt in our minds
while we are away from it and contrasts strongly with the dangerous
proposal which Menas makes to
Pompey (62–74) while the party conversation goes on in the background.

The audience is made privy to Menas'
plot and hence recognizes that the
conviviality of the scene is spurious.
Everyone reacts characteristically to
the occasion: Pompey appears the
genial host, Menas stays sober,
Antony drinks cheerfully, Caesar is
critical of his own intemperance and
Lepidus, the dupe, is carried off
insensible.

0.1 *banquet* dessert with wine. See note
to 1.2.12.

1 **plants** a pun. As well as signifying a
seedling, *plant* could also mean 'the
sole of the foot' (*OED sb.*[2]).

4 **high-coloured** red-faced; compare
'burnt our cheeks' (122).

5 **alms-drink**   meaning   uncertain.
OED's definition, 'the remains of
liquor reserved for alms-people'
(Alms *sb.* 4), is unsatisfactory. Riv
points out that it is explained in the
speech which follows. Every time the
guests make up their quarrels they
drink a toast, and Lepidus, joining in,
becomes increasingly intoxicated. 'His
drinking is an act of charity'
(Bevington).

2.7] *Pope*   1 their] *F2;* th'their *F*   4 high-coloured] *F2;* high Conlord *F*

2 SERVANT   As they pinch one another by the disposition, he cries out 'No more', reconciles them to
his entreaty, and himself to th' drink.

1 SERVANT   But it raises the greater war between him
and his discretion.   10

2 SERVANT   Why, this it is to have a name in great
men's fellowship. I had as lief have a reed that will
do me no service as a partisan I could not heave.

1 SERVANT   To be called into a huge sphere and not to
be seen to move in't, are the holes where eyes should   15
be, which pitifully disaster the cheeks.

A sennet sounded. Enter CAESAR, ANTONY, POMPEY,
LEPIDUS, AGRIPPA, MAECENAS, ENOBARBUS, MENAS *with
other Captains [and a* Boy Singer].

ANTONY
Thus do they, sir: they take the flow o'th' Nile

6–7 **As ... disposition** 'As they irritate
one another in accordance with their
personalities'. The servant recognizes
that the signatories to the peace treaty
are actually incompatible.

7 **No more** 'No more quarrelling'

8 **entreaty** i.e. to stop bickering

10 **discretion** prudence (*OED* 6)

11–12 **have ... fellowship** 'be a
member of an alliance of great men.'
Lepidus is a mere *name* and exercises
no power.

12 **had as lief** 'would just as soon'

13 **partisan** long-handled spear (*OED
sb.*² 1)

14–16 **To ... cheeks** 'To be called into
a high position (*sphere*) and visibly to
have no function in it is like having
eye sockets with no eyes, a condition
which would sadly ruin the face.' The
metaphor of the 'huge sphere' refers
to the spheres which, according to the
Ptolemaic astronomy, revolved round
the earth and influenced its inhabitants. *Pitifully* means both 'deserving
pity' and 'having pits or sockets

instead of eyes'. To *disaster* was to
'strike with calamity' (*OED v.*),
another word with planetary associations.

16 SD *sennet* notes sounded on a
trumpet to announce a ceremonial
entrance

17–20 **they ... follow** According to
Malone the source of this information
is Leo Africanus' *History and Description of Africa*, trans. John Pory, 1600,
Book VIII (Leo, 860). Leo describes
how 'the Egyptians according to the
increase of Nilus doe foresee the
plenty or dearth of the yeere following'. The rise and fall of the water
was calculated by the observation of
a scale inscribed on a pillar which
stood in a tank into which the water
of the Nile was conveyed through an
underground pipe. The practice is
also described, in words less close
to Shakespeare's, in Pliny, *Natural
History* 5.9, trans. Holland, 1601,
p. 98.

17 **take** measure

9 greater] *F2;* greatet *F*   12 lief] *Capell;* liue *F*   16.3 *and ...* Singer] *Jones subst.*

By certain scales i'th' pyramid. They know
By th'height, the lowness, or the mean, if dearth
Or foison follow. The higher Nilus swells,   20
The more it promises. As it ebbs, the seedsman
Upon the slime and ooze scatters his grain,
And shortly comes to harvest.

LEPIDUS   You've strange serpents there?

ANTONY   Ay, Lepidus.   25

LEPIDUS   Your serpent of Egypt is bred, now, of your
mud by the operation of your sun; so is your crocodile.

ANTONY   They are so.

POMPEY   Sit, and some wine! A health to Lepidus!
                                    [*They sit and drink.*]

LEPIDUS   I am not so well as I should be, but I'll ne'er   30
out.

ENOBARBUS   [*aside*] Not till you have slept. I fear me
you'll be in till then.

LEPIDUS   Nay, certainly, I have heard the Ptolemies'
pyramises are very goodly things. Without con-   35
tradiction I have heard that.

MENAS   [*aside to Pompey*]
Pompey, a word.

POMPEY   [*aside to Menas*]
                    Say in my ear what is't.

18 **pyramid** not of the kind usually
associated with Egypt but an obelisk
(*OED* 3). Cleopatra has a similar
structure in mind when she asks that
her country's 'high pyramides' should
be her gibbet (5.2.60).

19–20 **dearth / Or foison** famine or
plenty

26–7 **Your ... crocodile** It was widely
thought that organic life, such as
snakes and flies, could be created out
of vegetable matter. By way of
example Case quotes Sylvester's
translation of Du Bartas' Week 1, Day
2: 'As on the edges of some standing

lake ... / The foamy slime itselfe
transformeth oft / To green half-
Tadpoles ... / Half dead, half-living;
half a frog, half mud.' Jones points
out that 'the colloquial use of "your"
for "the" suggests a complacent
knowingness: Lepidus, now drunk, is
showing off.'

30–1 **I'll ne'er out** 'I shan't refuse to
join you'

32 **Not ... slept** a pun on *out*, meaning
'out of doors'. Hence *in* means both
'indoors' and 'in drink'.

35 **pyramises** a false plural derived by
the drunken Lepidus from *pyramis*,

29 SD] *Oxf subst.*   32 SD] *Capell*   37 SD *aside ... Pompey*] *Rowe   aside ... Menas*] *Capell
subst.*

MENAS [*Whispers in his ear.*]
    Forsake thy seat, I do beseech thee, captain,
    And hear me speak a word.
POMPEY [*aside to Menas*]
    Forbear me till anon. – This wine for Lepidus!   40
LEPIDUS What manner o' thing is your crocodile?
ANTONY It is shaped, sir, like itself, and it is as broad
    as it hath breadth. It is just so high as it is, and
    moves with it own organs. It lives by that which
    nourisheth it, and the elements once out of it, it   45
    transmigrates.
LEPIDUS What colour is it of?
ANTONY Of it own colour too.
LEPIDUS 'Tis a strange serpent.
ANTONY 'Tis so, and the tears of it are wet.   50
CAESAR Will this description satisfy him?
ANTONY With the health that Pompey gives him, else
    he is a very epicure.   [*Menas whispers again.*]
POMPEY [*aside to Menas*]
    Go hang, sir, hang! Tell me of that? Away!
    Do as I bid you. – Where's this cup I called for?   55
MENAS [*aside to Pompey*]
    If for the sake of merit thou wilt hear me,
    Rise from thy stool.

---

the Latin singular for 'pyramid'

40 Forbear ... anon 'Leave me until a little later'

44, 48 it own its own. This old form of the genitive is occasionally used by Shakespeare, as in *KL* 1.4.215–16, 'The hedge-sparrow fed the cuckoo so long, / That [it] had it head bit off by it young.'

45–6 it transmigrates 'its soul passes into another creature', an allusion to the Pythagorean doctrine of the transmigration of souls, the belief that after death the soul of one creature passes into the body of another. In reply to

the question 'What is the opinion of Pythagoras concerning wild fowl?' Malvolio replies, 'That the soul of our grandam might haply inhabit a bird' (*TN* 4.2.50–3). See also *AYL* 3.2.176–8.

53 epicure either (1) a man devoted to sensual pleasure and hence not easily *satisfied*, or (2) a follower of Epicurus who, believing there is no life after death, does not believe in 'transmigration'

56 merit 'my deserts'; 'my past services to you'

---

38 SD] *as Cam¹; opp.* anon *l. 40 F*   40 SD] *Capell subst.*   53 SD] *Cam¹*   54 SD] *Johnson subst.*   56 SD] *Johnson*

POMPEY   [*aside to Menas*]
                              I think thou'rt mad. The matter?
                              [*Rises and walks aside with Menas.*]
MENAS
    I have ever held my cap off to thy fortunes.
POMPEY
    Thou hast served me with much faith. What's else
        to say? –
    Be jolly, lords.
ANTONY   These quicksands, Lepidus,   60
    Keep off them, for you sink.
MENAS
    Wilt thou be lord of all the world?
POMPEY
    What sayst thou?
MENAS   Wilt thou be lord of the whole world?
    That's twice.
POMPEY   How should that be?
MENAS   But entertain it,
    And, though thou think me poor, I am the man   65
    Will give thee all the world.
POMPEY   Hast thou drunk well?
MENAS
    No, Pompey, I have kept me from the cup.
    Thou art, if thou dar'st be, the earthly Jove,

---

58 **held my cap off** i.e. 'behaved with
    deference'. In Shakespeare's time,
    servants, unlike their masters, usually
    went bareheaded indoors.
60–1 **These ... sink** Lepidus is tot-
    tering. By l. 86 he has collapsed com-
    pletely.
62–81 **Wilt ... drink** 'Menas the pirate
    came to Pompey, and whispering in
    his eare, said unto him: Shall I cut
    the gables [*sic*] of the ankers, and
    make thee Lord not only of Sicile and

Sardinia, but of the whole Empire of
Rome besides? Pompey having
pawsed a while upon it, at length
aunswered him: Thou shouldest have
done it, and never have told it me,
but now we must content us with that
we have. As for my selfe, I was never
taught to breake my faith, nor to be
counted a traitor' (North, 279).
64 **entertain it** consider it favourably
    (*OED v.* 14c)

57 SD *aside to Menas*] *Johnson   Rises ... Menas*] *Johnson subst.*

Whate'er the ocean pales or sky inclips
Is thine, if thou wilt ha't.

POMPEY   Show me which way.   70

MENAS

These three world-sharers, these competitors,
Are in thy vessel. Let me cut the cable,
And when we are put off, fall to their throats.
All then is thine.

POMPEY   Ah, this thou shouldst have done
And not have spoke on't. In me 'tis villainy;   75
In thee't had been good service. Thou must know
'Tis not my profit that does lead mine honour;
Mine honour, it. Repent that e'er thy tongue
Hath so betrayed thine act. Being done unknown,
I should have found it afterwards well done,   80
But must condemn it now. Desist and drink.

[Returns to the others.]

MENAS   *[aside]*

For this,
I'll never follow thy palled fortunes more.
Who seeks and will not take, when once 'tis offered,
Shall never find it more.

POMPEY   This health to Lepidus!   85

ANTONY

Bear him ashore. I'll pledge it for him, Pompey.

---

69 **pales** encloses (as with pales or
    stakes)
    inclips encircles
71 **competitors** 'associates, partners'.
    Compare 1.4.3; 5.1.42.
72 **cable** rope or chain attached to the
    anchor
74 * **then** F's 'there' makes sense,
    especially if Menas accompanies it
    with a gesture towards the world at
    large, but Pope's emendation *then*
    provides a fitting conclusion to this
    logically argued speech. Manuscript
    'then' and 'ther' could easily be

confused.
78 **Mine honour, it** 'My honour leads
    my profit'
79 **betrayed thine act** 'revealed (or
    been false to) your deed'
83 **palled** weakened, enfeebled (*OED*
    Pall *v.*[1] 7)
84–5 **Who … more** a variation of the
    proverb 'He that will not when he
    may, when he would he shall have
    nay' (Dent, N54)
86 **pledge it** i.e. respond to Pompey's
    toast (by drinking)

74 then] *Pope;* there *F*   81 SD] *Oxf*   82 SD] *Capell*

ENOBARBUS

Here's to thee, Menas!

MENAS   Enobarbus, welcome!

POMPEY

Fill till the cup be hid.

ENOBARBUS [*Points to the Attendant who carries off
  Lepidus.*] There's a strong fellow, Menas.

MENAS   Why?   90

ENOBARBUS

'A bears the third part of the world, man. Seest not?

MENAS

The third part then he is drunk. Would it were all,
That it might go on wheels!

ENOBARBUS

Drink thou! Increase the reels!

MENAS

Come!   95

POMPEY

This is not yet an Alexandrian feast.

ANTONY

It ripens towards it. Strike the vessels, ho!
Here's to Caesar!

CAESAR   I could well forbear't.
It's monstrous labour when I wash my brain
And it grows fouler.   100

ANTONY

Be a child o'th' time.

---

91 '**A** he (also at 135)
  third part i.e. one of the three tri-
    umvirs
93 **go on wheels** go fast; whirl giddily
  (*OED* Wheel *sb.* 12b), an allusion to
  the proverbial expression 'To drink
  until the world goes round' (Dent,
  W885.1)
94 **reels** (1) revels, (2) staggering motions
  (*OED* Reel *sb.²* 1, 1b)
97 **Strike the vessels** The most prob-

able meaning is 'strike the cups
together', as when drinking a toast.
Another suggestion has been 'tap the
casks' as in Beaumont and Fletcher's
'Home, Launce, and strike a fresh
piece of wine' (*Monsieur Thomas*,
5.10.42).
98 **forbear** abstain (from drinking the
  toast)
99 **wash my brain** 'a jocular expression
  for wine-drinking' (*OED* Wash *v.* 5c)

89 SD] *Steevens subst.*   100 And it grows] *F2;* and it grow *F;* An it grow *Oxf*

CAESAR   'Possess it', I'll make answer.
But I had rather fast from all, four days,
Than drink so much in one.
ENOBARBUS [*to Antony*]   Ha, my brave emperor,
Shall we dance now the Egyptian Bacchanals
And celebrate our drink?   105
POMPEY
Let's ha't, good soldier.
ANTONY   Come, let's all take hands
Till that the conquering wine hath steeped our sense
In soft and delicate Lethe.
ENOBARBUS   All take hands.
Make battery to our ears with the loud music,
The while I'll place you; then the boy shall sing.   110
The holding every man shall beat as loud
As his strong sides can volley.
                    Music plays. Enobarbus places them hand in hand.

The Song

BOY   Come, thou monarch of the vine,

101 **'Possess it'** ... **answer** 'My answer
is, "Be master of it."' Caesar, preferring to be in command of any
situation, disagrees with Antony.
104 **Bacchanals** dances in honour of
Bacchus, the god of wine
105 **celebrate** 'consecrate by religious
rites' (*OED v.* 2)
106 **ha't** do so
108 **Lethe** Lethè. See note to 2.1.27.
109 **Make battery to** 'make an assault
on'
110 **The while** 'in the meantime'
111 **holding** burden, or refrain, of a song
(*OED vbl. sb.* 5)
* **beat** Theobald emended this to
'bear' on the analogy of the expression
'bear the burden' ('sing the refrain')
and a misreading of manuscript *r* as *t*
was easily done. On the other hand,

beat follows logically from *battery*
(109) and 'one can also *beat* the
rhythm and emphasise it by singing
it loudly' (Sisson, 2.267). As Jones
points out, Horace's Cleopatra Ode
(1.37) begins with a reference to
'wine-heated dancers beating the
earth with their feet'. He visualizes 'a
very lively drunken ring-dance with
a great deal of rhythmic stamping'.
112 **volley** 'produce sounds simultaneously ... in a manner suggestive
of firearms or artillery' (*OED v.* 3a)
113–18 **Come** ... **round** Richmond
Noble (127) suggests that the song is
a parody of the Whit Sunday hymn
Veni creator spiritus. P. J. Seng (4–6),
however, argues that it is a parody
of another hymn, Stephen Langton's
Veni sancte spiritus: 'In a scene so

103 SD] *Capell*   111 beat] *F*; beate *Theobald*   113 SP BOY] *Jones; not in F*

Plumpy Bacchus with pink eyne!
In thy vats our cares be drowned;   115
With thy grapes our hairs be crowned.

ALL   Cup us till the world go round!
             Cup us till the world go round!

CAESAR

What would you more? Pompey, good night. Good
    brother,
Let me request you off. Our graver business   120
Frowns at this levity. Gentle lords, let's part.
You see we have burnt our cheeks. Strong Enobarb
Is weaker than the wine, and mine own tongue
Splits what it speaks. The wild disguise hath almost
Anticked us all. What needs more words? Good night. 125
Good Antony, your hand.

POMPEY   I'll try you on the shore.

ANTONY   And shall, sir. Give's your hand.

POMPEY

O, Antony, you have my father's house.
But what? We are friends! Come down into the boat.   130

ENOBARBUS

Take heed you fall not.

                        [*Exeunt all but Enobarbus and Menas.*]
                        Menas, I'll not on shore.

charged with ironic tensions it would
not be surprising to find a song
charged with ironic tensions of its
own.'
114 **pink eyne** 'having small, narrow,
or half-closed eyes; also squint-eyed'
(*OED* Pink-eyed *a.* 1)
117 **Cup us** 'fill our cups'. See note to
93.
119 **brother** brother-in-law
120 **request you off** 'ask you to come
ashore'
124 **Splits** mispronounces; 'mutilates'
(Onions)

wild disguise either 'riotous masque'
or 'drunken disorder'. See *OED* Disguise *sb.* 7.
125 **Anticked us all** 'made us all ridiculous, grotesque'
127 **try you** 'test your capacity for drink'
129 **you ... house** See 2.6.27 and note.
Pompey's hostility to Antony has now
been dispelled in drink and laughter.
130 **Come ... boat** i.e. the boat which
will take them from the ship to the
shore. Enobarbus' next line warns the
drunken Pompey and his guests to be
careful as they clamber down into it.

115 vats] *Pope; Fattes F*   117 SP ALL] *Staunton; not in F*   120 off. Our] *Rowe subst.; of our
F*   124 Splits] *F4; Spleet's F*   129 father's] *F2; Father F*   131 fall not. Menas, I'll] *Capell.; fall
not Menas: Ile F*   131 SD] *Capell subst.*

MENAS

No, to my cabin! These drums, these trumpets, flutes!
What!
Let Neptune hear we bid a loud farewell
To these great fellows. Sound and be hanged! Sound
out!   *Sound a flourish with drums.*
ENOBARBUS   Hoo, says 'a! There's my cap!   135
                                  [*Flings his cap in the air.*]
MENAS   Hoo! Noble captain, come!

                                                        Exeunt.

[**3.1**]   *Enter* VENTIDIUS *as it were in triumph,* [*with* SILIUS *and
other Romans, Officers and Soldiers,*] *the dead body of Pacorus
borne before him.*

VENTIDIUS

Now, darting Parthia, art thou struck, and now

132–4 * **No ... out** F gives these lines
to Enobarbus as a continuation of
his speech at 131 but, as a guest in
Pompey's galley, he would not have a
cabin there, whereas Menas, a supporter of Pompey, presumably did.
132 **These ... What** an order to the
musicians off stage to sound a flourish
as the guests leave in the boat. Menas'
incongruous command to both trumpets and flutes suggests that he is
drunk.
134 SD *Sound ... drums* a ceremonial
fanfare, played off stage and sounded
in response to Menas' order 'Sound
out!'

3.1 Location: Syria, on the eastern border
of the Roman empire. The vast distance between this location and that
of the previous episode indicates the
extent of the territory over which
the triumvirs hold power. This scene
(omitted from a great many
productions) is in ironical relationship
to the previous one. While the com-

manders are celebrating their spurious
concord, the subordinate is loyally
carrying out his orders, and, whereas
the previous scene leads up to the
carrying out of the drunken Lepidus,
this one starts with the carrying in of
the dead Pacorus.

0.1 *as ... triumph* Plutarch remarks that
'Ventidius was the only man that triumphed of the Parthians untill this
present day' (North, 281). 'In triumph' means 'triumphantly' and not
'as in a Roman triumph' or victory
procession.

1 **darting Parthia** The cavalry of
Parthia, a kingdom south-east of the
Caspian Sea, was celebrated for its
distinctive tactics. They would
advance hurling darts at the enemy
and then, retreating to avoid close
combat, turn in their saddles and
discharge flights of arrows.
struck punished (*OED* Strike *v.* 45).
The sense is of both a sharp blow and
a chastisement.

132 SP MENAS] *Capell; not in F which assigns 132–4 to Enobarbus.* What!] *Rowe;* what *F*
133 a loud] *Rowe²;* aloud *F*   135 SD] *Cam¹ subst.*

3.1] *Rowe*   0.1–0.2 *with ... Soldiers*] *Capell subst.*   1 struck] *F3* (strook); stroke *F*

Pleased Fortune does of Marcus Crassus' death
Make me revenger. Bear the King's son's body
Before our army. Thy Pacorus, Orodes,
Pays this for Marcus Crassus.
SILIUS   Noble Ventidius,   5
Whilst yet with Parthian blood thy sword is warm,
The fugitive Parthians follow. Spur through Media,
Mesopotamia, and the shelters whither
The routed fly. So thy grand captain Antony
Shall set thee on triumphant chariots and   10
Put garlands on thy head.
VENTIDIUS   O Silius, Silius,
I have done enough. A lower place, note well,
May make too great an act. For learn this, Silius:
Better to leave undone than, by our deed,
Acquire too high a fame when him we serve's away.   15
Caesar and Antony have ever won

2 **Marcus Crassus** a man of great wealth who, with Pompey and Julius Caesar, was a member of the first triumvirate. He led an army into Parthia, where he suffered a heavy defeat and in 53 BC was put to death. His head was cut off and sent to Orodes, King of Parthia and father of Pacorus, who poured molten gold into his mouth, a fate befitting a man who had thirsted for gold all his life (*OCD*; Spevack). Cleopatra threatens her Messenger with a similar punishment (2.5.34–5).

4 **Pacorus** the eldest son of Orodes, King of Parthia. It was his army which overcame the troops of Marcus Crassus. He was killed in battle against Ventidius in 39 BC on the same day (9 June) that Crassus had been defeated. Plutarch reports that 'a great number of the Parthians' were killed in this battle, 'and among them Pacorus, the kings owne sonne slaine.

This noble exployt as famous as ever any was, was a full revenge to the Romanes, of the shame and losse they had received before by the death of Marcus Crassus' (North, 281).

7 **The ... follow** 'follow the fleeing Parthians'
   Spur ride swiftly (using your spurs)

10 **triumphant** triumphal
   chariots The plural indicates that Silius visualizes an official victory procession in which Ventidius and his army will march through the streets of Rome.

12 **lower place** 'man of subordinate rank'

14–15 **Better ... away** 'Ventidius durst not undertake to follow them any further, fearing least he should have gotten Antonius displeasure by it' (North, 281).

16–20 **Caesar ... favour** 'Antonius and Caesar ... were alway more fortunate when they made warre by their

4 army. Thy] *F2 (Army, thy)*; Army thy *F*   5 SP SILIUS] *Theobald; Romaine F*   8 whither] *F (whether)*

More in their officer than person. Sossius,
One of my place in Syria, his lieutenant,
For quick accumulation of renown,
Which he achieved by th' minute, lost his favour.   20
Who does i'th' wars more than his captain can,
Becomes his captain's captain; and ambition,
The soldier's virtue, rather makes choice of loss
Than gain which darkens him.
I could do more to do Antonius good,   25
But 'twould offend him, and in his offence
Should my performance perish.

SILIUS

Thou hast, Ventidius, that
Without the which a soldier and his sword
Grants scarce distinction. Thou wilt write to Antony?   30

VENTIDIUS

I'll humbly signify what in his name,
That magical word of war, we have effected;
How, with his banners and his well-paid ranks,
The ne'er-yet-beaten horse of Parthia
We have jaded out o'th' field.

SILIUS   Where is he now?   35

VENTIDIUS

He purposeth to Athens, whither, with what haste

Lieutenants, then by them selves. For
Sossius, one of Antonius Lieu-
tenauntes in Syria, did notable good
service' (North, 282).

18 **place** position, rank
lieutenant 'i.e. the commanding
officer acting for Antony' (Bevington)

20 **by th' minute** 'every minute, incess-
antly' (Schmidt)

22–3 **ambition ... virtue** Compare *Oth*
3.3.349–50, 'the big wars / That
makes ambition virtue'.

24 **darkens** eclipses

26 **in his offence** 'because of the offence
he would take'

27 **perish** 'come to nothing' (Schmidt)

28–30 **that ... distinction** 'that quality
(discretion) without which a soldier
and his sword can scarcely allow any
distinction to be made between them'
(Jones). 'Soldier and his sword' are
the collective subject of the singular
verb *grants*. *OED* cites no example of
distinction in the sense of 'honour'
before the eighteenth century.

34 **horse** cavalry

35 **jaded** A jade is a worn-out horse;
hence to have *jaded* the Parthian
cavalry is to have worn them out
so that they are forced to retire in
exhaustion.

36 **purposeth** intends to go

28, 35 SPs SILIUS] *Theobald; Rom. F*

The weight we must convey with's will permit,
We shall appear before him. On there! Pass along!

Exeunt.

[**3.2**]   *Enter* AGRIPPA *at one door,* ENOBARBUS *at another.*

AGRIPPA   What, are the brothers parted?
ENOBARBUS
    They have dispatched with Pompey; he is gone.
    The other three are sealing. Octavia weeps
    To part from Rome; Caesar is sad, and Lepidus
    Since Pompey's feast, as Menas says, is troubled   5
    With the green-sickness.
AGRIPPA   'Tis a noble Lepidus.
ENOBARBUS
    A very fine one. Oh, how he loves Caesar!
AGRIPPA
    Nay, but how dearly he adores Mark Antony!
ENOBARBUS
    Caesar? Why he's the Jupiter of men!

3.2 Location: Rome. The cheerfully sarcastic opening dialogue (1–20) contrasts both with the heroism of the loyal Ventidius in the previous scene and with the pathos of Octavia's farewell to her brother (24–61). Throughout the scenes depicting the peace negotiations (2.6, 2.7, 3.2) it is strongly suggested, largely through Enobarbus and his friends, that the politicians' show of friendship conceals an actual self-interest and mistrust. Similarly in this scene the genuineness of Caesar's show of grief at losing his sister (24–41) is questioned by Enobarbus and Agrippa (51–9) and Antony's loyalty to his new wife has already been put in doubt by his earlier decision (2.3.37–9) to return to Egypt. Hence a distinction is constantly made between what is said and what may actually be felt or intended.

1 **brothers** not necessarily a reference to Antony and Octavius, who are now brothers-in-law, but to the triumvirate who, at the banquet, have made a show of love for one another **parted** departed

2 **dispatched with Pompey** 'settled the business with Pompey and sent him away' (*OED* Dispatch *v.* 3)

3 **The other three** the triumvirate
sealing 'putting their seals to the agreement' and, hence, 'finishing off their business' (Schmidt)

6 **green-sickness** 'an anaemic disease which mostly affects young women about the age of puberty and gives a pale or greenish tinge to the complexion' (*OED*). Enobarbus jokingly attributes the symptoms of Lepidus' hangover to his love for Caesar and Antony.

7 **fine** The Latin word *lepidus* means 'fine, elegant'.

AGRIPPA

What's Antony? The god of Jupiter!   10

ENOBARBUS

Spake you of Caesar? Hoo! The nonpareil!

AGRIPPA

O Antony! O thou Arabian bird!

ENOBARBUS

Would you praise Caesar, say 'Caesar'. Go no further.

AGRIPPA

Indeed, he plied them both with excellent praises.

ENOBARBUS

But he loves Caesar best. Yet he loves Antony.   15
Hoo! Hearts, tongues, figures, scribes, bards, poets,
    cannot
Think, speak, cast, write, sing, number – hoo! –
His love to Antony! But as for Caesar,
Kneel down, kneel down, and wonder!

AGRIPPA   Both he loves.

ENOBARBUS

They are his shards and he their beetle.

[Trumpet within.]
So,   20

---

11 **nonpareil** incomparable
12 **Arabian bird** i.e. unique. The
phoenix, a mythical bird, was said to
be the only one of its kind and to
live for several hundred years in the
Arabian desert, after which it burned
itself only to be reborn from its own
ashes.
16–17 **Hearts ... number** Steevens
points out that this series of nouns
followed by a series of corresponding
verbs is characteristic of the Elizabethan sonneteers, as in Sidney's
'Vertue, beawtie, and speach, did
strike, wound, charme / My hart,
eyes, eares, with wonder, love,
delight' (Sidney, *Poems*, 84). Eno-

barbus implies that Lepidus speaks
like a young man in love.
17 **cast** calculate (referring back to
figures)
number versify; put into 'numbers'
or verses
20 **They ... beetle** an allusion to the
proverb 'The beetle flies over many
sweet flowers and lights in a cow-
shard' (Tilley, B221). Steevens and
others mistakenly interpreted *shards*
as 'the wings of a beetle' owing to a
misunderstanding of *Mac* 3.2.42, 'the
shard-born beetle' ('shard-borne' in
F) which actually means 'the beetle
born out of dung'. A *shard* is a cow-
pat (*OED sb.*[2]).

10 SP AGRIPPA] *Rowe; Ant. F*   Antony? The ... Jupiter!] *Johnson subst.; Anthony,* the ... Iupiter?
F   11 Hoo!] *this edn;* How, *F;* Oh! *F2*   16 figures] *Hanmer;* Figure *F*   20 SD] *Capell*

175

This is to horse. Adieu, noble Agrippa.

AGRIPPA

Good fortune, worthy soldier, and farewell.

Enter CAESAR, ANTONY, LEPIDUS *and* OCTAVIA.

ANTONY

No further, sir.

CAESAR

You take from me a great part of myself.
Use me well in't. Sister, prove such a wife   25
As my thoughts make thee, and as my farthest bond
Shall pass on thy approof. Most noble Antony,
Let not the piece of virtue which is set
Betwixt us, as the cement of our love
To keep it builded, be the ram to batter   30
The fortress of it. For better might we
Have loved without this mean, if on both parts
This be not cherished.

ANTONY   Make me not offended
In your distrust.

CAESAR   I have said.

ANTONY   You shall not find,
Though you be therein curious, the least cause   35

21 **This ... horse** 'This trumpet calls us to mount our horses.' The *trumpet* may be a summons to mount or a short flourish for the entry of the triumvirs (which, as often in this play, is ironical in view of the preceding conversation). Either way, it indicates that departure is imminent.

23 **No further** Either (1) 'You must go no further' (i.e. 'We must part here') (Jones) or (2) 'You need not go on urging your points' (Bevington). The latter interpretation is the more Shakespearean in that it suggests a conversation continued from off stage.

26–7 **as my farthest ... approof** '[such a wife] that I could stake anything on

the trial of your conduct'. *Bond* (F 'band') is used in the sense of 'security, pledge' (*OED sb.*[1] 8c), *pass* in the sense of 'pledge' (*OED v.* 48) and *approof* in the sense of 'the act of proving, trial' (*OED* 1).

28 **piece** example (*OED sb.* 8c). Compare *Tem* 1.2.56, 'Thy mother was a piece of virtue.'

29 **cement** accented on the first syllable

32 **mean** intermediary (*OED sb.*[2] 9)

34 **In** By

   I have said 'I have finished.' Compare 2.6.109 and note.

35 **curious** 'inquisitive; minute in inquiry' (*OED* 5, 5b)

26 bond] *F (*Band*)   29 cement] *F (*Cyment*)

For what you seem to fear. So the gods keep you,
And make the hearts of Romans serve your ends.
We will here part.

CAESAR

Farewell, my dearest sister, fare thee well.
The elements be kind to thee, and make   40
Thy spirits all of comfort! Fare thee well.

OCTAVIA

My noble brother!   [*She weeps.*]

ANTONY

The April's in her eyes; it is love's spring
And these the showers to bring it on. Be cheerful.

OCTAVIA

Sir, look well to my husband's house, and –   45

CAESAR

What, Octavia?

OCTAVIA   I'll tell you in your ear.
                                    [*She whispers to Caesar.*]

ANTONY

Her tongue will not obey her heart, nor can
Her heart inform her tongue – the swan's-down
    feather
That stands upon the swell at full of tide,
And neither way inclines.   50

ENOBARBUS [*aside to Agrippa*]
Will Caesar weep?

AGRIPPA [*aside to Enobarbus*] He has a cloud in's face.

ENOBARBUS [*aside to Agrippa*]
He were the worse for that were he a horse;

---

40 **elements** seasons, weather. The idea develops into the metaphor of the April showers in 43.

43–4 **The ... on** a passing reference to the proverb 'April showers bring forth May flowers' (Dent, S411)

46 SD *She ... Caesar* Octavia and Caesar walk aside at this point, allow-

ing the audience to hear the remarks of Enobarbus and Agrippa. Lines 59–61 make it clear that she asked her brother to write to her regularly.

48 **inform** instruct, direct (*OED v.* 4c)

49 **at ... tide** i.e. on still water, just before the tide turns

52 **He were ... horse** a pun. A horse

---

42 SD] *Jones subst.* 46 SD *She ... Caesar*] *Oxf; taking him aside/Capell* 49 at full of] *F2; at the of full F uncorr.; at the full of F corr.* 51–7 SDs *aside] Capell*

177

So is he, being a man.
AGRIPPA   [*aside to Enobarbus*]
                              Why, Enobarbus,
When Antony found Julius Caesar dead,
He cried almost to roaring, and he wept   55
When at Philippi he found Brutus slain.
ENOBARBUS   [*aside to Agrippa*]
That year, indeed, he was troubled with a rheum.
What willingly he did confound he wailed,
Believe't, till I wept too.
CAESAR   No, sweet Octavia,
You shall hear from me still. The time shall not   60
Outgo my thinking on you.
ANTONY   Come, sir, come,
I'll wrestle with you in my strength of love.
Look, here I have you [*embracing him*]; thus I let
    you go,
And give you to the gods.
CAESAR   Adieu. Be happy!
LEPIDUS
Let all the number of the stars give light   65
To thy fair way!
CAESAR   Farewell, farewell!   *Kisses Octavia.*
ANTONY   Farewell!
                                    Trumpets sound. Exeunt.

---

with a dark spot on its face was said
to have a 'cloud' (*OED sb.* 6b). Such
a mark lessened its value.
54–6 **When ... slain** In his earlier play
Julius Caesar Shakespeare had portrayed Antony's grief on seeing the
murdered Caesar (3.1). He actually
showed no grief for the dead Brutus.
57 **rheum** watering of the eyes
58 **confound ... wailed** destroy ...
lamented
59 * **wept** Theobald's emendation of F

'weepe' has been generally accepted.
Capell's and Steevens's retention of
'weepe' depends on the correction of
the comma after *wailed* to a full stop.
The sense then is 'Believe it until I
myself weep (which will never
happen)'.
60 **still** regularly
60–1 **The ... you** 'Time will not over-
take my thoughts of you'; 'I shall
think of you constantly.'

59 wept] *Theobald;* weepe F   63 SD] *Hanmer subst.*

[3.3]   *Enter* CLEOPATRA, CHARMIAN, IRAS *and* ALEXAS.

CLEOPATRA
  Where is the fellow?
ALEXAS   Half afeard to come.
CLEOPATRA
  Go to, go to.

            Enter the Messenger *as before.*

            Come hither, sir.
ALEXAS   Good majesty,
  Herod of Jewry dare not look upon you
  But when you are well pleased.
CLEOPATRA   That Herod's head
  I'll have! But how, when Antony is gone,   5
  Through whom I might command it? – Come thou
      near.
MESSENGER
  Most gracious majesty!
CLEOPATRA   Didst thou behold
  Octavia?
MESSENGER   Ay, dread queen.
CLEOPATRA   Where?

3.3 Location: Alexandria. We have not
been in Egypt since 2.5 when we saw
Cleopatra's reception of the news of
Antony's marriage. Now, in this
scene, she is still interrogating the
same messenger. Whereas in the rest
of the world great events have been
taking place, Cleopatra's sole interest
is in Antony who, while he is away,
never mentions her by name. Her
ability to turn bad news into good
(and to transform the Messenger from
a 'horrible villain' (2.5.63) to a 'proper
man' (3.3.37)) is consistent with her
capacity in the final scene to transform
her suicide into a triumph. Such shifting and contradictory impressions are

characteristic of the whole play.
2 SD *as before* meaning either 'the same
  one who appeared in 2.5' or 'in the
  same dishevelled state'
3 **Herod of Jewry** The ruler of Judaea
  at the time of the events depicted in
  the play was Herod the Great (73–4
  BC). Shakespeare seems to have confused him with his successor, also
  Herod, who ruled at the time of the
  birth of Christ and, as the man
  responsible for the Slaughter of the
  Innocents, was regarded as a type
  of ferocious tyrant (*OCD*). Compare
  1.2.29.
5 **how** i.e. 'how can I have it?'

3.3] *Rowe*   2 SD *Enter ... before*] as *Ard²*; *after* Sir *F*

MESSENGER   Madam, in Rome.
  I looked her in the face, and saw her led
  Between her brother and Mark Antony.   10
CLEOPATRA
  Is she as tall as me?
MESSENGER   She is not, madam.
CLEOPATRA
  Didst hear her speak? Is she shrill-tongued or low?
MESSENGER
  Madam, I heard her speak; she is low-voiced.
CLEOPATRA
  That's not so good. He cannot like her long.
CHARMIAN
  Like her? O Isis! 'Tis impossible.   15
CLEOPATRA
  I think so, Charmian. Dull of tongue and dwarfish.
  What majesty is in her gait? Remember,
  If e'er thou look'dst on majesty.
MESSENGER   She creeps.
  Her motion and her station are as one.
  She shows a body rather than a life,   20
  A statue than a breather.
CLEOPATRA   Is this certain?
MESSENGER
  Or I have no observance.
CHARMIAN   Three in Egypt
  Cannot make better note.
CLEOPATRA   He's very knowing;
  I do perceiv't. There's nothing in her yet.
  The fellow has good judgement.

---

12 **shrill-tongued** i.e. like Fulvia. Compare 1.1.33.
14 **That ... good** Some commentators have taken this to mean 'That's not such good news', in which case 'He cannot like her long' expresses a sudden shift into optimism. On the other hand it could mean 'That's not in her favour', in which case the words which follow are simply a development of the same idea.
17 **gait** manner of walking
19 **station** remaining still
20 **shows ... life** 'looks like a dead body rather than a living one'

18 look'dst] *Pope;* look'st *F*

CHARMIAN   Excellent.   25
CLEOPATRA
  Guess at her years, I prithee.
MESSENGER   Madam,
  She was a widow –
CLEOPATRA   Widow? Charmian, hark!
MESSENGER
  And I do think she's thirty.
CLEOPATRA
  Bear'st thou her face in mind? Is't long or round?
MESSENGER
  Round, even to faultiness.   30
CLEOPATRA
  For the most part, too, they are foolish that are so.
  Her hair, what colour?
MESSENGER   Brown, madam, and her forehead
  As low as she would wish it.
CLEOPATRA   There's gold for thee.
  Thou must not take my former sharpness ill.
  I will employ thee back again; I find thee   35
  Most fit for business. Go, make thee ready;
  Our letters are prepared.   [*Exit Messenger.*]
CHARMIAN   A proper man.
CLEOPATRA
  Indeed, he is so. I repent me much
  That so I harried him. Why methinks, by him,
  This creature's no such thing.
CHARMIAN   Nothing, madam.   40

27 **widow** See 2.6.112 and note.
28 **thirty** Cleopatra's failure to comment on this information has been seen by some as significant. The historical Cleopatra was actually twenty-nine at this time but Shakespeare seems to visualize her as older (1.5.28–30), in which case she prefers not to linger on the subject.
33 **As low ... it** i.e. 'She wouldn't want it any lower.' A low forehead was considered unattractive. Compare *TGV* 4.4.192–3, where Julia compares herself to Silvia: 'Her eyes are grey as glass, and so are mine; / Ay, but her forehead's low, and mine's as high.'
37 **proper** 'excellent, fine' (*OED a.* 7)
39 **harried** harassed
   by him 'from what he says'
40 **no such thing** 'nothing remarkable'

37 SD] *Hanmer*

181

CLEOPATRA

    The man hath seen some majesty, and should know.

CHARMIAN

    Hath he seen majesty? Isis else defend,

    And serving you so long!

CLEOPATRA

    I have one thing more to ask him yet, good Charmian.

    But 'tis no matter; thou shalt bring him to me   45

    Where I will write. All may be well enough.

CHARMIAN

    I warrant you, madam.   *Exeunt.*

[3.4]   *Enter* ANTONY *and* OCTAVIA.

ANTONY

    Nay, nay, Octavia, not only that.

    That were excusable – that, and thousands more

    Of semblable import – but he hath waged

    New wars 'gainst Pompey; made his will, and read it

    To public ear;   5

42 **Isis else defend** 'May Isis forbid anything else'. The meaning is 'I certainly think so'.

43 **serving** The implied subject, as Jones points out, is 'he'. The Messenger, we now discover, has been serving Cleopatra for some time. The implication is that she had sent him to spy on Antony and report back to her. We learn later (3.6.63–4) that Caesar has agents spying on Antony.

3.4 Location: Athens. At 3.1.36 we learn that Antony intends to go to Athens and at 3.6.65 Octavia believes he is still there. According to Plutarch, Antony was in Tarentum (present-day Taranto) when Octavia spoke the words given to her in 12–20, but Shakespeare in this scene departs from Plutarch, who reports that she said them not to Antony but to Caesar. The dramatist presumably

wanted to avoid giving Octavia two similar scenes with her brother and decided to give her one with Antony (3.4) and one with Caesar (3.6). As a result this present scene prepares the audience for her meeting with her brother in 3.6. It shows the rift between Antony and Caesar starting to develop rapidly – much more rapidly than in historical fact. Enobarbus' prediction at the end of 2.6 is now proving correct.

3 **semblable** similar

3–4 **waged … Pompey** In 2.6.34–5 Pompey accepted the offer of Sicily and Sardinia, but now Caesar has made war against him 'to gette Sicilia into his handes' (North, 283).

4–5 **made … ear** Shakespeare here departs from Plutarch, who says that it was Antony's will which Caesar obtained from the custody of the vestal virgins and noting in it 'certaine

3.4] *Rowe*

Spoke scantly of me; when perforce he could not
But pay me terms of honour, cold and sickly
He vented them; most narrow measure lent me;
When the best hint was given him, he not took't,
Or did it from his teeth.

OCTAVIA   O, my good lord,   10
Believe not all, or if you must believe,
Stomach not all. A more unhappy lady,
If this division chance, ne'er stood between,
Praying for both parts.
The good gods will mock me presently   15
When I shall pray 'O, bless my lord and husband!';
Undo that prayer by crying out as loud

places worthy of reproch', he
assembled the Senate and 'red it
before them all' in order to arouse
their hostility towards Antony
(North, 293). Here Antony criticizes
Caesar for reading his *own* will in
public, presumably because it contained bequests which were beneficial
to the people. In *Julius Caesar*
(3.2.240–52) it was Antony who, in
order to sway the people, read
Caesar's will in public.

6 **scantly** grudgingly

8 **vented** 'expressed', often used con-
temptuously as in *Cor* 1.1.208–9,
'With these shreds / They vented
their complainings'
most ... me 'did me small justice'
(Jones)

9 **hint** opportunity; cue. Compare *Oth*
1.3.140–2, 'Wherein of antres vast
and deserts idle ... It was my hint to
speak.'

10 **from his teeth** Compare the proverbial expression 'From the teeth outwards' (i.e. not from the heart) (Dent,
T423).

12 **Stomach** resent. Compare 2.2.9.

12–20 **A more ... all** This passage is
adapted from a speech which, according to Plutarch, Octavia made to
Caesar, Maecenas and Agrippa. 'She
tooke them aside, and with all the
instance [*sic*] she could possible,
intreated them they would not suffer
her that was the happiest woman of
the world, to become nowe the most
wretched and unfortunatest creature
of all other. For now, said she, everie
mans eyes doe gaze on me, that am
the sister of one of the Emperours
and wife of the other. And if the
worst councell take place, (which the
goddes forbidde) and that they growe
to warres: for your selves, it is uncer-
taine to which of them two the goddes
have assigned the victorie, or over-
throwe. But for me, on which side
soever victorie fall, my state can be
but most miserable still' (North, 282).

13 **between** i.e. between Antony and
Caesar

15 **presently** at once

17 **Undo** 'and then undo'

6–7 me; when ... honour,] *Rowe;* me, / When ... Honour: *F*   8 them; most ... measure .lent]
Rowe; then most ... measure: lent *F*   9 him, he] *Rowe;* him: he *F*   took't] *Theobald (Thirlby);*
look't *F*

'O, bless my brother!' Husband win, win brother,
Prays and destroys the prayer; no midway
'Twixt these extremes at all.

ANTONY   Gentle Octavia,   20
Let your best love draw to that point which seeks
Best to preserve it. If I lose mine honour,
I lose myself; better I were not yours
Than yours so branchless. But, as you requested,
Yourself shall go between's. The meantime, lady,   25
I'll raise the preparation of a war
Shall stain your brother. Make your soonest haste,
So your desires are yours.

OCTAVIA   Thanks to my lord.
The Jove of power make me, most weak, most weak,
Your reconciler! Wars 'twixt you twain would be   30
As if the world should cleave, and that slain men
Should solder up the rift.

ANTONY

When it appears to you where this begins,
Turn your displeasure that way, for our faults
Can never be so equal that your love   35
Can equally move with them. Provide your going;
Choose your own company, and command what cost
Your heart has mind to.   *Exeunt.*

---

21 **draw ... point** 'induce you to that
place'. The image refers to the needle
of a compass.
24 **branchless** 'destitute, bare' (Schmidt).
Shakespeare may be thinking of the
crown of oak or laurel awarded to a
man who had won honour.
27 **stain** darken, eclipse. Compare *Son*
35.3, 'Clouds and eclipses stain both
moon and sun.'

28 **So ... yours** either 'so long as that is
what you want' or 'in order to fulfil
your desires'
33 **where this begins** 'who started this
quarrel'
34 **our faults** i.e. those of Antony and
Caesar
36 **Provide your going** 'Make your
preparations to leave'
37 **what** whatever

24 yours] *F2;* your *F*   27 stain] *F;* strain *Theobald*   30 Your] *F2;* You *F*   32 solder] *F*
(soader)   38 has] *F2;* he's *F*

[3.5]   *Enter* ENOBARBUS *and* EROS [*,meeting*].

ENOBARBUS   How now, friend Eros?

EROS   There's strange news come, sir.

ENOBARBUS   What, man?

EROS   Caesar and Lepidus have made wars upon Pompey.

ENOBARBUS   This is old. What is the success?   5

EROS   Caesar, having made use of him in the wars
'gainst Pompey, presently denied him rivality; would
not let him partake in the glory of the action, and,
not resting here, accuses him of letters he had formerly wrote to Pompey; upon his own appeal, seizes   10
him. So the poor third is up, till death enlarge his
confine.

ENOBARBUS

Then, world, thou hast a pair of chaps, no more,
And throw between them all the food thou hast,

3.5 Location: Alexandria. Several historical events are compressed into this
scene, including Caesar's dismissal of
Lepidus from the triumvirate (6–11)
and the murder of Pompey (18–19).
The Roman world is now divided
between Caesar and Antony, who are
coming closer to outright conflict (13–
15, 19–20).

4 **Caesar … Pompey** See 3.4.3–4 and
note.

5 **success** 'that which happens in the
sequel … the upshot, result' (*OED
sb.* 1)

6–12 **Caesar … confine** These details
come from Simon Goulart's 'Life of
Octavius', appended to the 1603
edition of North's translation of Plutarch's *Lives*, which describes how
Lepidus betrayed Octavius in the
struggle against Pompey. Lepidus'
soldiers deserted him and went over
to Octavius, who then deprived him
of his place as a triumvir but spared

his life and allowed him to live privately in Italy (Spevack, 465). Shakespeare leaves out Lepidus' treachery
and thereby places Octavius in a less
favourable light.

7 **rivality** equality. See *OED* Rival
sb.[2] 1, 'one who strives to equal or
outdo another'.

9 **resting here** 'stopping at that'

10 **his own appeal** i.e. Caesar's own
accusation

11 **up** 'shut up, imprisoned' (Schmidt,
6). Compare Beaumont and Fletcher,
The Island Princess 5.1, 'You hear
Armusia's up, honest Arm: / Clapt
up in prison.'

11–12 **enlarge his confine** 'sets him free
from prison' (a development from *up*)

13 * **world** Manuscript 'world' is easily
misread as 'would' (see textual
footnotes), and Hanmer's emendation
has been generally adopted.
   chaps chops, jaws

3.5] *Capell*   0.1 *meeting*] *Capell*   13 world, thou hast] *Hanmer subst.*; would thou hadst *F*

>   They'll grind the one the other. Where's Antony?   15

EROS

>   He's walking in the garden, thus, and spurns
>   The rush that lies before him; cries, 'Fool Lepidus!',
>   And threats the throat of that his officer
>   That murdered Pompey.

ENOBARBUS   Our great navy's rigged.

EROS

>   For Italy and Caesar. More, Domitius: 20
>   My lord desires you presently. My news
>   I might have told hereafter.

ENOBARBUS   'Twill be naught,

>   But let it be. Bring me to Antony.

EROS

>   Come, sir.   *Exeunt.*

[3.6]   *Enter* AGRIPPA, MAECENAS *and* CAESAR.

CAESAR

Contemning Rome, he has done all this, and more

---

15 * **They'll ... the other** 'They'll
grind one another down.' F's omission of 'the one' is presumably a
simple oversight, and Capell's emendation has been generally accepted.

16 **thus** Eros demonstrates Antony's
gesture. Bevington points out that
there were rushes on the floor of the
Jacobean stage.
spurns kicks (*OED* Spurn *v.*[1] 2). See
2.5.63 and note.

18–19 **his ... Pompey** Shakespeare is
here drawing on Simon Goulart's
'Life of Octavius', which describes
how Antony's lieutenant Titius
'found the meanes to lay hands upon
Sextus Pompeius that was fled into the
Ile of SAMOS, and then fortie yeares
old: whom he put to death by Antonius commandment' (Spevack, 466).

Shakespeare omits Antony's responsibility for Pompey's death and thereby
puts him in a more favourable light
than did his source.

21–2 **My ... hereafter** 'I could have
told you my news later'

22 **naught** either 'something worthless'
or 'something disastrous'

3.6 Location: Rome. In this scene Shakespeare again closely follows Plutarch,
who describes how Antony's arro-
gance and contempt for the Roman
people gradually aroused their hostility towards him. It is designed as a
parallel to 3.4. Whereas in the earlier
scene Antony makes accusations
against Caesar, in this one Caesar
accuses Antony. The link between the
two scenes is Octavia, who during 3.5

---

15 the one the other] *Capell (Johnson);* the other *F*

3.6] *Capell*

In Alexandria. Here's the manner of't:
I'th' market-place, on a tribunal silvered,
Cleopatra and himself in chairs of gold
Were publicly enthroned. At the feet sat   5
Caesarion, whom they call my father's son,
And all the unlawful issue that their lust
Since then hath made between them. Unto her
He gave the stablishment of Egypt; made her
Of lower Syria, Cyprus, Lydia,   10
Absolute Queen.
MAECENAS   This in the public eye?
CAESAR
I'th' common showplace where they exercise.

is given time to travel from Athens
to Rome. In the first part of the scene
(1–39) Caesar reveals his motives for
turning against Antony, but these are
redoubled in the second part (40–65),
where the unannounced arrival of his
sister provides him with further cause
for animosity. The roll-call of Near
Eastern monarchs (70–7) creates the
impression that the 'kings o'th' earth'
are assembling for the decisive battle.
1–19 **Contemning ... so** According to
Plutarch these accusations were made
by Octavius 'unto the Senate, and
oftentimes accusing him to the whole
people and assembly in Rome: he
thereby stirred up all the Romanes
against [Antony]' (North, 291).
1 **Contemning** despising, treating with
contempt
3 **tribunal** 'originally a raised platform
in a Roman basilica on which the
seats of the magistrates were placed;
a dais' (*OED sb.* 1)
6 **Caesarion** Cleopatra's son by Julius
Caesar. See note to 2.2.238.
my father Julius Caesar, who
adopted Octavius, the son of his niece,
as his own son and made him his heir
7 **unlawful issue** Caesar gives the
impression that Antony and Cleopatra

produced many children but Plutarch
mentions only a daughter and two
sons.
9 **stablishment** confirmed possession
(*OED* 1b)
12–16 **I'th' ... Phoenicia** According to
Plutarch, Antony 'assembled all the
people in the show place, where
younge men doe exercise them selves,
and there upon a high tribunall silvered, he set two chayres of gold, the
one for him selfe, and the other for
Cleopatra, and lower chaires for his
children: then he openly published
before the assembly, that first of all
he did establish Cleopatra Queene of
Aegypt, of Cyprus, of Lydia, and of
the lower Syria, and at that time also,
Caesarion king of the same Realmes.
... Secondly he called the sonnes he
had by her, the kings of kings, and
gave Alexander for his portion,
Armenia, Media, and Parthia ... and
unto Ptolomy for his portion, Phen-
icia, Syria, and Cilicia' (North, 290).
In Beerbohm Tree's production and
John Caird's Royal Shakespeare
Company production in 1992 this
episode was actually shown on the
stage as Octavius Caesar spoke the
lines. See Introduction, p. 68n.

His sons he there proclaimed the kings of kings:
Great Media, Parthia and Armenia
He gave to Alexander; to Ptolemy he assigned   15
Syria, Cilicia and Phoenicia. She
In th'habiliments of the goddess Isis
That day appeared, and oft before gave audience,
As 'tis reported, so.

MAECENAS

Let Rome be thus informed.   20

AGRIPPA

Who, queasy with his insolence already,
Will their good thoughts call from him.

CAESAR

The people knows it, and have now received
His accusations.

AGRIPPA   Who does he accuse?

CAESAR

Caesar; and that having in Sicily   25
Sextus Pompeius spoiled, we had not rated him
His part o'th' isle. Then does he say he lent me

---

13 * **he there** F's 'hither' probably arises from a misreading of manuscript 'he there' as 'hether', a variant spelling of 'hither'.

16–19 **She ... so** 'Now for Cleopatra, she did not onely weare at that time (but at all other times els when she came abroad) the apparell of the goddesse Isis, and so gave audience unto all her subjects' (North, 291). On the significance of this goddess for Cleopatra and the play generally, see pp. 67–9.

17 **habiliments** attire, dress (*OED* 1)

19 **so** i.e. dressed as Isis

21 **queasy** sickened, nauseated

22 **call from** withdraw

23 **knows** one of many examples in F of verbs in which the third person plural ends in 's' (Abbott, 333)

25–31 **Caesar ... revenue** 'The chiefest poyntes of his accusations ... were these: First, that having spoyled Sextus Pompeius in Sicile, he did not give him his parte of the Ile. Secondly, that he did deteyne in his hands the shippes he lent him to make that warre. Thirdly, that having put Lepidus their companion and triumvirate out of his part of the Empire, and having deprived him of all honors: he retayned for him selfe the lands and revenues thereof, which had bene assigned unto him for his part' (North, 291).

26 **spoiled** plundered; 'to strip (persons) of goods or possessions by violence or force' (*OED* Spoil $v.^1$ 2)
rated allotted (*OED* Rate $v.^1$ 1b)

13 he there] *Johnson;* hither *F*   kings of kings] *Rowe;* King of Kings *F*   16 Cilicia and Phoenicia] *F (*Silicia, and Phoenetia*)*   17 habiliments] *F (*abiliments*)*   23 knows] *F;* know *F3*   25 Sicily] *F2;* Cicilie *F*

Some shipping, unrestored. Lastly, he frets
That Lepidus of the triumvirate
Should be deposed and, being, that we detain   30
All his revenue.
AGRIPPA   Sir, this should be answered.
CAESAR
'Tis done already, and the messenger gone.
I have told him Lepidus was grown too cruel,
That he his high authority abused
And did deserve his change. For what I have
    conquered,   35
I grant him part; but then in his Armenia
And other of his conquered kingdoms, I
Demand the like.
MAECENAS   He'll never yield to that.
CAESAR
Nor must not then be yielded to in this.

Enter OCTAVIA *with her train.*

OCTAVIA
Hail, Caesar, and my lord! Hail, most dear Caesar!   40
CAESAR
That ever I should call thee castaway!
OCTAVIA
You have not called me so, nor have you cause.
CAESAR
Why have you stolen upon us thus? You come not

---

31 **revenue** pronounced with the accent
on the second syllable
33–5 **I ... change** 'Octavius Caesar aunswered him againe: that for Lepidus,
he had in deede deposed him, and
taken his part of the Empire from
him, bicause he did overcruelly use
his authoritie' (North, 291).
39 SD **train** retinue. Compare 1.1.56
SD.

40 * **lord** This is F3's expansion of F's
'L'. Ridley's emendation, 'lords', is
plausible on the grounds that Octavia
is greeting Maecenas and Agrippa as
well as Caesar, but her attention
throughout this episode is focused
largely on her brother.
41 **castaway** cast off, rejected
43 **stolen** 'come furtively' (Schmidt)

29 triumvirate] *F* (Triumpherate)   30 and, being, that] *Theobald;* And being that, *F*   40 lord]
F3; L. *F;* lords *Ard²*

189

Like Caesar's sister. The wife of Antony
Should have an army for an usher, and   45
The neighs of horse to tell of her approach
Long ere she did appear. The trees by th' way
Should have borne men, and expectation fainted,
Longing for what it had not. Nay, the dust
Should have ascended to the roof of heaven,   50
Raised by your populous troops. But you are come
A market maid to Rome, and have prevented
The ostentation of our love which, left unshown,
Is often left unloved. We should have met you
By sea and land, supplying every stage   55
With an augmented greeting.

OCTAVIA   Good my lord,
To come thus was I not constrained, but did it
On my free will. My lord, Mark Antony,
Hearing that you prepared for war, acquainted
My grieved ear withal, whereon I begged   60
His pardon for return.

CAESAR   Which soon he granted,
Being an abstract 'tween his lust and him.

OCTAVIA
Do not say so, my lord.

CAESAR   I have eyes upon him,
And his affairs come to me on the wind.
Where is he now?

OCTAVIA   My lord, in Athens.

---

52 **prevented** forestalled
53 **ostentation** public display
54 **Is ... unloved** 'is often thought to be unfelt'
55 **stage** 'a place in which rest is taken on a journey; ... a regular stopping place on a stage-coach route where horses are changed and travellers taken up and set down' (*OED sb.* 8)
60 **grieved** grievèd
61 **pardon for** permission to

62 abstract] *F;* obstruct *Theobald*

62 * **abstract** 'the removal of something which stood in the way' (Ridley). See *OED ppl. a.* and *sb.* B, 'Something abstracted or drawn from others'. This F reading makes sense if *Being* is taken to refer to *return*. Theobald's emendation, 'obstruct', adopted by many editors, makes sense if *Being* is taken to refer to Octavia herself, who had stood between Antony and the satisfaction of his 'lust'.

CAESAR   No,   65

  My most wronged sister. Cleopatra hath
  Nodded him to her. He hath given his empire
  Up to a whore, who now are levying
  The kings o'th' earth for war. He hath assembled
  Bocchus the King of Libya, Archelaus   70
  Of Cappadocia, Philadelphos King
  Of Paphlagonia, the Thracian King Adallas,
  King Manchus of Arabia, King of Pont,
  Herod of Jewry, Mithridates King
  Of Comagene, Polemon and Amyntas,   75
  The Kings of Mede and Lycaonia,
  With a more larger list of sceptres.

OCTAVIA

  Ay me, most wretched,
  That have my heart parted betwixt two friends
  That does afflict each other!

CAESAR   Welcome hither.   80

  Your letters did withhold our breaking forth
  Till we perceived both how you were wrong led
  And we in negligent danger. Cheer your heart.

---

67 **Nodded him** 'summoned him with a nod'

68 **who now are** 'and they are now'

69–77 **He ... sceptres** This list, with some confusion of kings and kingdoms, is taken directly from Plutarch (North, 296). Cappadocia, Paphlagonia, Pontus and Lycaonia were in Asia Minor, Thrace lay between the Aegean and the Black Sea, Comagena was a part of Syria, and Media lay to the east of Armenia. See map, Fig. 1.

73 * **Manchus** This is North's spelling. F's 'Mauchus' may have arisen from the compositor's having replaced a

letter *u* in the *n* section of his case. Manuscript *n* can also be mistaken for *u*. This page was set by Compositor B, whose spelling of proper names was unreliable.

80 **does** 'do'; another example of a verb in which the third person plural ends in 's'. Compare *smells* (1.4.21) and *knows* (3.6.23).

81 **our breaking forth** 'my breaking free from restraint.' Compare *KL* 1.4.203–4, 'breaking forth / In rank and not-to-be-endured riots'.

83 **negligent danger** 'danger through negligence'

70 Archelaus] *Theobald; Archilaus F*   72 Adallas] *North, Rowe; Adullas F*   73 Manchus] *North, Alexander; Mauchus F*   75 Comagene] *Rowe;* Comagena *North;* Comageat *F*   Polemon] *North, Theobald; Polemen F*   76 Lycaonia] *North, F2;* Licoania *F*   80 does] *F;* doe *F2*   82 wrong led] *F;* wrong'd *Capell*

Be you not troubled with the time, which drives
O'er your content these strong necessities,   85
But let determined things to destiny
Hold unbewailed their way. Welcome to Rome,
Nothing more dear to me! You are abused
Beyond the mark of thought, and the high gods,
To do you justice, makes his ministers   90
Of us and those that love you. Best of comfort,
And ever welcome to us.

AGRIPPA   Welcome, lady.

MAECENAS
Welcome, dear madam.
Each heart in Rome does love and pity you.
Only th'adulterous Antony, most large   95
In his abominations, turns you off
And gives his potent regiment to a trull
That noises it against us.

OCTAVIA   Is it so, sir?

CAESAR
Most certain. Sister, welcome. Pray you

---

84 **Be ... time** Compare the proverb
'Never grieve for that you cannot
help' (Dent, G453).
time state of affairs

86–7 **let ... way** 'let predestined events
continue unlamented on their fixed
course'. Caesar sees himself as the
agent of destiny, as did Plutarch, who
declares that 'it was predestined that
the government of all the world
should fall into Octavius Caesar's
handes' (North, 292).

88 **abused** deceived

89 **mark** boundary, limit (*OED sb.*¹ 1).
There may also be connotations of the
'mark' or 'target' at which contestants
aim in the game of archery. Compare
MA 2.1.246–7, 'I stood like a man at
a mark, with a whole army shooting
at me.'

90–1 **makes ... us** 'make us their
agents'. *Makes* is another example of
the third person plural ending in 's'.
It may be, as Case suggests, that the
use of *his* rather than 'their' arises
from the fact that *makes* can be singular as well as plural but misreading
of manuscript 'thir' (= their) as 'his'
would also be easy.

95 **large** unrestrained (*OED a.* and *adv.*
11)

96 **turns you off** turns you away

97 **potent regiment** powerful authority.
OED cites no example before the
nineteenth century of 'potent' used in
the sense of sexual potency.
trull whore

98 **noises it** clamours, cries out (*OED*
Noise *v.* 3a)

90 makes his] *F;* make his *F2;* make their *Theobald;* make them *Capell*   91 Best] *F;* Be *Rowe*   96
abominations] *F (*abhominations)

Be ever known to patience. My dear'st sister!   100

Exeunt.

[3.7]   *Enter* CLEOPATRA *and* ENOBARBUS.

CLEOPATRA
I will be even with thee, doubt it not.
ENOBARBUS   But why, why, why?
CLEOPATRA
Thou hast forspoke my being in these wars
And say'st it is not fit.
ENOBARBUS   Well, is it, is it?
CLEOPATRA
Is't not denounced against us? Why should not we   5
Be there in person?
ENOBARBUS   Well, I could reply
If we should serve with horse and mares together,

---

100 **known to patience** acquainted with
patience, patient

3.7 Location: Actium on the north-west
coast of Greece. Antony's preparations for battle begin ominously
with Enobarbus' prediction that
Antony will be distracted by the presence of Cleopatra (10–15) and
Antony's foolhardy decision to fight
by sea against the advice of Enobarbus
(34–48) and the hardened soldier (61–
6). Canidius' comment (69–70) that
his leader is led and 'we are women's
men' prepares us for the flight from
battle in 3.10.

2 **why, why, why** Enobarbus' insistent
repetitions suggest that he and Cleopatra have been discussing this question before entering the stage.

3–19 **Thou ... behind** According to
Plutarch, Enobarbus persuaded
Antony to send Cleopatra back to
Egypt, but she bribed Canidius to

speak to Antony, who was persuaded
to let her stay (North, 291–2).

3 **forspoke** spoken against (*OED* For-
speak *v.* 3)

5 * **denounced** declared (*OED* De-
nounce *v.* 1). Plutarch writes that
Caesar declared war not against
Antony and Cleopatra but against
Cleopatra alone (North, 295). Cleopatra here argues that, since war has
been declared specifically on her, she
ought to be present. Rowe's emendation, which I have adopted, is the
best solution to this much-disputed
line, and it would be easy for the
compositor to mistake manuscript
'Is't' for 'If'. The F reading, Wilson
remarks, 'is barely intelligible, giving
at best a sense tortuous and obscure'.

6–9 * **Well ... horse** Although Johnson's marking of this speech as an
aside has been followed by most
editors (Wilson inserts the SD
'mutters'), it would be characteristic

3.7] *Capell*   5 Is't not denounced ... us?] *Rowe;* If not, denounc'd ... us, *F*   6–9 Well ... horse]
aside / Johnson

The horse were merely lost. The mares would bear
A soldier and his horse.

CLEOPATRA   What is't you say?

ENOBARBUS

Your presence needs must puzzle Antony,   10
Take from his heart, take from his brain, from's time
What should not then be spared. He is already
Traduced for levity, and 'tis said in Rome
That Photinus, an eunuch and your maids
Manage this war.

CLEOPATRA   Sink Rome, and their tongues rot   15
That speak against us! A charge we bear i'th' war,
And, as the president of my kingdom, will
Appear there for a man. Speak not against it!
I will not stay behind.

Enter ANTONY *and* CANIDIUS.

ENOBARBUS   Nay, I have done.
Here comes the Emperor.

of Enobarbus' frankness to deliver it
directly to Cleopatra. Her question
which follows it could be motivated
by indignation or incomprehension
and not just failure to hear.
8 **merely** 'absolutely' (Schmidt).
  Compare 47. Enobarbus may be
  making a pun on *merely* and 'marely'.
8–9 **bear ... horse** 'carry the soldiers
  and copulate with the stallions'
  (Jones)
10 **puzzle** 'embarrass with difficulties ...
  perplex' (*OED v.* 1a)
13 **Traduced** blamed, censured
14 * **Photinus, an eunuch** The F punctuation does not make it clear whether
  Photinus and the eunuch are one and
  the same. The corresponding passage
  in North's Plutarch, however, shows
  that the eunuch is Mardian: 'Caesar

sayde furthermore, that ... they that
should make warre with them should
be Mardian the Euenuke, Photinus,
and Iras a woman of Cleopatraes bedchamber' (North, 295). The question
is complicated by the fact that Photinus (called 'Pothinus' by North) was
also a eunuch.
16 **charge** cost, expense. Cleopatra, says
  Plutarch, supplied Antony with two
  hundred ships and an immense
  amount of money to support his army
  (North, 295). Moreover Canidius
  advised Antony that 'there was no
  reason to send her from this warre,
  who defraied so great a charge'
  (North, 291–2).
19 SD * CANIDIUS For the various spellings of this name, see textual notes to
  List of Roles, p. 89.

14 Photinus, an] *Delius; Photinus* an *F*   19 SD CANIDIUS] *North, Rowe; Camidias F*

ANTONY   Is it not strange, Canidius,   20
That from Tarentum and Brundusium
He could so quickly cut the Ionian sea
And take in Toryne? You have heard on't, sweet?
CLEOPATRA
Celerity is never more admired
Than by the negligent.
ANTONY   A good rebuke,   25
Which might have well becomed the best of men,
To taunt at slackness. Canidius, we
Will fight with him by sea.
CLEOPATRA   By sea – what else?
CANIDIUS
Why will my lord do so?
ANTONY   For that he dares us to't.
ENOBARBUS
So hath my lord dared him to single fight.   30
CANIDIUS
Ay, and to wage this battle at Pharsalia,
Where Caesar fought with Pompey. But these offers,
Which serve not for his vantage, he shakes off,

---

20 **Emperor** According to Plutarch,
Octavius deprived Antony of this title
at the same time as he declared war
on Cleopatra (North, 291) but, as
Jones points out, Antony is called
'Emperor' three times in this scene
and 'in that way his stature is insisted
on immediately before his fall'.

20–3 **Is it ... Toryne** 'Whilest Antonius
rode at anker, lying idely in harber at
the head of Actium, in the place
where the citie of Nicopolis standeth
at this present: Caesar had quickly
passed the sea Ionium, and taken ...
Toryne, before Antonius understoode
that he had taken shippe' (North,
297). Tarentum and Brundusium
(North's 'Brundusium') are present-
day Taranto and Brindisi in the heel

of Italy. Toryne was a small town
across the Ionian Sea (the Adriatic)
in Epirus, close to Actium, where
Antony's battle against Octavius was
fought. Caesar has led his army down
to the southern tip of Italy and across
the Adriatic to the west coast of
Greece.

23 **take in** occupy, as in 1.1.24

24 **admired** wondered at

29 **For that** because

31 **Pharsalia** the plain in Thessaly
where Julius Caesar fought his decisive battle against Pompey the Great.
Antony challenged Octavius to 'fight
a battell with him in the fields of
Pharsalia, as Julius Caesar, and
Pompey had done before' (North,
297).

20, 27, 57, 79 Canidius] *North, Rowe;* Camidius *F*   21 Brundusium] *North, F2;* Brandusium
F   23 Toryne] *North, F2;* Troine *F*

And so should you.

ENOBARBUS   Your ships are not well manned,
Your mariners are muleteers, reapers, people   35
Engrossed by swift impress. In Caesar's fleet
Are those that often have 'gainst Pompey fought;
Their ships are yare, yours heavy. No disgrace
Shall fall you for refusing him at sea,
Being prepared for land.

ANTONY   By sea, by sea.   40
ENOBARBUS
Most worthy sir, you therein throw away
The absolute soldiership you have by land;
Distract your army, which doth most consist
Of war-marked footmen; leave unexecuted
Your own renowned knowledge; quite forgo   45
The way which promises assurance; and
Give up yourself merely to chance and hazard
From firm security.

ANTONY   I'll fight at sea.
CLEOPATRA
I have sixty sails, Caesar none better.
ANTONY
Our overplus of shipping will we burn,   50

35 * **muleteers** F's 'Militers' arose from a minim error for 'Muliters' (Wilson). A *muleteer* is a person who drives a mulet or small mule. Plutarch says that because Antony was short of seamen his captains conscripted 'all sortes of men out of Graece ... as travellers, muletters, reapers, harvest men, and younge boyes, and yet could they not sufficiently furnishe his gallies' (North, 297).

36 **Engrossed** gathered together (*OED* Engross *v.* 4)
impress conscription, compulsory enlistment

38 **yare** light, and hence easily manageable (*OED a.* 2b)

43 **Distract** divide, fragment (*OED v.*

1). In Plutarch Canidius argues that Antony 'would weaken his army by deviding them into shippes' (North, 298).

44 **footmen** foot soldiers
unexecuted unused

45 **renowned** renownèd

46 **assurance** certainty of success, as in *Mac* 4.1.83, 'I'll make assurance double sure.'

47 **merely** wholly

50 **overplus** surplus. Plutarch says that when Antony 'had determined to fight by sea, he set all the other shippes a fire, but three score shippes of Aegypt, and reserved onely but the best and greatest gallies' (North, 299). Bevington explains that he destroyed

35 muleteers] *F2 (*Muliters); Militers *F*

And with the rest full-manned, from th'head of
   Actium
Beat th'approaching Caesar. But if we fail,
We then can do't at land.

Enter a Messenger.

Thy business?

MESSENGER

The news is true, my lord; he is descried.
Caesar has taken Toryne.   55

ANTONY

Can he be there in person? 'Tis impossible;
Strange that his power should be. Canidius,
Our nineteen legions thou shalt hold by land
And our twelve thousand horse. We'll to our ship.
Away, my Thetis!

Enter a Soldier.

How now, worthy soldier?   60

SOLDIER

O noble Emperor, do not fight by sea.

his surplus ships so that he could
fully man the rest. On his shortage of
seamen, see note to 35.

51 **head** headland, promontory. North
writes of the 'harber at the head of
Actium' (297).

53 **business** presumably spoken with
three syllables, 'bus-i-ness'

57 **power** forces, as at 76

60 **Thetis** a sea-goddess and the mother
of Achilles. The term is appropriate
for Cleopatra because of her support
for the expedition by sea and her
association with a great warrior.
Thetis 'was often confused with her
grandmother Tethys, greatest of sea-
deities, wife of Oceanus, mother of
the Nile and other rivers' (Lloyd,
92). If 'Tethys' was what Shakespeare

meant, the name was again appropriate, since Tethys was one of the
names of Isis. On the significance of
the goddess Isis, see pp. 67–9.

SD **Soldier** Barroll ('Scarrus') argues
that he is the same character as Scarus
in 3.10 and 4.7–8.

61–6 **O noble ... foot** Plutarch
describes how a captain 'that had
served Antonius in many battels and
conflicts, and had all his body hacked
and cut ... cryed out unto him, and
sayd: O noble Emperor, how
commeth it to passe that you trust to
these vile brittle shippes? what, doe
you mistrust these woundes of myne,
and this sword? let the Aegyptians
and Phaenicians fight by sea, and set
us on the maine land, where we use

Trust not to rotten planks. Do you misdoubt
This sword and these my wounds? Let th'Egyptians
And the Phoenicians go a-ducking; we
Have used to conquer standing on the earth   65
And fighting foot to foot.

ANTONY   Well, well, away!
        Exeunt Antony, Cleopatra and Enobarbus.

SOLDIER
By Hercules, I think I am i'th' right.

CANIDIUS
Soldier, thou art. But his whole action grows
Not in the power on't. So our leader's led,
And we are women's men.

SOLDIER   You keep by land   70
The legions and the horse whole, do you not?

CANIDIUS
Marcus Octavius, Marcus Justeius,
Publicola and Caelius are for sea,
But we keep whole by land. This speed of Caesar's
Carries beyond belief.

SOLDIER   While he was yet in Rome,   75

to conquer, or to be slayne on our feete' (North, 299).

62 **misdoubt** mistrust; lack confidence in (*OED v.* 2)

64 **Phoenicians** a seafaring people who lived on the eastern shore of the Mediterranean in what is now Lebanon
go a-ducking get wet; fall into the sea

65 **Have used** are accustomed

66 **Well, well, away** 'Antonius passed by him, and sayd never a word, but only beckoned to him with his hand and head, as though he willed him to be of good corage, although in deede he had no great corage him selfe' (North, 299).

68–9 **his ... on't** 'his whole strategy is founded not on those resources in which he is strong'

71 **horse whole** cavalry undivided

72 SP * CANIDIUS Richard Proudfoot points out, privately, that the compositor's error in ascribing this speech to *Ven.* (see textual notes) presumably arose from its being his first encounter with the name as he started to set quire yy from the middle outwards.

72–3 **Marcus ... Caelius** The names are taken from Plutarch.

75 **Carries** shoots him forward. 'A bow, a gun or the like is said to *carry* an arrow, a ball, or other missile to a specified distance' (*OED* Carry *vb.* 9).

69 leader's led] *Theobald;* Leaders leade *F*   72 SP CANIDIUS] *Pope; Ven. F*   Justeius] *North, Theobald; Iusteus F*   73 Caelius] *North, Theobald; Celius F*

His power went out in such distractions as
Beguiled all spies.

CANIDIUS   Who's his lieutenant, hear you?

SOLDIER
They say one Taurus.

CANIDIUS   Well I know the man.

Enter a Messenger.

MESSENGER
The Emperor calls Canidius.

CANIDIUS
With news the time's in labour, and throws forth   80
Each minute some.   *Exeunt.*

[3.8]   *Enter* CAESAR [*and* TAURUS] *with his army, marching.*

CAESAR   Taurus!
TAURUS   My lord?
CAESAR
Strike not by land; keep whole; provoke not battle

---

76 **power** troops
   distractions divisions, separate
   groups (*OED sb.* 1b)
77 **Beguiled all spies** deceived all
   observers
78 **Taurus** a general, according to Plutarch, in charge of Caesar's land forces
   (North, 299). The reference to him
   here prepares us for his entrance at
   the beginning of the next scene.
80–1 * **With ... some** 'Every minute
   more news is delivered.' This reference to childbearing supports
   Rowe's emendation of F's 'with
   Labour' to *in labour.*

3.8 Location, scenes 8–10: Actium. In

these scenes depicting the battle no
fighting takes place on the stage. Since
it was a sea battle and involved thousands of men, it had to be left to
the imagination. Hence sound effects
were important and in the early performances the full battery of drums
and trumpets was no doubt brought
into action. Hodges (82) suggests that
when it was performed at the Globe
a cannon just outside the theatre was
fired. In several nineteenth-century
productions an actual sea fight was
mounted on the stage, usually to great
acclaim (see pp. 17–18).

3 **whole** intact. Compare 3.7.74.

78 Taurus] *North, Theobald;* Towrus *F passim*   Well I] *Rowe³;* Well, I *F*   80 in] *Rowe;* with
F   throws] *F (*throwes*);* throes *Theobald*

3.8] *Capell*   0.1 *and* TAURUS] *Capell subst.*

199

Till we have done at sea. Do not exceed
The prescript of this scroll. [*Gives him a scroll.*] Our   5
    fortune lies
Upon this jump.   *Exeunt.*

[3.9]   *Enter* ANTONY *and* ENOBARBUS.

ANTONY
Set we our squadrons on yond side o'th' hill
In eye of Caesar's battle, from which place
We may the number of the ships behold
And so proceed accordingly.   *Exeunt.*

[**3.10**] CANIDIUS *marcheth with his land army one way over the
stage, and* TAURUS, *the Lieutenant of Caesar, the other way. After
their going in, is heard the noise of a sea fight.*

Alarum. Enter ENOBARBUS.

ENOBARBUS
Naught, naught, all naught! I can behold no longer!
Th'Antoniad, the Egyptian admiral,

5 **prescript** instructions
6 **jump** venture, hazard (*OED sb.*[1] 6b),
the only occurrence of this noun in
Shakespeare's works. The verb is used
in a similar sense in *Mac* 1.7.7, 'We'd
jump the life to come.'

2 **eye** sight
battle main army, battalion

3.10 Shakespeare turns the limited theatrical resources of his theatre to his
advantage. He creates the Battle of
Actium by off-stage sounds and then
satisfies our curiosity by telling us,
first through Enobarbus, then through

Scarus, what has actually occurred.
No sooner has Antony fled after Cleopatra than his supporters begin to
abandon him. In this short scene we
learn that six kings have already left
him and that Canidius, the man in
charge of the land army, intends to
go over to the enemy (33–5). As the
scene ends, Enobarbus begins to consider the desertion he will carry out
in Act 4.
1 **Naught** lost, ruined (*OED sb.* B.4).
Compare *Cor* 3.1.229–30, 'Be gone,
away! / All will be naught else.'
2 **admiral** flagship. 'The Admirall
galley of Cleopatra, was called Anton-
iade' (North, 296).

5 SD] *Oxf subst.*   6 SD *Exeunt*] *F (exit)*

3.9] *Dyce*   4 SD *Exeunt*] *F (exit)*

3.10] *Dyce*   0.4 ENOBARBUS] *Rowe*[3]; *Enobarbus and Scarus F*

200

With all their sixty, fly and turn the rudder.
To see't mine eyes are blasted.

Enter SCARUS.

SCARUS   Gods and goddesses!
All the whole synod of them!
ENOBARBUS   What's thy passion?   5
SCARUS
The greater cantle of the world is lost
With very ignorance. We have kissed away
Kingdoms and provinces.
ENOBARBUS   How appears the fight?
SCARUS
On our side, like the tokened pestilence
Where death is sure. Yon ribaudred nag of Egypt –   10

4 **blasted** Shakespeare uses the verb 'blast' ('to strike with any pernicious influence' (Schmidt)) for a variety of different actions. Compare 3.13.110. Here it presumably means 'blinded'.

5 **synod** assembly. The word is almost always used, as here, of a gathering of all the gods. Compare *Cor* 5.2.68–9, 'The glorious gods sit in hourly synod about thy particular prosperity.'

6 **cantle** 'a segment of a circle or sphere' (*OED sb.* 3c)

7 **With ... ignorance** 'through sheer stupidity'. Compare *Oth* 3.3.404–5, 'fools as gross / As ignorance made drunk'.

9 **tokened pestilence** i.e. plague spot. The appearance of certain red spots on the body, commonly known as 'God's tokens', was a symptom of infection by the plague. Compare *LLL* 5.2.421–3, 'They have the plague, and caught it of your eyes. / These lords are visited; you are not free, / For the Lord's tokens on you do I see.'

10–15 **Yon ... flies** 'Howbeit the battell

was yet of even hand, and the victorie doubtfull, being indifferent to both: when sodainely they saw the three score shippes of Cleopatra busie about their yard masts, and hoysing saile to flie. So they fled through the middest of them that were in fight' (North, 301).

10 * **ribaudred** the only known occurrence of this word, described in *OED* as 'a corrupt reading in Shakespeare ... which has not yet been satisfactorily emended'. There has been no lack of emendations, the simplest of which is Rowe's 'ribauld', one of various spellings of 'ribald' (or 'licentious') of which *OED* gives several examples. This has the advantage of producing the ten syllables needed for the verse line. Cairncross argues that the manuscript wording was 'Yonder ribaud Nagge' and that the 'der' of 'Yonder' were accidentally transferred by the compositor to the end of 'ribaud' to produce 'Yon ribaudred Nagge'. Another plausible emendation is Steevens's 'ribald-rid', meaning 'ridden by a ribald man (or

10 ribaudred] *F;* ribauldred *F4;* ribauld *Rowe;* ribald-rid *Steevens;* riband-red *Oxf*

201

Whom leprosy o'ertake! – i'th' midst o'th' fight
When vantage like a pair of twins appeared
Both as the same – or, rather, ours the elder –
The breeze upon her, like a cow in June,
Hoists sails and flies.   15

ENOBARBUS
    That I beheld.
Mine eyes did sicken at the sight and could not
Endure a further view.

SCARUS   She once being loofed,
The noble ruin of her magic, Antony,
Claps on his sea-wing and, like a doting mallard,   20
Leaving the fight in height, flies after her.
I never saw an action of such shame.
Experience, manhood, honour, ne'er before
Did violate so itself.

ENOBARBUS   Alack, alack!

men)'. Schanzer ('Three notes', 22), supporting this emendation, connects it with Enobarbus' prediction that 'The mares would bear / A soldier and his horse' (3.7.8–9). Those editors who retain *ribaudred* without emendation (as here) tend to see it as a past participle. Furness defines it as 'made up of, or composed of ribaldry' and Sisson (2.269) as 'rotted by ribaldry and licence'. This last interpretation is supported by the allusions to the plague in the previous line and leprosy in the following one.

nag whore. Compare *2H4* 2.4.191, 'Know we not Galloway nags?' where Pistol appears to be referring to Doll Tearsheet. On this passage E. H. Sugden comments, 'Doll is like a Galloway nag because anyone may ride her'.

11 **leprosy** regarded as a venereal disease. Compare *Tim* 4.1.30, 4.3.36, and Ford, *'Tis Pity She's a Whore*, 1.1.74, 'Beg heaven to cleanse the leprosy of lust.'

12 **vantage** advantage, chance of success
13 **elder** i.e. therefore stronger. Cf. *JC* 2.2.46–7, 'We are two lions litter'd in one day, / And I the elder and more terrible.'
14 **breeze** gadfly, an insect which attacks cattle. Compare *TC* 1.3.48–9, 'The herd hath more annoyance by the breeze / Than by the tiger.'
18 **loofed** luffed; a nautical term meaning 'to bring the head of a ship nearer to the wind' (*OED* Luff *v.* 2). In its context, however, this does not appear to be the correct sense, for Cleopatra has already 'hoist sail' and flown. The meaning of *loofed* seems to be closer to 'aloof', another nautical term closely related to 'loof' which *OED* (Aloof *adv.* 3) defines as 'away at some distance'.
20 **Claps ... sea-wing** 'hoists his sails', a metaphor which leads naturally into *doting mallard*

14 June] *F2;* Inne *F*

Enter CANIDIUS.

CANIDIUS

Our fortune on the sea is out of breath   25
And sinks most lamentably. Had our general
Been what he knew – himself – it had gone well.
Oh, he has given example for our flight
Most grossly by his own!

ENOBARBUS   Ay, are you thereabouts?
Why then, good night indeed.   30

CANIDIUS

Toward Peloponnesus are they fled.

SCARUS

'Tis easy to't, and there I will attend
What further comes.

CANIDIUS   To Caesar will I render
My legions and my horse. Six kings already
Show me the way of yielding.

ENOBARBUS   I'll yet follow   35
The wounded chance of Antony, though my reason

---

27 **what ... himself** 'been what he
knew himself to be'. Plutarch comments on this episode, 'There Antonius shewed plainely, that he had not
onely lost the corage and hart of an
Emperor, but also of a valliant man,
and that he was not his owne man:
(proving that true which an old man
spake in myrth, that the soule of a
lover lived in another body, and not
in his owne)' (North, 301).
29 **grossly** flagrantly
are you thereabouts? 'is that what
you're thinking?'
30 **good night indeed** 'that really is the
end'
32 **'Tis ... to't** 'It's easy to get there'
attend wait and see (*OED v.* 13c)
33 **render** give up, hand over, as in 'She
rendered life' (4.14.33)
34 **legions ... horse** foot soldiers and

cavalry
34–5 **Six ... yielding** 'There were
certen kings also that forsooke him,
and turned on Caesars side' (North,
298). Historically Canidius did not
desert to Caesar, nor does Plutarch
say specifically that he did so: 'In the
ende Canidius, Antonius Lieuetenant,
flying by night, and forsaking his
campe: when [his soldiers] saw them
selves thus destitute of their heads and
leaders, they yelded themselves unto
the stronger' (North, 303). In fact Canidius fled back to Antony (*OCD*).
Shakespeare may have either, understandably, misunderstood North's
translation or invented Canidius'
desertion as the first of a series which
culminates in that of Enobarbus.
36 **wounded chance** 'broken fortunes'

27 knew – himself –] *this edn;* knew himselfe, *F*   28 he] *F2;* his *F*

Sits in the wind against me.

[*Exit at one door Canidius, at the other Scarus and Enobarbus.*]

[3.11]　　　　　*Enter* ANTONY *with Attendants.*

ANTONY

Hark! The land bids me tread no more upon't;
It is ashamed to bear me. Friends, come hither.
I am so lated in the world that I
Have lost my way for ever. I have a ship
Laden with gold. Take that, divide it. Fly　　　　　　　　　5
And make your peace with Caesar.

ALL　　　　　　　　　　　　　　　　　Fly? Not we.

ANTONY

I have fled myself and have instructed cowards
To run and show their shoulders. Friends, be gone.
I have myself resolved upon a course

---

37 **Sits ... me** 'urges me against it', a sailing metaphor growing out of those in 15–21. Shakespeare quite often uses *sit* with reference to the direction of the wind, as in *Ham* 1.3.56, 'The wind sits in the shoulder of your sail.'
SD **Exit ... Enobarbus** Canidius goes off towards Caesar and Scarus and Enobarbus towards Antony. Capell gives an exit to Canidius at 35 and Bevington suggests that, if this emendation is adopted, Scarus should exit at 33, leaving Enobarbus alone for the final three lines.

3.11 Location: unspecific. Plutarch says that this episode took place in 'Taenarus' (Taenarum), the central peninsula of southern Peloponnesus to which, we have been told (3.10.31), Antony and his men have fled. The impression that the discredited

Antony is being abandoned by his followers grows in this scene as he tells his attendants to leave him. His realization that he must now ignominiously bargain for terms with Caesar prepares us for the Ambassador's mission in the next scene. Antony recovers sufficiently to adopt a stoical defiance as the episode concludes.

3 **lated** belated; 'overcome by the lateness of the night; hence, overtaken by darkness, benighted' (*OED* Belated *ppl. a.* 1)

4–24 **I ... by** In Plutarch's account Antony 'toke one of his carects or hulks loden with gold and silver, and other rich cariage, and gave it unto his friends: commaunding them to depart, and to seeke to save them selves. They aunswered him weeping, that they would nether [*sic*] doe it, nor yet forsake him' (North, 302).

---

37 SD *Exit ... Enobarbus*] *this edn; Exeunt severally / Theobald*

3.11] *Dyce*

Which has no need of you. Be gone.   10
My treasure's in the harbour. Take it. Oh,
I followed that I blush to look upon.
My very hairs do mutiny, for the white
Reprove the brown for rashness, and they them
For fear and doting. Friends, be gone. You shall   15
Have letters from me to some friends that will
Sweep your way for you. Pray you, look not sad
Nor make replies of loathness; take the hint
Which my despair proclaims. Let that be left
Which leaves itself. To the sea-side straightway.   20
I will possess you of that ship and treasure.
Leave me, I pray, a little – pray you, now;
Nay, do so; for indeed I have lost command;
Therefore, I pray you. I'll see you by and by.
          [*Exeunt Attendants. Antony*] *sits down.*

Enter CLEOPATRA *led by* CHARMIAN, [IRAS] *and* EROS.

EROS   Nay, gentle madam, to him! Comfort him.   25
IRAS   Do, most dear queen.
CHARMIAN   Do? Why, what else?
CLEOPATRA   Let me sit down. O, Juno!
ANTONY   No, no, no, no, no!

---

12 **that** 'that which' (i.e. Cleopatra)
13–15 **My ... doting** *Doting* means 'infatuation' (compare *dotage* 1.1.1). Ridley compares these lines with 4.8.19–20 where Antony is in a very different mood.
17 **Sweep your way** 'clear your path'. Compare *Ham* 3.4.202–4, 'my two schoolfellows ... must sweep my way.'
18 **loathness** unwillingness. Compare *Tem* 2.1.131, 'Weigh'd between loathness and obedience'.
hint opportunity. Compare 3.4.9 and note.

19 **that** 'i.e. Antony (who is no longer himself)' (Jones)
23 **command** used in antithesis to 'pray'. He can no longer command his men and therefore begs them.
24 SD *sits down* Plutarch describes how Antony, having gone alongside Cleopatra's galley, was hoisted up into it and 'went and sate down alone in the prowe of his shippe, and said never a word, clapping his head betwene both his hands' (North, 301).

19–20 that ... leaves itself] *Capell;* them ... leaves it selfe *F;* them ... leave themselves *Rowe²*   24.1 *Exeunt ... Antony*] *Capell subst.*   24.2 IRAS] *Pope subst.*

EROS   See you here, sir?   30
ANTONY   O fie, fie, fie!
CHARMIAN   Madam!
IRAS   Madam! O, good empress!
EROS   Sir, sir!
ANTONY

    Yes, my lord, yes. He at Philippi kept   35
    His sword e'en like a dancer, while I struck
    The lean and wrinkled Cassius, and 'twas I
    That the mad Brutus ended. He alone
    Dealt on lieutenantry, and no practice had
    In the brave squares of war. Yet now – no matter.   40
CLEOPATRA   Ah, stand by.
EROS   The Queen, my lord! The Queen!
IRAS

    Go to him, madam; speak to him.
    He is unqualitied with very shame.
CLEOPATRA

    Well then, sustain me. Oh!   45

30–1 **See ... fie** Antony is so lost in remorse that he is unaware of Cleopatra's presence and fails to hear Eros' question. At 35 he seems unaware who Eros is.

31 **fie** an expression of contempt (for himself)

35 **kept** i.e. kept it in the scabbard. Compare *Oth* 1.2.59, 'Keep up your bright swords'. A dancer would wear a sword for ornament, not use. Plutarch says that when Antony and Octavius fought against Brutus and Cassius at Philippi, 'Caesar did no great matter, but Antonius had alway the upper hand, and did all' (North, 270). Compare *AW* 2.1.32–3, 'no sword worn / But one to dance with.'

36–8 **I struck ... ended** In denigrating Octavius, Antony exaggerates his own personal achievements. He did not

kill Cassius or Brutus, both of whom committed suicide (*JC* 5.3; 5.5).

37 **lean ... Cassius** Julius Caesar remarks that Cassius has a 'lean and hungry look' (*JC* 1.2.194).

38 **mad Brutus** In *JC* Brutus shows no symptoms of madness but this is presumably Antony's and not Shakespeare's opinion of him.
    alone 'was the only one who'

39 **Dealt on lieutenantry** i.e. 'made his subordinates do his fighting for him'

40 **brave** splendid
    squares disputes, contests (*OED sb.* 17)

41 **stand by** 'stand aside', as in *TS* 1.1.47 SD. In view of 'sustain me' at l. 45, it seems that Cleopatra is about to faint.

44 **unqualitied** unmanned; not himself
    very complete, absolute

38 mad] *F;* sad *Hanmer*   44 He is] *F2;* Hee's *F*

EROS

Most noble sir, arise. The Queen approaches.
Her head's declined, and death will seize her but
Your comfort makes the rescue.

ANTONY

I have offended reputation,
A most unnoble swerving.

EROS   Sir, the Queen!   50

ANTONY

O, whither hast thou led me, Egypt? See
How I convey my shame out of thine eyes
By looking back what I have left behind
'Stroyed in dishonour.

CLEOPATRA   O, my lord, my lord,
Forgive my fearful sails! I little thought   55
You would have followed.

ANTONY   Egypt, thou knewst too well
My heart was to thy rudder tied by th' strings
And thou shouldst tow me after. O'er my spirit
Thy full supremacy thou knewst, and that
Thy beck might from the bidding of the gods   60
Command me.

CLEOPATRA   Oh, my pardon!

ANTONY   Now I must

---

47 **but** unless
50 **most ... swerving** *Swerving* implies deviation from a norm or ideal. Antony 'stresses *unnoble* in dazed reply to Eros's "Most noble sir"' (Wilson).
51–4 **See ... dishonour** 'See how I try to cover up my shame from your sight by brooding on the ruins of my past' (Wilson).
53 **looking back** looking back at
57 **strings** heart strings. Antony expresses his total dependency on

Cleopatra by imagining that he is tied to her by the tendons or nerves which were thought to brace and sustain the heart.
58 * **shouldst tow** F's 'stowe' erroneously repeats the 'st' of the previous word, a not uncommon error in manuscript.
60 **beck** mute gesture. Antony contrasts the power of Cleopatra's silent gesture (which *commands* him) with that of the gods' spoken *bidding*.

47 seize] *F2;* cease *F*   51 whither] *F (*whether*)*   58 tow] *Rowe;* stowe *F*   59 Thy] *Theobald²;* The *F*

To the young man send humble treaties; dodge
And palter in the shifts of lowness, who
With half the bulk o'th' world played as I pleased,
Making and marring fortunes. You did know   65
How much you were my conqueror, and that
My sword, made weak by my affection, would
Obey it on all cause.

CLEOPATRA   Pardon, pardon!

ANTONY

Fall not a tear, I say; one of them rates
All that is won and lost. Give me a kiss. [*They kiss.*]   70
Even this repays me.
We sent our schoolmaster. Is 'a come back?
Love, I am full of lead. Some wine
Within there and our viands! Fortune knows
We scorn her most when most she offers blows.   75

                              Exeunt.

[**3.12**]   *Enter* CAESAR, AGRIPPA, DOLABELLA, [*and*
            THIDIAS] *with others.*

62 **young man** Compare 'boy Caesar' 3.13.17.
   treaties entreaties, requests (*OED sb.* 4)
   dodge 'haggle about terms' (*OED v.* 2)
63 **palter** 'shuffle or haggle in bargaining' (*OED* 3b)
   shifts of lowness tricks of a man brought low
65 **Making and marring** 'To make and mar' was a proverbial expression (Dent, M48). *Played* in the previous line develops into this metaphor from gambling in which fortunes are won and lost.
67 **affection** passion
68 **on all cause** 'whatever the reason'

69 **Fall ... tear** 'Do not let a tear fall'. Compare *Luc* 1551, 'For every tear he falls a Trojan bleeds.'
   rates is worth
71 **Even this** 'this alone' (Schmidt)
72 **schoolmaster** Plutarch identifies him as 'Euphronius the schoolemaister of their children' whom they had to send 'bicause they had no other men of estimacion about them, for that some were fledde, and those that remained, they did not greatly trust them' (North, 305–6).
   a he
73 **full of lead** heavy, sorrowful

3.12 Location: Caesar's camp outside Alexandria. This scene forms a par-

70 SD] *Oxf subst.*

3.12] *Dyce*   0.1 DOLABELLA, *and* THIDIAS] *Rowe; and Dolabello F*

CAESAR

Let him appear that's come from Antony.
Know you him?

DOLABELLA   Caesar, 'tis his schoolmaster;
An argument that he is plucked, when hither
He sends so poor a pinion of his wing,
Which had superfluous kings for messengers   5
Not many moons gone by.

Enter Ambassador *from Antony.*

CAESAR   Approach, and speak.

AMBASSADOR

Such as I am, I come from Antony.
I was of late as petty to his ends
As is the morn-dew on the myrtle leaf
To his grand sea.

CAESAR   Be't so. Declare thine office.   10

AMBASSADOR

Lord of his fortunes he salutes thee, and
Requires to live in Egypt; which not granted,
He lessens his requests and to thee sues

allel and contrast with the next one
in which Caesar's Ambassador comes
to Antony and Cleopatra and is given
a very different reception. The lowly
status of Antony's Ambassador adds
to the impression, already created in
3.10 and 3.11, that his followers are
all leaving him and that, now he is
defeated, he must 'dodge / And palter
in the shifts of lowness' (3.11.62–3).
Once their emissaries have returned
empty-handed, the opponents are left
with no means of resolving their conflict other than by battle. In rejecting
Antony's request but acceding to
Cleopatra's, Caesar plans to set them
against each other and, in the next
scene, he succeeds.

3 **argument** sign, evidence
4 **pinion** feather; specifically the out-
ermost feather of a bird's wing (*OED*

sb. 1). The metaphor develops out of
plucked in the previous line.
5 **Which** who
kings for messengers Compare
3.13.96–7 and 4.2.13.
6 SD **Ambassador** i.e. the schoolmaster
8 **petty ... ends** 'insignificant to his
purposes'
10 **his ... sea** 'the sea from which the
dew-drop is exhaled' (Steevens), or,
more probably, 'the great sea which
is Antony' (Ridley)
12, 28 **Requires** 'requests' (*OED v.* 2)
and not 'demands' (*OED* 4)
13 * **lessens** Some editors retain F's
'lessons', meaning 'schools' or 'disci-
plines', an appropriate word for a
schoolmaster. F2's *lessens*, however, is
a more likely reading.

13 lessens] *F2;* Lessons *F*

To let him breathe between the heavens and earth,
A private man in Athens. This for him.   15
Next, Cleopatra does confess thy greatness,
Submits her to thy might, and of thee craves
The circle of the Ptolemies for her heirs,
Now hazarded to thy grace.

CAESAR   For Antony,
I have no ears to his request. The Queen   20
Of audience nor desire shall fail, so she
From Egypt drive her all-disgraced friend
Or take his life there. This if she perform,
She shall not sue unheard. So to them both.

AMBASSADOR
Fortune pursue thee!

CAESAR   Bring him through the bands.   25
                              [*Exit Ambassador, attended.*]
[*to Thidias*]
To try thy eloquence now 'tis time. Dispatch.
From Antony win Cleopatra; promise,
And in our name, what she requires; add more,
From thine invention, offers. Women are not
In their best fortunes strong, but want will perjure   30

14–19 **To ... grace** 'They sent Ambassadors unto Octavius Caesar ... Cleopatra requesting the realme of Aegypt for her children, and Antonius praying that he might be suffered to live at Athens like a private man, if Caesar would not let him remaine in Aegypt' (North, 305).
18 **circle ... Ptolemies** 'crown of the kings of Egypt'
19 **hazarded ... grace** 'dependent for its fate on your favour.' A 'hazard' was a venture or risk (as in the game of dice of the same name) and the implication is that the crown has been staked and will be kept or lost depending on the extent of Caesar's generosity.

19–24 **For Antony ... unheard** 'Caesar would not graunt unto Antonius requests: but for Cleopatra, he made her aunswere, that he woulde deny her nothing reasonable, so that she would either put Antonius to death, or drive him out of her contrie' (North, 306).
21 **Of ... fail** 'shall be given a hearing and have her requests granted'
so provided that
22 **disgraced** disgracèd
25 **Bring ... bands** 'conduct him through the lines (of troops)'
28 **in our name** 'on my authority'
30 **In ... fortunes** 'even when they are most lucky'
30–1 **want ... vestal** 'need will make

25 SD] *Capell subst.*   26 SD] *Rowe*

The ne'er-touch'd vestal. Try thy cunning, Thidias;
Make thine own edict for thy pains, which we
Will answer as a law.

THIDIAS   Caesar, I go.

CAESAR

Observe how Antony becomes his flaw,
And what thou think'st his very action speaks   35
In every power that moves.

THIDIAS   Caesar, I shall.   *Exeunt.*

[3.13]   *Enter* CLEOPATRA, ENOBARBUS, CHARMIAN *and* IRAS.

CLEOPATRA

What shall we do, Enobarbus?

ENOBARBUS   Think, and die.

CLEOPATRA

Is Antony or we in fault for this?

ENOBARBUS

Antony only, that would make his will
Lord of his reason. What though you fled

---

the immaculate vestal virgin break her
vows' (Jones)
32 **Make ... pains** 'Decide for yourself
how much you should be paid for
your trouble'
33 **answer ... law** 'pay as if required by
law' (*OED* Answer *v.* 7)
34 **becomes his flaw** 'bears himself in
his misfortune'
35 **speaks** reveals
36 **power that moves** 'motion he
makes' (Riv)

3.13 Location: Alexandria. In the first
part of the scene a contrast is set up
between Antony's reception of his
own Ambassador and Cleopatra's
response to Caesar's. Whereas he is

defiant, she seems to be accom-
modating, and these different
responses indicate that Caesar's plan
to create a split between them is suc-
ceeding. Antony's challenge to Caesar
to meet him in single combat (25–8)
is a rashly heroic gesture (compare
3.7.30). His fury at discovering Cleopatra with Thidias arises from his
belief that she too has betrayed him,
and, in the last speech of the scene,
Enobarbus finally resolves to desert
him.
1 **Think** i.e. 'give way to despondency'.
In *Ham* 3.1.84, as Ridley points out,
melancholy is characterized as 'the
pale cast of thought'.
3 **will** desire, sexual passion

3.13] *Dyce*

From that great face of war, whose several ranges   5
Frighted each other? Why should he follow?
The itch of his affection should not then
Have nicked his captainship, at such a point,
When half to half the world opposed, he being
The mered question. 'Twas a shame no less   10
Than was his loss, to course your flying flags
And leave his navy gazing.
CLEOPATRA   Prithee, peace.

Enter the Ambassador *with* ANTONY.

ANTONY   Is that his answer?
AMBASSADOR   Ay, my lord.
ANTONY
The Queen shall then have courtesy, so she   15
Will yield us up.
AMBASSADOR   He says so.
ANTONY   Let her know't.
To the boy Caesar send this grizzled head,
And he will fill thy wishes to the brim
With principalities.
CLEOPATRA   That head, my lord?

5 **several ranges** different lines of troops (*OED* Range *sb.*[1] 1). The idea is that, when they came face to face, the opposing fleets were afraid of each other.

7 **affection** sexual passion. In combination with *itch* the word suggests mere lust.

8 **nicked** Wilson defines this as 'cut short' (*OED* Nick *v.*[2] 2), but the suggestion is that the 'itch of his affection' has emasculated him.

10 **The ... question** the sole ground of dispute. To 'mere' could also mean 'to mark out (land) by means of "meres" or boundaries' (*OED v.*[2] 1), and Johnson explained the phrase as

'the matter to which the dispute is limited'. This would relate back to the previous line and make Antony the disputed boundary between the two halves of the world.
mered merèd

11 **course** run after. Compare *Mac* 1.6.21, 'We cours'd him at the heels.'

12 **leave ... gazing** 'The enemies them selves', says Plutarch, 'wondred much to see them saile in that sort, with ful saile towards Peloponnesus' (North, 301).

15 **so** so long as

17 **boy Caesar** Compare 'young man', 3.11.62.

10 mered] *F (*meered*)*

ANTONY

    To him again! Tell him he wears the rose   20
    Of youth upon him, from which the world should note
    Something particular. His coin, ships, legions,
    May be a coward's, whose ministers would prevail
    Under the service of a child as soon
    As i'th' command of Caesar. I dare him therefore   25
    To lay his gay caparisons apart
    And answer me declined, sword against sword,
    Ourselves alone. I'll write it. Follow me.
                     [Exeunt Antony and Ambassador.]

ENOBARBUS   *[aside]*

    Yes, like enough high-battled Caesar will
    Unstate his happiness, and be staged to th' show   30
    Against a sworder! I see men's judgements are
    A parcel of their fortunes, and things outward
    Do draw the inward quality after them

20–1 **wears … him** 'is in the bloom of youth'

21–2 **from … particular** '(because he is young) everyone expects to see something remarkable in him personally'

23 **ministers** agents, subordinates

24 **soon** easily, as in *TGV* 2.7.19, 'Thou wouldst as soon go kindle fire with snow.'

26 * **gay caparisons** splendid trappings. Pope's emendation (*caparisons* for F's 'Comparisons') is appropriate as a description of Caesar's external advantages, his 'coins, ships, legions'. Shakespeare elsewhere uses *gay* in connection with exterior shows such as clothing ('gay ornaments', *3H6* 3.2.149). Alternatively, F's 'Comparisons' is also acceptable because those same advantages make Caesar appear superior in comparison with Antony.

27 **answer** 'meet in fight, encounter' (*OED v.* 26)
    declined 'brought as low as I am'

28 **Ourselves alone** This is Antony's second challenge to Caesar to fight in single combat. See 3.7.30.

29 **high-battled** 'commanding great armies'. 'Battle' is used elsewhere to signify 'army' (3.9.2).

30 **Unstate his happiness** 'divest himself of his good fortune' (*OED* Happiness *sb.* 1)
    be staged … show 'put on public display'

31 **sworder** usually glossed as 'gladiator'; but it could mean 'common soldier' (in comparison with the 'high-battled Caesar').

32 **parcel of** part of; 'of a piece with'
    things outward external circumstances

33 **inward quality** inherent quality; personality

26 caparisons] *Pope;* Comparisons *F*   28 SD] *Capell subst.*   29 SD] *Capell*

To suffer all alike. That he should dream,
Knowing all measures, the full Caesar will   35
Answer his emptiness! Caesar, thou hast subdued
His judgement too.

Enter a Servant.

SERVANT   A messenger from Caesar.
CLEOPATRA
What, no more ceremony? See, my women,
Against the blown rose they may stop their nose   40
That kneeled unto the buds. Admit him, sir.

[*Exit Servant.*]

ENOBARBUS   [*aside*]
Mine honesty and I begin to square.
The loyalty well held to fools does make
Our faith mere folly. Yet he that can endure
To follow with allegiance a fallen lord   45
Does conquer him that did his master conquer,
And earns a place i'th' story.

Enter THIDIAS.

CLEOPATRA   Caesar's will?
THIDIAS   Hear it apart.

---

34 **To … alike** 'so that both deteriorate together' (Wilson)
35 **Knowing all measures** 'having experienced every degree of fortune' (Jones). Plutarch comments that Antony had 'oftentimes proved both the one and the other fortune' and had been 'throughly acquainted with the divers chaunges and fortunes of battells' (North, 302). *Measures* refers to the words *full* and *emptiness* which follow.
36 **Answer** respond to
40 **blown rose** rose that has bloomed and withered

42 **square** quarrel. Compare 2.1.46 and note.
44 **faith** fidelity
46 **him … conquer** i.e. Fortune. The ability to overcome the hazards of Fate by defying or rising above them is a characteristic of Shakespeare's Roman heroes such as Brutus in *JC*, Coriolanus and Antony as he was formerly. See 1.4.69–72, where Caesar praises him for enduring misfortune 'like a soldier'.
47 **story** chronicle; history book
49 **apart** in private

34 alike. That] *Rowe;* alike, that *F*   41 SD] *Capell subst.*   42 SD] *Hanmer*

CLEOPATRA   None but friends. Say boldly.   50
THIDIAS
    So haply are they friends to Antony.
ENOBARBUS
    He needs as many, sir, as Caesar has,
    Or needs not us. If Caesar please, our master
    Will leap to be his friend. For us, you know,
    Whose he is we are, and that is Caesar's.
THIDIAS   So.   55
    Thus then, thou most renowned: Caesar entreats
    Not to consider in what case thou stand'st
    Further than he is Caesar.
CLEOPATRA   Go on; right royal.
THIDIAS
    He knows that you embrace not Antony
    As you did love, but as you feared him.
CLEOPATRA   Oh!   60
THIDIAS
    The scars upon your honour, therefore, he
    Does pity as constrained blemishes,
    Not as deserved.
CLEOPATRA   He is a god and knows
    What is most right. Mine honour was not yielded
    But conquered merely.   65

---

50 **None but friends** 'Only friends are
   here.'
51 **haply** perhaps
53 **Or ... us** 'or has no need of friends',
   i.e. 'his case is beyond hope'
   (Deighton)
57 **in what ... stand'st** 'the situation
   you are in'.
58 **Further ... Caesar** This is deliberately ambiguous. It could mean 'and
   therefore, by definition, magnanimous', or 'and therefore has you
   at his mercy'.
   right royal This is usually taken to

mean 'a truly generous gesture', but
Cleopatra could as well be ironically
addressing Thidias.
59–60 **He knows ... him** Ridley points
   out that in North's Plutarch (314)
   Cleopatra says this about herself
   during the episode (5.2.140–74) in
   which she deceives Caesar about her
   treasure. Shakespeare transfers the
   argument to the persuasive Thidias.
62 **constrained** (constrainèd); forced,
   received under compulsion.
65 **merely** utterly

54 us, you] *Steevens subst.;* us you *F;* as you *F2*   58 Caesar] *F2; Caesars F*

ENOBARBUS   [*aside*]
  To be sure of that, I will ask Antony.
  Sir, sir, thou art so leaky
  That we must leave thee to thy sinking, for
  Thy dearest quit thee.   *Exit Enobarbus.*
THIDIAS   Shall I say to Caesar
  What you require of him? For he partly begs   70
  To be desired to give. It much would please him
  That of his fortunes you should make a staff
  To lean upon. But it would warm his spirits
  To hear from me you had left Antony
  And put yourself under his shroud,   75
  The universal landlord.
CLEOPATRA   What's your name?
THIDIAS
  My name is Thidias.
CLEOPATRA   Most kind messenger,
  Say to great Caesar this in deputation:
  I kiss his conqu'ring hand. Tell him I am prompt
  To lay my crown at's feet, and there to kneel   80
  Till from his all-obeying breath I hear
  The doom of Egypt.
THIDIAS   'Tis your noblest course.
  Wisdom and fortune combating together,
  If that the former dare but what it can,

67–9 **Sir … quit thee** Enobarbus sees
  Antony as a sinking ship which the
  rats, including his *dearest* Cleopatra,
  are all leaving. He, of course, is thinking of joining the rats himself (42–4).
70 **require** request
75 **shroud** 'protection' (*OED sb.*[1] 6); but
  the word inevitably has sinister over-
  tones.
78 * **in deputation** 'as my rep-
  resentative'. Compare *1H4* 4.3.86–7,
  'All the favourites that the absent
  King / In deputation left behind him
  here.' Case suggests that the com-

positor substituted 'dis' for 'de' 'as a
  result of the proximity of *this* and
  kiss'.
79 **prompt** ready and willing
81 **all-obeying** obeyed by everyone
82 **The … Egypt** 'his judgement on the
  Queen of Egypt'
84–5 **If that … shake it** 'If the wise
  man is resolute enough to remain
  wise, no fortune can upset him' (a
  Stoic sentiment). 'Thidias gives the
  saying a pragmatic turn entirely
  characteristic of Caesar the politician:
  Play along with fortune – i.e. Caesar –

66 SD] *Hanmer*   78 this in deputation:] *Ard¹*; this in disputation, *F*; this; in Deputation *Theobald*
(*Warburton*)   80–1 kneel / Till from] *Jones (Muir)*; kneele. / Tell him, from *F*

No chance may shake it. Give me grace to lay   85
My duty on your hand.
CLEOPATRA   [*Offers him her hand.*]
                          Your Caesar's father oft,
When he hath mused of taking kingdoms in,
Bestowed his lips on that unworthy place
As it rained kisses.

Enter ANTONY *and* ENOBARBUS.

ANTONY   Favours? By Jove that thunders!   90
What art thou, fellow?
THIDIAS   One that but performs
The bidding of the fullest man and worthiest
To have command obeyed.
ENOBARBUS   [*aside*] You will be whipped.
ANTONY   [*Calls for servants.*]
Approach there! – Ah, you kite! – Now, gods and
    devils,
Authority melts from me. Of late when I cried
    'Ho!',   95
Like boys unto a muss, kings would start forth

and you won't get hurt' (Bevington).
86 **duty** homage
88 **taking ... in** conquering. Compare
1.1.24.
90 **As** as if
90–109 **Favours ... to him** '[Thidias]
    was longer in talke with her then any
    man else was, and the Queene her
    selfe also did him great honor: inso-
    much as he made Antonius gealous
    of him. Whereupon Antonius caused
    him to be taken and well favoredly
    whipped, and so sent him unto
    Caesar' (North, 306).
90 **Jove that thunders** In Ovid's *Meta-
    morphoses* Jupiter is referred to as 'the
    thunderer' ('Jupiter tonans'). See, for
    example, *Metamorphoses*, 1.170.
92 **fullest** most fortunate. Compare *full*

in 35.
94 **kite** literally a bird of prey, but used
    figuratively to mean a whore.
    Compare *H5* 2.1.76, 'Fetch forth the
    lazar kite of Cressid's kind.'
96 **muss** a game in which children
    scramble for small objects thrown on
    the ground. Randle Cotgrave, *Dic-
    tionarie of the French and English
    Tongues*, 1611, mentions in his defi-
    nition of the word *Groee*, 'the boyish
    scrambling for nuts, etc.; cast on the
    ground; a Musse'. In Jonson's *Bar-
    tholomew Fair* (4.1.33), Cokes cries, 'a
    muss, a muss, a muss, a muss' as he
    'falls a-scrambling' for a basket of
    peas which has fallen to the ground.
    For the reference to kings, compare
    3.12.5.

87 SD] *Capell subst.*   93 SD] *Capell*   94 SD] *Cam¹ subst.*   95 me. Of late when] *Johnson subst.;*
me of late. When *F*

And cry 'Your will?'

Enter Servant[s].

                  Have you no ears? I am
Antony yet. Take hence the jack and whip him!
ENOBARBUS   [*aside*]
   'Tis better playing with a lion's whelp
   Than with an old one dying.
ANTONY   Moon and stars!   100
   Whip him! Were't twenty of the greatest tributaries
   That do acknowledge Caesar, should I find them
   So saucy with the hand of she here – what's her name
   Since she was Cleopatra? Whip him, fellows,
   Till like a boy you see him cringe his face   105
   And whine aloud for mercy. Take him hence!
THIDIAS
   Mark Antony –
ANTONY   Tug him away! Being whipped,
   Bring him again. The jack of Caesar's shall
   Bear us an errand to him.

                   Exeunt [Servants] with Thidias.
   You were half blasted ere I knew you. Ha?   110
   Have I my pillow left unpressed in Rome,
   Forborne the getting of a lawful race,
   And by a gem of women, to be abused
   By one that looks on feeders?

98 **jack** Of the many definitions given by *OED* the closest is 'a low-bred or ill-mannered fellow, a knave' (*sb.*[1] 2).

99–100 **'Tis better ... dying** a variation on the proverb 'It is dangerous to play with lions' (Dent, L321.1)

101 **tributaries** men who pay tribute

105 **cringe** distort (*OED v.* 1)

110 **blasted** withered, blighted (*OED* Blast *v.* 7)

112 **Forborne ... race** Shakespeare here departs from Plutarch, who mentions two daughters that Octavia had by Antony. In view of the ease with which he left her, this statement sounds hypocritical, but at the same time Antony is aware at this moment of the duplicity of the woman for whom he has left his wife.

113 **abused** deceived

114 **feeders** parasites. Compare *Tim* 2.2.158–9, 'When all our offices have been oppress'd / With riotous feeders.'

97 SD *Servants*] *as Capell subst.*; *a Servant (after* him *l.* 98) *F*   99 SD] *Capell*   108 The] *F*; this *Pope*   109 errand] *F (*arrant)

CLEOPATRA   Good my lord –

ANTONY

You have been a boggler ever.   115
But when we in our viciousness grow hard –
Oh, misery on't! – the wise gods seel our eyes,
In our own filth drop our clear judgements, make us
Adore our errors, laugh at's while we strut
To our confusion.

CLEOPATRA   Oh, is't come to this?   120

ANTONY

I found you as a morsel, cold upon
Dead Caesar's trencher – nay, you were a fragment
Of Gnaeus Pompey's, besides what hotter hours,
Unregistered in vulgar fame, you have
Luxuriously picked out. For I am sure,   125
Though you can guess what temperance should be,
You know not what it is.

CLEOPATRA   Wherefore is this?

---

115 **boggler** 'waverer; inconstant woman' (*OED* Boggle *v.* 3). Henn (120) explains *boggler* as 'a hawk that does not select and keep to any one quarry, but turns backwards and forwards from one to another as [Cleopatra] has turned from lover to lover'. If this is the case, then the allusion to falconry probably gave rise to *seel* two lines later.

116–20 **But when ... confusion** Several passages in the Bible express this idea, including John 12:40, 'He hath blinded theyr eyes, and hardened their hart, that they should not see with their eyes, and lest they should understand with theyr heart', and Psalms 2:4, 'He that dwelleth in heaven shall laugh them to scorne: the Lord wyl have them in derision.' It is also close to the proverb 'When God shall punish he will first take away the understanding' (Dent,

G257).

117 **seel** a term in falconry for sewing up a hawk's eyelids temporarily in preparation for receiving the hood

120 **confusion** 'ruin, overthrow' (Schmidt)

121–2 **morsel ... trencher** Earlier Cleopatra has described herself as 'a morsel for a monarch' (1.5.32) and Enobarbus has called her Antony's 'Egyptian dish' (2.6.128). For her liaisons with Julius Caesar and Gnaeus Pompey, see 1.5.30–5 and notes on List of Roles, p. 87.

122 **trencher** wooden platter
fragment leftover

124 **Unregistered ... fame** 'unknown to common rumour'

125 **Luxuriously ... out** wantonly collected. Compare *1H4* 2.4.367–8, 'Could the world pick thee out three such enemies again?'

---

117 seel] *F (seele)*; seale *F3*   117–18 eyes, / In ... filth drop] *Warburton subst.*; eyes / In ...
filth, drop *F*

ANTONY

To let a fellow that will take rewards
And say 'God quit you!' be familiar with
My playfellow, your hand, this kingly seal   130
And plighter of high hearts! O that I were
Upon the hill of Basan, to outroar
The horned herd! For I have savage cause,
And to proclaim it civilly were like
A haltered neck which does the hangman thank   135
For being yare about him.

Enter a Servant *with* THIDIAS.

Is he whipped?

SERVANT

Soundly, my lord.

ANTONY   Cried he? And begged 'a pardon?

SERVANT

He did ask favour.

ANTONY   [*to Thidias*]

If that thy father live, let him repent
Thou wast not made his daughter; and be thou
sorry   140

---

129 **quit** repay. 'God quit you' appears to have been a common way of expressing thanks (*OED v.* 10).

130 **seal** 'token (something which confirms a covenant)' (Jones). Compare *MND* 3.2.143–4, 'thy hand … This princess of pure white, this seal of bliss.'

131 **plighter** that which pledges
high noble

131–3 **O … herd** The hill of Basan is described in Psalms 68:15 as 'a high hill', and in Psalms 22:12 it is said that 'Many bulls are come about me: fat bulls of Basan close me in on every side'. Antony sees himself as a cuckold, a horned beast, like one of the bulls of Basan.

133 **horned** hornèd
savage cause 'cause enough to behave wildly'

134 **civilly** politely

135 **A haltered neck** i.e. someone with a noose round his neck

136 **yare** brisk and quick. Compare 5.2.282.

137 **Cried … 'a pardon** 'Antony jeeringly treats Thidias as a schoolboy who has been flogged for a misdemeanour' (Jones)
a the common abbreviation of 'he', as in 2.7.91, 135, or possibly the indefinite article

136 SD *as Collier; after* whipt *F*   139 SD] *Oxf*

To follow Caesar in his triumph, since
Thou hast been whipped for following him. Hence-
     forth
The white hand of a lady fever thee;
Shake thou to look on't. Get thee back to Caesar;
Tell him thy entertainment. Look thou say   145
He makes me angry with him. For he seems
Proud and disdainful, harping on what I am,
Not what he knew I was. He makes me angry,
And at this time most easy 'tis to do't,
When my good stars that were my former guides   150
Have empty left their orbs and shot their fires
Into th'abysm of hell. If he mislike
My speech and what is done, tell him he has
Hipparchus, my enfranched bondman, whom
He may at pleasure whip or hang or torture,   155
As he shall like to quit me. Urge it thou.
Hence with thy stripes! Be gone!

                              Exit Thidias [with Servant].

143 **fever** 'put you into a fever' (*OED
    v.* 1)
145 **entertainment** reception; 'how you
    have been treated'
145–52 **Look ... hell** '[Antony] bad him
    tell him that he made him angrie with
    him, bicause he shewed him selfe
    prowde and disdainfull towards him,
    and now specially when he was easie
    to be angered, by reason of his present
    miserie' (North, 306).
150–2 **When ... hell** a reference to the
    Ptolemaic system of astronomy
    according to which the earth, at the
    centre of the universe, was sur-
    rounded by a series of concentric
    spheres, in each of which moved a
    planet which influenced human
    affairs. Antony says that the planets
    (*stars*) which have hitherto given him
    good fortune have now fallen out of
    their spheres and left him unpro-

tected. As Seaton (222) points out,
the images are apocalyptic: 'And the
fifth angel blewe, and I sawe a starre
fal from heaven unto the earth, and
to him was given the keye of the
bottomlesse pit. And he opened the
bottomlesse pit' (Revelation 9:1–2).
154–6 **Hipparchus ... me** Plutarch
refers to 'Hipparchus ... the first
of all his infranchised bondmen that
revolted from him, and yelded unto
Caesar' (North, 302). 'If this mislike
thee said he, thou hast Hipparchus
one of my infranchised bondmen with
thee: hang him if thou wilt, or whippe
him at thy pleasure, that we may crie
quittaunce' (North, 306). An 'enfranched bondman' is a former slave who
has been given his freedom.
154 **enfranched** enfranchèd
156 **quit** requite, repay

142 whipped for] *Rowe subst.;* whipt. For *F*   him.] *Rowe;* him, *F*   157 SD *with Servant*] *Oxf
subst.*

CLEOPATRA   Have you done yet?

ANTONY

Alack, our terrene moon is now eclipsed

And it portends alone the fall of Antony.

CLEOPATRA

I must stay his time.   160

ANTONY

To flatter Caesar would you mingle eyes

With one that ties his points?

CLEOPATRA   Not know me yet?

ANTONY

Cold-hearted toward me?

CLEOPATRA   Ah, dear, if I be so,

From my cold heart let heaven engender hail

And poison it in the source, and the first stone   165

Drop in my neck; as it determines, so

Dissolve my life! The next Caesarion smite,

Till by degrees the memory of my womb,

Together with my brave Egyptians all,

---

158 **terrene moon** Cleopatra, Antony's earthly moon, associated with Isis, the Egyptian moon-goddess (compare 3.6.16–19 and pp. 67–9). An eclipse was thought to be a portent of imminent disaster, as in *KL* 1.2.103–4, 'These late eclipses of the sun and moon portend no good to us.'

160 **I ... time** 'I must wait for him', but whether Cleopatra implies 'wait for him to recover' or 'wait for his final defeat' is unclear. In view of her question at 157, the former is the more likely.

162 **one ... points** i.e. a mere servant or valet. *Points* were laces with metal tags with which men and women tied their clothes (*OED* Point *sb.* II.5).

164–72 **From my ... prey** 'Shakespeare may have recalled the account in Exodus of the plagues that God inflicted on the Egyptians. These included the plagues of hail and of flies as well as

the plague on the first-born. "I ... will smite all the first-born of Egypt", says Jehovah (Exodus 12:12); compare Cleopatra's "the next Caesarion smite" – Caesarion was her first child. These biblical resonances may have been felt to lend conviction to Cleopatra's words: hence Antony's "I am satisfied"' (Jones). See also Walter, 138.

166 **in my neck** 'in my throat' or 'on my head' (*OED* Neck *sb.*[1] 1d)

determines concludes; i.e. melts

167 * **smite** Rowe's emendation of F's 'smile' has been universally accepted and is supported by Exodus 9:25, 'And the hail smote throughout all the land of Egypt' (Walter, 138).

168 **memory ... womb** i.e. 'all my children'

169 **brave** fine, splendid. Compare 1.5.23 and note.

160 time.] *F3*; time? *F*   167 Caesarion] *North, Hanmer*; Caesarian *F*   smite] *Rowe*; smile *F*

By the discandying of this pelleted storm   170
Lie graveless, till the flies and gnats of Nile
Have buried them for prey!
ANTONY   I am satisfied.
Caesar sets down in Alexandria, where
I will oppose his fate. Our force by land
Hath nobly held; our severed navy too   175
Have knit again, and fleet, threat'ning most sea-like.
Where hast thou been, my heart? Dost thou hear,
    lady?
If from the field I shall return once more
To kiss these lips, I will appear in blood.
I and my sword will earn our chronicle.   180

170 * **discandying** 'to melt or dissolve out of a candied or solid condition' (*OED* Discandy *v.*) *OED* describes the word as 'rare' and cites only two examples, both from this play (see 4.12.22). The predominant meaning is of hail which melts ('the poison in the hail is liberated by the melting' (Case)), but the word is inescapably associated with 'candy', or crystallized sugar, as in 'sugar candy', especially in 4.12.22 where Antony's followers are said to *discandy* and 'melt their *sweets*'. Harrier suggests a link between the two: in fifteenth- and sixteenth-century pageants hail and snow were represented by sweets and 'cumfittes'. A pageant of 1583 has 'a tempest wherein it hailed small comfects, rained rose water and snewed [snowed] an artificial kind of snew'. Cleopatra thinks simultaneously of the melting of hail and of the sugar candy which was used to represent it. The few editors who retain F's 'discandering' are not convincing, and Theobald's emendation has been generally adopted.

172 **buried them** i.e. by eating them

173 **sets down** encamps. Compare *Cor* 5.3.1–2, 'We will before the walls of Rome tomorrow / Set down our host.' Plutarch says that Caesar 'came, and pitched his campe hard by the city, in the place where they runne and manage their horses' (North, 307).

174 **oppose his fate** resist his destiny

174–5 **Our force ... held** Plutarch records that Antony's soldiers, his land army, 'after they certainly knewe he was fled, ... kept them selves whole together seven daies' (North, 303).

176 **fleet** are afloat (*OED v.*[1] 5)
    most sea-like 'in sea-going trim' (Onions)

177 **hast thou** Antony's change of mood from fury to tenderness is indicated by his shift from the formal *you* (161) to the intimate *thou*.
    heart possibly 'courage', but the reference is more probably addressed to Cleopatra, who, in offering her favours to Thidias, has been 'away'

179 **in blood** 'in full vigour'. The phrase is used of hounds, as in *Cor* 4.5.210–11, 'They shall see, sir, his crest up again and the man in blood.'

180 **chronicle** 'place in history'. Compare Enobarbus' desire to 'earn a place i'th' story' (3.13.47).

170 discandying] *Theobald (Thirlby)*; discandering *F*   176 fleet] *F* (Fleete); float *Rowe*

There's hope in't yet.

CLEOPATRA

That's my brave lord!

ANTONY

I will be treble-sinewed, hearted, breathed,
And fight maliciously. For when mine hours
Were nice and lucky, men did ransom lives   185
Of me for jests. But now, I'll set my teeth
And send to darkness all that stop me. Come,
Let's have one other gaudy night. Call to me
All my sad captains. Fill our bowls once more.
Let's mock the midnight bell.

CLEOPATRA   It is my birthday.   190
I had thought t'have held it poor, but since my
          lord
Is Antony again, I will be Cleopatra.

ANTONY

We will yet do well.

CLEOPATRA   [*to Charmian and Iras*]
Call all his noble captains to my lord!

ANTONY

Do so, we'll speak to them; and tonight I'll force   195
The wine peep through their scars. Come on, my
          queen,
There's sap in't yet! The next time I do fight

---

182 **brave** See 1.5.23 and note.
184 **maliciously**   violently,   fiercely
    (*OED adv.* 2)
185 **nice** easy-going; 'wanton' (*OED
    a.* 2)
185–6 **ransom ... jests** 'bought their
    lives from me for no more than the
    price of a joke' (Jones)
188 **gaudy** festive; 'luxurious' (*OED
    a.²* 1)
190–2 **It ... Cleopatra** Plutarch writes
    that whereas Cleopatra 'did solemnise
    the day of her birth very meanely and

sparingly, fit for her present misfortune: she now in contrary maner
did keepe it with such solemnitie, that
she exceeded all measure of sump-
tuousnes and magnificence' (North,
306). Shakespeare's introduction of
this unexpected and intimate detail
suggests that, after their violent argument, the two of them are reconciled
again.
197 **sap** life. The sense is of the sap
    rising in the spring.

194 SD *to ... Iras*] *this edn; To Attendants Cam²*

I'll make Death love me, for I will contend
Even with his pestilent scythe.

Exeunt [all but Enobarbus].

ENOBARBUS
Now he'll outstare the lightning. To be furious   200
Is to be frighted out of fear, and in that mood
The dove will peck the estridge; and I see still
A diminution in our captain's brain
Restores his heart. When valour preys on reason,
It eats the sword it fights with. I will seek   205
Some way to leave him.   *Exit.*

[4.1]   *Enter* CAESAR, AGRIPPA *and* MAECENAS, *with his army,
Caesar reading a letter.*

CAESAR
He calls me boy, and chides as he had power
To beat me out of Egypt. My messenger

198–9 **I will … scythe** 'I will destroy
as many as death does in times of
plague'. *Contend* is used in the sense
of 'compete'.
200 **furious** 'desperate in frenzy'
(Wilson)
202 **estridge** goshawk (a large, short-
winged hawk). Douce (436) was the
first person to establish this interpretation, in support of which he referred
to *3H6* 1.4.41, 'So doves do peck the
falcon's piercing talons.' Some quite
recent editors (and *OED*) continue to
define *estridge* as 'an ostrich'.
    still constantly
203–4 **A diminution … heart** 'As
Antony's reason fails him, his courage
revives'
204 **heart** courage. Compare 177 above.

4.1 Location: outside Alexandria, where
Caesar has 'pitched his campe hard

by the city, in the place where they
runne and manage their horses'
(North, 307). Antony's despair
(3.13.149–52, 158–9), his gradual
abandonment by his followers and the
reckless bravado with which he meets
his ruin create the impression that his
end is near. Caesar and his advisers
sense this and, in this scene, Caesar
prepares to fight 'the last of many
battles'.
1 **boy** Antony calls him 'the boy Caesar'
in the previous scene (3.13.17). Later
(4.12.48) he calls him 'the young
Roman boy'. Jones points out that,
according to Suetonius' *Life of Augustus*, Caesar was, in fact, contemp-
tuously referred to as 'the boy' by
his enemies (*Historie of the Twelve
Caesars*, trans. Philemon Holland,
1606, p. 42).
    as as if

198 Death] *Cam²; death F*   199 SD *all but Enobarbus*] *Capell subst.*   204 on] *Rowe; in F*   206
SD *Exit*] *F (Exeunt)*

4.1] *Rowe*

225

> He hath whipped with rods; dares me to personal
>   combat,
> Caesar to Antony. Let the old ruffian know
> I have many other ways to die; meantime   5
> Laugh at his challenge.
>
> MAECENAS
>   Caesar must think,
> When one so great begins to rage, he's hunted
> Even to falling. Give him no breath, but now
> Make boot of his distraction. Never anger   10
> Made good guard for itself.
>
> CAESAR   Let our best heads
> Know that tomorrow the last of many battles
> We mean to fight. Within our files there are,
> Of those that served Mark Antony but late,
> Enough to fetch him in. See it done,   15
> And feast the army. We have store to do't
> And they have earned the waste. Poor Antony!   *Exeunt.*

[4.2]   *Enter* ANTONY, CLEOPATRA, ENOBARBUS, CHARMIAN,
IRAS, ALEXAS *with others.*

3–5 **dares ... die** 'Antonius sent againe
to chalenge Caesar, to fight with him
hande to hande. Caesar aunswered
him, that he had many other wayes
to dye then so' (North, 307). This is
a mistranslation of Plutarch's original
Greek version in which Caesar says
that Antony can find many other ways
to die.

4 **old ruffian** The words suggest that
Caesar has an affection for Antony
which he has not hitherto expressed.
'Poor Antony' (17) creates a similar
impression.

6 **Laugh** 'that I laugh'

8–9 **he's ... falling** The image is of a
stag at bay.

9 **breath** 'time to breathe'

10 **Make ... distraction** 'take advantage
of his frenzy'. Compare *2H6* 4.1.13,
'Thou that art his mate, make boot
of this.'

10–11 **Never ... itself** Compare the
proverb 'Nothing is well said or done
in anger' (Tilley, N307; not in Dent).

11 **best heads** chief officers

13 **files** ranks, as in 1.1.3

15 **fetch him in** surround and take him
(*OED* Fetch *v.* 15b)

16 **store** plenty

4.2 Location: Alexandria. The sense of
an ending which Shakespeare has
steadily built up from 3.10 onwards
now deepens as Antony takes leave of
his personal servants and tells them

3 combat,] *Rowe;* Combat. *F*

4.2] *Rowe*

ANTONY

  He will not fight with me, Domitius?

ENOBARBUS   No.

ANTONY

  Why should he not?

ENOBARBUS

  He thinks, being twenty times of better fortune,

  He is twenty men to one.

ANTONY   Tomorrow, soldier,

  By sea and land I'll fight. Or I will live,   5

  Or bathe my dying honour in the blood

  Shall make it live again. Woo't thou fight well?

ENOBARBUS

  I'll strike, and cry 'Take all!'

ANTONY   Well said! Come on!

  Call forth my household servants.   [*Exit Alexas.*]

                        Let's tonight

  Be bounteous at our meal.

Enter three or four Servitors.

                     Give me thy hand.   10

  Thou hast been rightly honest; so hast thou,

(24–33) that he may no longer be alive for them to serve him. The banquet which he calls on them to prepare is, as Middleton Murry comments, 'the Last Supper of Antony' (Murry, 362).

1 **Domitius** This is the only time that Antony addresses Enobarbus by his first name and it suggests a growing intimacy between them. Ironically, Enobarbus has already resolved to desert him (3.13.205–6).

4–5 **Tomorrow ... fight** 'Then Antonius seeing there was no way more honorable for him to dye, then fighting valliantly: he determined to sette up his rest [i.e. "decide the matter"],

both by sea and lande' (North, 307).

5–6 **Or ... Or** Either ... or

6–7 **bathe ... again** Blood baths were supposed to be 'a very powerful tonic in great debility from long-continued diseases' (*OED* Blood *sb.* 19). Antony hopes to regain the honour which he lost at Actium by dying valiantly.

7 **Woo't** colloquial for 'wilt'. Compare *Ham* 5.1.275, 'Woo't weep, woo't fight, woo't fast, woo't tear thyself?'

8 **Take all** a gambler's cry as he stakes everything on the last throw of the dice. Lear is said to run 'unbonneted' through the storm and 'bid what will take all' (*KL* 3.1.15).

1 Domitius] *North, Rowe; Domitian F*   9 SD] *this edn*   10 SD *Enter ... Servitors*] *as Dyce; after* to night *l. 9 F*

Thou, and thou, and thou. You have served me well
And kings have been your fellows.

CLEOPATRA [*aside to Enobarbus*]   What means this?

ENOBARBUS [*aside to Cleopatra*]

'Tis one of those odd tricks which sorrow shoots
Out of the mind.

ANTONY   And thou art honest too.   15

I wish I could be made so many men,
And all of you clapped up together in
An Antony, that I might do you service
So good as you have done.

ALL THE SERVANTS   The gods forbid!

ANTONY

Well, my good fellows, wait on me tonight;   20
Scant not my cups, and make as much of me
As when mine empire was your fellow too
And suffered my command.

CLEOPATRA [*aside to Enobarbus*]

                                    What does he mean?

ENOBARBUS [*aside to Cleopatra*]

To make his followers weep.

ANTONY   Tend me tonight.

May be it is the period of your duty.   25
Haply you shall not see me more, or if,

---

13 **fellows** fellow servants. Compare
  3.13.96–7.
14 **tricks** whims
  shoots produces, emits. The metaphor may be derived from either
  plants ('to put forth buds or shoots',
  OED Shoot *v.* 7) or archery.
17 **clapped up** 'put together hastily'
  (*OED* Clap *v.* 13a)
21–8 **Scant ... master** 'So being at
  supper, (as it is reported) he commaunded his officers and household
  servauntes that waited on him at his
  bord, that they should fill his cuppes

full, and make as muche of him as
they could: for said he, you know not
whether you shall doe so much for
me to morrow or not, or whether you
shall serve an other maister: and it
may be you shall see me no more, but
a dead bodie' (North, 307–8).
21 **Scant ... cups** 'give me plenty to
  drink'
23 **suffered my command** 'was subject
  to my authority (as you have been)'
25 **period** end, as in 4.14.108
26 **if** if you do

13 SD] *Capell*   14 SD] *Johnson*   19 SP ALL THE SERVANTS] *Jones; Omnes.* F   23 SD] *Capell*   24
SD] *Capell*

A mangled shadow. Perchance tomorrow
You'll serve another master. I look on you
As one that takes his leave. Mine honest friends,
I turn you not away, but, like a master   30
Married to your good service, stay till death.
Tend me tonight two hours – I ask no more –
And the gods yield you for't!
ENOBARBUS   What mean you, sir,
To give them this discomfort? Look, they weep,
And I, an ass, am onion-eyed. For shame!   35
Transform us not to women!
ANTONY   Ho, ho, ho!
Now the witch take me if I meant it thus!
Grace grow where those drops fall! My hearty friends,
You take me in too dolorous a sense,
For I spake to you for your comfort, did desire you   40
To burn this night with torches. Know, my hearts,
I hope well of tomorrow, and will lead you
Where rather I'll expect victorious life

27 **mangled shadow** 'hideously dis-
figured ghost (like the ghost of Hector
when he appears to Aeneas in Book 2
of Virgil's *Aeneid*)' (Jones)
33 **yield** reward
33–6 **What mean ... women** 'Per-
ceiving that his frends and men fell a
weeping to heare him say so: to salve
that he had spoken, he added this
more unto it, that he would not leade
them to battell, where he thought not
rather safely to returne with victorie,
then valliantly to dye with honor'
(North, 308).
34 **discomfort** 'deprivation of comfort;
... distress, grief' (*OED sb.* 2)
35 **onion-eyed** Compare 1.2.176–7 and
note.
37 **the ... me** 'may I be bewitched'.
Take in the sense of 'bewitch' occurs

in *Ham* 1.1.163, 'No fairy takes, nor
witch hath power to charm.' The
word is often used to indicate infection by a disease.
38 **Grace** herb of grace, a popular name
for rue, a bitter-tasting herb used as
a medicine. Compare *R2* 3.4.104–5,
'Here did she fall a tear, here in this
place / I'll set a bank of rue, sour
herb of grace.' By a punning connection rue was associated with
repentance and also, as here, with
'ruth' or pity. The tears of Antony's
servants are an expression of their
pity for him and, by a conceit, the
herb of pity will grow where the tears
fall.
hearty loving, 'big-hearted'
40 **for your comfort** 'to support,
reassure, you'

38 fall! My ... friends,] *Theobald;* fall (my ... Friends) F

Than death and honour. Let's to supper, come,
And drown consideration.   *Exeunt.*   45

[**4.3**]   *Enter [through one door,* First Soldier *and his Company,
through the other door,* Second Soldier].

1 SOLDIER
Brother, good night. Tomorrow is the day.
2 SOLDIER
It will determine one way. Fare you well.
Heard you of nothing strange about the streets?
1 SOLDIER   Nothing. What news?
2 SOLDIER   Belike 'tis but a rumour. Good night to you.   5
1 SOLDIER   Well sir, good night.

[*Other* Soldiers *enter and join Second Soldier.*]

45 **consideration** serious thought, self-
examination, as in *H5* 1.1.28–9, 'Consideration like an angel came / And
whipt th'offending Adam out of him.'

4.3 Location: Alexandria. Shakespeare
creates an impression of time passing
as he prepares us for the decisive
battle. Caesar has already said
(4.1.12–13) that *tomorrow* he intends
to fight the last battle, and Antony
has warned his servants that *tomorrow*
they may serve another master
(4.2.27–8). The first line of this scene
tells that it is now night and that
tomorrow will be the decisive day.
According to Plutarch, the episode
took place 'within litle of midnight,
when all the citie was quiet, full of
feare and sorrowe, thinking what
would be the issue and ende of this
warre' (North, 308). To convey this
sense of apprehension Shakespeare
created the dialogue of the soldiers,
who do not appear in Plutarch. The
mysterious departure of Antony's
supposed ancestor and guardian
spirit, Hercules, makes his defeat

seem certain.
0.1–0.2 *Enter ...* **Second Soldier** The
precise way in which the soldiers
dispose themselves on the stage is not
altogether clear, and the editors have
proposed various possibilities. It looks
as though the First Soldier has been
on guard and is handing over to the
Second Soldier, his relief. The First
Soldier, about to leave, is prevented
by the arrival of the other group.
The Second Soldier, now in charge,
instructs the newcomers to be attentive (7) as they take up their positions
in the two corners on one side of the
stage. The Second Soldier, taking up
his place ('Here we') in a corner on
the opposite side, discusses the forth-
coming battle with the First Soldier
(9–12). The latter is again about to
leave but is interrupted by the sound
of the music. All the soldiers gather
together at 24 to discuss what they
have heard.
1 **the day** i.e. 'of the decisive battle'
2 **determine** either 'decide' or 'end'
   one way 'one way or the other'
5 **Belike** Probably

4.3] *Hanmer*   0.1–0.2 *through ...* Second Soldier] *this edn; a* Company of Soldiours *F*
6 SD *Other ... Soldier*] *this edn;* They meete other Soldiers *F*

230

2 SOLDIER   Soldiers, have careful watch.

3 SOLDIER   And you. Good night, good night.

> *They place themselves in every corner of the stage.*

2 SOLDIER

Here we. And if tomorrow

Our navy thrive, I have an absolute hope   10

Our landmen will stand up.

1 SOLDIER

'Tis a brave army and full of purpose –

> *Music of the hautboys is under the stage.*

2 SOLDIER   Peace! What noise?

1 SOLDIER   List, list!

2 SOLDIER   Hark!   15

1 SOLDIER   Music i'th' air.

3 SOLDIER   Under the earth.

4 SOLDIER   It signs well, does it not?

3 SOLDIER   No.

1 SOLDIER   Peace, I say! What should this mean?   20

2 SOLDIER

'Tis the god Hercules whom Antony loved

---

12 SD *hautboys* oboes. They would produce an eerie, supernatural sound as they also did in *Mac* 4.1.106 when the witches' cauldron sinks beneath the stage (Jones). On the use of music in this play, see p. 9.

13–22 **Peace ... leaves him** 'It is said that sodainly they heard a marvelous sweete harmonie of sundrie sortes of instrumentes of musicke, with the crie of a multitude of people, as they had bene dauncing, and had song as they use in Bacchus feastes, with movinges and turninges after the maner of the Satyres: and it seemed that this daunce went through the city unto the gate that opened to the enemies, and that all the troupe that made this noise they heard, went out of the city at that gate' (North, 308).

14 **List** listen; hark

18 **signs well** 'is a good omen'

21 **Hercules** Antony fostered the idea that he was a descendant of Hercules (see pp. 64–5). According to Plutarch 'It was sayd that Antonius came of the race of Hercules ... and in the manner of his life he followed Bacchus: and therefore he was called the new Bacchus' (North, 295). In Plutarch's account of this episode the music is associated not with Hercules but with Bacchus (note to 13–22). Shakespeare presumably made the change because, whereas Bacchus was associated with wine and festivity, Hercules was the embodiment of manly strength, the attribute which Antony most needs at this point. Having been deserted by his followers, he is now being abandoned by his guardian spirit.

8 SP 3 SOLDIER] *Capell;* 1 *F*

Now leaves him.

1 SOLDIER   Walk. Let's see if other watchmen
    Do hear what we do.

2 SOLDIER   How now, masters?   *Speak together.*

ALL   How now? How now? Do you hear this?   25

1 SOLDIER   Ay. Is't not strange?

3 SOLDIER   Do you hear, masters? Do you hear?

1 SOLDIER

    Follow the noise so far as we have quarter.

    Let's see how it will give off.

ALL   Content. 'Tis strange.

                                                        Exeunt.

[4.4]   *Enter* ANTONY *and* CLEOPATRA *with* [CHARMIAN *and*]
                                others.

ANTONY

    Eros! Mine armour, Eros!

CLEOPATRA   Sleep a little.

ANTONY

    No, my chuck. Eros! Come, mine armour, Eros!

                    Enter EROS [*with armour*].

28 **so ... quarter** 'as far as our watch
    extends'. For *quarter* meaning
    'watch', see *KJ* 5.5.20, 'Keep good
    quarter and good care tonight.'
29 **give off** cease

4.4 Location: Alexandria. Shakespeare
    continues to convey the impression of
    time passing. The first line suggests
    that Antony and Cleopatra have just
    woken. By l. 18 it is morning and
    the soldiers start to arrive and the
    trumpets to blow in preparation for
    battle. Cleopatra's arming of Antony
    (which is not in Plutarch) is a brief

moment of intimacy.

1 **Eros** 'a man whom [Antony] loved
    and trusted much' (North, 309).
    Antony's repetition of his name, like
    his reference to him as 'good fellow'
    establishes the closeness of their
    relationship (his name is the Greek
    word for sexual love), and also pre-
    pares us for the episode (4.14) in
    which Antony asks Eros to kill him.
2 **chuck** 'chick'; an intimate term of
    endearment, as in Macbeth's injunc-
    tion to his wife, 'Be innocent of the
    knowledge, dearest chuck' (*Mac*
    3.2.45).

4.4] *Hanmer*   0.1 CHARMIAN *and*] *Capell subst.*   2 SD *with armour*] *Capell*

Come, good fellow, put thine iron on.
If fortune be not ours today, it is
Because we brave her. Come!

CLEOPATRA   Nay, I'll help too.   5
What's this for?

ANTONY   Ah, let be, let be! Thou art
The armourer of my heart. False, false! This, this!

CLEOPATRA
Sooth, la, I'll help. Thus it must be.

ANTONY   Well, well!
We shall thrive now. Seest thou, my good fellow?
Go put on thy defences.

EROS   Briefly, sir.   10

CLEOPATRA
Is not this buckled well?

ANTONY   Rarely, rarely!
He that unbuckles this, till we do please
To doff't for our repose, shall hear a storm.
Thou fumblest, Eros, and my queen's a squire
More tight at this than thou. Dispatch. O love,   15

---

3 **thine iron** 'the armour which you are holding for me'. Antony is not telling Eros to put on his own armour. He does so at l. 10.

5–8 * **Nay … must be** F assigns all these lines to Cleopatra. In F (and, presumably, the manuscript copy) both proper names and speech prefixes were italicized. It may be that initially the speech prefix *Ant.* was accidentally omitted from the manuscript but was later added between the lines. Hence the compositor mistook the speech prefix at l. 6 for a proper name and read 5–6 as 'Nay, Ile helpe too, *Antony.* / What's this for? Ah, let be, let be, thou art ...' Malone's emendation, as here, has been generally adopted.

7 **False … this** Cleopatra has tried to put a wrong piece of armour on Antony, who then shows her which is the right one.

8 **Sooth, la** indeed. *Sooth* means 'in truth' and *la* is emphatic.
Well, well 'Cleopatra is doing better' (Wilson)

10 **Briefly** shortly, in a moment

11 **Rarely** Splendidly

13 **doff't** take it off

14 **squire** in the Middle Ages, a young man of noble birth who served as an attendant on a knight. The term has associations with chivalric romance, as has *dame* (29).

15 **tight** skilful (*OED a.* 3)
Dispatch 'Hurry up!' Compare 4.5.17.

3 thine] *F;* mine *Hanmer*   5 too] *Hanmer;* too, *Anthony F*   6–7 Ah … This, this!] *as Malone (Capell); F assigns to Cleopatra*   8 SP CLEOPATRA] *Hanmer; not in F*   13 doff't] *F (*daft*)*

That thou couldst see my wars today and knew'st
The royal occupation, thou shouldst see
A workman in't.

Enter an armed Soldier.

Good morrow to thee! Welcome!
Thou look'st like him that knows a warlike charge.
To business that we love we rise betime   20
And go to't with delight.
SOLDIER   A thousand, sir,
Early though't be, have on their riveted trim
And at the port expect you.   *Shout. Trumpets flourish.*

Enter Captains *and* Soldiers.

CAPTAIN

The morn is fair. Good morrow, General!
ALL THE SOLDIERS

Good morrow, General!
ANTONY   'Tis well blown, lads!   25

16 **That** if only
    knew'st understood
17 **occupation** trade, business; usually
    applied to manual work as in *Cor*
    4.1.13–14, 'Now the red pestilence
    strike all trades in Rome, / And occu-
    pations perish.'
18 **workman** true craftsman
19 **charge** responsibility. Wilson para-
    phrases the line as 'a man who has
    been ordered to deliver a warlike
    message'.
20–1 **To ... delight** Compare the
    proverb 'What we do willingly is easy'
    (Dent, D407).
20, 27 **betime, betimes** early. 'The next
    morning by breake of day, he went to
    set those few footemen he had in
    order upon the hills adjoyning unto
    the citie' (North, 308).

22 **trim** trappings, armour (*OED sb.* 3).
    The various pieces of a suit of armour
    were held together by rivets. Cf. *H5*
    4 Prol. 12–13, 'The armourers,
    accomplishing the knights, / With
    busy hammers closing rivets up.'
23 **port** gate
    expect await
24 SP* CAPTAIN The F speech prefix
    '*Alex.*' is clearly wrong because, as we
    shortly learn (4.6.12–13), Alexas has
    deserted to Caesar some time ago.
    Case suggests that the roles of Alexas
    and the Captain were doubled and
    Spevack that the prefix might have
    stood for Alexander Cooke, the actor,
    but, as Spevack adds, both possi-
    bilities are remote and there is no
    evidence for either.
25 **'Tis well blown** i.e. the flourish of

24 SP CAPTAIN] *Rowe; Alex. F*   25 SP ALL THE SOLDIERS] *Jones; All. F*

This morning, like the spirit of a youth
That means to be of note, begins betimes.
[*to Cleopatra*] So, so. Come, give me that. This way.
Well said.
Fare thee well, dame. Whate'er becomes of me,
This is a soldier's kiss. [*Kisses her.*] Rebukable   30
And worthy shameful check it were, to stand
On more mechanic compliment. I'll leave thee
Now like a man of steel. – You that will fight,
Follow me close, I'll bring you to't. Adieu.
                              Exeunt [all but Cleopatra and Charmian].

CHARMIAN
Please you retire to your chamber?
CLEOPATRA   Lead me.   35
He goes forth gallantly. That he and Caesar might
Determine this great war in single fight!
Then Antony – but now –. Well, on.   *Exeunt.*

[**4.5**]   *Trumpets sound. Enter* ANTONY *and* EROS [*, a* Soldier
                        meeting them].

trumpets which they have just
sounded. Some commentators
(including Wilson) paraphrase the
sentence as 'The morning blossoms
well', and this is possible since
Antony then compares the morning
to 'a youth that ... begins betimes'.
28 **So ... that** addressed to Cleopatra,
who is having difficulty in putting on
Antony's armour. He asks her to give
it to him and shows her ('This way')
how to fit it.
Well said Well done. Compare *1H4*
5.4.75, 'Well said, Hal! to it, Hal!',
where Hal is fighting and not saying
anything.
31 **shameful check** 'reprimand, deserving shame'

31–2 **stand / On** insist on; 'make much
of' (Schmidt), as in *Mac* 3.4.118,
'Stand not upon the order of your
going'
32 **mechanic compliment** i.e. the kind
of prolonged leave-taking indulged in
by commoners
34 **Follow ... close** 'if you will follow
me close'
36 **That** 'if only', as at 16

4.5 Location: Alexandria. In practically
every scene from 3.10 onwards, following the disaster at Actium, Shakespeare has made us aware that
Antony's supporters are leaving him
and that Enobarbus is contemplating
desertion. In Plutarch the desertion

28 SD] *this edn*   30 SD] *Johnson*   32 compliment. I'll leave thee] *Theobald subst.;* Complement,
Ile leaue thee. *F*   33 steel. You] *Rowe;* Steele, you *F*   34 SD *all ... Charmian*] *Capell subst.*

4.5] *Hanmer*   0.1–0.2 *a ... them*] *Theobald (Thirlby)*

SOLDIER
  The gods make this a happy day to Antony!
ANTONY
  Would thou and those thy scars had once prevailed
  To make me fight at land!
SOLDIER   Hadst thou done so,
  The kings that have revolted and the soldier
  That has this morning left thee would have still   5
  Followed thy heels.
ANTONY   Who's gone this morning?
SOLDIER   Who?
  One ever near thee. Call for Enobarbus,
  He shall not hear thee, or from Caesar's camp
  Say 'I am none of thine.'
ANTONY   What sayest thou?
SOLDIER   Sir,
  He is with Caesar.
EROS   Sir, his chests and treasure   10
  He has not with him.
ANTONY   Is he gone?
SOLDIER   Most certain.
ANTONY
  Go, Eros, send his treasure after. Do it.
  Detain no jot, I charge thee. Write to him –
  I will subscribe – gentle adieus and greetings.
  Say that I wish he never find more cause   15
  To change a master. Oh, my fortunes have

occurs much earlier, before the Battle of Actium, but by shifting it here Shakespeare presents the departure of Antony's closest and most trusted officer as the culmination of a process which has been developing steadily for some time.

0.1 **Soldier** It is clear from 2–3 that this is the soldier who appeared at 3.7.60.

1 SP* SOLDIER F assigns this line and 3–6 and 6–9 to Eros, presumably because the Soldier was omitted from the opening entry direction and, with only Antony and Eros on the stage, Eros was apparently the only character who could say them.

1 **happy** lucky
2 **once** previously
4 **revolted** deserted
14 **subscribe** 'sign the letter'

1 SP SOLDIER] *Theobald (Thirlby); Eros F*   3, 6 SPs SOLDIER] *Capell; Eros F*

Corrupted honest men! Dispatch. – Enobarbus!   *Exeunt.*

[**4.6**]   *Flourish. Enter* AGRIPPA, CAESAR, *with* ENOBARBUS
and DOLABELLA.

CAESAR

Go forth, Agrippa, and begin the fight.
Our will is Antony be took alive.
Make it so known.

AGRIPPA

Caesar, I shall.   [*Exit.*]

CAESAR

The time of universal peace is near.   5

---

17 **Dispatch** 'Get on with it'

4.6 Location: Caesar's camp outside
Alexandria. The last word to be
spoken in the previous scene was
Antony's 'Enobarbus', said, no doubt,
with affection and grief. Within
moments, Enobarbus enters in the
company of Antony's enemies.
Hearing Caesar's order that the
deserters should be placed in the van-
guard (8–11), he thinks of other
deserters who have been badly treated
(12–18), and Caesar's cold strategy
contrasts with Antony's liberality in
sending Enobarbus' treasure after him
(21–3). The difference between his
two masters makes him wish to die,
thereby preparing us for his death in
4.9. Shakespeare created the character
and history of Enobarbus out of one
sentence in Plutarch: '[Domitius]
being sicke of an agewe when he
went and tooke a litle boate to goe to
Caesars campe, Antonius was very
sory for it, but yet he sent after him
all his caryage, trayne, and men: and

the same Domitius, as though he gave
him to understand that he repented
his open treason, he died immediatly
after' (North, 298).

5 **universal peace** the *pax Romana*
which Augustus was said to have
created throughout the world. Holinshed, in his account of Cymbeline,
twice mentions the time of universal
peace in which 'not only the Bri-
taynes, but in manner all other nations
were contented to be obedient to the
Romayne empire' and 'the whole
world, through meanes of this same
Augustus, was now in quiet, without
all warres or troublesome tumults'
(*Chronicles*, 2 vols, 1577, vol. 1, p.
47). Since Christ was born in the time
of Caesar Augustus, the *pax Romana*
was said to be a fulfilment of the
prophecies both of Isaiah (2:4) and of
Virgil's fourth *Eclogue*. 'It was predestined', says Plutarch, 'that the
government of all the world should
fall into Octavius Caesars handes'
(North, 292).

---

17 Dispatch. – Enobarbus!] *Steevens subst.;* Dispatch *Enobarbus. F;* Dispatch *Eros. F2;* Despatch!
To Enobarbus! *Johnson conj.*   17 SD *Exeunt*] *F (Exit)*

4.6] *Hanmer*   4 SD] *Capell subst.*

Prove this a prosp'rous day, the three-nooked world
Shall bear the olive freely.

Enter a Messenger.

MESSENGER   Antony
Is come into the field.
CAESAR   Go charge Agrippa
Plant those that have revolted in the van
That Antony may seem to spend his fury   10
Upon himself.   *Exeunt [all but Enobarbus]*.
ENOBARBUS
Alexas did revolt and went to Jewry on
Affairs of Antony; there did dissuade
Great Herod to incline himself to Caesar
And leave his master Antony. For this pains   15
Caesar hath hanged him. Canidius and the rest
That fell away have entertainment but

6 **three-nooked** divided into three parts. Case quotes several examples of the idea that the world was divided into three. It is probably derived from the 'so-called "T in O" maps: a "T" circumscribed by an "O", with the top half (nook) of the circle representing Asia, and lower left-hand and right-hand quadrants (nooks) representing, respectively, Europe and Africa' (Blakiston, 868). See also Donald K. Anderson (103–6).

7 **bear the olive** bring forth the olive tree (the symbol of peace). Compare *2H4* 4.4.87, 'But Peace puts forth her olive everywhere.'
freely plentifully, abundantly (*OED adv.* 4)

8–9 **charge ... Plant** 'command Agrippa to place'

12–16 **Alexas ... him** Plutarch writes of Alexas that Antony sent him to Herod of Jewry, 'hoping still to keepe him his frend, that he should not revolt from him. But he remained

there, and betrayed Antonius. For where he should have kept Herodes from revolting from him, he perswaded him to turne to Caesar: and trusting king Herodes, he presumed to come in Caesars presence. Howbeit Herodes did him no pleasure: for he was presently taken prisoner, and sent in chaines to his owne contrie, and there by Caesars commaundement put to death' (North, 306).

13 * **dissuade** persuade. Rowe and other editors emend this to 'persuade' (the word used by North; see previous note), but *dissuade* compresses into one word both the idea of persuasion and the idea of dissuasion from Antony's service.

16–18 **Canidius ... trust** See 3.10.33–4 and note to 3.10.34–5.

17 **entertainment** employment (*OED sb.* 2), as in *AW* 4.1.14–15, 'He must think us some band of strangers i'th' adversary's entertainment'

9 van] *F (*Vant*)* 11 SD *all ... Enobarbus] Capell subst.; Exeunt F* 12 Jewry] *F (*Iewrij*)* 13 dissuade] *F (*disswade*); perswade Rowe* 16 Canidius] *F2; Camindius F*

No honourable trust. I have done ill,
Of which I do accuse myself so sorely
That I will joy no more.   20

Enter a Soldier *of Caesar's.*

SOLDIER
Enobarbus, Antony
Hath after thee sent all thy treasure, with
His bounty overplus. The messenger
Came on my guard, and at thy tent is now
Unloading of his mules.   I give it you.   25
ENOBARBUS
SOLDIER
Mock not, Enobarbus.
I tell you true. Best you safed the bringer
Out of the host. I must attend mine office
Or would have done't myself. Your emperor   29
Continues still a Jove.   *Exit.*
ENOBARBUS
I am alone the villain of the earth,
And feel I am so most. O Antony,
Thou mine of bounty, how wouldst thou have paid
My better service, when my turpitude
Thou dost so crown with gold! This blows my heart. 35

---

23 **bounty overplus** gift in addition.
   Bounty implies not simply a gift but
   a generous one as in 'mine of bounty'
   (33).
24 **on my guard** 'while I was on guard'
27–8 **safed ... host** 'gave the man who
   brought it safe conduct through the
   troops'. For *safe* meaning 'make safe',
   see 1.3.56.
28 **attend mine office** 'get on with my
   duties'
30 **a Jove** The sense implies 'bountiful,
   generous'. Jove, as the god of the sky,
   was responsible for the falling of rain,

but Shakespeare may have had in
mind the myth in which Jove impreg-
nated Danae in the form of a shower
of gold (Ovid, *Metamorphoses*, 4.610–
11; Apollodorus, 2.4.1).
31 **alone** the only, the worst
32 **feel ... most** 'feel it more than
   anyone else'
33 **mine** store. Shakespeare is probably
   thinking of the rich mines of India,
   as in *1H4* 3.1.166–7, 'as bountiful /
   As mines of India'.
35 **blows my heart** 'makes my heart
   swell'

19 sorely] *F (forely)*   20 more] *F2;* mote *F*   35–6 heart. / If ... not, a] *Rowe subst.;* hart, / If
... not: a *F*

If swift thought break it not, a swifter mean
Shall outstrike thought, but thought will do't, I feel.
I fight against thee? No, I will go seek
Some ditch wherein to die; the foul'st best fits   39
My latter part of life.   *Exit.*

[4.7]   *Alarum. Drums and Trumpets. Enter* AGRIPPA [*and
others*].

AGRIPPA
Retire! We have engaged ourselves too far.
Caesar himself has work, and our oppression
Exceeds what we expected.   *Exeunt.*

         Alarums. Enter ANTONY, *and* SCARUS *wounded.*

SCARUS
O, my brave emperor, this is fought indeed!
Had we done so at first, we had droven them home   5
With clouts about their heads.
ANTONY   Thou bleed'st apace.

---

36 **thought** melancholy. See note to
3.13.1.
mean means. Presumably he is thinking of suicide.

4.7 Location: the battlefield outside
Alexandria. Such are the fortunes of
war that when Antony seems destined
to be defeated he wins a victory.
Shakespeare creates a contrast
between the misery of the deserter
Enobarbus in the previous scene and
the joyfulness in this scene of the
loyal Scarus, who, with his wit and
courage, to some extent takes Enobarbus' place. Strictly speaking, since
the stage is cleared at l. 3, a new scene
should start with the entry of Antony
and Scarus, but traditionally editors
have not divided the play at this point.
The succession of short battle scenes

in effect constitutes a single unit with
the forces of each side passing briefly
across the stage.
0.1 *Alarum* a call to battle with drums
and trumpets. The Jacobean audience
would recognize these as a signal that
the long-expected battle had started.
2 **has work** 'is having to work hard'
our oppression 'the pressure on us'
3 SD SCARUS Barroll ('Scarrus', 31–9)
identifies Scarus as the Soldier who
appears at 3.7.60.
4 **brave** 'courageous' and also 'splendid', as in 3.13.169
fought indeed 'real fighting'
5 **had droven** would have driven.
Droven is an old form of the past
participle 'driven'.
6 **clouts** both 'cloths, bandages' (*OED
sb.*[1] 4) and 'heavy blows' (*OED* 7)

37–8 do't, I feel. / I … thee?] *Rowe subst.;* doo't. I feele / I … thee: F

4.7] *Hanmer*   0.1–0.2 *and others] Capell subst.*   3 SD *Exeunt*]; F (*Exit*)

SCARUS

> I had a wound here that was like a T
> But now 'tis made an H.   *[Sound retreat] far off.*

ANTONY   They do retire.

SCARUS

> We'll beat 'em into bench-holes. I have yet
> Room for six scotches more.   10

Enter EROS.

EROS

> They're beaten, sir, and our advantage serves
> For a fair victory.

SCARUS   Let us score their backs
> And snatch 'em up as we take hares – behind!
> 'Tis sport to maul a runner.

ANTONY   I will reward thee
> Once for thy sprightly comfort, and tenfold   15
> For thy good valour. Come thee on!

SCARUS   I'll halt after.   *Exeunt.*

[**4.8**]   *Alarum. Enter* ANTONY *again in a march;* SCARUS *with others.*

8 **an H** Steevens points out that the pronunciation of *H* was similar to that of 'ache' (compare *MA* 3.4.56; Cercignani, 324). Moreover, as Ridley remarks, 'a T with an extra stroke (wound) at the bottom is an H on its side.'

9 **bench-holes** the holes in a privy, as in *The Precepts of Cato*, 1560, 'Such braggers will be readyer to creepe in at a bench-hoole then to shew theyr heads, or bide one stroke in a field.'

10 **scotches** gashes (*OED sb.*[1] 1)

11 **beaten** thrashed

11–12 **our advantage ... victory** 'our advantage over them will help us to win a fine victory'

12 **score** cut notches in. *OED* (v. 1c) says 'mark by cuts of a whip', and the image may indeed be one of flogging.

13 **snatch ... hares** The image is of a dog in pursuit of a hare. The *runner* should be visualized as dashing away in terror.

15 **sprightly** spirited, cheerful

17 **halt after** 'limp after you'

4.8 Location: Alexandria. Like a knight in a medieval romance, Antony returns in triumph to his lady. Shakespeare makes the most of the victory by showing first Antony's exhilaration

8 SD *Sound ... off*] *Capell subst.; Far off (opp.* heads *l. 6) F*

4.8] *Capell*

ANTONY

We have beat him to his camp. Run one before
And let the Queen know of our gests.   [*Exit a Soldier.*]
                                    Tomorrow,
Before the sun shall see's, we'll spill the blood
That has today escaped. I thank you all,
For doughty-handed are you, and have fought   5
Not as you served the cause, but as't had been
Each man's like mine. You have shown all Hectors.
Enter the city; clip your wives, your friends;
Tell them your feats, whilst they with joyful tears
Wash the congealment from your wounds, and kiss   10
The honoured gashes whole.

Enter CLEOPATRA.

[*to Scarus*] Give me thy hand.
To this great fairy I'll commend thy acts,

and then Cleopatra's delight at his return. The willingness with which he commands her to offer her hand to Scarus contrasts with his fury when she offered the same hand to Thidias in 3.13. With characteristic liberality (which contrasts strongly with Caesar's parsimony in 4.1.15–17), he wishes he could feast the entire army, and a scene which had begun with an alarum of battle concludes with a fanfare of triumph.

1 **We have … camp** 'Antonius made a saly upon [Caesar], and fought verie valliantly, so that he drave Caesars horsemen backe, fighting with his men even into their campe' (North, 307).

2 * **gests** notable deeds. If this emendation by Theobald of F's 'guests' is correct, this is Shakespeare's only use of the word. By this time it was associated with the 'knightly gests' of the heroes of medieval romance and

Antony presumably sees himself in such a role. Compare *squire*, 4.4.14, and note.

5 **doughty-handed** 'valiant in action'. Like *gests* it has associations of epic and romance as in *Faerie Queene*, 1.5.1, 'How that doughtie turnament / With greatest honour he atchieven might.'

7 **shown all Hectors** 'all shown yourselves to be as brave as Hector'. Doll Tearsheet tells Falstaff that he is 'as valorous as Hector of Troy' (*2H4* 2.4.219).

8 **clip** hug (*OED v.*[1] 1)

9 **feats** achievements; another word associated with medieval chivalry, as in 'feats of arms' (*OED* Feat *sb.* 2)

11 **whole** well, fully healed

12 **fairy** 'enchantress, to whose influence our victory must be ascribed' (Wilson). Warburton notes that the word was 'often used in this sense in the old romances'.

2 gests] *Theobald (Warburton);* guests *F* SD] *Oxf* 11 SD *to Scarus*] *Rowe*

Make her thanks bless thee. [*to Cleopatra*] O thou
    day o'th' world,
Chain mine armed neck! Leap thou, attire and all,
Through proof of harness to my heart, and there   15
Ride on the pants triumphing!   [*They embrace.*]

CLEOPATRA   Lord of lords!
O infinite virtue! Com'st thou smiling from
The world's great snare uncaught?

ANTONY   My nightingale,
We have beat them to their beds. What, girl! Though
    grey
Do something mingle with our younger brown, yet
    have we   20
A brain that nourishes our nerves and can
Get goal for goal of youth. Behold this man.

13 **day** light
15 **proof of harness** armour which has
been 'proved' or tested and found
impenetrable. For *harness* meaning
'armour', see *1H4* 3.2.101, 'He doth
fill fields with harness in the realm.'
16 **pants triumphing** 'triumphantly on
my panting breast'. Antony visualizes
his heart as a triumphal chariot in
which Cleopatra will ride. Case notes
that this passage was imitated by
Fletcher in *The False One*, 4.2.126,
where Caesar says to Cleopatra, 'My
heart shall be the chariot that shall
bear ye.'
    Lord of lords An echo of Revelation
17:14: 'The Lamb shall overcome
them: For he is Lorde of Lordes, and
King of Kinges: and they that are on
his syde, are called, and chosen, and
faythfull.'
17 **virtue** courage (Latin *virtus*)
18 **snare** a string with a running noose
used to catch small wild animals or
birds (*OED sb.* 1). War is similarly
imagined in *1H6* 4.2.21–2, 'The
Dauphin, well-appointed, / Stands
with the snares of war to tangle thee.'
Compare *toil*, 5.2.347.

* **My nightingale** F's 'Mine Nightingale', like 'should'st stowe' (3.11.58)
and 'mine Nailes' (5.2.222), derives
from the accidental repetition of
letters in the manuscript copy of a
kind which is not infrequent. Plutarch
remarks that Cleopatra's 'voyce and
words were marvelous pleasant: for
her tongue was an instrument of
musicke to divers sports and pastimes'
(North, 275).
21 **nerves** muscles
22 **Get ... of youth** 'win as many victories as a young man'. The allusion
could be to running in a race (where
the *goal* was the finishing line) or
to football. Either interpretation is
supported by *OED*.
22–6 **Behold ... shape** '[Antony] came
againe to the pallace, greatly boasting
of this victorie, and sweetely kissed
Cleopatra, armed as he was, when he
came from the fight, recommending
one of his men of armes unto her, that
had valliantly fought in this skirmish.
Cleopatra to reward his manlines,
gave him an armor and head peece of
cleane gold' (North, 307).

13 SD] *Oxf*   16 SD] *Oxf subst. (after* bless thee *l. 13)*   18 My] *F2*; Mine *F*   20 have] *Hanmer;*
ha *F*

Commend unto his lips thy favouring hand.

            [*She offers Scarus her hand.*]

Kiss it, my warrior. He hath fought today

As if a god in hate of mankind had   25

Destroyed in such a shape.

CLEOPATRA   I'll give thee, friend,

An armour all of gold. It was a king's.

ANTONY

He has deserved it, were it carbuncled

Like holy Phoebus' car. Give me thy hand.

Through Alexandria make a jolly march;   30

Bear our hacked targets like the men that owe them.

Had our great palace the capacity

To camp this host, we all would sup together

And drink carouses to the next day's fate

Which promises royal peril. Trumpeters,   35

With brazen din blast you the city's ear;

Make mingle with our rattling taborins

That heaven and earth may strike their sounds together,

Applauding our approach.   [*Trumpets sound.*] *Exeunt.*

---

25 **mankind** accented on the first syllable

26 **such a shape** 'a form (or image) like his'

28 **carbuncled** embossed with jewels. The name *carbuncle* is given to various precious stones, chiefly red ones. Ovid describes the yoke of Phoebus' chariot as set with chrysolites and gems (*Metamorphoses*, 2.106–10).

31 **targets** shields

    like ... them either 'with spirit and exaltation, such as becomes the brave warriors that own them' (Johnson) or 'hacked as much as the men are to whom they belong' (Warburton)

33 **camp this host** 'accommodate this army'

34 **carouses** toasts. To 'drink carouse' was to drain the glass to the bottom

(*OED* Carouse *adv.*) Plutarch describes Antony's way of drinking 'souldierlike' with his men (North, 257).

35 **royal peril** 'danger fit for kings'; extreme risk. Compare 'royal occupation', 4.4.17.

35–9 **Trumpeters ... approach** 'This military command, delivered in a stentorian parade-ground voice, gives the scene a brilliant climax. The command is of course instantly obeyed. It marks Antony's last heroic moment in the play' (Jones).

37 **taborins** small drums. The 'March into Alexandria', actually presented on the stage, was a regular and popular feature of nineteenth-century productions of the play. See p. 18.

---

23 favouring] *Theobald;* sauouring *F*   SD] *Oxf subst.*   39 SD *Trumpets sound*] *Jones*

[4.9] *Enter a* Sentry *and his Company [of* Watch]. ENOBARBUS
follows.

SENTRY
If we be not relieved within this hour,
We must return to th' court of guard. The night
Is shiny, and they say we shall embattle
By th' second hour i'th' morn.
1 WATCH   This last day was a shrewd one to's.   5
ENOBARBUS   O bear me witness, night –
2 WATCH   What man is this?
1 WATCH   Stand close and list him.   [*They stand aside.*]
ENOBARBUS
Be witness to me, O thou blessed moon,
When men revolted shall upon record   10
Bear hateful memory, poor Enobarbus did
Before thy face repent.
SENTRY   Enobarbus?
2 WATCH   Peace! Hark further.
ENOBARBUS
O sovereign mistress of true melancholy,   15

4.9 Location: Caesar's camp outside Alexandria. This scene is a companion to 4.3, which is also for a group of sentries. Both take place at night and are solemn in tone, and both form a prelude to battle. In the earlier scene Antony is deserted by the 'god Hercules' and in this one another deserter, Enobarbus, dies. The silence here contrasts strongly with the loud fanfare which precedes it. Compressing historical events, Shakespeare conveys the impression that Antony's defeat in 4.12 occurs the day after his victory in 4.8. This scene takes place during the intervening night.

2 **court of guard** guard house
3 **shiny** bright
3–4 **we ... morn** In the previous scene

(4.8.2–4) Antony says that they will fight *tomorrow* before dawn.
3 **embattle** prepare for battle (*OED v.*[1] 1)
5 **shrewd** difficult, irksome, 'tough' (*OED a.* 4)
8 **close** in hiding. Compare *H8* 2.1.55, 'Let's stand close and behold him.'
list listen to
10–11 **When ... memory** 'when other deserters shall be given infamous reports in the history books'. *Record* is accented on the second syllable.
15 **sovereign ... melancholy** The address is to the moon, whose influence was thought to produce mental disorders. Compare *Oth* 5.2.109–11, 'It is the very error of the moon. / She comes more nearer earth than she was wont, / And makes men mad.'

4.9] *Capell*   0.1 Sentry] *F (Centerie)*   *of* Watch] *Cam*[2]   8 SD] *Cam*[1] *subst.*

The poisonous damp of night disponge upon me,
That life, a very rebel to my will,
May hang no longer on me. Throw my heart
Against the flint and hardness of my fault,
Which, being dried with grief, will break to powder   20
And finish all foul thoughts. O Antony,
Nobler than my revolt is infamous,
Forgive me in thine own particular,
But let the world rank me in register
A master-leaver and a fugitive.   25
    O Antony! O Antony!   [*He sinks down.*]

1 WATCH   Let's speak to him.

SENTRY   Let's hear him, for the things he speaks may
concern Caesar.

2 WATCH   Let's do so. But he sleeps.   30

SENTRY   Swoons rather, for so bad a prayer as his was
never yet for sleep.

1 WATCH   Go we to him.

16 **disponge** 'drop as from a sponge'.
On the dangers of exposure to the
'rheumy and unpurged air' of night,
see Portia's advice to Brutus (*JC*
2.1.261–7). Tilley (A93) associates
this passage with the proverb 'Fresh
air is ill for the diseased or wounded
man.'

17 **my will** Enobarbus' will is to die.

19 **flint** 'Enobarbus adapts to his use
the proverbial metaphor "A heart of
flint"' (Dent, H311) (Bevington).

20 **dried with grief** 'Dry sorrow drinks
our blood' explains Romeo (*RJ*
3.5.59), and Oberon (*MND* 3.2.97)
speaks of 'sighs of love, that costs
the fresh blood dear'. Each sigh was
thought to cost one drop of blood.
'Grief means loss of blood and
increase of melancholy. Since cold
and dryness, the qualities of melancholy, are inimical to life, the grief-
stricken person becomes thin and ill.
He may die. Immoderate sorrow is a

disease' (Babb, 103).

23 **in ... particular** 'as far as you yourself are concerned' (Case)

24 **rank ... register** 'place me in its
records'

25 **fugitive** deserter (*OED a.* and *sb.* 1b)

26 SD *He sinks down* Editors generally
supply the SD *He dies* at this point
and, if a precise moment occurs when
Enobarbus does die, it is here after
he has said the words 'O Antony!'
(compare Cleopatra's feigned dying
word at 4.13.8). Nevertheless, in spite
of the Sentry's verdict at l. 36, the
Second Watch's closing line (40) suggests that Enobarbus may not be quite
dead. There is a similar uncertainty
about the precise moment of Antony's
death at 4.15.61–5. Plutarch says that
Enobarbus was 'sick of an ague' but
the physiological explanation in 15–
21 shows that he dies of melancholy.

32 **for** 'a preparation for'

26 SD] *this edn; Dies / Rowe*

246

2 WATCH   Awake sir! Awake! Speak to us!
1 WATCH   Hear you, sir?   35
SENTRY
 The hand of death hath raught him.   *Drums afar off.*
           Hark! The drums
 Demurely wake the sleepers. Let us bear him
 To th' court of guard. He is of note. Our hour
 Is fully out.
2 WATCH   Come on, then. He may recover yet.   40
          Exeunt [with the body].

[**4.10**] *Enter* ANTONY *and* SCARUS *with their army.*

ANTONY
 Their preparation is today by sea;
 We please them not by land.
SCARUS   For both, my lord.
ANTONY
 I would they'd fight i'th' fire or i'th' air;

---

36 **raught** seized (an old form of 'reached'). See *OED* Reach *v.*[1] 4c, 'To seize in the hand, to take or lay hold of; to carry off'.

37 **Demurely** 'gravely, quietly' (*OED*). This expressive word has been subjected to needless emendation such as 'Din early' (Hanmer), 'Do early' (Collier), 'Do merrily' (Dyce) and even 'Clam'rously' (Singer).

38 **of note** an important man

38–9 **Our ... out** 'Our period on duty is completely finished'

4.10 Location: the battlefield outside Alexandria. As usual, Shakespeare creates a link with the preceding scene and, as the watchmen go off with the body of Enobarbus, we hear the ominous news that Caesar is pre-paring to fight by sea. As the scene ends, Antony sets off for the hills from which he will shortly see the naval battle. In his production for the Royal Shakespeare Company in 1978 Peter Brook staged this and the following scene without a break and with all four characters on the stage throughout. By this means continuity of performance was sustained and Caesar and Antony were shown practically face to face.

2 **both** i.e. both sea and land

3 **i'th' fire or i'th' air** i.e. in the other two elements of which, in addition to earth (*land*) and water (*sea*), all matter was thought to be composed. As Cleopatra prepares herself for death (5.2.288) she sees herself as 'fire and air'.

40 SD *with the body*] *Capell*

4.10] *Capell*

We'd fight there too. But this it is: our foot
Upon the hills adjoining to the city   5
Shall stay with us – order for sea is given;
They have put forth the haven –
Where their appointment we may best discover
And look on their endeavour.   *Exeunt.*

[**4.11**]   *Enter* CAESAR *and his army.*

CAESAR

But being charged we will be still by land,
Which, as I take't, we shall, for his best force
Is forth to man his galleys. To the vales,
And hold our best advantage.   *Exeunt.*

[**4.12**]   *Alarum afar off, as at a sea fight. Enter* ANTONY *and*
SCARUS.

4–9 **our ... endeavour** 'The next
morning by breake of day, he went to
set those few footemen he had in
order upon the hills adjoyning unto
the citie: and there he stoode to
behold his gallies which departed
from the haven, and rowed against
the gallies of his enemies, and so
stoode still, looking what exployte his
souldiers in them would do' (North,
308).
4 **foot** infantry
7 **put ... haven** 'set out from the harbour'
8 **appointment** 'resolution, purpose'
(*OED* 5, where this passage is
quoted). *Their* refers to Antony's
naval forces, as the passage in North's
Plutarch makes clear.

1 **But ... charged** 'unless we are
attacked'
2 **we shall** i.e. 'be still'

4 **hold ... advantage** 'stay in the most
favourable position'

4.12 Location: uncertain. Lines 1–29
appear to take place 'upon the hills
adjoyning to the citie' from which
Antony can watch the sea fight, but
Cleopatra's entry at l. 30 suggests
that the location has moved into
Alexandria, to which, according to
Plutarch, Antony fled (see note to 10–
15). On the Jacobean stage questions
of precise location did not arise.
Neither Plutarch nor Shakespeare
says that Cleopatra in fact betrayed
Antony but, after her flight at Actium
and her reception of Thidias in 3.13,
he is easily convinced that she has.
Shakespeare creates the maximum
effect from Antony's rage by first
allowing him to express it to Scarus
(10–17) and then bringing on Cleopatra to receive its full force. The

6–7 us – order ... haven –] *Knight subst.;* vs. Order ... Haven: *F*

4.11] *Dyce*

4.12] *Dyce*

ANTONY

Yet they are not joined. Where yond pine does stand
I shall discover all. I'll bring thee word
Straight how 'tis like to go.   *Exit.*

SCARUS   Swallows have built
In Cleopatra's sails their nests. The augurs
Say they know not, they cannot tell; look grimly,   5
And dare not speak their knowledge. Antony
Is valiant and dejected, and by starts
His fretted fortunes give him hope and fear
Of what he has and has not.

Enter ANTONY.

desertion of his remaining troops marks the conclusion of a process which has been proceeding steadily from 3.10.31 onwards. Now only Eros, the man 'whom he loved and trusted much', and for whom he calls at 30 and 49, is left to support him.

0.1 * *Alarum . . . sea fight* Most editors have interpreted this stage direction as meaning that the actual sound of the sea fight is heard off stage and have moved the SD from its place (as here) in F either to l. 3, immediately after Antony's exit (Wilson), or to l. 9, just before his re-entry (Steevens, Case). Walter is apparently alone in recognizing that the alarum is only the prelude to the sea fight and not the fight itself, as Antony's first sentence makes clear. Contrast this SD with that at the opening of 3.10 in which the actual *noise of a sea fight* is heard. Having heard the alarum, Antony goes off to the vantage point near the pine tree on the hill (see headnote) in order to observe the battle. Shakespeare lets the audience know that the battle is about to begin but waits until Antony's re-entry at l. 9 before

revealing its outcome.

1 **joined** i.e. in battle

3–4 **Swallows ... nests** In Plutarch's account this episode occurs before the Battle of Actium: 'There chaunced a marvelous ill signe. Swallowes had bred under the poope of her shippe, and there came others after them that drave away the first, and plucked downe their neasts' (North, 296).

4 **sails** ships, as in 2.6.24, 3.7.49
   augurs soothsayers. They were Roman officials 'whose duty it was to predict future events ... in accordance with omens derived from the flight, singing and feeding of birds' and other portents (*OED* Augur *sb.* 1). There are allusions to them in the other Roman plays (*JC* 2.1.200; *Cor* 2.1.1). Richard Proudfoot has pointed out (privately) that manuscript 'Augurres' could account for F's 'Auguries' as well as validating Capell's emendation 'augurers'.

8 **fretted** chequered, as in *JC* 2.1.103–4, 'Yon grey lines / That fret the clouds are messengers of day.' Alternatively it could mean 'wasted, decayed' (*OED* Fret *v.*[1] 7).

4 augurs] *Pope;* Auguries *F;* Augurers *Capell*

ANTONY   All is lost!
This foul Egyptian hath betrayed me.   10
My fleet hath yielded to the foe, and yonder
They cast their caps up and carouse together
Like friends long lost. Triple-turned whore! 'Tis thou
Hast sold me to this novice, and my heart
Makes only wars on thee. Bid them all fly!   15
For when I am revenged upon my charm,
I have done all. Bid them all fly! Be gone!

                                    [Exit Scarus.]

O sun, thy uprise shall I see no more.
Fortune and Antony part here; even here
Do we shake hands. All come to this! The hearts   20
That spanieled me at heels, to whom I gave
Their wishes, do discandy, melt their sweets
On blossoming Caesar, and this pine is barked

10–15 **This foul … on thee** 'When Antonius sawe that his men did forsake him, and yeelded unto Caesar, and that his footemen were broken and overthrowen: he then fled into the citie, crying out that Cleopatra had betrayed him unto them, with whom he had made warre for her sake' (North, 308).

10 **betrayed** betrayèd

13 **Triple-turned** 'From Julius Caesar to Gnaius Pompey, from Pompey to Antony, and, as he now suspects, from him to Octavius Caesar' (Staunton)

16 **charm** enchantress, witch, as at 25

20 **hearts** men. It is not so much the men as their loyalties which have proved traitors.

21 * **spanieled** 'fawned on me like spaniels'. Compare *JC* 3.1.43, 'base spaniel fawning'. Hanmer's emendation of F's 'pannelled' is supported by the fact that an alternative spelling of 'spaniel' was 'spannell' (*OED sb.*¹). Spaniels were proverbially said to fawn and flatter (Dent, S704). Hulme (102–8) defends F's 'pannelled' on the grounds that a 'pannel' was a term for a prostitute. In other words, Antony's followers, notably Cleopatra, had, like prostitutes, made protestations of love to him and then broken them.

22 **discandy** literally 'melt' as in 3.13.170, but the image is of dogs which, having been given sweetmeats, allow them to melt and dribble from their mouths. Shakespeare is thinking of 'the unclean practice of feeding dogs at meals under the table' (Wilson). A similar cluster of images occurs in *1H4* 1.3.251–2, 'Why, what a candy deal of courtesy / This fawning greyhound then did proffer me.'

23 **this pine** i.e. himself, as distinct from 'yond pine' (l. 1) beside which he has observed the fight
    barked stripped of its bark and hence killed

17 SD] *Capell*   20 hands.] *Capell;* hands? *F*   this!] *F* (this?)   21 spanieled] *Hanmer;* pannelled *F*

That overtopped them all. Betrayed I am.
O this false soul of Egypt! This grave charm   25
Whose eye becked forth my wars and called them
    home,
Whose bosom was my crownet, my chief end,
Like a right gipsy hath at fast and loose
Beguiled me to the very heart of loss.
What, Eros, Eros!

Enter CLEOPATRA.

           Ah, thou spell! Avaunt!   30
CLEOPATRA
Why is my lord enraged against his love?
ANTONY
Vanish, or I shall give thee thy deserving
And blemish Caesar's triumph. Let him take thee
And hoist thee up to the shouting plebeians!
Follow his chariot like the greatest spot   35
Of all thy sex; most monster-like be shown

---

25 **false** unfaithful, treacherous
grave at the same time 'potent or commanding' (Case), 'formidable' (*OED a.*[1] 2b) and 'deadly' (Steevens). Vindice in *Revenger's Tragedy* (3.5.137) says that the skeleton of his dead mistress 'has a somewhat grave look with her' (ed. R.A. Foakes, 1966).

27 **my crownet ... end** 'the crown and end of my endeavours'

28 **right** true, typical. For Cleopatra as a gipsy see 1.1.10 and note.
fast and loose a proverbial image (Dent, P401). 'Fast and Loose' was a cheating game supposedly played by gipsies on their unsuspecting dupes. Compare John Lyly, *Euphues and his England* ed. Edward Arber, 1868, p. 326, 'Thus with the Aegyptian thou playest fast and loose.' Scot describes the game in *Discoverie of Witchcraft* (1584), 3.29.336–7. An object, tied in a trick knot, appears to be held fast,

but can be released when the conjurer pulls the string.

30 **Avaunt** 'be gone'; frequently used to ward off evil spirits as in *CE* 4.3.79, 'Avaunt, thou witch', and *Mac* 3.4.92, where Macbeth says it to Banquo's ghost.

33 **Caesar's triumph** As Jones remarks, this is the first reference to the triumphal procession through Rome to which Caesar would be entitled in celebration of his victory over Antony. If Antony gave Cleopatra 'her deserving' and killed her, Caesar would be deprived of the satisfaction of leading her in triumph.

34 **plebeians** accented on the first syllable

35 **spot** stain, blemish

36 **monster-like** Monsters of various kinds (deformed creatures, Indians, etc.) were regularly exhibited at Bartholomew Fair and in travelling shows. Trinculo in *Tem* thinks of

For poor'st diminutives, for dolts, and let
Patient Octavia plough thy visage up
With her prepared nails!   *Exit Cleopatra.*
                        'Tis well thou'rt gone
If it be well to live. But better 'twere   40
Thou fell'st into my fury, for one death
Might have prevented many. Eros, ho!
The shirt of Nessus is upon me. Teach me
Alcides, thou mine ancestor, thy rage;
Let me lodge Lichas on the horns o'th' moon,   45
And with those hands that grasped the heaviest club
Subdue my worthiest self. The witch shall die.
To the young Roman boy she hath sold me, and I fall
Under this plot. She dies for't. Eros, ho!   *Exit.*

[**4.13**] *Enter* CLEOPATRA, CHARMIAN, IRAS, MARDIAN.

exhibiting Caliban as a monster: 'There would this monster make a man; any strange beast there makes a man. When they will not give a doit to relieve a lame beggar, they will lay out ten to see a dead Indian' (2.2.30–3).

37 * **For … dolts** Sisson (2.271) argues for retaining this F reading and interprets 'for' as 'instead of': 'Cleopatra will be put on show instead of dwarfs and idiots.' Some editors accept Warburton's emendation of F's *dolts* to 'doits' ('small coins') and interpret *diminutives* as 'small pieces of money', though there is no known example of this meaning. 'Doits' is supported by the passage in *Tem* quoted in the note to 36.

39 **prepared** (preparèd); i.e. which she had allowed to grow (or had sharpened) for this purpose

41 **fell'st into** 'hadst fallen victim to'

43–5 **shirt … moon** Antony recalls the death of Hercules (otherwise called

Alcides), whom he claimed as his ancestor (see 1.3.85 and note). The centaur Nessus, whom Hercules had shot with a poisoned arrow, gave to Deianira, Hercules' wife, a shirt soaked in his own poisoned blood, claiming that it would work as a love charm. She accordingly sent his servant Lichas to Hercules with the shirt. When he put it on it burned and destroyed him. In his agony he hurled Lichas into the sea where the gods, moved by compassion, turned him into a rock (Ovid, *Metamorphoses*, 9.211–38). The death of Hercules is the subject of Seneca's tragedy *Hercules Oetaeus* with which Shakespeare may have been acquainted.

46 **heaviest club** Hercules' club, which he cut from the forest of Nemaea, was celebrated and he is often depicted carrying it.

47 **worthiest** 'most deserving of death'

4.13 Location: Alexandria. '[Cleopatra]

37 dolts] *F;* doits *Warburton (Thirlby)*

4.13] *Dyce*

CLEOPATRA

Help me, my women! Oh, he's more mad
Than Telamon for his shield; the boar of Thessaly
Was never so embossed.

CHARMIAN   To th' monument!

There lock yourself and send him word you are dead.
The soul and body rive not more in parting   5
Than greatness going off.

CLEOPATRA   To th' monument!

Mardian, go tell him I have slain myself.
Say that the last I spoke was 'Antony',
And word it, prithee, piteously. Hence, Mardian,   9
And bring me how he takes my death. To
    th' monument!   *Exeunt.*

being affraied of his fury, fled into the
tombe which she had caused to be
made, and there locked the dores unto
her, and shut all the springes of the
lockes with great boltes, and in the
meane time sent unto Antonius to tell
him that she was dead' (North, 308).
Our knowledge that she is not actually
dead creates, needless to say, a simple
but painfully absurd dramatic irony
in the next scene as Antony attempts
to commit suicide. The repeated commands, 'To th' monument', prepare
us for 4.15 and 5.2, which are set
there.

2 **Telamon** Ajax, son of Telamon.
After the fall of Troy, he went mad
and killed himself when the shield
and armour of the dead Achilles were
awarded not to himself but to Ulysses.
boar of Thessaly When King
Oeneus of Caledon, a country in
Thessalia in eastern Greece, failed to
make the proper sacrifices to Diana,
she retaliated by sending a giant boar
to ravage his country. It was destroyed
by Hercules. The image may have

developed from the reference to Hercules' club five lines earlier.

3 **embossed** 'of a hunted animal:
Driven to extremity; foaming at the
mouth from exhaustion' (*OED*
Embossed *ppl. a.*)
monument 'a sepulchre, place of
sepulture' (*OED sb.* 1). North (309)
calls it 'the tombe'. Tybalt is said to
lie in 'a dim monument' (*RJ* 3.5.201).

5–6 **The soul ... off** Case compares this
idea with Chapman, *Bussy D'Ambois*
(1604), 2.2.45–7, 'I must utter that /
That will in parting break more
strings in me, / Than death when life
parts.'

5 **rive** split, cleave

6 **going off** departing

9 **piteously** 'so as to arouse pity'

10 **bring me** bring me word
* **death. To th' monument!** The F
punctuation (see textual notes) makes
good sense but the imperative has
already been spoken twice (3 and 6)
like a refrain and should presumably
be repeated now, as in Pope's emendation.

10 death. To th' monument!] *Pope subst.;* death to'th' Monument. *F*

[**4.14**]   *Enter* ANTONY *and* EROS.

ANTONY
Eros, thou yet behold'st me?
EROS   Ay, noble lord.
ANTONY
Sometime we see a cloud that's dragonish,
A vapour sometime like a bear or lion,
A towered citadel, a pendent rock,
A forked mountain, or blue promontory   5
With trees upon't that nod unto the world
And mock our eyes with air. Thou hast seen these
    signs?
They are black vesper's pageants.

4.14 Location: Alexandria. Defeated in battle and betrayed, as he believes, by the woman for whom he has fought, Antony has no further purpose for which to live. Hence, he feels his identity slipping away from him (2–20) and decides to commit suicide (21–2), a decision which is strengthened and lent irony by Mardian's announcement that Cleopatra has killed herself (28–34). Shakespeare, assisted by Plutarch, then subjects him to a gradual process of humiliation. Even as he expresses his admiration for her courage, we know that it is utterly misplaced; his remaining servant, Eros, first refuses to kill him (70–2), then outdoes his master in courage by killing himself (95); Antony then attempts to do the deed himself but fails (103–4); the guards refuse to give him the fatal stroke and finally, in this abject state, he learns that Cleopatra is still alive. It is from this wretched condition that, in her imagination, Cleopatra raises him in the last scene.

1 **thou ... behold'st me?** 'can you still see me?' (a question which may well perplex Eros). The question is explained in 14, where Antony says he

can't hold on to his 'visible shape'.

2–8 **Sometime ... pageants** This is the fullest expression in the play of the phenomena of transformation and melting. A great many sources for the idea have been cited, including Aristophanes, *The Clouds*, 346–7, Pliny, *Natural History*, 2.3.7, and Chapman, *Bussy D'Ambois*, 3.1.21–3: 'empty clouds / In which our faulty apprehensions forge / The forms of dragons, lions, elephants' (ed. Nicholas Brooke, 1964). Hamlet also discusses with Polonius the changing shapes of clouds (*Ham* 3.2.376–82) and, in terms similar to those used here, Prospero speaks of the 'insubstantial pageant' of the world (*Tem* 4.1.148–56).

2 **dragonish** shaped like a dragon
4 **pendent** overhanging
5 **forked** forkèd
8 **black vesper's pageants** 'the spectacular displays of dark evenings'. *Pageants* was originally the name given to the movable stages or floats on which the miracle plays were performed. The word was subsequently applied to the plays themselves and to movable stage machinery. *OED* (Pageant *sb*. 2b) cites Giovanni Tor-

4.14] *Dyce*   4 towered] *Rowe;* toward *F*

EROS   Ay, my lord.

ANTONY

That which is now a horse, even with a thought
The rack dislimns and makes it indistinct   10
As water is in water.

EROS   It does, my lord.

ANTONY

My good knave Eros, now thy captain is
Even such a body. Here I am Antony,
Yet cannot hold this visible shape, my knave.
I made these wars for Egypt, and the Queen –   15
Whose heart I thought I had, for she had mine,
Which, whilst it was mine, had annexed unto't
A million more, now lost – she, Eros, has
Packed cards with Caesar, and false-played my glory
Unto an enemy's triumph.   20
Nay, weep not, gentle Eros. There is left us
Ourselves to end ourselves.

Enter MARDIAN.

O thy vile lady!

riano, *A Dictionary of Italian and English, formerly compiled by John Florio*, 1611, 'a frame or pageant, to rise, moove, or goe it selfe with vices'. Shakespeare may have envisaged the court masques, very popular at this time, of which transformation scenes created by elaborate movable scenery were a prominent feature.

9 **with a thought** as quick as thought
10 **The rack dislimns** 'the cloud changes its shape'. A *rack* is 'a mass of cloud, driven before the wind, in the upper air' (*OED sb.*[1] 3). To 'limn' is to paint a picture and, hence, to *dislimn* is to do the reverse and obliterate it. The transformation scenes of the court masques are probably still in Shakespeare's mind. 'There is also

wordplay involving the idea of a *body* (compare line 13) being "dislimbed" – torn limb from limb – on a rack' (Jones).

12 **knave** lad; servant
17–18 **whilst ... lost** 'while it was still my own (and I had not lost it to her) had a million more hearts (of my followers) attached to it which are now lost'
19–20 **Packed ... triumph** 'Shuffled the cards in Caesar's favour and treacherously allowed my enemy to trump (= triumph over) my glory' (Wilson). 'Trump' is a corruption of 'triumph' and both words were used for a winning card (*OED* Triumph *sb.* 8). *Knave* and *Queen* may have suggested the card-game metaphor.

10 dislimns] *Rowe;* dislimes *F*   18 now lost –] *Capell subst.;* (now lost:) *F*   19 Caesar] *Rowe;* Caesars *F*

She has robbed me of my sword.

MARDIAN   No, Antony,
My mistress loved thee and her fortunes mingled
With thine entirely.

ANTONY   Hence, saucy eunuch! Peace!   25
She hath betrayed me and shall die the death.

MARDIAN

Death of one person can be paid but once,
And that she has discharged. What thou wouldst do
Is done unto thy hand. The last she spake
Was 'Antony! Most noble Antony!'   30
Then, in the midst, a tearing groan did break
The name of Antony; it was divided
Between her heart and lips. She rendered life,
Thy name so buried in her.

ANTONY   Dead, then?

MARDIAN   Dead.

ANTONY

Unarm, Eros. The long day's task is done   35
And we must sleep. [*to Mardian*] That thou depart'st
   hence safe
Does pay thy labour richly. Go.   *Exit Mardian.*
Off! Pluck off!   [*Eros unarms him.*]
The sevenfold shield of Ajax cannot keep

---

23 **robbed ... sword** 'taken away my soldiership'; emasculated me

25 **saucy** impudent

27 **Death ... once** Two proverbs expressed this idea: 'A man can die but once' (Dent, M219) and 'I owe God a death' (with a pun on 'death' and 'debt') (Dent, G237). Compare *2H4* 3.2.234–5, 'A man can die but once, we owe God a death.'

29 **Is ... hand** 'has already been done for you' (*OED* Hand *sb.* 34c)

32–3 **it was ... lips** 'only half of it was spoken by her lips; the other half

remained in her heart'

33 **rendered** surrendered, gave up

35 **Unarm** 'He went into a chamber and unarmed him selfe, and being naked said thus: O Cleopatra, it grieveth me not that I have lost thy companie, for I will not be long from thee: but I am sory, that having bene so great a Captaine and Emperour, I am in deede condemned to be judged of lesse corage and noble minde, then a woman' (North, 309).

39 **sevenfold ... Ajax** Ajax carried a

36 SD] *Hanmer*   38 SD] *Cam¹ subst.*

The battery from my heart. O, cleave, my sides!   40
Heart, once be stronger than thy continent;
Crack thy frail case! Apace, Eros, apace!
No more a soldier; bruised pieces go;
You have been nobly borne. From me awhile.

Exit Eros.

I will o'ertake thee, Cleopatra, and   45
Weep for my pardon. So it must be, for now
All length is torture; since the torch is out,
Lie down and stray no farther. Now all labour
Mars what it does – yea, very force entangles
Itself with strength. Seal then, and all is done.   50
Eros! – I come, my queen. – Eros! – Stay for me.
Where souls do couch on flowers we'll hand in hand
And with our sprightly port make the ghosts gaze.
Dido and her Aeneas shall want troops,
And all the haunt be ours. Come Eros! Eros!   55

Enter EROS.

shield of bronze backed with seven layers of bull's hide (*Iliad*, 7.222–3).

40 **battery ... heart** 'bombardment from assaulting my heart'

41 **once** for once
thy continent 'that which contains you'; the *case* or the body. For *case* used in this sense, see 4.15.93 and compare *KL* 2.4.197–8, 'O sides, you are too tough! / Will you yet hold?'

42 **Apace** 'Hurry!' Eros is unarming him in response to his order in 35.

43 **bruised** bruisèd
bruised pieces 'battered pieces of armour.' Antony sees his disarming as a sign that he is no longer a soldier.

44 **From me** leave me

47 **length** i.e. of life; duration

49–50 **very ... strength** 'The fiercer the struggle, the more tangled and exhausted he becomes – like a trapped animal' (Jones). Wilson compares this image with *Son* 23.3–4, 'Some fierce

thing replete with too much rage, / Whose strength's abundance weakens his own heart.'

50 **Seal** finish. See 3.2.3 and note.

53 **sprightly** lively and also 'ghostly'
port 'bearing, demeanour'

54 **Dido ... troops** Warburton and successive commentators have pointed out that when in Virgil's *Aeneid* Aeneas visits Dido in the underworld she refuses to meet him, and wishes to remain with her husband Sychaeus (*Aeneid*, 6.467–74). Antony prefers to see them as celebrated lovers. For the significance of the story of Dido and Aeneas in the play generally, see pp. 66–7.

55 **all ... ours** 'they will all accompany us'. *Haunt* survives in the sense of 'a place of frequent resort' (*OED*) in the expression 'my usual haunt', and here there is a pun referring back to *ghosts* two lines earlier.

EROS
    What would my lord?

ANTONY   Since Cleopatra died,
    I have lived in such dishonour that the gods
    Detest my baseness. I, that with my sword
    Quartered the world and o'er green Neptune's back
    With ships made cities, condemn myself to lack   60
    The courage of a woman; less noble mind
    Than she which, by her death, our Caesar tells
    'I am conqueror of myself.' Thou art sworn, Eros,
    That when the exigent should come – which now
    Is come indeed – when I should see behind me   65
    Th'inevitable prosecution of
    Disgrace and horror, that on my command
    Thou then wouldst kill me. Do't. The time is come.
    Thou strik'st not me; 'tis Caesar thou defeat'st.
    Put colour in thy cheek.

EROS   The gods withhold me!   70
    Shall I do that which all the Parthian darts,
    Though enemy, lost aim and could not?

ANTONY   Eros,
    Wouldst thou be windowed in great Rome and see
    Thy master thus with pleached arms, bending down

---

59 **Quartered** cut into quarters
60 **With ... cities** Compare *H5* 3 Chorus 14–16, 'behold / A city on th'inconstant billows dancing; / For so appears this fleet majestical.'
60–3 **condemn ... of myself** taken from North's Plutarch. See note to 35.
63 **I ... myself** i.e. 'I, and not you, am my own conqueror.' Antony makes a similar boast in 4.15.15–16, 57–60.
63–8 **Thou art ... come** 'He had a man of his called Eros ... whom he had long before caused to sweare unto him, that he should kill him when he did commaunde him: and then he willed him to keepe his promise. His man drawing his sworde, lift it up as though he had ment to have striken

his maister: but turning his head at one side, he thrust his sword into him selfe, and fell downe dead at his maisters foote' (North, 309). This is Plutarch's first reference to Eros, but Shakespeare introduces him as early as 3.11.24 and gives his name repeatedly in 4.4.
64 **exigent** 'state of pressing need, emergency' (*OED a.* and *sb.*[1] B.1)
66 **inevitable prosecution** inescapable pursuit (*OED* Prosecution *sb.* 4)
70 **The gods ... me** 'The gods forbid'
71 **Parthian darts** See note to 3.1.1 ('darting Parthia').
73 **windowed** placed in a window
74 **pleached** intertwined; crossed and tied together as a captive. The reference is to the process of 'pleaching'

His corrigible neck, his face subdued   75
To penetrative shame, whilst the wheeled seat
Of fortunate Caesar, drawn before him, branded
His baseness that ensued?

EROS   I would not see't.

ANTONY

Come, then! For with a wound I must be cured.
Draw that thy honest sword which thou hast worn   80
Most useful for thy country.

EROS   O sir, pardon me!

ANTONY

When I did make thee free, swor'st thou not then
To do this when I bade thee? Do it at once,
Or thy precedent services are all
But accidents unpurposed. Draw, and come!   85

EROS

Turn from me then that noble countenance
Wherein the worship of the whole world lies.

ANTONY   [*Turns from him.*]
Lo thee!

EROS

My sword is drawn.

ANTONY   Then let it do at once
The thing why thou hast drawn it.

EROS   My dear master,   90
My captain and my emperor, let me say,
Before I strike this bloody stroke, farewell.

whereby the branches of young trees
are bent down and interlaced to form
a hedge.

75 **corrigible** submissive. The word
means, literally, 'liable to be corrected
or punished'.

76 **penetrative** penetrating, piercing
wheeled seat i.e. chariot

77 **branded** 'made conspicuous as by a
brand'

78 **His ... ensued** 'the humiliation of
the man who followed (the chariot)'

84 **precedent** previous. Pronounced
with a long 'e' (as in 'precede') and
with the emphasis on the second syllable.

85 **accidents unpurposed** casual or
fortuitous deeds performed to no
purpose

87 **worship** worth, honour. The implication is not simply that all the value
of the world is embodied in his face
but that the world reveres it.

88 **Lo thee** 'Look; see' (*OED* Lo *int.* b)

88 SD] *Rowe subst.*

ANTONY

'Tis said, man, and farewell.

EROS

Farewell, great chief. Shall I strike now?

ANTONY   Now, Eros.

EROS

Why, there then!   *Kills himself.*

                        Thus I do escape the sorrow   95

Of Antony's death.

ANTONY   Thrice nobler than myself!

Thou teachest me, O valiant Eros, what

I should and thou couldst not! My queen and Eros

Have by their brave instruction got upon me

A nobleness in record. But I will be   100

A bridegroom in my death and run into't

As to a lover's bed. Come then! And, Eros,

Thy master dies thy scholar. To do thus

                                    [Falls on his sword.]

I learned of thee. How? Not dead? Not dead?

The guard, ho! O, dispatch me.

Enter a [Company of the] Guard [, one of them DERCETUS].

96–8 **Thrice ... not** 'Then said Antonius, O noble Eros, I thanke thee for
this, and it is valliantly done of thee,
to shew me what I should doe to my
selfe, which thou couldest not doe for
me. Therewithall he tooke his sworde,
and thrust it into his bellie, and so
fell downe upon a litle bed' (North,
309).

99 **instruction** 'teaching by example'
  got upon me 'gained advantage over
  me'

100 **nobleness in record** 'noble reputation in history'. Compare Enobarbus' desire to 'earn a place i'th'
story' (3.13.47).

102 **As to ... bed** a proverbial

expression: 'To go to one's grave
(death) like a bed' (Dent, B192.1).
Compare *Ham* 4.4.62.

105 **The guard ... me** 'The wounde he
had killed him not presently, for the
blood stinted a litle when he was
layed: and when he came somwhat to
him selfe againe, he praied them that
were about him to dispatch him. But
they all fled out of the chamber, and
left him crying out and tormenting
him selfe' (North, 309).

SD * DERCETUS For the various
spellings of this name, see notes on
List of Roles and textual notes, pp.
88 and 89.

95 SD] *as Rowe; opp.* Eros *l. 94 F*   103 SD] *Rowe subst.*   105 ho!] *Theobald subst.;* how? *F*   SD
Enter ... DERCETUS] Rowe subst.; Enter a Guard F

1 GUARD   What's the noise?   105

ANTONY

    I have done my work ill, friends. O make an end
    Of what I have begun.

2 GUARD   The star is fallen.

1 GUARD

    And time is at his period.

ALL THE GUARD   Alas and woe!

ANTONY

    Let him that loves me strike me dead.

1 GUARD   Not I!

2 GUARD

    Nor I!   110

3 GUARD

    Nor any one!   *Exeunt [all the Guard but Dercetus].*

DERCETUS

    Thy death and fortunes bid thy followers fly.
    This sword but shown to Caesar with this tidings
    Shall enter me with him.   *[Takes up Antony's sword.]*

Enter DIOMEDES.

DIOMEDES   Where's Antony?   115

107 **The star is fallen** Schanzer (*Problem Plays*, 137) comments: 'The reference here is presumably to the day-star, the sun, which measures time, and to which Antony has been repeatedly compared.' The words also suggest Revelation 8:10,13: 'And there fel downe a great starre from heaven, burning as it were a lampe ... And I behelde and heard an angel fleeing through the middes of heaven, sayeing with a loud voyce, Wo, wo, wo, to the inhabitants of the earth' (Seaton, 219–20).

108 **period** end, as in 4.2.25

113–14 **This sword ... him** 'After Antonius had thrust his sworde in

him selfe, as they caried him into the tombes and monuments of Cleopatra, one of his gard called Dercetaeus, tooke his sword with the which he had stricken him selfe, and hidde it: then he secretly stale away, and brought Octavius Caesar the first newes of his death, and shewed him his sword that was bloodied' (North, 310).

113 **this tidings** 'Tidings' and 'tiding' were used interchangeably as the singular form of the word. Compare *R2* 3.4.80, 'this ill tidings'.

114 **enter ... him** 'admit me favourably to his service'

108 SP ALL THE GUARD] *Jones; All. F*   111 SD *all ... Dercetus] Capell subst.*   114 SD] *Cam²*

DERCETUS There, Diomed, there!

DIOMEDES Lives he? Wilt thou not answer, man?

       [Exit Dercetus with the sword of Antony.]

ANTONY

Art thou there, Diomed? Draw thy sword and
· give me

Sufficing strokes for death.

DIOMEDES   Most absolute lord,

My mistress Cleopatra sent me to thee.   120

ANTONY

When did she send thee?

DIOMEDES   Now, my lord.

ANTONY   Where is she?

DIOMEDES

Locked in her monument. She had a prophesying
 fear

Of what hath come to pass, for when she saw –
Which never shall be found – you did suspect

She had disposed with Caesar, and that your rage 125

Would not be purged, she sent you word she was
 dead,

But fearing since how it might work, hath sent

Me to proclaim the truth, and I am come,

I dread, too late.

ANTONY

Too late, good Diomed. Call my guard, I prithee. 130

---

120 **My mistress ... thee** 'At last there came a secretarie unto him called Diomedes, who was commaunded to bring him into the tombe or monument where Cleopatra was. When he heard that she was alive, he verie earnestlie prayed his men to carie his bodie thither, and so he was caried in his mens armes into the entry of the monument' (North, 309).

124 **be found** be seen; happen

125 **disposed** come to an agreement, made terms (*OED* Dispose *v.* 7b)

126 **purged** Antony's rage is visualized as a disease which needs a purgative drug to prevent it from destroying him, or 'working' (127).

117 SD] *Capell subst.*

DIOMEDES

What ho! The Emperor's guard! The guard, what ho!
Come, your lord calls!

Enter four or five of the Guard *of Antony.*

ANTONY

Bear me, good friends, where Cleopatra bides.
'Tis the last service that I shall command you.

1 GUARD

Woe, woe are we, sir! You may not live to wear   135
All your true followers out.

ALL THE GUARD   Most heavy day!

ANTONY

Nay, good my fellows, do not please sharp fate
To grace it with your sorrows. Bid that welcome
Which comes to punish us, and we punish it,
Seeming to bear it lightly. Take me up.   140
I have led you oft; carry me now, good friends,
And have my thanks for all.

Exeunt, bearing Antony [and Eros].

[**4.15**] *Enter* CLEOPATRA *and her Maids aloft, with* CHARMIAN
and IRAS.

135–6 **live ... out** 'outlive all your faithful followers (who would willingly let
you wear them out in your service)'
(May)

137 **sharp** severe; merciless

138 **To grace it** 'by honouring it', an
example of the Shakespearean use of
the infinitive as a gerund (Abbott,
356)
Bid 'if we bid'

138–40 **Bid ... lightly** Compare the
proverb 'He that endures is not overcome' (Dent, E136). Wilson comments that this stoical principle is

similar to the one followed by Brutus
on hearing of his wife's death (*JC*
4.3.190–2).

4.15 Location: outside Cleopatra's
monument. Plutarch says that Cleopatra 'had long before made many
sumptuous tombes and monumentes,
as well for excellencie of worke-
manshippe, as for height and greatnes
of building, joyning hard to the
temple of Isis' (North, 307). We are
prepared for Antony's arrival first by
his request (4.14.133) to the guard to

135 SP ALL THE GUARD] *Jones; All. F*   142 SD *Exeunt*] *F (Exit)   and Eros*] *Oxf*

4.15] *Dyce*

CLEOPATRA

O Charmian, I will never go from hence.

CHARMIAN

Be comforted, dear madam.

CLEOPATRA   No, I will not.

All strange and terrible events are welcome,
But comforts we despise. Our size of sorrow,
Proportioned to our cause, must be as great   5
As that which makes it.

Enter DIOMEDES [*below*].

How now? Is he dead?

DIOMEDES

His death's upon him, but not dead.
Look out o'th' other side your monument;
His guard have brought him thither.

Enter [*below*] ANTONY [*borne by*] *the* Guard.

CLEOPATRA

O sun,   10

carry him there, then by Diomedes' announcement (8–9) that he is coming. Their last reunion is painfully delayed by her fear of coming down to him (22–4) and the difficulty the women have in lifting him up into the monument. When they are at last reunited, the two of them are, characteristically, at odds as Antony tries to deliver his dying words and Cleopatra interrupts him to curse their fortune (43–52), but finally she allows him to speak and, like Othello just before his suicide, he asks her (and the audience) to remember him not for his sorry end but for his former achievements (53–60). Those, he hopes, will constitute his 'place in the story'. Like Antony when he believed her to be dead, Cleopatra

finds life meaningless without him (62–70) and, like him, begins to contemplate suicide (84–6, 90–5). The last two lines are therefore a preparation for 5.2.

0.1 *aloft* See LN, p. 304.

4–6 **Our ... it** Cleopatra uses the royal plural (*we ... our*).

8 **o'th' other side** Diomedes has entered through one of the doors at the rear of the Jacobean stage and Antony is carried through the other. To see Antony, Cleopatra must turn away from Diomedes.

10–12 **O sun ... world** According to the Ptolomaic astronomy, the sun moved round the earth in a crystalline sphere, as did the other planets in their own particular spheres. If it burned its sphere it would fly off into space and

6 SD DIOMEDES] *F (Diomed)*   *below*] *Collier*   9 SD *below*] *Collier*   *borne by*] *Rowe; and F*

Burn the great sphere thou mov'st in! Darkling stand
The varying shore o'th' world! O Antony,
Antony, Antony! Help, Charmian! Help, Iras, help!
Help, friends below! Let's draw him hither.

ANTONY   Peace!
Not Caesar's valour hath o'erthrown Antony,   15
But Antony's hath triumphed on itself.

CLEOPATRA
So it should be that none but Antony
Should conquer Antony, but woe 'tis so.

ANTONY
I am dying, Egypt, dying. Only

leave the world in darkness (*darkling*).
There are echoes in this passage of
Revelation 8:12: 'And the fourth angel
blewe, and the thirde part of the Sunne
was smitten, and the thirde part of
the Moone, and the thirde part of [the]
starres, that the thirde part of them
shoulde be darkened: and the day was
smitten that the thirde part of it should
not shine' (Seaton, 220).

12 **varying shore** 'the earth where light
and darkness made an incessant variation' (Warburton). This is acceptable
in view of the previous line calling
for the destruction of the sun which
created such variations. There is also
the suggestion of the ebb and flow of
the tides. Jones, however, interprets
shore as 'a term of contempt, meaning
"sewer". "Common shore" was regularly used for "common sewer" in
Shakespeare's day (*OED* Shore *sb.*⁴).
Cleopatra would then mean that the
world without Antony is nothing but
a ceaselessly flowing sewer – just as
later, when Antony dies, she finds
"this dull world ... no better than a
sty".'

13–14 **Help ... hither** Wilson points
out that Cleopatra's instruction to the
women to draw Antony up are
repeated at 31–2, and that Antony's
'I am dying, Egypt, dying' (19) is
repeated at 43. He deduces from this

evidence that Shakespeare made a cut
from 14 to 32 ('Peace ... good
friends') but, finding that by the omission of 19–22 ('I am dying ... lips')
he had not sufficiently emphasized
that Antony's death was imminent,
he tried to remedy this by transferring
part of it to 43. Ridley conjectures
that Shakespeare originally intended
to have Antony hoisted up after l. 13,
but, seeing the possibilities of a brief
dialogue before the hoisting, wrote
14–32 omitting to delete Cleopatra's
first request to raise him. The F text
is, in fact, perfectly acceptable as it
stands, as David Galloway argues
(*N&Q* 203 (1958): 330–5), and, as
Jones comments, conveys the
impression of the untidiness and anti-
climaxes of real life: 'If the passage
seems confused and repetitive, that
may be exactly what Shakespeare
intended.'

15–16 **Not ... itself** Antony has earlier
(4.14.61–3) attributed this stoical attitude to Cleopatra.

17–18 **none ... conquer Antony**
Compare Ovid, *Metamorphoses*, trans.
Arthur Golding (1567), 13.390, 'None
may Ajax overcome save Ajax', and
JC 5.5.56–7, 'For Brutus only overcame himself, / And no man else hath
honor by his death.'

I here importune death awhile until   20
Of many thousand kisses the poor last
I lay upon thy lips.

CLEOPATRA   I dare not, dear.
Dear my lord, pardon. I dare not
Lest I be taken. Not th'imperious show
Of the full-fortuned Caesar ever shall   25
Be brooched with me. If knife, drugs, serpents, have
Edge, sting or operation, I am safe.
Your wife Octavia, with her modest eyes
And still conclusion, shall acquire no honour
Demuring upon me. But come, come Antony –   30
Help me, my women – we must draw thee up.
Assist, good friends!   *[They begin lifting.]*

ANTONY   O quick, or I am gone!

CLEOPATRA

Here's sport indeed! How heavy weighs my lord!
Our strength is all gone into heaviness;
That makes the weight. Had I great Juno's power,   35
The strong-winged Mercury should fetch thee up
And set thee by Jove's side. Yet come a little;

---

20 **importune death** 'beg death (to delay)'

22 **dare not** i.e. come down to him. 'Cleopatra would not open the gates, but came to the high windowes, and cast out certaine chaines and ropes, in the which Antonius was trussed: and Cleopatra her owne selfe, with two women only, which she had suffered to come with her into these monumentes, trised Antonius up' (North, 309).

26 **brooched** adorned (as with a brooch). Compare *Ham* 4.7.93–4, 'He is the brooch indeed / And gem of all the nation.'

29 **still conclusion** impassive judgement. Compare 'the sober eye / Of dull Octavia' (5.2.53–4).

30 **Demuring** The word may derive either from 'demur', in which case it means 'dwelling upon, gazing at with pondering eyes' (*OED* Demur *v.* 1), or from 'demure', in which case it means 'looking at demurely' (Jones, who adds 'with an irritatingly complacent sobriety').

32 SD *They begin lifting* 'It was a hard thing for these women to do, to lift him up: but Cleopatra stowping downe with her head, putting to all her strength to her uttermost power, did lift him up with much a doe, and never let goe her hold, with the helpe of the women beneath that bad her be of good corage, and were as sorie to see her labor so, as she her selfe' (North, 310).

34 **heaviness** both 'sorrow' and 'weight'

26 me. If] *Rowe subst.*; me, if *F*   27 operation, I] *F2*; operation. I *F*   32 SD] *Cam¹ subst.*

Wishers were ever fools. O come, come, come,
> *They heave Antony aloft to Cleopatra.*
And welcome, welcome! Die when thou hast lived;
Quicken with kissing. Had my lips that power,   40
Thus would I wear them out.   [*Kisses him.*]

ALL THE GUARD
    Ah, heavy sight!

ANTONY
    I am dying, Egypt, dying.
    Give me some wine and let me speak a little –

CLEOPATRA
    No, let me speak, and let me rail so high   45
    That the false huswife Fortune break her wheel,
    Provoked by my offence –

ANTONY   One word, sweet queen:
    Of Caesar seek your honour with your safety. Oh!

CLEOPATRA
    They do not go together.

ANTONY   Gentle, hear me.
    None about Caesar trust but Proculeius.   50

CLEOPATRA
    My resolution and my hands I'll trust;

---

38 **Wishers** ... **fools** proverbial: 'Wishers and woulders are never good householders' (Tilley, W539; not in Dent)

39 **Die ... lived** 'Don't die before you have lived'

40 **Quicken** come to life

45 **rail so high** curse so violently

46 **false huswife** 'treacherous hussy'
    wheel (1) spinning-wheel used by a 'housewife' and (2) the wheel by turning which the Roman goddess of Fortune determined the fates of men. 'Fortune', says Fluellen, 'is painted ... with a wheel, to signify to you, which is the moral of it, that she is turning, and inconstant, and mut-

ability, and variation' (*H5* 3.6.30–5). In *AYL* Rosalind proposes to Celia that they should 'mock the good huswife Fortune from her wheel'.

47 **offence** i.e. her insults

48–50 **Of Caesar ... Proculeius** 'When he had dronke, he earnestly prayed her, and perswaded her, that she would seeke to save her life, if she could possible, without reproache and dishonor: and that chiefly she should trust Proculeius above any man else about Caesar' (North, 310).

49 **They ... together** Compare the proverb 'The more danger the more honour' (Dent, D35).

---

39 when] *F*; where *Pope*   41 SD] *Cam¹ subst.*   42 SP ALL THE GUARD] *Jones; All. F* Ah] *Cam¹*; A *F*; Oh *Rowe*

None about Caesar.

ANTONY

The miserable change now at my end,
Lament nor sorrow at, but please your thoughts
In feeding them with those my former fortunes   55
Wherein I lived the greatest prince o'th' world,
The noblest; and do now not basely die,
Not cowardly put off my helmet to
My countryman; a Roman by a Roman
Valiantly vanquished. Now my spirit is going;   60
I can no more.

CLEOPATRA   Noblest of men, woo't die?
Hast thou no care of me? Shall I abide
In this dull world, which in thy absence is
No better than a sty? O see, my women,
The crown o'th' earth doth melt. My lord!   65

[Antony dies.]

O withered is the garland of the war,
The soldier's pole is fallen; young boys and girls

53–60 **The ... vanquished** According
to Plutarch, Antony told Cleopatra
that 'she should not lament nor
sorowe for the miserable chaunge of
his fortune at the end of his dayes:
but rather that she should thinke him
the more fortunate, for the former
triumphes and honors he had
received, considering that while he
lived he was the noblest and greatest
Prince of the world, and that now
he was overcome, not cowardly, but
valiantly, a Romane by an other
Romane' (North, 310).

59–60 **A Roman ... vanquished**
Brower (336) comments that this
could mean simply that Antony had
fought bravely until beaten by Caesar,
but more probably means that he has

overcome himself, as both he and
Cleopatra have said earlier (4.15.15–
18).

61 **woo't** 'wilt', as at 4.2.7

66 **garland** The literal meaning is
'crown', but the crown of oak awarded
by the Romans to a successful general
is probably imagined, in which case
the meaning is closer to 'hero'.
Compare *Cor* 1.1.183–4, 'And call
him noble, that was now your hate; /
Him vile that was your garland.'

67 **pole** variously interpreted as 'standard', 'lodestar' (supported by
4.14.107, 'The star is fallen') and
'maypole'. None of these interpretations is wholly plausible, however,
and it is more likely that *pole* is used
in the sense of 'measuring rod' (*OED*

---

56 lived the] *Theobald;* liued. The *F*   65 SD *Antony dies*] *Capell (opp.* women *l. 64)*

Are level now with men; the odds is gone
And there is nothing left remarkable
Beneath the visiting moon.   [*She faints.*]
CHARMIAN   O quietness, lady!   70
IRAS She's dead too, our sovereign.
CHARMIAN Lady!
IRAS Madam!
CHARMIAN O madam, madam, madam!
IRAS Royal Egypt! Empress!   [*Cleopatra stirs.*]
CHARMIAN Peace, peace, Iras.   76
CLEOPATRA

No more but e'en a woman, and commanded
By such poor passion as the maid that milks
And does the meanest chares. It were for me
To throw my sceptre at the injurious gods   80
To tell them that this world did equal theirs
Till they had stolen our jewel. All's but naught;

sb[1] 3): 'the standard by which soldiering was measured has collapsed',
or, in other words, 'the odds is gone'.
68 **the ... gone** 'There is no distinction
left between great and small' (Ridley)
69 **remarkable** extraordinary, wonderful
70 **visiting moon** 'The moon is seen,
because of its regular waxing and
waning and its rapid rotation about
the earth, as a visitor to it' (May)
77 **No ... woman** 'No longer anything
but a mere woman (and not an
"Empress")'
* **e'en** Since F's 'in' for *e'en* occurs
also in *CE* 2.2.102, *MV* 3.5.22 and
AW 3.2.18, it was evidently a Shakespearean spelling.
78 **passion** Perhaps not simply 'grief'

but, according to Walter (138–9), the
condition of *hysterica passio* by which
women were thought to be commonly
afflicted, the symptoms of which
included swooning.
79 **chares** chores, household tasks. The
spelling survives in 'charwoman'.
were would be fitting
81 **this world ... theirs** Cleopatra
amplifies this statement when she
describes the godlike Antony in
5.2.81–91.
82 **naught** either 'worthless' (*OED* B.1)
or 'nothing' (nought) (*OED* A.1). The
latter ('Everything has been reduced
to nothing') is the more bold and
paradoxical and therefore the more
Shakespearean.

70 SD] *Rowe*   75 SD] *Cam¹ subst.*   77 e'en] *Capell (Johnson); in F*

Patience is sottish, and impatience does
Become a dog that's mad. Then is it sin
To rush into the secret house of death   85
Ere death dare come to us? How do you, women?
What, what, good cheer! Why, how now, Charmian?
My noble girls! Ah, women, women! Look,
Our lamp is spent, it's out. Good sirs, take heart.
We'll bury him, and then what's brave, what's noble,   90
Let's do't after the high Roman fashion
And make death proud to take us. Come, away.
This case of that huge spirit now is cold.
Ah, women, women! Come, we have no friend
But resolution and the briefest end.   95
                    Exeunt, bearing off Antony's body.

[5.1] *Enter* CAESAR *with his Council of War:* AGRIPPA,
DOLABELLA, MAECENAS [, PROCULEIUS, GALLUS].

83 **sottish** stupid
83–4 **does / Become** befits
89 **sirs** used in Shakespeare's day of women as well as men, as in 'Sirrah Iras' (5.2.228)
91 **after ... fashion** i.e. committing suicide, an act which, according to Roman stoical principles, was seen as noble. Antony regards the suicide of Eros and the supposed suicide of Cleopatra in this way (4.14.96–100).
95 **briefest** swiftest

5.1 Location: Caesar's camp outside Alexandria. The announcement to Caesar of Antony's death has been prepared for by Dercetus' decision (4.14.112–14) to take Antony's sword to him. We therefore await Dercetus' arrival in Caesar's camp but do not see it until after the end of 4.15. This sequence of scenes allows Shakespeare to create a contrast between Cleopatra's desolation and Caesar's more public, formal grief. His reaction to the death of his rival shows how 'the ebbed man ... comes deared by being lacked' (1.4.43–4). Moved though he is by Antony's death, Caesar takes care to deny responsibility for it (74–5) and to appear magnanimous toward Cleopatra (56–9) while actually contriving to take her prisoner. The dispatching of Proculeius and Gallus to Cleopatra (61–9) prepares the way for the next scene.

0.2 * MAECENAS F's *Menas* is clearly an error, since Menas, one of the 'famous pirates' associated with Pompey in 2.1, has no place in Caesar's camp. Theobald, pointing out that two of the speeches in this scene are assigned to '*Mec.*', substituted Maecenas for Menas in this entry direction, and his emendation has been universally accepted.

86 us?] *F2;* vs. *F*   87 what, good] *Theobald;* what good *F*

5.1] *Pope*   0.1–0.2] *Riv; Enter Caesar, Agrippa, Dollabella, Menas, with his Counsell of Warre F*   0.2 MAECENAS] *Theobald (Thirlby); Menas F*

CAESAR

Go to him, Dolabella, bid him yield.
Being so frustrate, tell him, he mocks
The pauses that he makes.

DOLABELLA   Caesar, I shall.   [*Exit.*]

Enter DERCETUS *with the sword of Antony.*

CAESAR

Wherefore is that? And what art thou that dar'st
Appear thus to us?

DERCETUS   I am called Dercetus.   5
Mark Antony I served, who best was worthy
Best to be served. Whilst he stood up and spoke
He was my master, and I wore my life
To spend upon his haters. If thou please
To take me to thee, as I was to him   10
I'll be to Caesar. If thou pleasest not,
I yield thee up my life.

CAESAR   What is't thou say'st?

DERCETUS

I say, O Caesar, Antony is dead.

CAESAR

The breaking of so great a thing should make
A greater crack. The round world   15

2 **frustrate** ineffectual (*OED pa. pple.* B.2)

2–3 **he mocks … makes** 'his delays in surrendering are merely ridiculous'

3 SD *Enter* DERCETUS Presumably the scene was staged with the convention that one of the two tiring-house doors led to Caesar's quarters and the other to the rest of the world. Caesar and his supporters came in through one door and Dercetus and the Egyptian (48 SD) through the other.

5 **thus** i.e. with a bloody sword. Bevington points out that it was a treasonable offence in medieval and Tudor England to enter the monarch's pres-

ence with weapons drawn. When in *2H6* Warwick and Suffolk do so, the King exclaims, 'Why, how now, lords? your wrathful weapons drawn / Here in our presence? Dare you be so bold?' (3.2.237–8).

9 **spend** expend

14 **breaking** destruction (*OED* Break *v.* 9) and disclosure (as in 'break the news')

15 **crack** both 'rift' and 'explosive sound' (as in 'crack of doom', *Mac* 4.1.117). 'Formerly applied to the roar of a cannon, of a trumpet and of thunder' (*OED sb.* 1).

2 he mocks] *F;* he but mocks *Hanmer*   3 SD] *Theobald subst.*

271

Should have shook lions into civil streets
And citizens to their dens. The death of Antony
Is not a single doom; in the name lay
A moiety of the world.

DERCETUS   He is dead, Caesar,
Not by a public minister of justice,   20
Nor by a hired knife, but that self hand
Which writ his honour in the acts it did
Hath, with the courage which the heart did lend it,
Splitted the heart. This is his sword;
I robbed his wound of it. Behold it stained   25
With his most noble blood.

CAESAR   [*Points to the sword.*] Look you, sad friends.
The gods rebuke me, but it is tidings
To wash the eyes of kings.

AGRIPPA   And strange it is
That nature must compel us to lament
Our most persisted deeds.

MAECENAS   His taints and honours   30
Waged equal with him.

AGRIPPA   A rarer spirit never
Did steer humanity; but you gods will give us

---

16 **civil** city, urban
19 **moiety** half
21 **hired** hirèd. See Cercignani, 25, 356–7.
   self selfsame
26 * **Look ... friends** The punctuation – or, rather, lack of it – in F
   allows of several interpretations of
   this line, and different editors have
   adopted different readings (see textual
   notes).
27 * **tidings** F2's 'a Tydings' may be
   correct because it regularizes the
   rhythm of the line. The lack of a
   syllable may, however, indicate that
   the actor should make a pause

(brought about by the pressure of
grief) after *me*.
28, 31 SP * AGRIPPA F assigns these
   two speeches to Dolabella, who left
   the stage at l. 3. The error is more
   likely to be Shakespeare's than the
   compositor's.
30 **most persisted deeds** 'those deeds
   we have most persistently tried to
   accomplish'
31 **Waged equal with him** 'were
   equally matched in him'. Compare
   Per 4.2.31, 'The commodity wages
   not with the danger.'
32 **humanity** a human being

18 the] *F;* that *Pope*   26 SD] *this edn* you, sad friends. *F3 subst.;* you sad Friends, *F;* you sad,
friends: *Theobald*   27 tidings] *F;* a Tydings *F2*   28 SP AGRIPPA] *Theobald; Dol. F*   31 Waged]
F; way *F2;* weigh'd *Rowe*   SP AGRIPPA] *Theobald; Dola. F*

Some faults to make us men. Caesar is touched.

MAECENAS

When such a spacious mirror's set before him,
He needs must see himself.

CAESAR   O Antony,   35
I have followed thee to this; but we do launch
Diseases in our bodies. I must perforce
Have shown to thee such a declining day
Or look on thine. We could not stall together
In the whole world. But yet let me lament   40
With tears as sovereign as the blood of hearts
That thou, my brother, my competitor
In top of all design, my mate in empire,
Friend and companion in the front of war,
The arm of mine own body, and the heart   45
Where mine his thoughts did kindle, that our stars,
Unreconciliable, should divide
Our equalness to this. Hear me, good friends –

34 **mirror** 'looking glass' and also 'example', as in 'the mirror of all Christian kings' (*H5* 2 Chorus 6). It is called *spacious* because of the scope of Antony's achievements.

36 **followed ... this** 'pursued you to this (catastrophe)'
launch lance. ' "Launch" and "lance" are both derived from Latin *lancere*, to handle a lance, but developed along slightly divergent paths' (Bevington).

38 **shown** exhibited

39 * **look** F's 'looke' may have been a misreading of 'looked', the emendation made by Hanmer (see textual notes).
stall dwell. Since the word was used by Shakespeare of animals ('stalling of an ox', *AYL* 1.1.10), the image is probably of two horses sharing the same stable, but *OED* also defines 'stall with' as 'tolerate the presence of

(another)' (Stall *v.*[1] 1) and this may be the meaning here.

40–8 **But ... this** Plutarch writes, 'Caesar hearing these newes, straight withdrewe him selfe into a secret place of his tent, and there burst out with teares, lamenting his hard and miserable fortune, that had bene his frende and brother in law, his equall in the Empire, and companion with him in sundry great exploytes and battells' (North, 310).

41 **sovereign** potent (as in 'sovereign remedy')

42 **competitor** partner, as in 1.4.3

43 **In ... design** 'in the most lofty enterprises'

44 **front** 'battle-front' and 'forehead', as in 1.1.6

46 **his** its

47–8 **divide ... this** 'separate us, who were so equally matched, to this extent'

36 launch] *F*; lance *Theobald*   39 look] *F* (looke); look'd *Hanmer*

Enter an Egyptian.

But I will tell you at some meeter season.
The business of this man looks out of him; 50
We'll hear him what he says. Whence are you?
EGYPTIAN

A poor Egyptian yet. The Queen, my mistress,
Confined in all she has, her monument,
Of thy intents desires instruction,
That she preparedly may frame herself 55
To th' way she's forced to.
CAESAR   Bid her have good heart.
She soon shall know of us, by some of ours,
How honourable and how kindly we
Determine for her. For Caesar cannot lean
To be ungentle.
EGYPTIAN   So the gods preserve thee! *Exit.*
CAESAR

Come hither, Proculeius. Go and say 61
We purpose her no shame. Give her what comforts
The quality of her passion shall require,

50 **looks ... him** 'shines out from his
looks'. Compare *Cym* 5.5.23, 'There's
business in these faces.'
52 * **Egyptian yet. The** Most editors
have adopted Rowe's emendation of
F's 'Egyptian yet, the'. The meaning
then is 'from what is yet Egypt (till
you pronounce on its fate)'. Wilson's
emendation creates a different
meaning: 'a poor man from Egypt
whom the Queen has nevertheless
employed'. Either version is acceptable.
57 **by ... ours** 'from some of my representatives'
59 * **lean** 'incline or tend towards, some
quality or condition' (*OED v.* 5).

Richard Proudfoot points out
(privately) that F's 'leaue' is more
probably a misreading of MS 'leane'
than of 'leue' (= 'live', the emendation made by Rowe).
61–8 **Come ... of her** 'After this, he
sent Proculeius, and commaunded
him to doe what he could possible
to get Cleopatra alive, fearing least
otherwise all the treasure would be
lost: and furthermore, he thought that
if he could take Cleopatra, and bring
her alive to Rome, she would mar-
velously beawtifie and sette out his
triumphe' (North, 310–11).
63 **require** 'render necessary' (Schmidt)

48 SD *Enter ...* Egyptian] *as Capell; after* sayes *1.* 51 *F*   52 Egyptian yet. The] *Rowe³ subst.;*
Egyptian yet, the *F;* Egyptian, yet the *Cam¹*   53 all she has, her] *Rowe;* all, she has her *F*   54
intents desires] *Pope;* intents, desires, *F*   59–60 lean ... ungentle] *this edn;* leaue ... vngentle *F;*
live ... ungentle *Rowe²;* leaue ... gentle *Capell;* learn ... ungentle *Dyce (Tyrwhitt)*

Lest, in her greatness, by some mortal stroke
She do defeat us. For her life in Rome   65
Would be eternal in our triumph. Go,
And with your speediest bring us what she says
And how you find of her.
PROCULEIUS   Caesar, I shall.
CAESAR   Gallus, go you along.   *Exeunt Proculeius [and Gallus].*
                                   Where's Dolabella

To second Proculeius?
ALL BUT CAESAR   Dolabella!   70
CAESAR
Let him alone, for I remember now
How he's employed. He shall in time be ready.
Go with me to my tent, where you shall see
How hardly I was drawn into this war,
How calm and gentle I proceeded still   75
In all my writings. Go with me and see
What I can show in this.   *Exeunt.*

[5.2]   *Enter* CLEOPATRA, CHARMIAN *and* IRAS.

65–6 her ... triumph 'her presence alive in Rome in my triumph would make it famous for ever' (Jones)

67 with ... speediest 'as quickly as you can'. Compare *Oth* 2.3.7, 'with your earliest'.

68 how ... her 'what you find out about her'. For examples of *how* = 'concerning, about', see Abbott, 174.

73–6 where ... writings 'Then he called for all his frendes, and shewed them the letters Antonius had written to him, and his aunsweres also sent him againe, during their quarrell and strife: and how fiercely and prowdly the other answered him, to all just and reasonable matters he wrote unto him' (North, 310).

74 hardly reluctantly
75 still constantly

5.2 Location: inside Cleopatra's monument. At the end of 4.15 (84–6, 90–5), following the death of Antony, Cleopatra begins to contemplate suicide (as Antony did on hearing of the supposed death of Cleopatra). In 5.1 (62–6) Caesar foresees this possibility and makes plans to forestall it. Then, at the opening of this scene, Cleopatra considers suicide in a more positive way as a means of defeating Caesar and overcoming the onslaughts of fortune. This long scene is divided into short episodes, each one introduced by the arrival of a new

---

69 SD *Exeunt Proculeius and Gallus*] *this edn.; Exit Proculeius F (opp. shall l. 68)*   70 SP ALL
BUT CAESAR] *Oxf; All. F*

5.2] *Pope*   0.1 *and* IRAS] *Capell; Iras, and Mardian F*

CLEOPATRA

My desolation does begin to make
A better life. 'Tis paltry to be Caesar.
Not being Fortune, he's but Fortune's knave,
A minister of her will. And it is great
To do that thing that ends all other deeds,   5
Which shackles accidents and bolts up change,
Which sleeps and never palates more the dung,
The beggar's nurse and Caesar's.

character (Proculeius, the Soldiers, Dolabella, Caesar, Seleucus, the Countryman) who attempts either to prevent or to assist her. Cleopatra is the only character who remains on the stage throughout. The tension in the scene arises from our uncertainty whether Cleopatra will manage to 'fool their preparation and ... conquer / Their most absurd intents' (224–5) by killing herself. It is a contest between Caesar and Cleopatra for Cleopatra's life. When therefore, having obtained the asps and dressed herself in her robes, she prepares to die, she appears to have won a final victory, as Caesar himself admits (334–6).

0.1 * *Enter ...* IRAS Mardian is also included in the F entry direction but he says nothing throughout the scene, nobody mentions him and his presence would be a distraction during the intimate episodes between Cleopatra and her women. Moreover Plutarch emphasizes that Cleopatra was alone apart from her two women (North, 309). The actor playing Mardian may have doubled the role of Seleucus, a possibility which is strengthened by Cleopatra's hint (173–4) that Seleucus, too, is a eunuch. Shakespeare presumably intended to include

Mardian in the dialogue but then found that the scene was better without him and neglected to delete his entry (compare note to 1.2.0.1). The opening stage direction does not say that they come on 'aloft' (as in 4.15.0.1) and we can assume that the scene was played on the main stage.

1 **desolation** a word with many associations: 'ruin' (*OED* 1), 'solitariness' (*OED* 3) and 'grief' (*OED* 4)

3 **Fortune's knave** Compare the proverbial expression 'He is Fortune's fool' (Dent, F617.1). See also *RJ* 3.1.136. A *knave* is a servant, as in 4.14.12.

6 **shackles accidents** 'prevents chance happenings (as if by fettering them with *shackles*)' (May)
   bolts up locks up; imprisons with a bolt

7 **palates** tastes, as in *TC* 4.1.60, 'Not palating the taste of her dishonor'
   * **dung** Theobald's emendation 'dugg', prompted by association with *nurse* in the next line, makes sense but is unnecessary. *Dung* expresses a contempt for mere earthly life and is consistent with 'our dungy earth' (1.1.36) and 'this dull world, which in thy absence is / No better than a sty' (4.15.63–4).

7 dung] *F;* dugg *Theobald (Warburton)*

276

Enter PROCULEIUS.

PROCULEIUS
  Caesar sends greeting to the Queen of Egypt,
  And bids thee study on what fair demands   10
  Thou mean'st to have him grant thee.

CLEOPATRA   What's thy name?

PROCULEIUS
  My name is Proculeius.

CLEOPATRA   Antony
  Did tell me of you, bade me trust you, but
  I do not greatly care to be deceived
  That have no use for trusting. If your master   15
  Would have a queen his beggar, you must tell him
  That majesty, to keep decorum, must
  No less beg than a kingdom. If he please
  To give me conquered Egypt for my son,
  He gives me so much of mine own as I   20
  Will kneel to him with thanks.

PROCULEIUS   Be of good cheer.
  You're fallen into a princely hand; fear nothing.

8 SD * ***Enter*** PROCULEIUS Some editors have amplified this F stage direction (see textual notes) in accordance with Plutarch's statement that 'Proculeius came to the gates that were very thicke and strong, and surely barred, but yet there were some cranewes through the which her voyce might be heard, and so they without understoode' (North, 311). Assuming that this scene, unlike 4.15, takes place on the main stage and not on the gallery, a fence or grille could easily be fitted across one of the tiring-house doors and Proculeius could remain behind it. On the other hand, Shakespeare could have chosen not to follow Plutarch in this detail but simply to bring on Proculeius as an ambassador from Caesar whom Antony has advised Cleopatra to trust.

10 **study ... demands** 'think seriously about requests for favourable terms'
14 **to be deceived** 'whether I am deceived or not'
15 **That have no use** 'since I have no need'
16 **queen his beggar** 'have a queen beg from him', seemingly an allusion to the ballad of 'King Cophetua and the Beggar Maid' in which a king woos a beggar maid and makes her his queen. There are references to it in *RJ* 2.1.4 and *LLL* 1.2.109–10. Cleopatra is amused to find the roles have been reversed.
17 **keep decorum** act appropriately. Compare 1.2.75–6.
18–28 **If he ... kneeled to** 'Cleopatra demaunded the kingdome of Aegypt for her sonnes: and ... Proculeius

8 SD *Enter* PROCULEIUS] *F; Enter Proculeius and Gallus below* / *Hanmer; Enter Proculeius and Gallus, with Soldiers, at the Door of the Monument, without* / *Capell*

Make your full reference freely to my lord,
Who is so full of grace that it flows over
On all that need. Let me report to him   25
Your sweet dependency, and you shall find
A conqueror that will pray in aid for kindness
Where he for grace is kneeled to.

CLEOPATRA   Pray you tell him
I am his fortune's vassal and I send him
The greatness he has got. I hourly learn   30
A doctrine of obedience, and would gladly
Look him i'th' face.

PROCULEIUS   This I'll report, dear lady.
Have comfort, for I know your plight is pitied
Of him that caused it.

> [*Enter* GALLUS *and* Roman Soldiers.]

[*to the Soldiers*] You see how easily she may be
        surprised.   35
Guard her till Caesar come.

IRAS   Royal queen!

---

aunswered her, that she should be of
good cheere, and not be affrayed to
referre all unto Caesar' (North, 311).
23 **Make ... freely** 'refer yourself
   wholly and frankly' (Wilson); 'Put
   yourself wholly into his hands' (Jones)
24 **grace** favour, good will
26 **sweet dependency** meek sub-
   missiveness. Compare *TS* 3.2.195,
   'this most patient, sweet, and virtuous
   wife'.
27 **pray in aid** 'crave your assistance'
   (originally a legal term; *OED* Pray *v.*
   6). Hence 'pray ... kindness' means
   'beg you to help him in being kind to
   you' (May).
29–30 **I am ... got** 'I submit myself to
   his good fortune and I acknowledge
   the power he has achieved.'

31 **doctrine** 'lesson; such as could be
   found in the Elizabethan homily "Of
   Order and Obedience"' (Bevington)
34 SD * *Enter ...* **Soldiers** See LN,
   pp. 304–5.
35–6 * **You ... come** The speech prefix
   Pro., already supplied at 32, is
   repeated here in F and some editors,
   following Malone (see textual notes),
   emend it to *Gallus*. It is clear,
   however, that there was a stage direction in the manuscript at 34 which
   was omitted for compositorial reasons
   (see p. 76) and that the speech prefix
   Pro. was repeated after it. Both 32–4
   and 35–6 should therefore be assigned
   to Proculeius (Hosley, 65–6).
35 **surprised** captured

34 SD *Enter* ... Soldiers] *This edn; Here Gallus, and* Guard, *ascend the Monument by a Ladder, and
enter at a back-Window* / Theobald   35 SD] *Oxf*   35–6 You ... come] *F; Malone assigns to Gallus*

CHARMIAN

O Cleopatra, thou art taken, queen!

CLEOPATRA

Quick, quick, good hands.   [*Draws a dagger.*]

PROCULEIUS   Hold, worthy lady, hold!

[*Disarms her.*]

Do not yourself such wrong, who are in this
Relieved, but not betrayed.

CLEOPATRA   What, of death too,   40

That rids our dogs of languish?

PROCULEIUS   Cleopatra,

Do not abuse my master's bounty by
Th'undoing of yourself. Let the world see
His nobleness well acted, which your death
Will never let come forth.

CLEOPATRA   Where art thou, Death?   45

Come hither, come! Come, come and take a queen
Worth many babes and beggars!

PROCULEIUS   O temperance, lady!

CLEOPATRA

Sir, I will eat no meat; I'll not drink, sir;
If idle talk will once be necessary,

37–45 **O Cleopatra ... forth** 'She
thought to have stabbed her selfe in
with a short dagger she ware of
purpose by her side. But Proculeius
came sodainly upon her, and taking
her by both the hands, said unto her:
Cleopatra, first thou shalt doe thy
selfe great wrong, and secondly unto
Caesar: to deprive him of the occasion
and oportunitie, openly to shew his
bountie and mercie ... So even as he
spake the word, he tooke her dagger
from her, and shooke her clothes for
feare of any poyson hidden about her'
(North, 311).

40 **relieved** rescued (*OED* Relieve *v.* 1).
In her reply, Cleopatra interprets the
word in the sense of 'eased of' (*OED*
Relieve *v.* 5c).

41 **languish** suffering; 'to continue in a
state of feebleness and suffering'
(*OED v.* 1)

45 **let come forth** 'allow to show itself'

47 **babes and beggars** i.e. people who
are seized by death in large numbers.

49 **once** ever

49–50 * **If ... neither** Line 49 seems
inconsistent with those which
immediately precede and follow it,
both of which are about renunciation.
Malone suggested that it was originally followed by another line,
omitted by the compositor, the sense
of which was 'I won't speak so much
as a syllable'. Another suggestion is
that the line itself was deleted by
Shakespeare but retained by the compositor. Capell's proposal was to

---

38 SD *Draws a dagger*] *Theobald subst. Disarms her*] *Malone subst.*

I'll not sleep neither. This mortal house I'll ruin,   50
Do Caesar what he can. Know, sir, that I
Will not wait pinioned at your master's court,
Nor once be chastised with the sober eye
Of dull Octavia. Shall they hoist me up
And show me to the shouting varletry   55
Of censuring Rome? Rather a ditch in Egypt
Be gentle grave unto me! Rather on Nilus' mud
Lay me stark naked, and let the water-flies
Blow me into abhorring! Rather make
My country's high pyramides my gibbet   60
And hang me up in chains!

PROCULEIUS   You do extend
These thoughts of horror further than you shall
Find cause in Caesar.

Enter DOLABELLA.

DOLABELLA   Proculeius,
What thou hast done thy master Caesar knows,
And he hath sent for thee. For the Queen,   65
I'll take her to my guard.

PROCULEIUS   So, Dolabella,
It shall content me best. Be gentle to her.

emend *sleep* to 'speak'. Sense can be
made of F, however, as it stands: 'If
it is necessary for me to engage in
trivial chatter in order to stay awake,
then I won't sleep either.'
50 **mortal house** i.e. her body
52 **pinioned** 'with my arms bound;
shackled' (*OED* Pinion *v.* 2)
53 **chastised** spoken with the emphasis
on the first syllable
55 **varletry** common people; mob
59 **Blow ... abhorring** 'deposit their
eggs on me and make me abhorrent'.
OED Blow *v.*¹ 28 cites Edward
Topsell, *History of Four-footed Beasts*,
1607, p. 49, 'Worms ... which are
not bigger then such as flyes blow in

rotten flesh'.
60 **pyramides** plural of Latin *pyramis*
('pyramid'). This form was common
at the time, though Shakespeare elsewhere uses 'pyramids' (*Mac* 4.1.57).
It is pronounced with four syllables,
with the accent on the second
(Cercignani, 43). The pyramid Cleopatra has in mind is not of the shape
we think of today but an obelisk. See
2.7.18 and note.
63 SD *Enter* DOLABELLA Shakespeare
greatly expands Plutarch's account of
this episode and creates a character for
Dolabella who in Plutarch's version is
little more than a name (North, 314).

50 sleep] *F;* speak *Capell*   58 naked] *F (*nak'd*)*

[*to Cleopatra*] To Caesar I will speak what you shall
   please,
If you'll employ me to him.

CLEOPATRA   Say I would die.

Exit Proculeius [with Gallus and Soldiers].

DOLABELLA
Most noble empress, you have heard of me?   70

CLEOPATRA
I cannot tell.

DOLABELLA   Assuredly you know me.

CLEOPATRA
No matter, sir, what I have heard or known.
You laugh when boys or women tell their dreams;
Is't not your trick?

DOLABELLA   I understand not, madam.

CLEOPATRA
I dreamt there was an emperor Antony.   75
O, such another sleep, that I might see
But such another man!

DOLABELLA   If it might please ye –

CLEOPATRA
His face was as the heavens, and therein stuck

---

74 **trick** 'custom; characteristic quality'
(*OED sb.* 7)

78–91 **His face … pocket** Adelman
(*Essay*) points out the similarity of
this passage to Cartari's description
of the representations of Jove:
'*Orpheus* … ascribed thus much unto
Jove … He sitteth on the highest
part of [the world], whose feet reach
downe to the lowest and basest corner
thereof, within whom is contained
earth, water, aire, fire, day, and night:
whose Image he thus setteth forth,
his head (sayth hee) with those his
golden-hued lockes, is the beauteous
firmament gloriously adorned with
such infinite armies of translucent
stars, and from ech side of his temples

peepe forth two yong golden hornes,
signifying by the one the East, and
by the other the West, his eies are the
Sunne and the Moone, his shoulders
and breast the spacious compasse of
the aire, and the wings thereon
infixed, intend the furious swiftnesse
of the winds, his bellie downe to the
knee, is the wide earth circumcinct
with the waters of the sea, and his
feet discend down throgh the bowels
of the lower center' (*Imagines Deorum*,
Lyon, 1581, trans. Richard Linche as
The Fountaine of Ancient Fiction 1599,
Iij verso). Seaton (219–24) remarks
that the passage calls to mind the
account in Revelation 10:1–2 of the
'myghtie angel' which 'came downe

68 SD] *Hanmer*   69 SD *Exit Proculeius*] *as Pope; after* to him *l.*   69 F   *with … Soldiers*] *Capell
subst.*   78 heavens *F (*Heau'ns)

A sun and moon which kept their course and lighted
The little O, the earth.

DOLABELLA   Most sovereign creature –   80

CLEOPATRA

His legs bestrid the ocean; his reared arm
Crested the world; his voice was propertied
As all the tuned spheres, and that to friends;
But when he meant to quail and shake the orb,
He was as rattling thunder. For his bounty,   85
There was no winter in't; an autumn it was
That grew the more by reaping. His delights
Were dolphin-like: they showed his back above
The element they lived in. In his livery
Walked crowns and crownets; realms and islands
    were   90

from heaven, clothed with a cloude,
and the raynbow upon his head, and
his face as it were the Sunne, and his
feete as it were pillars of fyre ... and
he put his right foote upon the sea,
and his left foote on the earth.'
Bevington compares it to Marlowe's
account of Tamburlaine in *1 Tamburlaine*, 2.1 and to Lady Percy's
eulogy of the dead Hotspur (*2H4*
2.3.18–38).

80 * **O, the earth** Steevens's emendation of F's 'o'th' earth' is supported by
Shakespeare's use of 'O' for anything
circular, as in *H5* Prologue 13,
'Within this wooden O', referring to
the Globe theatre, a round (or, at
least, polygonal) building.

81 **His ... ocean** Shakespeare is thinking
of the Colossus of Rhodes, a bronze
statue of Apollo which was one of the
Seven Wonders of the World. It is
said to have been more than 100 feet
high and to have stood astride the
harbour of Rhodes. Compare *JC*
1.2.135–6, 'he doth bestride the
narrow world / Like a colossus'.

81–2 **reared ... world** 'The image is
taken from heraldry: sometimes a

raised arm, perhaps holding a sword,
was mounted on the helmet as a crest'
(May). Hence *Crested* means 'dominated', 'crowned'.

82 **propertied / As** had the qualities of

83 **tuned spheres** (tunèd). There was a
belief, attributed to Pythagoras, that
each of the seven planetary spheres,
in their rotation round the earth,
produced a musical note and that
together they produced a perfectly
harmonious   sound   which   was,
however, inaudible to human ears.
The idea is explained in *MV* 5.1.58–
65.

84 **quail** 'bring into subjection by fear'
(*OED v.*[1] 5)
    orb world

86 * **autumn** See LN, p. 305.

87–9 **His delights ... in** 'as the dolphin
shows his back above the water, so
Antony rose superior to the pleasures
which were his element'

89 **livery** retinue. A livery was a suit of
clothes given by a master to his servants as a token by which they could
be identified.

90 **crowns and crownets** i.e. kings and
princes. Compare 3.13.95–7.

80 O, the] *Steevens subst.*; o'th' *F*; O o'th' *Theobald*   86 autumn] *Theobald*; *Anthony F*

As plates dropped from his pocket.

DOLABELLA   Cleopatra –

CLEOPATRA

Think you there was or might be such a man
As this I dreamt of?

DOLABELLA   Gentle madam, no.

CLEOPATRA

You lie up to the hearing of the gods!
But if there be nor ever were one such,   95
It's past the size of dreaming. Nature wants stuff
To vie strange forms with fancy; yet t'imagine
An Antony were nature's piece 'gainst fancy,
Condemning shadows quite.

DOLABELLA   Hear me, good madam.

Your loss is as yourself, great, and you bear it   100
As answering to the weight. Would I might never
O'ertake pursued success, but I do feel,
By the rebound of yours, a grief that smites
My very heart at root.

CLEOPATRA   I thank you, sir.

Know you what Caesar means to do with me?   105

---

91 **plates** silver coins (*OED* Plate *sb.* 13)
95 **if ... such** 'if there neither is nor ever was such a man'. 'This reading keeps F's "nor", and takes the construction to be "neither [understood] ... nor" ' (Jones).
96 **It's past ... dreaming** 'no dream could measure up to the reality'
96–7 **Nature ... fancy** 'Nature lacks the material to compete with the imagination in the creation of wonderful forms'. *Strange* implies not only 'extraordinary' and 'exotic' but also 'exceptional to a degree which excites wonder and astonishment' (*OED a.* 10).
97–9 **t'imagine ... quite** 'to imagine an Antony would be to create a masterpiece (*piece*), which would be

natural rather than a fantasy and would entirely discredit the insubstantial creations (*shadows*) of fancy'. Compare 2.2.210–11, where Cleopatra is said to be more beautiful than a picture of Venus in which the imaginary surpasses reality.
101 **As answering ... weight** 'in proportion to its gravity'
101–2 **Would ... feel** 'may I never achieve my aim if I do not feel' (Ridley)
103 **rebound** reflection
103–4 **smites ... root** 'strikes to the very bottom of my heart'
105 **Know ... me** Cleopatra catches Dolabella at this unguarded moment and puts to him the vital question.

95 nor] *F;* or *F3*   103 smites] *Capell;* suites *F;* shoots *Pope*

DOLABELLA

    I am loath to tell you what I would you knew.

CLEOPATRA

    Nay, pray you, sir.

DOLABELLA   Though he be honourable –

CLEOPATRA

    He'll lead me, then, in triumph.

DOLABELLA

    Madam, he will. I know't.

Flourish. Enter PROCULEIUS, CAESAR, GALLUS, MAECENAS
           and others of his train.

ALL   Make way there! Caesar!   110

CAESAR   Which is the Queen of Egypt?

DOLABELLA   It is the Emperor, madam.   *Cleopatra kneels.*

CAESAR

    Arise! You shall not kneel.

    I pray you rise. Rise, Egypt.

CLEOPATRA   Sir, the gods

    Will have it thus. My master and my lord   115

    I must obey.   *[She stands.]*

CAESAR   Take to you no hard thoughts.

    The record of what injuries you did us,

    Though written in our flesh, we shall remember

    As things but done by chance.

CLEOPATRA   Sole sir o'th' world,

    I cannot project mine own cause so well   120

    To make it clear, but do confess I have

111 **Which ... Egypt** Caesar's apparent inability to recognize Cleopatra is interpreted by Wilson as his 'opening shot in the duel of wits', but the question may not be addressed to the company in general but to his emissary Dolabella, who then introduces him formally to the Queen of Egypt (Bevington).

119 **sir** master

120 **project** set forth; present in words (*OED v.* 3). The word is emphasized on the first syllable.

121 **clear** spotless, innocent. Compare *Mac* 1.7.16–18, 'Duncan ... hath been / So clear in his great office.'

106 what I] *Rowe³;* what, I F   116 SD *She stands*] *this edn; rising* / *Oxf (after* Egypt *l. 114)*

Been laden with like frailties which before
Have often shamed our sex.

CAESAR   Cleopatra, know
We will extenuate rather than enforce.
If you apply yourself to our intents,   125
Which towards you are most gentle, you shall find
A benefit in this change; but if you seek
To lay on me a cruelty by taking
Antony's course, you shall bereave yourself
Of my good purposes, and put your children   130
To that destruction which I'll guard them from
If thereon you rely. I'll take my leave.

CLEOPATRA

And may through all the world! 'Tis yours, and we,
Your scutcheons and your signs of conquest, shall
Hang in what place you please. Here, my good lord.   135
                                    [*Hands him a paper.*]

CAESAR

You shall advise me in all for Cleopatra.

CLEOPATRA

This is the brief of money, plate and jewels

---

124 **extenuate ... enforce** 'excuse
rather than stress (your frailties)'.
Compare *JC* 3.2.38–40, 'his glory not
extenuated, wherein he was worthy;
nor his offences enforc'd, for which
he suffer'd death'. In both passages
the language is legalistic.
125 **apply yourself** conform
128 **lay ... cruelty** 'make me appear
cruel'; 'inflict on me the appearance
of being cruel'
132 **I'll ... leave** Caesar is about to make
an exit but Cleopatra detains him in
order to introduce the subject of her
treasure, a subject she is evidently
anxious to discuss. This indicates that

Seleucus' supposed betrayal of her
has been deliberately contrived. See
11.140–74 and notes.
134 **scutcheons** 'shields bearing the
coats of arms of their owners' (May).
A victor in battle would commonly
display the scutcheons he had captured from his opponents.
135 **Hang** Bevington suggests a pun
here. It is not necessarily the shields
but Caesar's prisoners who will hang.
In 60–1, Cleopatra imagines herself
being hung up in chains.
136 **in ... Cleopatra** 'about all matters
pertaining to Cleopatra'

135 SD] *Cam¹ subst.*

I am possessed of. 'Tis exactly valued,
Not petty things admitted. Where's Seleucus?

[*Enter* SELEUCUS.]

SELEUCUS   Here, madam.   140
CLEOPATRA

This is my treasurer. Let him speak, my lord,
Upon his peril, that I have reserved
To myself nothing. Speak the truth, Seleucus.
SELEUCUS

Madam,

---

137 **brief** summary, inventory
139 **not ... admitted** 'not including
trivial items'
SD * *Enter* SELEUCUS F provides no
direction for Seleucus to enter and it
would be inappropriate for him to
come on either with Caesar and his
supporters or with Cleopatra and her
women at the beginning of the scene
where he is not identified in the dialogue. Plutarch says that Cleopatra
'caused to be brought all the treasure
and pretious things she had of the
auncient kings her predecessors' into
the monument (North, 307) and that
at this point 'by chaunce there stoode
Seleucus by, one of her Treasorers'
(North, 314). It appears, then, that
the monument was the place where
Seleucus worked and that he entered,
as it were, from his office.
140–74 **Here ... on me** Cleopatra has
already learned from Dolabella (108–
9) that Caesar intends to exhibit her in
his triumphal procession. It is likely,
then, that she tries deliberately to
deceive him into believing that she
does not intend to kill herself and that
she has already instructed Seleucus to
support her in this plan. This is what
Shakespeare implies when she pre-

vents Caesar's exit at 132 (see note).
Plutarch is unambiguous: '[Seleucus],
to seeme a good servant, came straight
to Caesar to disprove Cleopatra, that
she had not set in al, but kept many
things back of purpose. Cleopatra was
in such a rage with him, that she flew
upon him, and tooke him by the
heare of the head, and boxed him
wellfavoredly. Caesar fell a laughing,
and parted the fray. Alas, said she, O
Caesar: is not this a great shame and
reproche, that thou having vouche-
saved to take the peines to come unto
me, and hast done me this honor,
poore wretche, and caitife creature,
brought into this pitiefull and miserable estate: and that mine owne
servaunts should come now to accuse
me, though it may be I have reserved
some juells and trifles meete for
women, but not for me (poore soule)
to set out my selfe withall, but
meaning to geve some pretie presents
and gifts unto Octavia and Livia, that
they making meanes and intercession
for me to thee, thou mightest yet
extend thy favor and mercie upon
me? Caesar was glad to heare her say
so, perswading him selfe thereby that
she had yet a desire to save her life

137–8 brief of ... of. 'Tis] *Pope subst.*; breefe: of ... of, 'tis *F*   139 admitted] *F*; omitted *Theobald*
SD *Enter* SELEUCUS] *Ard²*   145 seel] *F* (seele); seale *F3*; seal *F4*

I had rather seel my lips than to my peril   145
Speak that which is not.

CLEOPATRA   What have I kept back?

SELEUCUS

Enough to purchase what you have made known.

CAESAR

Nay, blush not, Cleopatra. I approve
Your wisdom in the deed.

CLEOPATRA   See, Caesar! O behold
How pomp is followed! Mine will now be yours   150
And, should we shift estates, yours would be mine.
The ingratitude of this Seleucus does
Even make me wild. O slave, of no more trust
Than love that's hired! What, go'st thou back?
    Thou shalt
Go back, I warrant thee! But I'll catch thine eyes   155
Though they had wings! Slave! Soulless villain!
    Dog!
O rarely base!

CAESAR   Good queen, let us entreat you.

CLEOPATRA

O Caesar, what a wounding shame is this,
That – thou vouchsafing here to visit me,
Doing the honour of thy lordliness   160
To one so meek – that mine own servant should
Parcel the sum of my disgraces by

... And so he tooke his leave of her,
supposing he had deceived her, but
in deede he was deceived him selfe'
(North, 314).

145 * **seel** a term used in falconry for
sewing up the eyelids of a hawk (as
in 3.13.117), here used figuratively of
the lips. Some editors adopt F4's
'seal', which was an alternative spelling of *seel* but in modern English loses
its metaphorical connotations.

150 **How ... followed** either 'how people
in power are served' or 'how people only
serve those who are in power'. In

view of what follows ('Mine will now
be yours') the latter meaning is the
more likely.
Mine my followers (i.e. people like
Seleucus)

151 **shift estates** change positions

154 **hired** paid for, bought

157 **rarely** exceptionally

159 **thou** Cleopatra, becoming more
ingratiating, shifts from the formal
you of her previous address to Caesar
to the more intimate *thou*.

162 **Parcel** 'enumerate by items, specify'
(Schmidt)

Addition of his envy! Say, good Caesar,
That I some lady trifles have reserved,
Immoment toys, things of such dignity   165
As we greet modern friends withal; and say
Some nobler token I have kept apart
For Livia and Octavia, to induce
Their mediation, must I be unfolded
With one that I have bred? The gods! It smites me   170
Beneath the fall I have. [*to Seleucus*] Prithee go hence,
Or I shall show the cinders of my spirits
Through th'ashes of my chance. Wert thou a man,
Thou wouldst have mercy on me.

CAESAR   Forbear, Seleucus.
                                        [*Exit Seleucus.*]

CLEOPATRA

Be it known that we, the greatest, are misthought   175
For things that others do, and when we fall,
We answer others' merits in our name,
Are therefore to be pitied.

CAESAR   Cleopatra,
Not what you have reserved nor what acknowledged
Put we i'th' roll of conquest. Still be't yours;   180
Bestow it at your pleasure, and believe

---

164 **lady** suitable for a lady, feminine
165 **Immoment toys** insignificant trifles. *OED* describes *immoment* as 'rare' and cites only this example.
166 **modern** ordinary (*OED a.* A.4). Compare *AW* 2.3.2–3, 'to make modern and familiar, things supernatural and causeless'.
168 **Livia** Caesar's wife
169–70 **unfolded / With** revealed, betrayed by (*OED* Unfold *v.*[1] 2)
170 **With** by
bred 'brought up (as my servant)', as in *MM* 4.2.130–1, 'A Bohemian born,

but here nurs'd up and bred'
172 **cinders** embers
173 **chance** fortune
Wert … man This may imply that Seleucus is a eunuch. His role could well have been doubled with that of Mardian.
174 **Forbear** withdraw, as at 1.2.128
175 **misthought** misjudged
177 **We … name** 'we are held to be accountable for the misdeeds which others have committed in our name'
merits 'deserts, whether good or bad (here bad)' (Wilson)

170 With] *F*; By *Rowe*[2] 171 SD] *Johnson* 174 SD] *Capell* 177 merits … name,] *Johnson subst.*; merits, … name *F*

Caesar's no merchant to make prize with you
Of things that merchants sold. Therefore be cheered;
Make not your thoughts your prisons. No, dear queen,
For we intend so to dispose you as   185
Yourself shall give us counsel. Feed and sleep.
Our care and pity is so much upon you
That we remain your friend; and so, adieu.

CLEOPATRA
My master and my lord!   Not so. Adieu.

CAESAR
Flourish. Exeunt Caesar and his train.

CLEOPATRA
He words me, girls, he words me, that I should not   190
Be noble to myself. But hark thee, Charmian.
                              [*Whispers to Charmian.*]

CHARMIAN
Finish, good lady. The bright day is done
And we are for the dark.

CLEOPATRA   Hie thee again.
I have spoke already and it is provided.
Go put it to the haste.

CHARMIAN   Madam, I will.   195

Enter DOLABELLA.

DOLABELLA
Where's the Queen?

CHARMIAN   Behold, sir.   [*Exit.*]

CLEOPATRA   Dolabella!

182 **make prize** Wilson points out that
  prize was an alternative spelling of
  'price' (*OED* Prize). 'Make prize with
  you' therefore means 'bargain, haggle
  with you'.
184 **Make … prisons** 'don't imagine
  you are a prisoner'
187 **care … is** an example of the 's'
  inflection with two singular nouns as
  subject (Abbott, 336), as in *Cym*

3.6.21, 'Plenty and peace breeds cowards.'
190 **words me** 'offers me words (with
  no substance)'
191 **Be … myself** i.e. by committing
  suicide. Like Antony when he has
  been defeated (4.14.96), Cleopatra
  regards suicide as a noble act.
193 **Hie thee again** hurry back
195 **put … haste** do it quickly

191 SD] *Theobald* 196 SD] *Capell*

DOLABELLA

> Madam, as thereto sworn by your command,
> Which my love makes religion to obey,
> I tell you this: Caesar through Syria
> Intends his journey, and within three days   200
> You with your children will he send before.
> Make your best use of this. I have performed
> Your pleasure and my promise.

CLEOPATRA   Dolabella,

> I shall remain your debtor.

DOLABELLA   I, your servant.

> Adieu, good queen. I must attend on Caesar.   205

CLEOPATRA

> Farewell and thanks.   *Exit [Dolabella].*
>   Now, Iras, what think'st thou?
> Thou an Egyptian puppet shall be shown
> In Rome as well as I. Mechanic slaves
> With greasy aprons, rules and hammers shall
> Uplift us to the view. In their thick breaths,   210
> Rank of gross diet, shall we be enclouded
> And forced to drink their vapour.

IRAS   The gods forbid!

CLEOPATRA

> Nay, 'tis most certain, Iras. Saucy lictors

197–206 **Madam … thanks** '[Dol-
abella] sent her word secretly as she
had requested him, that Caesar determined to take his jorney through
Suria, and that within three dayes he
would sende her away before with her
children' (North, 314).
207 **puppet** 'an actor in a pantomime'
(*OED sb.* 3c). 'She sees herself and
her maids as figures on an Egyptian
"pageant" or platform drawn after
Caesar's car in the triumph' (Wilson).
208 **Mechanic slaves** common artisans
209 **rules** rulers used by carpenters for
drawing straight lines. Compare *JC*
1.1.5–7: '*Flavius.* Speak, what trade

art thou? *Carpenter.* Why, sir, a carpenter. *Murellus.* Where is thy leather
apron and thy rule?'
211 **Rank … diet** 'stinking of coarse
food'. In his other Roman plays
Shakespeare imagined the plebeians
as having bad breath (*JC* 1.2.246–7;
Cor 2.1.236).
212 **drink** inhale (*OED v.*[1] 5)
213 **Saucy** both 'insolent' and 'lascivious' (*OED a.*[1] 2a, 2b)
lictors Roman officers who attended
on a magistrate and carried out sen-
tences on offenders. Wilson suggests
that Shakespeare thinks of them as
beadles whose duty it was to deal with

206 SD *Exit Dolabella*] Capell; *Exit F (opp. Caesar l. 205)*   207 shall] *F*; shalt *F2*

Will catch at us like strumpets, and scald rhymers
Ballad us out o'tune. The quick comedians   215
Extemporally will stage us and present
Our Alexandrian revels; Antony
Shall be brought drunken forth; and I shall see
Some squeaking Cleopatra boy my greatness
I'th' posture of a whore.

IRAS   O the good gods!   220

CLEOPATRA

Nay, that's certain.

IRAS

I'll never see't, for I am sure my nails
Are stronger than mine eyes!

CLEOPATRA   Why, that's the way

To fool their preparation and to conquer
Their most absurd intents.

Enter CHARMIAN.

                                     Now, Charmian!   225
Show me, my women, like a queen. Go fetch
My best attires. I am again for Cydnus

strumpets. Compare *2H4* 5.4, where the Hostess and Doll Tearsheet have been handed over to the beadles to be whipped.

214 **scald** scabby, scurvy (*OED a.*[1] 2). It originally meant 'affected with the scall', a scaly disease of the skin, but in this context implies 'contemptible'.

215 **Ballad us** Ballads on topical subjects were sold in the streets by ballad-singers and exhibited on the walls of taverns. During the Gadshill robbery, Falstaff threatens to have ballads made on Prince Hal and Poins and 'sung to filthy tunes' (*1H4* 2.2.44–6). See Firth, 511–38.

quick quick-witted

219 **boy my greatness** 'reduce my greatness to what a boy actor can manage' (Jones). Shakespeare shows

extraordinary boldness in giving these lines to a boy actor who must, presumably, have done justice to the role of Cleopatra.

222 * **my nails** F's 'mine Nailes' erroneously repeats the 'N' of 'Nailes'. Compare 'should'st stowe' (3.11.58) and 'mine Nightingale' (4.8.18).

226 **Show me** make me appear; display me

227 **Cydnus** the place of her first meeting with Antony (2.2.197). In putting on her robes of state, Cleopatra wishes not simply to die like a queen but to prepare herself for the grand reunion with Antony, whom she imagines as *curled* (300) by the barber.

215 Ballad] *F2*; Ballads *F*   out o'] *Theobald;* out a *F*   222 my] *F2;* mine *F*   227 Cydnus] *Rowe (Cidnus); Cidrus F*

291

To meet Mark Antony. Sirrah Iras, go.
Now, noble Charmian, we'll dispatch indeed,
And when thou hast done this chare, I'll give thee
    leave   230
To play till doomsday. Bring our crown and all.

                                       [Exit Iras.]
                                     A noise within

Wherefore's this noise?

             Enter a Guardsman.

GUARDSMAN   Here is a rural fellow
That will not be denied your highness' presence.
He brings you figs.
CLEOPATRA
Let him come in.   *Exit Guardsman.*
                   What poor an instrument   235
May do a noble deed! He brings me liberty.
My resolution's placed, and I have nothing

228 **Sirrah** a term of address used to a servant or other inferior and applied to both women (as here) and men
229 **dispatch** (1) hurry, as in 4.4.15, and (2) finish, as in 5.2.321. The meaning of 'we'll dispatch indeed' is therefore 'we'll hurry and we really will finish'.
230 **chare** task, chore, as in 4.15.79
231 SD * F has no stage direction here but it is clear that Iras must leave in order to re-enter with the robe and crown at l. 278. Ridley, who discusses the question at length (255–7), has Charmian exit with Iras, leaving Cleopatra to interview the countryman alone. This is an attractive idea but if Charmian remains on the stage, Cleopatra has a companion with whom to share the ironies in the dialogue with the countryman. Moreover when Iras has returned it is she alone that Cleopatra addresses (282), the implication being that it is only she who has been away.

232–4 **Here ... figs** Plutarch writes, 'Nowe, whilest she was at dinner, there came a contrieman, and brought her a basket. The souldiers that warded at the gates, asked him straight what he had in his basket. He opened the basket, and tooke out the leaves that covered the figges, and shewed them that they were figges he brought. They all of them marvelled to see so goodly figges. The countrieman laughed to heare them, and bad them take some if they would. They beleved he told them truely, and so bad him carie them in. After Cleopatra had dined, she sent a certaine table written and sealed unto Caesar, and commaunded them all to go out of the tombes where she was, but the two women, then she shut the dores to her' (North, 315–16).
235 **What poor an** 'what a poor'
237 **placed** fixed

231 SD] *Capell*

Of woman in me. Now from head to foot
I am marble-constant. Now the fleeting moon
No planet is of mine.

Enter Guardsman *and* Clown [*with a basket*].

GUARDSMAN   This is the man.   240

CLEOPATRA
  Avoid, and leave him.   *Exit Guardsman.*
Hast thou the pretty worm of Nilus there
That kills and pains not?

CLOWN   Truly, I have him; but I would not be the
party that should desire you to touch him, for his   245
biting is immortal. Those that do die of it do seldom
or never recover.

CLEOPATRA   Remember'st thou any that have died on't?

CLOWN   Very many; men and women too. I heard of
one of them no longer than yesterday – a very honest   250
woman, but something given to lie, as a woman

239 **fleeting moon** The moon is said to
be *fleeting* (or 'inconstant') because
of its regular waxing and waning.
Cleopatra believes she is transforming
herself into a being beyond change.
She is several times associated with
the moon and with Isis, the Egyptian
moon-goddess and equivalent of the
Roman Diana (see pp. 67–9). The
expression 'fleeting moon' was proverbial (Dent, M1111).

240 SD **Clown** a word regularly used
for a countryman or rural labourer.
Costard in *LLL* is referred to as 'a
swain, a most simple clown' (4.1.140).
Bowers (285) argues that the Clown
embodies the traditional figure of
Death, who arrives at a banquet with
a platter of food or drink.

241 **Avoid** go

242–78 **Hast ... worm** According to
Plutarch, Cleopatra 'was verie carefull
in gathering all sorts of poysons
together to destroy men. Now to make

proofe of those poysons which made
men dye with least paine, she tried it
upon condemned men in prison ...
She afterwardes went about to prove
the stinging of snakes and adders, and
made some to be applied unto men
in her sight ... She found none of all
them she had proved so fit, as the
biting of an Aspicke, the which only
causeth a heavines of the head,
without swounding or complaining,
and bringeth a great desire also to
sleepe' (North, 305).

242 **worm** a word regularly used to mean
'snake', as in *Cym* 3.4.34–5, 'whose
tongue / Outvenoms all the worms
of Nile'.

246 **immortal** The Clown, of course,
means 'mortal' but at 280 Cleopatra
sees the asp as making her 'immortal'.

251 **lie** (1) tell lies, (2) lie with men.
The Clown's dialogue is full of sexual
innuendoes.

239 marble-constant] *Capell;* Marble constant *F*   240 SD *with a basket*] *Rowe*

should not do but in the way of honesty – how she
died of the biting of it, what pain she felt. Truly, she
makes a very good report o'th' worm; but he that
will believe all that they say shall never be saved by   255
half that they do. But this is most falliable, the
worm's an odd worm.

CLEOPATRA   Get thee hence. Farewell.

CLOWN   I wish you all joy of the worm.

[*Sets down his basket.*]

CLEOPATRA   Farewell.   260

CLOWN   You must think this, look you, that the worm
will do his kind.

CLEOPATRA   Ay, ay. Farewell.

CLOWN   Look you, the worm is not to be trusted but
in the keeping of wise people; for, indeed, there is   265
no goodness in the worm.

CLEOPATRA   Take thou no care; it shall be heeded.

CLOWN   Very good. Give it nothing, I pray you, for it
is not worth the feeding.

CLEOPATRA   Will it eat me?   270

CLOWN   You must not think I am so simple but I know
the devil himself will not eat a woman. I know that
a woman is a dish for the gods if the devil dress her
not. But truly, these same whoreson devils do the
gods great harm in their women, for in every ten that   275
they make, the devils mar five.

CLEOPATRA   Well, get thee gone. Farewell.

---

252 **honesty** (1) truthfulness, (2) chastity
252–3 **how ... felt** The Clown's sexual
  punning continues: *die* is used in both
  its literal and its sexual senses, as in
  1.2.145.
256 **they** i.e. women
  falliable another of the Clown's mistakes. He means 'infallible'.
259 **I wish ... joy** The evidence of *MA*
  2.1.191–5 suggests that the usual
  context for these words was in the
  sale of animals: '*Benedick* The Prince

hath got your Hero. *Claudio* I wish
him joy of her. *Benedick* Why, that's
spoken like an honest drovier; so they
sell bullocks.' It is an expression with
which the countryman would be familiar (Richard Proudfoot, privately).
262 **do his kind** 'act according to his
  nature'
267 **Take ... care** don't worry
273 **dress her** (1) 'prepare her for cook-
  ing' and (2) 'put her clothes on'

259 SD] *Capell subst.*

CLOWN   Yes, forsooth. I wish you joy o'th' worm.   *Exit.*

[*Enter* IRAS *with a robe, crown and other jewels.*]

CLEOPATRA

Give me my robe. Put on my crown. I have
Immortal longings in me. Now no more   280
The juice of Egypt's grape shall moist this lip.
                              [*The women dress her.*]
Yare, yare, good Iras! Quick! Methinks I hear
Antony call. I see him rouse himself
To praise my noble act. I hear him mock
The luck of Caesar, which the gods give men   285
To excuse their after wrath. Husband, I come!
Now to that name my courage prove my title!
I am fire and air; my other elements
I give to baser life. So, have you done?
Come, then, and take the last warmth of my lips.   290
Farewell, kind Charmian. Iras, long farewell.
                  [*Kisses them. Iras falls and dies.*]
Have I the aspic in my lips? Dost fall?

---

280 **Immortal longings** longings for
immortality
282 **Yare** quick. The word, often used
as a term in seamanship, also meant
'nimble, deft'. Compare 2.2.221 and
3.7.38.
286 **To excuse ... wrath** 'to justify the
anger they show in bringing them low
later'
287 **title** right
288 **fire and air** the more spiritual of
the four elements. She relinquishes
her baser elements of earth and water
to the *dungy earth* (1.1.36) out of
which she was created. Case compares
these lines with the Dauphin's
account of his horse (*H5* 3.7.21–2).
'He is pure air and fire; and the dull
elements of earth and water never

appear in him.'
291 SD *Iras ... dies* The cause of her
death is not explained by either Plutarch or Shakespeare. Steevens suggests that 'Iras must be supposed to
have applied an asp to her arm while
her mistress was settling her dress.'
Others argue that she dies 'of the
grief which taking leave of her mistress caused her' (Delius), and this is
the most plausible explanation, not
only because it would avoid some
complicated stage business but because Iras' death would thereby parallel that of Enobarbus (4.9.18–26).
292 **aspic** asp. This form of the word
(used by North) was not uncommon,
as *OED* illustrates.

278 SD *Enter ... jewels*] *Ard¹ subst.; Re-enter* Iras *Capell*   281 SD] *Cam²*   291 SD] *Capell subst.*

If thou and nature can so gently part,
The stroke of death is as a lover's pinch
Which hurts and is desired. Dost thou lie still? 295
If thus thou vanishest, thou tell'st the world
It is not worth leave-taking.

CHARMIAN

Dissolve, thick cloud, and rain, that I may say
The gods themselves do weep!

CLEOPATRA   This proves me base.
If she first meet the curled Antony, 300
He'll make demand of her, and spend that kiss
Which is my heaven to have.

[*to the asp; applying it to her breast*]
                         Come, thou mortal wretch,
With thy sharp teeth this knot intrinsicate
Of life at once untie. Poor venomous fool,
Be angry and dispatch. O, couldst thou speak, 305
That I might hear thee call great Caesar ass
Unpolicied!

CHARMIAN   O eastern star!

CLEOPATRA   Peace, peace!

---

299 **This ... base** i.e. the death of Iras. Compare Antony's comment on Eros, 'Thrice nobler than myself' (4.14.96).

300 **curled** curlèd. 'Probably she thinks of Antony as she first saw him "barber'd ten times o'er" (2.2.234)' (Case).

302 **mortal** deadly

303 **intrinsicate** The word was in use before the play was written and appears to have been synonymous with 'intricate'. There is also the suggestion of 'intrinsic' meaning 'situated within' (*OED*). The 'knot intrinsicate' is the one which ties the soul to the 'baser life' of the body, or what Donne ('The Exstasie', l. 64) calls 'That subtile knot that makes us man'.

304–5 **Poor ... dispatch** Cleopatra is deliberately arousing the asp to make

it bite her more fiercely. Plutarch writes of reports that Cleopatra 'did pricke and thrust it with a spindell of golde, so that the Aspicke being angerd withall, lept out with great furie, and bitte her in the arme' (North, 316). She is, of course, anxious to kill herself during this brief period when she is alone. *Fool* is an affectionate term used normally of children.

305 **couldst thou speak** 'if only you could speak'

307 **Unpolicied** 'outwitted in "policy" or statecraft' (Jones)
eastern star Venus, the morning star which is visible in the east before sunrise. Similarly Antony's Guard, seeing him close to death, exclaims, 'The star is fallen' (4.14.107).

302 SD] *Capell subst.*

Dost thou not see my baby at my breast
That sucks the nurse asleep?

CHARMIAN   O break! O break!

CLEOPATRA

As sweet as balm, as soft as air, as gentle –   310
O Antony! – Nay, I will take thee too.

> [*Applies another asp to her arm.*]

What should I stay –   *Dies.*

CHARMIAN

In this vile world? So fare thee well.
Now boast thee, Death, in thy possession lies
A lass unparalleled. Downy windows, close,   315
And golden Phoebus, never be beheld
Of eyes again so royal! Your crown's awry;
I'll mend it, and then play.

Enter the Guard, *rustling in.*

1 GUARD

Where's the Queen?

CHARMIAN   Speak softly. Wake her not.

308 **at my breast** Plutarch says (North, 316) that she was bitten in the arm, but by the time the play was written the idea had developed that she applied the asp to her breast (see p. 74). Case refers to Thomas Nashe's *Christ's Tears*, 1593–4, 'At thy breasts (as at Cleopatraes) aspisses shall be put out to nurse' (Nashe, 2.140).

309 **asleep** See note to 242–78.

312 **What** why

313 * **vile** F's 'wilde' is probably a misreading of 'vilde', a common form of 'vile' (*OED*), but some editors retain 'wild'. *Vile* is consistent with Antony's and Cleopatra's expressions of contempt for the world, such as 'dungy earth' (1.1.36) and 'dull world' (4.15.63).

315 **windows** i.e. eyelids

317 * **awry** F's 'away', emended by Rowe, is an *a:r* error of which there are several in this play (Wilson, 126).

318 **play** an allusion to 230–1, 'I'll give thee leave / To play till doomsday'
SD * **Enter . . . in** The F stage direction brings on Dolabella with the Guard, but he is also required to enter shortly afterwards (327). Evidently Shakespeare initially brought him on here, then realized that it would be more telling dramatically to bring him on alone later.
rustling clattering, as in Holland, *Plutarch's Moralia*, 1603, p. 437, 'The great rustling and clattering that harneis and armor made'

311 SD] *Theobald subst.*   313 vile] *Capell;* wilde *F*   317 awry] *Rowe³;* away *F*   318 SD *rustling*] *F;* rushing / *Rowe in*] *Rowe; in, and Dolabella F*

1 GUARD
Caesar hath sent –

CHARMIAN   Too slow a messenger.   320
                        [Applies an asp.]
O come apace! Dispatch! I partly feel thee.

1 GUARD
Approach ho! All's not well. Caesar's beguiled.

2 GUARD
There's Dolabella sent from Caesar. Call him.
                       [Exit a Guardsman.]

1 GUARD
What work is here, Charmian? Is this well done?

CHARMIAN ·
It is well done, and fitting for a princess   325
Descended of so many royal kings.
Ah, soldier!   *Charmian dies.*

Enter DOLABELLA.

DOLABELLA
How goes it here?

2 GUARD   All dead.

DOLABELLA   Caesar, thy thoughts
Touch their effects in this. Thyself art coming

---

320 **Caesar hath sent** Plutarch writes that when Caesar had received the letter from Cleopatra, 'and began to read her lamentation and petition, requesting him that he would let her be buried with Antonius, founde straight what she ment, and thought to have gone thither him selfe: howbeit he sent one before in all hast that might be, to see what it was ... But when they had opened the dores, they founde Cleopatra starke dead, layed upon a bed of gold, attired and arraied in her royall robes, and one of her two women, which was called Iras, dead at her feete: and her other woman called Charmion halfe dead,

and trembling, trimming the diademe which Cleopatra ware upon her head' (North, 316).

322 **All's not well** The Guard's unfavourable reaction, repeated in his question at 324, prompts Charmian's retort, 'It is well done' (325).

324–6 **What ... kings** 'One of the souldiers seeing her, angrily sayd unto her: Is that well done Charmion? Verie well sayd she againe, and meete for a Princes discended from the race of so many noble kings. She sayd no more, but fell downe dead hard by the bed' (North, 316).

328–9 **thy ... effects** 'your thoughts meet with their realisation'

320 SD] *Pope subst.*   323 SD] *Oxf*

To see performed the dreaded act which thou   330
So sought'st to hinder.

Enter CAESAR *and all his train, marching.*

ALL BUT CAESAR
A way there! A way for Caesar!
DOLABELLA
O sir, you are too sure an augurer:
That you did fear is done.
CAESAR   Bravest at the last,
She levelled at our purposes and, being royal,   335
Took her own way. The manner of their deaths?
I do not see them bleed.
DOLABELLA   Who was last with them?
1 GUARD
A simple countryman that brought her figs.
This was his basket.
CAESAR   Poisoned, then.
1 GUARD   O Caesar,
This Charmian lived but now; she stood and spake.   340
I found her trimming up the diadem
On her dead mistress. Tremblingly she stood,
And on the sudden dropped.
CAESAR   O noble weakness!
If they had swallowed poison, 'twould appear
By external swelling; but she looks like sleep,   345

---

334 **Bravest** The primary sense is 'most
courageous' but 'brave' in Shakespeare's day had a number of implications such as 'splendid', 'excellent',
'fine', which are also present here
(*OED a*. 1, 3).
335 **levelled at** guessed correctly. The
image is of 'levelling' or 'aiming' a
weapon at a target as in *MV* 1.2.37–
8, 'I will describe them and according

to my description level at my affection.'
344–5 **If … swelling** Even at this
moment of crisis Caesar remains
coolly perceptive. Plutarch notes that
there was 'no marke seene of her
bodie, or any signe discerned that she
was poysoned' (North, 316).
345 **like sleep** 'as though she were
asleep'

332 SP ALL BUT CAESAR] *this edn; All F* 341–2 diadem / On … mistress. Tremblingly]
Theobald subst.; Diadem; / On … Mistris tremblingly *F*

As she would catch another Antony
In her strong toil of grace.

DOLABELLA   Here on her breast
There is a vent of blood, and something blown;
The like is on her arm.

1 GUARD
This is an aspic's trail, and these fig leaves   350
Have slime upon them such as th'aspic leaves
Upon the caves of Nile.

CAESAR   Most probable
That so she died, for her physician tells me
She hath pursued conclusions infinite
Of easy ways to die. Take up her bed,   355
And bear her women from the monument.
She shall be buried by her Antony.
No grave upon the earth shall clip in it
A pair so famous. High events as these
Strike those that make them, and their story is   360
No less in pity than his glory which
Brought them to be lamented. Our army shall
In solemn show attend this funeral,

347 **toil** snare; literally a noose in which game or other quarry is trapped (*OED sb.*[2] 1)
  grace 'charm, beauty', and also with the religious implication of 'transcendence'
348 **vent** discharge, emission
  blown often explained as 'swollen', but this is unlikely, since Caesar has just pointed out that there is apparently no 'external swelling'. Jones is more probably right in glossing it as 'deposited' and referring back to l. 59: 'In the next speech the First Guard explains what the *something* is.'
354 **conclusions infinite** innumerable experiments (*OED* Conclusion 8). For Cleopatra's experiments with poisons, see note to 242–78.

355 **bed** Plutarch says that when Caesar came to Cleopatra in her monument she was 'layed upon a litle low bed in poore estate' (North, 313).
357 **buried ... Antony** Plutarch writes that Cleopatra, in her letter to Caesar, had asked to be buried with Antony. See note to 320.
358 **clip** enfold, clasp, as in 4.8.8
359 **events** outcomes. Hence 'high events' can be paraphrased as 'tragic catastrophes'.
360 **Strike ... them** 'affect with grief the people who cause them'
360–2 **their ... lamented** 'the pity which their tale arouses is no less than the glory of the man who made them so lamentable'. *Their* refers to Antony and Cleopatra and *his* to Caesar.

And then to Rome. Come, Dolabella, see
High order in this great solemnity.   365
    Exeunt omnes [, *the Soldiers bearing the dead bodies*].

365 **solemnity** ceremony (*OED* 2)

365 SD *the Soldiers ... bodies*] *Cam¹ subst.*

LONGER NOTES

1.2.118–21 *At ... appear The F stage directions here are insufficient in a way characteristic of manuscript copy (see pp. 75–6) and create several problems. These are: (1) in F four messengers are required to speak but are identified as *Mes.*, *1. Mes.*, *2. Mes.* and *3. Mes.* (here referred to as First, Second, Third and Fourth); (2) after l. 118, following the exit of the First Messenger, two messengers are required to speak but only one has entered; (3) since between ll. 118 and 121 only one messenger is on the stage (the Second), to whom does Antony address his question 'The man from Sicyon, is there such a one?' and who delivers the reply? (4) although the Second Messenger must clearly exit at the end of l. 121, no exit direction is given.

Various methods of dealing with these problems have been proposed (see textual footnotes), most of them requiring the addition of attendants who either are present from the beginning of the scene or come on with Antony at l. 91. These additional actors would not only stretch the resources of the acting company in an already thickly populated play (though the parts could easily be doubled with others) but detract from the essentially private, intimate nature of the episode. The simplest solution, adopted here, is provided by the Oxford editors, who give the first half of l. 120 ('The man from Sicyon –') to the Second Messenger, the second half ('Is there such a one?') to Antony and the reply to the Second Messenger. The Second Messenger thus delivers a single speech ('The man from Sicyon ... stays upon your will') which is broken by Antony's interjection. This is the most satisfactory solution in that it leaves F's stage directions intact and entails no additional actors. The only emendations required are the addition of the SP 'ANTONY' halfway through l. 120 and an exit direction for the Second Messenger.

2.1.16, 18, 39 SP * MENAS F gives all the speeches in this scene which are not allotted to Pompey or Varrius to '*Mene*', which, assuming that this is an abbreviation of *Menecrates*, leaves Menas with nothing to say. Yet it is clear from Pompey's reply (l. 43) that 39–43 should be spoken by Menas. The problem is complicated by the fact that F spells Menas '*Menes*' in the entry direction at 2.7.16 and he could therefore have been given a speech prefix identical to that of his associate. Alternatively Compositor B, whose spelling of proper names is often inaccurate (see p. 79), may have overlooked the difference between the spellings of the two speech prefixes in the manuscript copy. The solution is either to allot all the relevant speeches in this scene to Menas, as Johnson did ('Menas can do all'), or to divide them between the two characters, as Rowe, Capell and Malone did, though in different ways. Sisson (2.264) remarks that the two men have distinct and different personalities, 'the first two speeches being of a philosophical turn of thought, the rest those of a man concerned with facts and soldiering'. In accordance with this suggestion, the first two are here given to Menecrates and the remaining three to Menas.

4.15.0.1 *aloft* There have been many hypotheses about how this scene was staged. Some scholars believe that Cleopatra and her maids entered on the gallery, as the stage direction *aloft* usually indicates. Others object that the gallery was seldom used in Shakespeare's plays and, even then, was occupied by one or, at the most, two characters (though it should be pointed out that in *R2* 3.3.61 five characters appear there and more in Act 1 of *Tit*. They propose that the monument was represented by some kind of portable structure with a flat roof which was brought on to the stage. The various arguments are summarized in detail by Spevack (778–85). Bevington (45) includes drawings which illustrate the different ways in which the scene could have been staged. It is likely that the simplest method was adopted and that it made use of the available facilities of the playhouse. Hosley describes how this could have been done. Cleopatra and her maids appeared at one of the windows of the gallery over the stage. Diomedes entered through one of the two tiring-house doors (l. 6) and Antony was carried in (l. 9) on a litter or in a chair through the other door. He was hauled up by the women with ropes which were either run round a winch inside the stage superstructure or passed through a pulley of the kind regularly used to 'fly' characters up and down. If Antony were brought in on a chair it would be simple to attach the ropes to it and if the pulley were equipped with a counterweight, as it probably was, no great effort was needed to lift him up.

5.2.34 SD * *Enter … Soldiers* F has no stage direction here. It was probably omitted by the compositor for practical reasons (see p. 76). The dialogue which follows, however, clearly indicates that Cleopatra has been captured, and if the scene was played on the main stage the soldiers could simply walk on. Plutarch describes how Gallus came and deliberately 'held her with talke' while Proculeius 'did set up a ladder against that high windowe, by the which Antonius was trised up, and came downe into the monument with two of his men' (North 311). Theobald constructed a stage direction on the basis of Plutarch's details (see textual footnotes) and many editors have followed him, but there is no need for anything so complicated. Plutarch gave a realistic account of the episode but Shakespeare's stage was not a realistic one. That it was Gallus who led the soldiers is likely from Caesar's order to him (5.1.69) to accompany Proculeius. Departing slightly from Plutarch, Shakespeare has Proculeius 'hold her with talke' while Gallus forces an entry. It has already been established at 4.15.8 that the two tiring-house doors were placed on either side of the monument. Maintaining this convention, the conversation with Proculeius (9–34) takes place on one side of the stage so as to distract Cleopatra from the approach of Gallus and the soldiers through the door on the other side. Such simple staging would make it possible to perform the play practically anywhere if it went on tour.

5.2.86 * **autumn** Although Theobald's emendation of F's '*Anthony*' has been accepted by the majority of editors, either reading is possible. In defence of *Anthony*, Jones says that Cleopatra 'is speaking rhapsodically and with startlingly abrupt metaphors. . . . The idea of Antony as a perpetually plenteous harvest is amply prepared for in *bounty* and *winter*.' Harold Brooks writes (privately), 'He was such an Antony that his nature as a source of bounty was that the more he gave the more he had to give. Of benefactors on the merely ordinary human level it has to be said that the more they give the less the resources from which they can go on giving, but, paradoxically, miraculously, with Antony it was the reverse. The paradox sets him beyond the bounds of what is normal. That is what Cleopatra constantly reiterates about this Antony she dreamed of: he transcended the normal limitations of human nature.' Wilson defends the emendation on the grounds that manuscript 'Autome' could easily be misread as 'Antonie'. Ridley objects, however, that what the compositors had in front of them was regularly 'Anthony' (very occasionally 'Anthonie') and not, as Wilson assumes, 'Antonie' and that, since the manuscript appears to have indicated that proper names were to be printed in italics, the compositor would scarcely have read the hypothetical 'Autome' without italics as a proper name. Proudfoot (1987), defending *autumn*, points out that the word is printed in italics in the Quarto of *TC* (1.2.126) and that the italicization may in both cases have been derived from Shakespeare's manuscript. 'Antony' is certainly more boldly imaginative ('there is no other word with which to describe him than his own name') but *autumn* is more consistent with the pattern of the images and has the two syllables required by the verse line.

APPENDIX
FOLIO LINEATION

In the following passages the lineation of the text of this edition differs from that of the First Folio. After the act, scene and line references to this edition, the name is given of the editor who first introduced the lineation here adopted. Minor errors in F are silently corrected.

1.1.4	Have glowed ... turn	*Rowe*
	Haue glow'd like plated Mars:	
	Now bend, now turne.	*Folio*
1.1.43–4	I'll seem ... himself.	*Pope*
	One line	*Folio*
1.1.53–4	No messenger ... note	*Rowe*
	No Messenger but thine, and all alone, to night	
	Wee'l wander through the streets, and note	*Folio*
1.1.60–3	I am full ... happy!	*Capell*
	Prose	*Folio*
1.2.10–11	In nature's ... read.	*Theobald*
	Prose	*Folio*
1.2.35–6	You have seen ... approach.	*Capell*
	Prose	*Folio*
1.2.40–1	If every ... million.	*Rowe*
	Prose	*Folio*
1.2.88	A Roman ... Enobarbus!	*Rowe*
	A Romane thought hath strooke him.	
	Enobarbus?	*Folio*
1.2.92	We will ... with us.	*Rowe*
	We will not looke vpon him:	
	Go with vs.	*Folio*
1.2.93	Fulvia ... field.	*Rowe*
	Fuluia thy Wife,	
	First came into the Field.	*Folio*
1.2.95–6	Ay ... state	*Rowe*
	I: but soone that Warre had end,	
	And the times state	*Folio*
1.2.105–10	Labienus ... Whilst	*Steevens*
	Labienus (this is stiffe-newes)	
	Hath with his Parthian Force	

306

	Extended Asia: from Euphrates his conquering	
	Banner shooke, from Syria to Lydia,	
	And to Ionia, whil'st –	*Folio*
1.2.111–12	Speak to me ... Rome;	*Rowe*
	Speake to me home,	
	Mince not the generall tongue, name	
	Cleopatra as she is call'd in Rome:	*Folio*
1.2.126–7	In Sicyon ... serious	*Pope*
	In *Scicion*, her length of sicknesse,	
	With what else more serious,	*Folio*
1.2.183	No more ... officers	*Rowe*
	No more light Answeres:	
	Let our Officers	*Folio*
1.3.3	See ... does.	*Rowe*
	See where he is,	
	Whose with him, what he does:	*Folio*
1.3.30	Who have ... madness,	*Rowe*
	Who haue beene false to *Fuluia?*	
	Riotous madnesse,	*Folio*
1.3.34	But bid ... staying,	*Rowe*
	But bid farewell, and goe:	
	When you sued staying,	*Folio*
1.3.103–4	Let us ... flies	*Pope*
	Let vs go.	
	Come: Our separation so abides and flies,	*Folio*
1.4.7–9	More womanly ... faults	*Capell*
	More Womanly then he. Hardly gaue audience	
	Or vouchsafe to thinke he had Partners. You	
	Shall finde there a man, who is th'abstracts of all faults,	*Folio*
1.4.10–11	I must ... goodness.	*Capell*
	I must not thinke	
	There are, euils enow to darken all his goodnesse:	*Folio*
1.4.43	And the ... worth love,	*Rowe*
	And the ebb'd man,	
	Ne're lou'd, till ne're worth loue,	*Folio*
1.4.80–1	Till which ... Farewell.	*Capell*
	One line	*Folio*
1.4.84–5	Doubt ... bond.	*Capell*
	One line	*Folio*
1.5.3–4	Ha, ha ... mandragora,	*Steevens*
	One line	*Folio*
1.5.66–70	Who's born ... Caesar so?	*Rowe*
	Prose	*Folio*
1.5.80–1	He shall ... Egypt!	*Johnson*
	Prose	*Folio*

2.1.2–5	Know ... sue for.	*Rowe*
	Prose	*Folio*
2.1.16–17	Caesar ... carry.	*Hanmer*
	Caesar and *Lepidus* are in the field,	
	A mighty strength they carry.	*Folio*
2.2.8–9	'Tis not ... stomaching.	*Hanmer*
	One line	*Folio*
2.2.9–10	Every ... born in't	*Pope*
	Prose	*Folio*
2.2.12–14	Your speech ... Antony.	*Pope*
	Your speech is passion: but pray you stirre	
	No Embers vp. Heere comes the Noble *Anthony.*	*Folio*
2.2.35–6	I must ... little, I	*Rowe*
	One line	*Folio*
2.2.40–1	My being ... to you?	*Capell*
	One line	*Folio*
2.2.59–61	You praise ... excuses.	*Pope*
	Prose	*Folio*
2.2.76–7	I wrote ... Alexandria. You	*Rowe*
	One line	*Folio*
2.2.79–80	Sir ... admitted, then.	*Capell*
	One line	*Folio*
2.2.86–8	You have broken ... me with.	*Rowe*
	Prose	*Folio*
2.2.94–5	To lend ... denied.	*Fourth Folio*
	Prose	*Folio*
2.2.125–31	Thou hast ... further speak.	*Theobald*
	Prose	*Folio*
2.2.136–7	No worse ... speak	*Second Folio*
	No worse a husband then the best of men: whose	
	Vertue, and whose generall graces, speake	*Folio*
2.2.151–2	The power ... Octavia.	*Theobald*
	The power of *Caesar*,	
	And his power, vnto *Octauia.*	*Folio*
2.2.172–3	Great ... master.	*Theobald*
	Great, and encreasing:	
	But by Sea he is an absolute Master.	*Folio*
2.2.204	The winds ... silver,	*Pope*
	The Windes were Loue-sicke.	
	With them the Owers were Siluer,	*Folio*
2.2.253–5	Let us ... abide here.	*Rowe*
	Prose	*Folio*
2.3.1–2	The world ... bosom.	*Rowe*
	The world, and my great office, will	
	Sometimes deuide me from your bosome.	*Folio*

2.3.2–4	All which … for you.	*Rowe*
	Prose	*Folio*
2.3.14–15	Say … mine?	*Capell*
	Say to me, whose Fortunes shall rise higher	
	Caesars or mine?	*Folio*
2.4.1–2	Trouble … after.	*Rowe*
	Prose	*Folio*
2.4.2–3	Sir … follow.	*Theobald*
	Prose	*Folio*
2.4.5–7	We shall … Lepidus	*Pope*
	Prose	*Folio*
2.4.7–9	Your way … upon me.	*Rowe*
	Prose	*Folio*
2.5.1–2	Give … love.	*Rowe*
	Prose	*Folio*
2.5.5–6	As well … sir?	*Rowe*
	Prose	*Folio*
2.5.8	And when … short,	*Rowe*
	And when good will is shewed,	
	Though't come to short	*Folio*
2.5.15–18	'Twas merry … drew up.	*Pope*
	Prose	*Folio*
2.5.26–8	Antonio's … here	*Dyce*
	Anthonyo's dead,	
	If thou say so Villaine, thou kil'st thy Mistris:	
	But well and free, if thou so yeild him.	
	There is Gold, and heere	*Folio*
2.5.62–3	What … eyes	*Capell*
	What say you?	
	Hence horrible Villaine, or Ile spurne thine eyes	*Folio*
2.5.92	The gods … still?	*Rowe*
	The Gods confound thee,	
	Dost thou hold there still?	*Folio*
2.5.105–6	Are all … by 'em.	*Capell*
	Are all too deere for me:	
	Lye they vpon thy hand, and be vndone by em.	*Folio*
2.5.108–9	I am … hence	*Capell*
	One line	*Folio*
2.6.2–3	Most meet … have we	*Rowe*
	Most meete that first we come to words,	
	And therefore haue we	*Folio*
2.6.32–4	Which do … fortune.	*Rowe*
	Which do not be entreated too,	
	But waigh what it is worth imbrac'd	
	And what may follow to try a larger Fortune.	*Folio*

2.6.39–40	Know ... prepared	*Pope*
	Know then I came before you heere,	
	A man prepar'd	*Folio*
2.6.52–3	Since ... upon you.	*Rowe*
	One line	*Folio*
2.6.62–5	No, Antony ... feasting there.	*Rowe*
	Prose	*Folio*
2.6.71–2	Well ... perceive	*Theobald*
	One line	*Folio*
2.6.75–6	Sir ... praised ye	*Pope*
	One line	*Folio*
2.7.59–60	Thou hast ... lords.	*Hanmer*
	Prose	*Folio*
2.7.64–6	But entertain ... world.	*Pope*
	Prose	*Folio*
2.7.82–3	For this ... more.	*Pope*
	For this, Ile neuer follow	
	Thy paul'd Fortunes more,	*Folio*
2.7.86	Bear ... Pompey.	*Pope*
	Beare him ashore,	
	Ile pledge it for him *Pompey.*	*Folio*
2.7.92–3	The third ... wheels!	*Theobald*
	Prose	*Folio*
2.7.98–100	I could ... fouler.	*Pope*
	Prose	*Folio*
2.7.101–3	Possess ... one.	*Knight*
	Prose	*Folio*
2.7.103–5	Ha ... drink?	*Johnson*
	Prose	*Folio*
2.7.119	What would ... brother,	*Rowe*
	What would you more?	
	Pompey goodnight. Good Brother	*Folio*
2.7.130	But what ... boat.	*Rowe*
	But what, we are Friends?	
	Come downe into the Boate.	*Folio*
2.7.132	No ... What!	*Rowe*
	No to my Cabin: these Drummes,	
	These Trumpets, Flutes: what	*Folio*
3.1.28–30	Thou hast ... Antony?	*Capell*
	Prose	*Folio*
3.2.16	Hoo ... cannot	*Rowe*
	Hoo, Hearts, Tongues, Figure,	
	Scribes, Bards, Poets, cannot	*Folio*
3.2.33–4	Make ... distrust.	*Rowe*
	One line	*Folio*

3.2.48	Her heart ... feather	*Rowe*
	Her heart informe her tongue.	
	The Swannes downe feather	*Folio*
3.2.52–3	He were ... man.	*Pope*
	Prose	*Folio*
3.3.2–6	Good majesty ... near.	*Pope*
	Prose	*Folio*
3.3.7–8	Didst ... Octavia?	*Theobald*
	One line	*Folio*
3.3.8–10	Madam ... Antony.	*Theobald*
	Prose	*Folio*
3.3.12	Didst ... low?	*Rowe*
	Didst heare her speake?	
	Is she shrill tongu'd or low?	*Folio*
3.3.18–19	She creeps ... one.	*Rowe*
	One line	*Folio*
3.3.22–4	Three ... yet.	*Theobald*
	Three in Egypt cannot make better note.	
	He's very knowing, I do perceiu't,	
	There's nothing in her yet.	*Folio*
3.3.26–7	Madam ... widow	*Capell*
	One line	*Folio*
3.3.31–2	For ... colour?	*Third Folio*
	Prose	*Folio*
3.3.42–6	Hath he ... enough.	*Rowe*
	Prose	*Folio*
3.4.5–6	To public ... not	*Capell*
	To publicke eare, spoke scantly of me,	
	When perforce he could not	*Folio*
3.5.13–15	Then, world ... Antony?	*Hanmer*
	Prose	*Folio*
3.5.22–3	'Twill ... Antony.	*Hanmer*
	One line	*Folio*
3.6.10–11	Of lower ... Queen.	*Rowe*[2]
	One line	*Folio*
3.6.23–4	The people ... accusations.	*Pope*
	The people knowes it,	
	And haue now receiu'd his accusations.	*Folio*
3.6.29–31	That Lepidus ... revenue.	*Rowe*
	That *Lepidus* of the Triumpherate, should be depos'd,	
	And being that, we detaine all his Reuenue.	*Folio*
3.6.37–8	And other ... like.	*Rowe*
	One line	*Folio*
3.6.64–5	And his ... now?	*Rowe*
	One line	*Folio*

3.6.65–7	No ... to her.	*This edition*
	No my most wronged Sister, *Cleopatra*	
	Hath nodded him to her.	*Folio*
3.6.80–1	Welcome ... forth	*Fourth Folio*
	One line	*Folio*
3.7.19–20	Nay ... Emperor.	*Hanmer*
	One line	*Folio*
3.7.70–1	You keep ... you not?	*Rowe*
	Prose	*Folio*
3.7.76–7	His power ... spies.	*Pope*
	His power went out in such distractions,	
	As beguilde all Spies.	*Folio*
3.7.80–1	With news ... some.	*Rowe*
	With Newes the times with Labour,	
	And throwes forth each minute, some.	*Folio*
3.8.3	Strike ... battle	*Rowe*
	Strike not by Land,	
	Keepe whole, prouoke not Battaile	*Folio*
3.10.4–5	Gods ... them!	*Theobald*
	One line	*Folio*
3.10.29–30	Ay ... indeed.	*Dyce*
	Prose	*Folio*
3.10.32–3	'Tis easy ... comes.	*Hanmer*
	'Tis easie toot,	
	And there I will attend what further comes.	*Folio*
3.13.15–16	The Queen ... up.	*Malone*
	The Queene shall then haue courtesie,	
	So she will yeeld vs vp.	*Folio*
3.13.55–6	So ... entreats	*Pope*
	One line	*Folio*
3.13.63–5	He is ... merely.	*Pope*
	He is a God,	
	And knowes what is most right. Mine Honour	
	Was not yeelded, but conquer'd meerely.	*Folio*
3.13.75–6	And put ... landlord.	*Hanmer*
	One line	*Folio*
3.13.90–1	Favours ... fellow?	*Fourth Folio*
	One line	*Folio*
3.13.97–8	Have you ... whip him!	*Capell*
	Haue you no eares?	
	I am *Anthony* yet. Take hence this Iack, and whip him.	*Folio*
3.13.195–6	Do so ... queen,	*Rowe*
	Do so, wee'l speake to them,	
	And to night Ile force	
	The Wine peepe through their scarres.	

	Come on (my Queene)	*Folio*
4.1.11–12	Let ... battles	*Theobald*
	Let our best heads know,	
	That to morrow, the last of many Battailes	*Folio*
4.4.8–10	Well, well ... defences.	*Hanmer*
	Well, well, we shall thriue now.	
	Seest thou my good Fellow. Go, put on thy defences.	*Folio*
4.4.21–3	A thousand ... expect you.	*Rowe*
	A thousand Sir, early though't be, haue on their	
	Riueted trim, and at the Port expect you.	*Folio*
4.5.6–7	Who's gone ... Enobarbus,	*Pope*
	Whose gone this morning?	
	Who? one euer neere thee, call for *Enobarbus*,	*Folio*
4.5.9–11	What sayest ... certain.	*Theobald*
	Prose	*Folio*
4.6.7–8	Antony ... field.	*Capell*
	One line	*Folio*
4.8.1–2	We have ... gests.	*Rowe*
	We haue beate him to his Campe: Runne one	
	Before, & let the Queen know of our guests:	*Folio*
4.9.28–9	Let's hear ... Caesar.	*Knight*
	Let's heare him, for the things he speakes	
	May concerne *Caesar*.	*Folio*
4.9.31–2	Swoons ... sleep.	*Knight*
	Swoonds rather, for so bad a Prayer as his	
	Was neuer yet for sleepe.	*Folio*
4.9.36–9	Hark ... fully out.	*Malone*
	Hearke the Drummes demurely wake the sleepers:	
	Let vs beare him to'th'Court of Guard: he is of note:	
	Our houre is fully out.	*Folio*
4.12.1–3	Yet ... to go.	*Capell*
	Yet they are not ioyn'd:	
	Where yon'd Pine does stand, I shall discouer all.	
	Ile bring thee word straight, how 'tis like to go.	*Folio*
4.13.3–4	To th' monument ... dead.	*Pope*
	To'th' Monument, there locke your selfe,	
	And send him word you are dead:	*Folio*
4.14.7	And mock ... signs?	*Rowe*
	And mocke our eyes with Ayre.	
	Thou hast seene these Signes,	*Folio*
4.14.22–3	O thy ... sword.	*Rowe*
	One line	*Folio*
4.14.25–6	Hence ... death.	*Hanmer*
	Hence sawcy Eunuch peace, she hath betraid me,	
	And shall dye the death.	*Folio*

313

4.14.66–70	Th'inevitable ... cheek.	*Capell*
	Th'ineuitable prosecution of disgrace and horror,	
	That on my command, thou then would'st kill me.	
	Doo't, the time is come: Thou strik'st not me,	
	'Tis *Caesar* thou defeat'st. Put colour in thy Cheeke.	*Folio*
4.14.95–6	Thus I ... death.	*Pope*
	One line	*Folio*
4.14.106–7	I have ... begun.	*Capell*
	I haue done my worke ill Friends:	
	Oh make an end of what I haue begun.	*Folio*
4.14.118	Art thou ... give me	*Rowe*
	Art thou there *Diomed*?	
	Draw thy sword, and giue mee,	*Folio*
4.14.131–2	What ho ... calls!	*Pope*
	What hoa: the Emperors Guard,	
	The Guard, what hoa? Come, your Lord calles.	*Folio*
4.15.12–14	The varying ... hither.	*Malone*
	The varrying shore o'th'world. O *Antony, Antony, Antony*	
	Helpe *Charmian*, helpe *Iras* helpe: helpe Friends	
	Below, let's draw him hither.	*Folio*
4.15.17–18	So it ... 'tis so.	*Rowe*
	So it should be,	
	That none but *Anthony* should conquer *Anthony*,	
	But woe 'tis so.	*Folio*
4.15.33	Here's ... my lord!	*Rowe*
	Heere's sport indeede:	
	How heauy weighes my Lord?	*Folio*
5.1.2–3	Being ... makes.	*Hanmer*
	Being so frustrate, tell him,	
	He mockes the pawses that he makes.	*Folio*
5.1.11–12	I'll be ... life.	*Fourth Folio*
	One line	*Folio*
5.1.30–1	His taints ... with him.	*Pope*
	One line	*Folio*
5.1.47–8	Unreconciliable ... friends–	*Pope*
	Vnreconciliable, should diuide our equalnesse to this.	
	Heare me good Friends,	*Folio*
5.1.59–60	Determine ... ungentle.	*Pope*
	One line	*Folio*
5.1.69–70	Gallus ... Proculeius?	*Pope*
	Prose	*Folio*
5.2.40–1	What ... languish?	*Capell*
	One line	*Folio*
5.2.41–2	Cleopatra ... bounty by	*Capell*
	One line	*Folio*

5.2.114–16	Sir ... obey.	*Pope*
	Sir, the Gods will haue it thus,	
	My Master and my Lord I must obey,	*Folio*
5.2.144–6	Madam ... is not.	*Capell*
	Madam, I had rather seele my lippes,	
	Then to my perill speake that which is not.	*Folio*
5.2.190–1	He words ... Charmian.	*Hanmer*
	He words me Gyrles, he words me,	
	That I should not be Noble to my selfe.	
	But hearke thee *Charmian*.	*Folio*
5.2.223–5	Why that's ... intents.	*Rowe*
	Why that's the way to foole their preparation,	
	And to conquer their most absurd intents.	*Folio*
5.2.306–7	That I ... Unpolicied!	*Pope*
	One line	*Folio*
5.2.322	Approach ... beguiled.	*Theobald*
	Approach hoa,	
	All's not well: *Caesar*'s beguild.	*Folio*
5.2.324	What work ... done?	*Rowe*
	What worke is heere *Charmian*?	
	Is this well done?	*Folio*
5.2.350–2	This is ... Nile.	*Johnson*
	This is an Aspickes traile,	
	And these Figge-leaues haue slime vpon them, such	
	As th'Aspicke leaues vpon the Caues of Nyle.	*Folio*

ABBREVIATIONS AND REFERENCES

Unless otherwise stated, the place of publication is London.

ABBREVIATIONS

Abbreviations used in notes

* Precedes commentary notes involving readings altered from the early edition(s) on which the edition is based.

LN	Longer notes
SD	stage direction
SP	speech prefix
subst.	substantively (i.e. ignoring accidentals of spelling and punctuation)
this edn	a reading adopted for the first time in this edition
TLN	through line numbering in *The First Folio of Shakespeare*, ed. Charlton Hinman, Norton Facsimile (1968)
t.n.	textual notes at the foot of the page

Shakespeare's works

AC	*Antony and Cleopatra*
AW	*All's Well That Ends Well*
AYL	*As You Like It*
CE	*The Comedy of Errors*
Cor	*Coriolanus*
Cym	*Cymbeline*
Ham	*Hamlet*
1H4	*King Henry IV Part 1*
2H4	*King Henry IV Part 2*
H5	*King Henry V*
1H6	*King Henry VI Part 1*
2H6	*King Henry VI Part 2*
3H6	*King Henry VI Part 3*
H8	*King Henry VIII*

JC	*Julius Caesar*
KJ	*King John*
KL	*King Lear*
LLL	*Love's Labour's Lost*
Luc	*The Rape of Lucrece*
MA	*Much Ado About Nothing*
Mac	*Macbeth*
MM	*Measure for Measure*
MND	*A Midsummer Night's Dream*
MV	*The Merchant of Venice*
MW	*The Merry Wives of Windsor*
Oth	*Othello*
Per	*Pericles*
PP	*The Passionate Pilgrim*
R2	*King Richard II*
R3	*King Richard III*
RJ	*Romeo and Juliet*
Son	*Sonnets*
TC	*Troilus and Cressida*
Tem	*The Tempest*
TGV	*The Two Gentlemen of Verona*
Tim	*Timon of Athens*
Tit	*Titus Andronicus*
TN	*Twelfth Night*
TNK	*The Two Noble Kinsmen*
TS	*The Taming of the Shrew*
VA	*Venus and Adonis*
WT	*The Winter's Tale*

REFERENCES

Editions of Shakespeare collated

References to Shakespeare's works other than Antony and Cleopatra *are to the* Riverside Shakespeare *(Boston, 1974)*.

Alexander	*William Shakespeare: The Complete Works*, ed. Peter Alexander, 4 vols (1951), vol. 4
Ard[1]	*Antony and Cleopatra*, ed. R. H. Case, The Arden Shakespeare (1906)
Ard[2]	*Antony and Cleopatra*, ed. M. R. Ridley, The Arden Shakespeare, Ninth Edition (1954)
Bevington	See Cam[2]
Cam[1]	*Antony and Cleopatra*, ed. John Dover Wilson, The New Shakespeare (Cambridge, 1950)

317

Cam[2]   *Antony and Cleopatra*, ed. David Bevington, New Cambridge Shakespeare (Cambridge, 1990)

Capell   *Mr. William Shakespeare His Comedies, Histories and Tragedies*, ed. Edward Capell, 10 vols (1767–8), vol. 8

Case   See Ard[1]

Collier   *The Works of William Shakespeare*, ed. John Payne Collier, 8 vols (1842–4), vol. 8

Collier[2] *The Works of Shakespeare*, ed. John Payne Collier, 8 vols (1853), vol. 8

Delius   *Shakspere's Werke*, ed. Nicolaus Delius, 7 vols (Elberfeld, 1844–53), vol. 2

Dyce   *The Works of William Shakespeare*, ed. Alexander Dyce, 6 vols (1857), vol. 6

Dyce[2]   *The Works of William Shakespeare*, ed. Alexander Dyce, 9 vols (1864–7), vol. 7

F   *Mr. William Shakespeares Comedies, Histories, and Tragedies*, First Folio (1623)

F corr.   corrected state in the First Folio

F uncorr. uncorrected state in the First Folio

F2   *Mr. William Shakespeares Comedies, Histories, and Tragedies*, Second Folio (1632)

F3   *Mr. William Shakespeares Comedies, Histories, and Tragedies*, Third Folio (1663)

F4   *Mr. William Shakespeares Comedies, Histories, and Tragedies*, Fourth Folio (1685)

Facsimile *The First Folio of Shakespeare*, ed. Charlton Hinman, The Norton Facsimile (London etc., 1968)

Furness   *The Tragedie of Anthonie, and Cleopatra*, ed. Horace Howard Furness, New Variorum Shakespeare (Philadelphia, 1907)

Hanmer   *The Works of Shakespear*, ed. Thomas Hanmer, 6 vols (Oxford, 1743–4), vol. 5

Johnson   *The Plays of William Shakespeare*, ed. Samuel Johnson, 8 vols (1765), vol. 7

Jones   *Antony and Cleopatra*, ed. Emrys Jones, New Penguin Shakespeare (1977)

Knight   *The Pictorial Edition of the Works of Shakespeare*, ed. Charles Knight, 8 vols (1838–43), vol. 6

Malone   *The Plays and Poems of William Shakespeare*, ed. Edmond Malone, 10 vols (1790), vol. 7

Oxf   *William Shakespeare: The Complete Works*, ed. Stanley Wells and Gary Taylor (Oxford, 1986)

Pope   *The Works of Shakespear*, ed. Alexander Pope, 6 vols (1723–5), vol. 5

Pope[2]   *The Works of Shakespear*, ed. Alexander Pope, 8 vols (1728), vol. 7

References

Ridley	See Ard[2]
Riv	*The Riverside Shakespear*, ed. G. Blakemore Evans and others (Boston, 1974)
Rowe	*The Works of Mr. William Shakespear*, ed. Nicholas Rowe, 6 vols (1709), vol. 6
Rowe[2]	*The Works of Mr. William Shakespear*, ed. Nicholas Rowe, 6 vols (1709), vol. 6
Rowe[3]	*The Works of Mr. William Shakespear*, ed. Nicholas Rowe, 8 vols (1714), vol. 7
Singer	*The Dramatic Works of William Shakespeare*, ed. S. W. Singer, 10 vols (1826), vol. 10
Spevack	*Antony and Cleopatra*, ed. Marvin Spevack, New Variorum Shakespeare (1990)
Staunton	*The Works of William Shakespeare*, ed. Howard Staunton, 3 vols (1858–60), vol. 3
Steevens	*The Plays of William Shakespeare*, notes by Samuel Johnson and George Steevens, 10 vols (1773), vol. 8
Steevens[2]	*The Plays of William Shakespeare*, 10 vols (1778), vol. 8
Steevens[3]	*The Plays of William Shakespeare*, 10 vols (1785), vol. 8
Theobald	*The Works of Shakespeare*, ed. Lewis Theobald, 7 vols (1733), vol. 6
Theobald[2]	*The Works of Shakespeare*, ed. Lewis Theobald, Second Edition, 8 vols (1740), vol. 7
Walter	*Antony and Cleopatra*, ed. J. H. Walter, The Players' Shakespeare (1969)
Warburton	*The Works of Shakespeare*, ed. William Warburton, 8 vols (1747), vol. 7
Wilson	See Cam[1]

Other works

Abbott	E. A. Abbott, *A Shakespearean Grammar* (1886)
Adelman, *Essay*	Janet Adelman, *The Common Liar: An Essay on Antony and Cleopatra* (New Haven and London, 1973)
Adelman, *Mothers*	Janet Adelman, *Suffocating Mothers: Fantasies of Maternal Origin in Shakespeare's Plays* (New York and London, 1992)
Anderson	Donald K. Anderson, Jr, 'A new gloss for the "three-nook'd world" of *Antony and Cleopatra*', *ELN* 17 (1979), 103–6
J. Anderson	James R. Anderson, *An Actor's Life* (1902)
Anton	Robert Anton, *The Philosophers Satyrs* (1616)
Appian	Appianus Alexandrinus, *Bella Civilia*, trans. W. B., ed. Ernest Schanzer (Liverpool, 1956)

References

Apuleius	Apuleius, *The Golden Asse*, trans. William Adlington (1596)
Aristophanes	Aristophanes, *Works*, trans. B. B. Rogers, Loeb Classical Library, 3 vols (Cambridge, MA, and London, 1960–1)
Arnold	Matthew Arnold, 'The study of poetry', in *Essays in Criticism*, 2nd series (1888) (1988)
Babb	Lawrence Babb, *The Elizabethan Malady: A Study of Melancholia in English Literature from 1580 to 1642* (East Lancing, MI, 1951)
Bacon	Francis Bacon, *Novum Organum*, in *Works*, ed. Spedding, vol. 4 (1870)
Barnes	Barnabe Barnes, *The Divils Charter*, ed. R. B. McKerrow, in *Materialen zur Kunde des älteren Englischen Dramas* (Louvain, 1904)
Barroll, 'Scarrus'	Leeds Barroll, 'Scarrus and the Scarred Soldier', *HLQ* 22 (1958–9), 31–9
Barroll, *Politics*	Leeds Barroll, *Politics, Plague, and Shakespeare's Theater* (Ithaca and London, 1991)
Barton	Anne Barton, *'Nature's piece 'gainst fancy': The Divided Catastrophe in Anthony and Cleopatra*, inaugural lecture, Bedford College (1973)
Bayley	John Bayley, *Shakespeare and Tragedy* (1981)
Bible	All biblical references are to the Bishop's Bible (1572)
Blakiston	J. M. G. Blakiston, 'The three nook'd world', *TLS*, 17 September (1964), 868
Bono	Barbara J. Bono, *Literary Transvaluation: From Vergilian Epic to Shakespearean Tragicomedy* (Berkeley and Los Angeles, 1984)
Bowers	John M. Bowers, ' "I am marble-constant": Cleopatra's Monumental End', *HLQ* 46 (1983), 283–97
Bradley, *Tragedy*	A. C. Bradley, *Shakespearean Tragedy* (1904)
Bradley, *Lectures*	A. C. Bradley, *Oxford Lectures on Poetry* ((1909)
Bradshaw	Graham Bradshaw, *Shakespeare's Scepticism* (Brighton, 1987)
Brathwait	Richard Brathwait, *The English Gentlewoman* (1631)
Brower	Reuben A. Brower, *Hero and Saint: Shakespeare and the Graeco-Roman Heroic Tradition* (Oxford, 1971)
Brown	*Shakespeare: Antony and Cleopatra*, ed. John Russell Brown, Casebook Series (1968)
Bullough	*Narrative and Dramatic Sources of Shakespeare*, ed. Geoffrey Bullough, 8 vols (1957–75), vol. 5 (1964)
Byrne	Muriel St Clare Byrne, Notes on the illustrations to Harley Granville-Baker, *Prefaces to Shakespeare*, 4 vols (1963)

320

References

Cairncross	Andrew S. Cairncross, '*Antony and Cleopatra* III.x.10', *N&Q* 220 (1975), 173
Cantor	Paul Cantor, *Shakespeare's Rome: Republic and Empire* (Ithaca and London, 1976)
Castelvetro	Lodovico Castelvetro, *Poetica d'Aristotele vulgarizzata et sposta* (Basle, 1576), trans. Allan H. Gilbert, in Gilbert, *Literary Criticism: Plato to Dryden* (Detroit, 1962)
Cercignani	Fausto Cercignani, *Shakespeare's Works and Elizabethan Pronunciation* (Oxford, 1981)
Chambers, *Stage*	E. K. Chambers, *The Elizabethan Stage*, 4 vols (Oxford, 1923)
Chambers, *Study*	E. K. Chambers, *William Shakespeare: A Study of Facts and Problems*, 2 vols (Oxford, 1930)
Charney	Maurice Charney, *Shakespeare's Roman Plays: The Function of Imagery in the Drama* (Cambridge, MA, 1961)
Coates	John Coates, '"The Choice of Hercules" in *Antony and Cleopatra*', *SS* 31 (1978), 45–52
Coleridge	Samuel Taylor Coleridge, *Coleridge's Shakespearean Criticism*, ed. T. M. Raysor, 2 vols (Cambridge, MA, 1930)
Colie	Rosalie Colie, *Shakespeare's Living Art* (Princeton, NJ, 1974)
Collier	Constance Collier, *Harlequinade* (1929)
Cook	Dutton Cook, *Nights at the Play: A View of the English Stage* (1883)
Danby	John F. Danby, *Poets on Fortune's Hill* (1952)
Davies	H. Neville Davies, Introduction to *Shakespeare's Antony and Cleopatra, 1813* (1970)
T. Davies	Thomas Davies, *Dramatic Miscellanies*, 3 vols (1783–4)
Dawson	R. M. Dawson, 'But why Enobarbus?' *N&Q* 232 (1987), 216–17
Deighton	Kenneth Deighton, *The Old Dramatists: Conjectural Readings* (Calcutta, 1898)
Dent	R. W. Dent, *Shakespeare's Proverbial Language: An Index* (Berkeley and London, 1981)
Dickey	Franklin M. Dickey, *Not Wisely but Too Well: Shakespeare's Love Tragedies* (San Marino, CA, 1957)
Douce	Francis Douce, *Illustrations of Shakespeare*, 2 vols, vol. 1 (1807)
Dowden	Edward Dowden, *Shakspere: A Critical Study of his Mind and Art* (1875), (1967)
Dryden, *Works*	John Dryden, *Works*, 20 vols (Berkeley and Los Angeles, 1956–89)

Dryden, *Essays*	John Dryden, *Essays*, ed. W. P. Ker, 2 vols (New York, 1961)
Dryden, *Love*	John Dryden, *All for Love*, in *Works*, vol. 13 (Berkeley and Los Angeles, 1984)
ELN	*English Language Notes*
Erickson	Peter Erickson, *Patriarchal Structures in Shakespeare's Drama* (Berkeley and Los Angeles, 1985)
Farnham	Willard Farnham, *Shakespeare's Tragic Frontier: The World of his Final Tragedies* (Berkeley and Los Angeles, 1950)
Firth	C. H. Firth, 'Ballads and broadsides', in *Shakespeare's England*, 2 vols, vol. 2 (1916)
Fisch	Harold Fisch, '*Antony and Cleopatra*: the limits of mythology', *SS* 23 (1970), 59–67
Gilbert	Allan H. Gilbert, *Literary Criticism: Plato to Dryden* (Detroit, MI, 1962)
Goldman	Michael Goldman, *Acting and Action in Shakespearean Tragedy* (Princeton, NJ, 1985)
Granville-Barker, 'Note'	Harley Granville-Barker, 'A note upon chapters XX and XXI of *The Elizabethan Stage*', *RES* 1 (1925), 63–4
Granville-Barker, *Prefaces*	Harley Granville-Barker, *Prefaces to Shakespeare*, 2nd series (1930)
Greg, *Bibliography*	W. W. Greg, *A Bibliography of the English Printed Drama to the Restoration*, vol. 1 (London, 1939)
Greg, *Pericles*	*Shakespeare's Quartos in Collotype Facsimile*, ed. W. W. Greg, vol. 5: *Pericles* (Oxford, 1940)
Greg, *Editorial Problem*	W. W. Greg, *The Editorial Problem in Shakespeare* (Oxford, 1942)
Greg, *First Folio*	W. W. Greg, *The Shakespeare First Folio* (Oxford, 1955)
Gurr	Andrew Gurr, *Playgoing in Shakespeare's London* (Cambridge, 1987)
Harrier	Richard C. Harrier, 'Cleopatra's end', *SQ* 13 (1962), 63–5
Hazlitt	William Hazlitt, 'On Shakespeare and Milton', *Lectures on the English Poets (1818)*, in *Complete Works*, 21 vols, vol. 5 (1930–4)
Heath	Benjamin Heath, *A Revisal of Shakespeare's Text* (1765)
Henn	T. R. Henn, *The Living Image: Shakespearean Essays* (1972)
Hinman	Charlton Hinman, *The Printing and Proof-Reading of the First Folio of Shakespeare*, 2 vols (Oxford, 1963)
HLQ	*Huntingdon Library Quarterly*
Hodges	C. Walter Hodges, *The Globe Restored* (1968)
Holland	Plutarch, *The Philosophie, commonly called The Morals*, trans. Philemon Holland (1603)

Homer	Homer, *The Odyssey*, trans. A. T. Murray, Loeb Classical Library, 2 vols (Cambridge, MA, and London, 1953)
Honigmann	E. A. J. Honigmann, *Shakespeare, Seven Tragedies: The Dramatist's Manipulation of Response* (1976)
Hosley	Richard Hosley, 'The Staging of the Monument Scenes in *Antony and Cleopatra*', *Library Chronicle* 30 (1964), 62–71
Howard-Hill	T. H. Howard-Hill, *A Reassessment of Compositors B and E in the First Folio Tragedies* (Columbia, SC, 1977)
Hughes-Hallett	Lucy Hughes-Hallett, *Cleopatra* (1991)
Hulme	Hilda M. Hulme, *Explorations in Shakespeare's Language* (1962)
Hunter	G. K. Hunter, 'A. C. Bradley's *Shakespearean Tragedy*', in *Dramatic Identities and Cultural Tradition* (Liverpool, 1978)
Jackson	Zachariah Jackson, *Shakespeare's Genius Justified* (1819)
Johnson	Samuel Johnson, *Johnson on Shakespeare*, ed. Walter Raleigh (Oxford, 1908)
Jones, *Form*	Emrys Jones, *Scenic Form in Shakespeare* (Oxford, 1971)
Jones, *Origins*	Emrys Jones, *The Origins of Shakespeare* (Oxford, 1977)
Kaula	David Kaula, 'The time sense of *Antony and Cleopatra*', *SQ* 15 (1964), 211–23
King	T. J. King, *Casting Shakespeare's Plays: London Actors and their Roles 1590–1642* (Cambridge, 1992)
Kinnear	Benjamin Kinnear, *Cruces Shakespeareanae: Difficult Passages in the Works of Shakespeare* (1883)
Knight	G. Wilson Knight, *The Imperial Theme* (1931), (1965)
Knights	L. C. Knights, *Some Shakespearean Themes* (1959)
Krook	Dorothea Krook, *Elements of Tragedy* (New Haven, CT, 1969)
Lamb	Margaret Lamb, *Antony and Cleopatra on the English Stage* (London and Toronto, 1980)
Leo	Leo Africanus, *History and Description of Africa*, trans. John Pory (1600), Hakluyt Society, 3 vols, vol. 3 (1896)
Lives	Plutarch, *Lives of the Noble Grecians and Romans*, trans. Sir Thomas North, ed. W. E. Henley, 6 vols (1895–6)
Lloyd	Michael Lloyd, 'Cleopatra as Isis', *SS* 12 (1959), 88–94
Long	John H. Long, *Shakespeare's Use of Music: The Histories and the Tragedies* (Gainesville, FL, 1971)
Lowen	Tirzah Lowen, *Peter Hall Directs Antony and Cleopatra* (1990)
Lucretius	Lucretius, *De Rerum Natura*, trans. F. J. Miller, Loeb

	Classical Library, 2 vols (Cambridge, MA, and London, 1982)
MacCallum	M. W. MacCallum, *Shakespeare's Roman Plays and their Background* (1967 (1910))
Mack	Maynard Mack, 'The Jacobean Shakespeare', in *Jacobean Theatre*, eds John Russell Brown and Bernard Harris, Stratford-upon-Avon Studies 1 (1960)
McKerrow	R. B. McKerrow, *Prolegomena for the Oxford Shakespeare* (Oxford, 1939)
Markels	Julian Markels, *The Pillar of the World: Antony and Cleopatra in Shakespeare's Development* (Columbus, OH, 1968)
Mason	H. A. Mason, *Shakespeare's Tragedies of Love* (1970)
May	Graham May, Glossary to *Antony and Cleopatra*, BBC Television Shakespeare (1981)
Merchant	W. M. Merchant, 'Classical costume in Shakespeare productions', *SS* 10 (1957), 71–6
Middleton	Thomas Middleton, *Black Book* (1604), in *Works*, ed. A. H. Bullen, 8 vols, vol. 8 (1885)
Miola	Robert S. Miola, *Shakespeare's Rome* (Cambridge, 1983)
MLR	*Modern Language Review*
Montaigne	Michel de Montaigne, 'An Apologie of Raymond Sebond', *Essayes*, trans. John Florio (1603), 3 vols, vol. 2 (1965)
Murry	John Middleton Murry, *Shakespeare* (1936)
N&Q	*Notes and Queries*
Nashe	Thomas Nashe, *Christ's Tears* (1593–4), in *Works*, ed. R. B. McKerrow, vol. 2 (1910)
Noble	Richmond Noble, *Shakespeare's Use of Song* (Oxford, 1923)
Norman	Arthur M. Z. Norman, 'Source material in *Antony and Cleopatra*', *N&Q* 201 (1956), 59–61
North	Plutarch, 'The Life of Marcus Antonius' and 'The Life of Julius Caesar' trans. Sir Thomas North, in *Narrative and Dramatic Sources of Shakespeare*, ed. Geoffrey Bullough, vol. 5 (1964)
OCD	*The Oxford Classical Dictionary*, ed. N. G. L. Hammond and H. H. Scullard (Oxford, 1970)
Odell	George C. D. Odell, *Shakespeare: From Betterton to Irving*, 2 vols (New York, 1920)
OED	*The Oxford English Dictionary*, 11 vols (Oxford, 1888–1933)
Onions	C. T. Onions, *A Shakespeare Glossary*, enlarged and revised by Robert D. Eagleson (Oxford, 1986)
Ornstein	Robert Ornstein, 'The ethic of the imagination: love

	and art in *Antony and Cleopatra*', in *Later Shakespeare*, eds John Russell Brown and Bernard Harris, Stratford-upon-Avon Studies 8 (1966)
Ovid, *Fasti*	Ovid, *Fasti*, ed. and trans. J. G. Frazer, 5 vols (1929)
Ovid, *Metamorphoses*	Ovid, *Metamorphoses*, trans. F. J. Miller, Loeb Classical Library, 2 vols (Cambridge, MA, and London, 1953)
Ovid, *Heroides*	Ovid, *Heroides*, trans. Grant Showerman, Loeb Classical Library (Cambridge, MA, and London, 1977)
Panofsky	Irwin Panofsky, *Herkules am Scheidewege* (Leipzig, 1930)
Partridge	Eric Partridge, *Shakespeare's Bawdy: A Literary and Psychological Essay* (1955)
Pelling	Plutarch, *Life of Antony*, ed. C. B. R. Pelling (Cambridge, 1988)
Pitcher	'Samuel Daniel's occasional and dedicatory verse: A critical edition', ed. John Pitcher, D. Phil. thesis (Oxford, 1978)
Pliny	Pliny, *Natural History*, Loeb Classical Library, 10 vols (Cambridge, MA, and London, 1949–62)
Primrose	James Primrose, *Popular Errours, or the Errours of the People in Physick* (1651)
Proudfoot	Richard Proudfoot, 'Two notes on Shakespeare's text', *K. M. 80: A Birthday Album for Kenneth Muir, Tuesday May 5, 1987* (Department of English, University of Liverpool, 1987)
Rees	Joan Rees, *Samuel Daniel, a Critical and Biographical Study* (Liverpool, 1964)
RES	*The Review of English Studies*
Riemer	A. P. Riemer, *A Reading of Shakespeare's Antony and Cleopatra* (Sydney, 1968)
Schanzer, 'Pembroke'	Ernest Schanzer, '*Antony and Cleopatra* and the Countess of Pembroke's *Antonius*', *N&Q* 201 (1956), 152–4
Schanzer, 'Daniel's revision'	Ernest Schanzer, 'Daniel's revision of his *Cleopatra*', *RES*, NS 8 (1957), 375–81
Schanzer, 'Three notes'	Ernest Schanzer, 'Three notes on *Antony and Cleopatra*', *N&Q* 205 (1960), 20–2
Schanzer, *Problem Plays*	Ernest Schanzer, *The Problem Plays of Shakespeare: A Study of Julius Caesar, Measure for Measure and Antony and Cleopatra* (1963)
Schmidt	Alexander Schmidt, *Shakespeare Lexicon and Quotation Dictionary*, 2 vols (Berlin, 1902; New York, 1971)
Seaton	Ethel Seaton, '*Antony and Cleopatra* and the Book of Revelation', *RES* 22 (1946): 219–24
Seng	P. J. Seng, 'Shakespearean hymn parody?', *Renaissance News* 18 (1965), 4–6

Sidney, *Poems*	Sir Philip Sidney, *Poems*, ed. Ringler (Oxford, 1962)
Sidney, *Defence*	Sir Philip Sidney, *A Defence of Poetry*, in *Miscellaneous Prose*, ed. Katherine Duncan-Jones and Jan van Dorsten (Oxford, 1973)
Simmons	J. L. Simmons, *Shakespeare's Pagan World: The Roman Tragedies* (Charlottesville, VA, 1973)
Sisson	Charles J. Sisson, *New Readings in Shakespeare*, 2 vols (Cambridge, 1956)
Southern	Richard Southern, *Changeable Scenery* (1952)
Spenser	Edmund Spenser, *The Faerie Queene*, ed. A. C. Hamilton (1977)
SQ	*Shakespeare Quarterly*
SS	*Shakespeare Survey*
SSt	*Shakespeare Studies*
Stone	George Winchester Stone, 'Garrick's presentation of *Antony and Cleopatra*', *RES* 13 (1937), 20–38
Sugden	E. H. Sugden, *Topographical Dictionary of the Works of Shakespeare* (Manchester, 1925)
Swinburne, *Study*	A. C. Swinburne, *A Study of Shakespeare* (1880)
Swinburne, *Shakespeare*	A. C. Swinburne, *Shakespeare* (Oxford, 1909)
Thistleton	Alfred E. Thistleton, *Some Textual Notes on the Tragedie of Antony and Cleopatra* (1899)
Tilley	M. P. Tilley, *The Proverbs in England in the Sixteenth and Seventeenth Centuries* (Ann Arbor, MI, 1950)
TLS	*The Times Literary Supplement*
TN	*Theatre Notebook*
Traci	Philip J. Traci, *The Love Play of Antony and Cleopatra: A Critical Study of Shakespeare's Play*, Studies in English Literature 64 (The Hague, 1970)
Traversi	Derek Traversi, *Shakespeare: The Roman Plays* (1963)
Tyrwhitt	Thomas Tyrwhitt, *Observations and Conjectures upon Some Passages of Shakespeare* (1766)
Upton	John Upton, *Critical Observations on Shakespeare* (1746)
Virgil	Virgil, *Aeneid*, trans. H. R. Fairclough, Loeb Classical Library, 2 vols (Cambridge, MA, and London, 1954)
Waddington	Raymond B. Waddington, '*Antony and Cleopatra*: "What Venus did with Mars"', *SSt* 2 (1966), 210–27
Waith	Eugene Waith, *The Herculean Hero in Marlowe, Chapman, Shakespeare and Dryden* (New York and London, 1962)
Walter	J. H. Walter, 'Four notes on *Antony and Cleopatra*', *N&Q* 214 (1969), 137–9
Wells, *Re-editing*	Stanley Wells, *Re-editing Shakespeare for the Modern Reader* (Oxford, 1984)

'Wells, *Companion* Stanley Wells and Gary Taylor, *William Shakespeare: A Textual Companion* (Oxford, 1987)

Wind Edgar Wind, *Pagan Mysteries in the Renaissance* (Oxford, 1980)

Xenophon Xenophon, *Memorabilia*, trans. E. C. Marchant, Loeb Classical Library (London and New York, 1923)

INDEX
TO INTRODUCTION AND COMMENTARY